Fit for a King

The Royal Garage of the Shahs of Iran

Borzou Sepasi

with Ramin Salehkhou and Gautam Sen

DALTON WATSON FINE BOOKS

Fit for a King
The Royal Garage of the Shahs of Iran

Borzou Sepasi
with Ramin Salehkhou and Gautam Sen

First published 2022

ISBN: 978-1-85443-292-6

All rights reserved. Apart from any fair dealing for the purpose of private study, research, criticism or review, as permitted under the terms of the Copyright, Design and Patents Act of 1988, no part of this book may be reproduced or transmitted in any form or by any means, electronic, electrical, chemical, mechanical, optical including photocopying, recording or by any other means placed in any information storage or retrieval system, without prior permission of the publisher.

All reasonable steps have been taken to locate the appropriate copyright holders of photographic and other material. The author and publisher apologise for any errors or omissions. Certain words, names of models and designations that are mentioned in the text are the property of the rights holders of the marque in question. Such words, model names and designations are used for identification purposes only.

Design: Jodi Ellis Graphics

Printed by: Interpress Co. Ltd., Hungary

for the publisher:
Dalton Watson Fine Books
Glyn and Jean Morris

Deerfield, IL 60015 USA
www.daltonwatson.com

To my wife Mahnaz, son Yara and I.M
who were always by my side
with their love and support.

Table of Contents

6	**PREFACE**	
8	**FOREWORD**	
	Nick Mason	
9	**FOREWORD**	
	Simon Kidston	
10	**FAMILY TREE**	
12	**CHAPTER 1**	
	Iran enters the Automotive Age ~ The Qajar Dynasty	
30	**CHAPTER 2**	
	The Sheikh Khazal Rebellion and the Rise of the Pahlavi Dynasty	
50	**CHAPTER 3**	
	The Pahlavi Garage Comes of Age	
58	**CHAPTER 4**	
	In his Father's Footsteps	
64	**CHAPTER 5**	
	A new Modern Iran begins to Emerge, 1925 to 1936	
94	**CHAPTER 6**	
	The Winds of War and a Special Gift from the Third Reich	
104	**CHAPTER 7**	
	The Royal Wedding ~ an Egyptian Princess fit for an Iranian Prince	
130	**CHAPTER 8**	
	Iran and the Second World War	
142	**CHAPTER 9**	
	The Shah adjusts to a New World	
166	**CHAPTER 10**	
	Reza Shah returns Home	
174	**CHAPTER 11**	
	The 1950s ~ a New decade, a New Era, a New Queen	
184	**CHAPTER 12**	
	1953 ~ the Year of the Coup and Drophead Coupe	
188	**CHAPTER 13**	
	Surviving the Coup	
212	**CHAPTER 14**	
	The Rise of Shah Mohammad Reza Pahlavi	
248	**CHAPTER 15**	
	House cleaning in the Royal Garage	
258	**CHAPTER 16**	
	Farah Diba, the new Queen of Iran	
272	**CHAPTER 17**	
	Farah bears a Crown Prince	
282	**CHAPTER 18**	
	Queen Elizabeth II visits Iran and the Shah visits France	

296	**CHAPTER 19**	The Start of the 1960s
336	**CHAPTER 20**	More Toys for the (Royal) Boy
346	**CHAPTER 21**	The Mercedes 600 dominates the Royal Fleet
350	**CHAPTER 22**	1967 ~ The Year of the Coronation and the global search for a Carriage Maker
358	**CHAPTER 23**	The Lamborghini Miura and the Iranian Royal Family
378	**CHAPTER 24**	The Shah of Iran and the Birth of the G-Class Mercedes
384	**CHAPTER 25**	The Shah's "Utilitarian" Tastes and the Cars of Summer
390	**CHAPTER 26**	An Aston Martin for Summer Fun
394	**CHAPTER 27**	The Shah's affinity for the Range Rover
400	**CHAPTER 28**	Celebrating 2,500 Years of the Persian Empire
408	**CHAPTER 29**	The Shah Tries a 1971 Mercedes-Benz 300SEL 6.3
414	**CHAPTER 30**	The Crown Prince receives a Mini Benz
420	**CHAPTER 31**	Visiting with an American President
420	**CHAPTER 32**	Six Daimlers join the Royal Garage
420	**CHAPTER 33**	A Camargue for the Shah and… one for Queen Farah?
434	**CHAPTER 34**	The Crown Prince graduates to an Italian Supercar
440	**CHAPTER 35**	The Shah and Crown Prince's Last Rides
446	**APPENDIX 1**	The Story Continues
528	**APPENDIX 2**	Honorable Mentions
544	**APPENDIX 3**	Planes, Rail Carriages and More
554	**INDEX, BIBLIOGRAPHY AND ACKNOWLEDGMENTS**	

Preface

As a young boy during the early 1990s, I would accompany my father during his daily trips to the newsstand to buy the evening newspaper. Even though the Iran-Iraq war, one of the longest wars in modern history, had ended several years earlier, the effects of the war were still visible, and access to foreign periodicals was still very limited.

It was during one of these daily excursions that I saw that the newsstand had old back issues of foreign periodicals on display, probably passed on from a foreign embassy. As I flipped through them, I came across the May 18, 1988 issue of *Autocar*, and being an enthusiast even then, convinced my father to buy the magazine for me.

Once home, I voraciously read the contents using an English-Farsi dictionary when I came across an advertisement for a car which astounded me by its beauty. The advertisement was for a Maserati Ghibli, and, what further caught my attention, was the fact that it stated that the car was once owned by the Shah of Iran, the former monarch who had left Iran before I was born.

Having heard many stories of the enormous wealth that the Shah had at his disposal during his reign, I concluded that there must have been other cars like the Ghibli as well. It was from this point that my quest to uncover the history of the royal cars of Iran started.

At first, there was an absolute dearth of information. At times I would receive word of a certain car being claimed to have been once owned by the Shah of Iran, only to discover that the information was false, and that the owner was attempting to push up the price.

It was several years later, on March 13, 1997, where I read, purely by chance, in the state-owned newspaper *Keyhan*, an article titled, "Today the Most Beautiful cars belonging to the Deposed Shah were put on Auction in Geneva".

When reading the article, two points immediately caught my attention. The first was that the article stated that among the vehicles put up for auction were a Lamborghini and a Rolls-Royce, marques that I have always had a particular affinity for. Even more importantly, the article went on to claim that the Shah owned one of the largest car collections in the world.

With this article, I found the renewed energy to carry on my quest and, shortly thereafter, upon entering university, I gained access to the internet, a technology which was still in its infancy in Iran. I still remember my first online search as if it was yesterday, as I immediately began searching for the royal cars of Iran, tracking down four of them on that very day.

The information that I gathered gave me the confidence to write my first article at the age of 24, about the royal cars of Iran, for one of Iran's highest circulation newspapers. At the end of the article,

Author Borzou Sepasi, pictured in the former Shah's Lamborghini Miura, chassis number 3303, during the 2019 Rétromobile event.

I provided my email, and was overwhelmed by the interest that was generated. Of the emails I received, one came from a gentleman claiming to be the head of a soon-to-be-established museum to house the cars which were in the hands of the Bonyad Mostazafan, the organization mandated with managing the property and assets of the former Shah and those associated with him.

He stated that he had over 180 cars in his care but had no idea about the history or the background of any of them and asked if I could help identify each of these vehicles. He then invited me to visit the warehouse where the cars were kept.

Upon the opening of the doors, I was overwhelmed by the breathtaking sight of rows and rows of the most exotic cars I had ever laid my eyes on, including a multitude of Rolls-Royces, numerous Mercedes-Benz 600s, Porsches, Ferraris, and the like. In between were a number of cars which were immediately identifiable by their rarity, such as the famed Mercedes-Benz 500K Autobahnkurier, Bizzarrini 5300 GT Strada and a Porsche 934 RSR. The cars were covered with layers and layers of dust, but nothing could hide their beauty.

It was from then on that I was brought onboard by the museum to try to uncover the history of each of these cars. While some were relatively simple, others were far more complicated and shrouded in mystery. I visited a multitude of libraries, going through numerous texts and periodicals, spending hours trying to spot and identify cars in pictures often related to historical events.

The next step was paying visits to dozens of governmental organizations which may have had information pertaining to these cars in their archives. In many cases I would return empty handed, but one day, purely coincidentally on one of my visits, when I mentioned what I was searching for, much to my utter surprise, the manager of that organization took out a small album with pictures of a number of cars, stating that these cars had been in their possession since their confiscation following the revolution.

Having earlier uncovered the list of all the Rolls-Royces sold to the royal court, I spotted a Rolls-Royce Silver Cloud III, known as the "Chinese Eyes", among the cars in his photo album. When I recited the VIN number by heart, the manager immediately granted me first-hand access to the cars in their possession.

In 2002, following my initial success in gaining access to the warehouses of the Bonyad Mostazafan, I was permitted entry to the storage area of the Saad Abad Palace, one of the primary abodes of the royal family. Among the cars in their care, the most notable were a Rolls-Royce Phantom VI and Mercedes-Benz 300SL Roadster. What shocked me was the state of these cars, many of which were exposed to the elements, as well as numerous articles from the palaces, both large and small, which due to a lack of storage space, had been stored on and around the cars. As a result, I was only successful in taking a few pictures.

In 2005, with the opening of the Shah's primary palace, Niavaran, to the public as a museum, I submitted a request to visit the former parking garage which, at that time, was still under lock and key. Though I was aware that a number of cars, such as the fabled Lamborghini Miura SVJ, had been removed and sold off, I was hoping that perhaps some of the other cars may still be there.

Several months after my initial request, I was finally granted access. To my surprise, I came across the Shah's Rolls-Royce Phantom V Landaulette and Phantom VI, both in time capsule condition.

That same year, after stubbornly making innumerable requests, I became the first private citizen to be able to see first-hand and inspect the Shah's private rail carriages, the results of which can be seen in this book.

Of course, much of the material gathered for this book could not have been achieved had it not been for the kindness and assistance of numerous people. I will never forget the day when I received a phone call from Mrs. Tadjbakhshian, the head of the archives of the Saad Abad Palace informing me that she had discovered a new photograph in their archives. The picture in question turned out to be none other than that of the Shah's first Lamborghini Miura. I remember dropping everything and driving out to the Palace.

Then there was the time when I endured the smirks of Mrs. Afarin Emami, the manager of the Niavaran Palace and Mrs. Zarrin Majidi, head of archives of the Palace who, after allowing me access to the Palace archives, stood by and watched with a smile when I jumped for joy like a four-year old when I discovered a photo of the Mercedes-Benz 500K Autobahnkurier dating back to 1938.

This does not mean that the process was not fraught with problems. Not only were there the usual problems of bureaucracy and red tape, but also the fact that four decades after the revolution, there is still much sensitivity about the rule of Mohammad Reza Pahlavi. Many times I was faced with suspicion as to why I was gathering these materials, only to assuage all by showing the documents and information that I was gathering for this book, and that all my efforts were for a strictly non-political historical project.

Today, many of the vehicles that are covered in this book are spread across the world. I long for the day when they could all be on display in our national auto museum where they could be enjoyed by all Iranians, as well as visitors from elsewhere. If that day should ever come, I will know that this book will have achieved its aim.

I wish to use this opportunity to express my sincere thanks to two people who were instrumental in putting this book together, for without them, the publication would have been pushed back for years. My good friend Ramin Salehkhou, who has devoted nearly a quarter of a century of his life towards preserving the historical vehicles of Iran and is a founder of an association that has garnered international recognition for its activities in this field. His tireless editing, translating and numerous inputs to the book helped to bring this book to an international level. Gautam Sen, whom, for many in the historical vehicle universe needs no introduction, is an award-winning automotive historian, author, journalist and all-round good guy. Gautam was instrumental in solving many of the gaps in my research that without him, we would have drawn a blank. I cannot thank them both enough for their extensive contributions to bringing this book to fruition.

I also wish to mention that both gentlemen are extensively involved in the activities of FIVA (Fédération Internationale Vehicules Anciens) an organization dedicated to preserving historical vehicles across the world for the next generation. I hope that with this book, I have done my part for this most worthy endeavor.

Lastly, I cannot thank my family enough for all their support. My wife, Mahnaz Beedel, who supported me unconditionally, my son Yara, who time and time again had to give up play time with me to allow me to wrap up this book. My mother, Mitra Sehat who encouraged me since the very beginning, my father Behrouz and my brother Barzin, who helped whenever they could. I also wish to thank my good friend Shahed Valad Beigi and my former editor at *Machine Magazine,* Saied Shobeiri, who always lent their support and encouragement.

Borzou Sepasi
Tehran
December 2021

Foreword *by Nick Mason*

Every car enthusiast has a "what if" moment. To this day, I still ponder what if I had not sold my Alfa 8C to pay off a tax bill and had chosen prison instead. I am sure that the number of enthusiasts making a "what if" decision between incarceration and the sale of a cherished car are a very small minority. On the other hand, I can say without a doubt that a "what if" moment shared virtually by almost every die-hard car enthusiast is the fantasy of being able to go back in time to take delivery from the factory some of the world's most iconic cars.

Imagine such a journey starting with Germany, where one could choose a Mercedes 500K, in fact, one of a total of six Autobahnkuriers and the only one with a supercharged prototype 540 engine designed to speed down the Autobahn at speeds over 180kph. For good measure one could also add a Gullwing, a 300SL Roadster and even a 300S to this fantasy.

From Germany, one could then travel on to Spain where they could enjoy the pleasures of a Pegaso Z-102 Berlinetta Touring Prototipo, the actual New York show car and Carrera Panamerica competitor.

Hopping over to France, as I have the personal pleasure of owning a Type 35B, I, for one, would then personally complement the Type 35 with the breathtakingly beautiful Bugatti Type 57C by Vanvooren.

From France, this journey would continue by crossing the channel where one could pick up a bevy of Rolls-Royces, including the only Phantom IV Drophead coupe and one of five Phantom V State Landaulettes. All of that luxury would then be topped off with the performance of a 1955 Bentley R-Type Continental and the brutal power of the first production Aston Martin V8.

In Italy, one would first travel to Sant'Agata to pick up not just any Miura, but the first Miura SVJ and then be off to Maranello where one could choose among others, a Ferrari 410 Superamerica, a 500 Superfast and then round it out with a BB Boxer, another car which I personally have had the pleasure of ownership, but this one would be different, as it would be the one picked up by King Hussein of Jordan to be gifted to a "special friend". Finally, in Modena, no fantasy car collection would be complete without the first Maserati 5000GT, especially as it came equipped with an engine from the 450S, making it a virtual racing car dressed in street clothing.

While still in Italy, one could reach out across the Atlantic to secure the right to pick up from Ghia among the best that Virgil Exner would have to offer, namely a Chrysler K-300.

While for any enthusiast this would have been the ultimate fantasy, in reality, there is one man in the world who has actually lived this automotive life, having owned not only all of the cars mentioned above, but a broad array of other truly unique cars as well. This man is none other than the last Monarch of Iran, Mohammad Reza Pahlavi, also known as the 'Shah'.

(Paddy Balls/Martin Griffin)

I can relate to the Shah's passion for speed, as evidenced by the fact that he would specify the most high-performance versions of many of the cars he owned. When not available, he had them built to his exacting specifications. His high-speed jaunts from Tehran to his palace on the shores of the Caspian Sea are legendary. Had royal duties not prevailed, I am convinced he would, at a minimum, have become a gentleman racer. This passion for speed was also evident in the fact that he was also an avid pilot, having sat behind the cockpit of everything from fighter jets to the Concorde, a subject which this book also covers in detail.

Complementing this passion for speed was his appreciation of style, which first manifested itself at the ripe age of twelve when he personally handpicked his first car, a Saoutchik-bodied Hispano-Suiza J12.

This is not in any way a political book. It is a work of history which otherwise would have been lost to time, and any judgement of his rule is left to the opinion of the pundits. What is clear is that the Shah comes across as a true driving enthusiast, not a rich poseur, and would use every opportunity afforded to him to sit behind the wheel and actually enjoy the cars he purchased over the years, whether it was through the snowy back roads of St. Moritz or high-speed midnight runs in Tehran. Nothing exemplifies this point more than the fact that, despite having a bevy of the latest automotive exotica available to him at the royal garage located nearby, when the Niavaran Palace fell to the revolutionaries, they were surprised to discover that the car used by the Shah to sneak out at night for his jaunts across Tehran was not the latest offering of exotica from the world's manufacturers, but an Italian sports car at the time nearing its tenth year of spirited use. It was the Lamborghini Miura SVJ. Enough said.

Nick Mason
December 2021

Foreword *by Simon Kidston*

Many of the motoring world's greatest masterpieces would never receive the adulation that greets them today had it not been for the patronage, influence and very deep, state-assisted pockets of one man: His Imperial Majesty Mohammad Reza Pahlavi, Shahinshah of Persia, better known simply as The Shah of Iran.

The expression 'Car of Kings' is oft-used. It's true that Prince Leopold of Belgium, Prince Bernhard of the Netherlands, the King of Morocco and Prince Bertil of Sweden were passionate buyers of very fast and costly hand-built European sports cars. Even the heir to our own throne drives an Aston Martin DB6 Vantage Volante gifted to him by his mother, Her Majesty The Queen. But no ruler can match the range and depth of the vast Tehran garage maintained for the Shah, a world where the 'everyday' was a fleet of Mercedes 600 Pullmans, Rolls-Royce or Cadillac limousines, and truly 'special' referred to bespoke creations from Spanish firm Pegaso, French thoroughbred Bugatti and the Italian greats, Ferrari, Maserati and Lamborghini.

Naturally, merely expensive sports cars such as the Mercedes 300 SL Gullwing and Roadster, and production Ferraris, Bentleys and Aston Martins feature in this book. Moving up a gear, the Shah owned not one but two Ferrari 500 Superfasts, topping the elevated company of a list of plutocrats that included the Aga Khan, actor Peter Sellers and the Sachs and Livanos families. Only a few years earlier, visits to Italy had yielded a Ferrari 410 Superamerica and the first car to be referred to by his name in its prefix: 'The Shah of Iran' Maserati 5000GT, a striking *granturismo* powered by a detuned (to 340bhp…) V8 450S racing engine.

A little over a decade later, another exotic Italian one-off with racing car credentials was offered to the offices of His Imperial Majesty. You can imagine the telex machines chattering, the uniformed courtiers whispering and, in an office far away in Sant'Agata, near Modena, Lamborghini marketing and engineering high command drawing up a sales proposal for a very special Miura, the Shah's third, and the first-ever SVJ.

I was to discover at first-hand the extraordinary background to ten special cars ordered by the Shah or his close relatives when, in March 1997, I auctioned this long-lost Miura in Geneva. The buyer was US actor Nicolas Cage, who paid a price of $497,500, triple its pre-sale estimate and setting a record for the most valuable Lamborghini yet sold. Six months of contract negotiations, historical research and visits to the region preceded the sale. I remember the day in Dubai when I first saw it in an anonymous warehouse: its metallic burgundy paint was faded; the once-brilliant white leather interior muted under a quarter century of grime; the odometer read just 2,900 km.

That famous Lamborghini Miura, and some of the significant other cars amassed by the Iranian Royal Family during the Shah's rule, survive today. Some do not. This fascinating book is a tribute to them all, and a fascinating insight into a world where anything was possible and only the best would do: each one truly 'Fit for a King'.

Simon Kidston
December 2021

Reza Shah Pahlavi
1878-1944

FIRST MARRIAGE

NO AVAILABLE PHOTOGRAPH

Maryam Savadkoohi
1882-1904

Fatima
1903-1992

SECOND MARRIAGE

Tadj ol-Molouk Ayromlu
1896-1982

Shams
1917-1996

Mohammad Reza
1919-1980

Ashraf
1919-2016

Ali Reza
1922-1954

THIRD MARRIAGE

Turan Amirsoleimani
1905-1995

Gholam Reza
1923-2017

FOURTH MARRIAGE

Esmat ol-Molouk Dowlatshahi
1905-1995

Abdul Reza
1924-2004

Ahmad Reza
1925-1981

Mahmoud Reza
1926-2001

Fatemeh
1928-1987

Hamid Reza
1928-1992

Mohammad Reza Shah Pahlavi
1919-1980

FIRST MARRIAGE

Fawzia Fuad
1921-2013

SECOND MARRIAGE

Soraya Esfandiary-Bakhtiary
1932-2001

THIRD MARRIAGE

Farah Diba
1938-

Shahnaz
1940-

**Reza
(Crown Prince)**
1960-

Farahnaz
1963-

Ali Reza
1966-2011

Leila
1970-2001

CHAPTER 1

Iran enters the Automotive Age ~
The Qajar Dynasty

Chapter 1: Iran enters the Automotive Age ~ The Qajar Dynasty

The Gardner-Serpollet ~ a car fit for a (Persian) King

A glimpse at Iranian history will show that through the ages, the automobile and the Iranian monarchy have been intertwined and it is not uncommon to see the presence of one or more unique automobiles, whether symbolically or otherwise, having a prominent role in many of the historical events pertaining to the monarchy over the years.

The first such event was the entry of the automobile into Iran. The country, which until 1935, was commonly known as Persia, saw the first automobile proverbially rolled into Iranian history by Mozaffar ad-Din Shah, the fifth King of the Qajar dynasty (1785 to 1925). He had come to the throne on May 1, 1896 following the assassination of his father, Nasser ad-Din Shah who had ruled Iran for over half a century.

The new monarch, whose title in Farsi was "Shah", meaning King, had spent his years as the Crown Prince, living a life of luxury and leisure. Not surprisingly, he ascended to the throne ill-equipped to rule the country, as he had had virtually no experience or knowledge in affairs of the state. Exacerbating matters, the young Shah was out of touch with his citizens and was facing a serious financial crisis after inheriting a government, which not only ran massive deficits, but was also heavily indebted to Imperial Russia and England.

The young King belatedly undertook several attempts at fiscal and other reform-oriented measures but could not overcome the legacy of crushing debts which, as time proceeded, would be further exacerbated by his own actions.

The Shah looked to the West as a source of inspiration and followed closely the latest technological developments underway at the time. He began to emulate the European lifestyle, aspiring to visit France one day, which, at the time, stood out as the zenith of European culture for Iranians.

In order to manage the fiscal affairs, which, not surprisingly, were further aggravated by the lavish spending of his own

Portrait of Mozaffar ad-Din Shah. *(Golestan Palace)*

court, Mozaffar ad-Din Shah resorted to the granting of economic concessions to foreign powers as a means of securing funds. These concessions served not only to finance his government, but also his own increasingly lavish lifestyle. As the number of concessions grew, foreign powers gained monopolistic control of various Iranian industries and markets.

The most notable of these was the D'Arcy Oil Concession, awarding the full rights of discovery, extraction and sales of a newly discovered substance that became known as "oil". When justifying his decision to grant this concession, the Shah was reported to have

Fit for a King ~ The Royal Garage of the Shah of Iran

responded that he was simply getting rid of "that nasty and dangerously flammable substance".[1]

In 1900, while rounding out his fourth year on the throne, Mozaffar ad-Din Shah finally achieved his dream of visiting France. To finance this trip, he secured a loan of 23.5 million Rubles from the last Tsar of Russia, Nicholas II, to cover the expenses required for a trip fit for a king, and his retinue of ministers, high-ranking officials, acolytes and guards.

Rubles in hand and plunging his country further into debt to a foreign power, the Shah and his retinue set out by royal carriage to the border city of Tabriz, where the Qajar dynasty traced its lineage. The arrival of the Shah, to what could be called his "hometown", was met with great enthusiasm from the local populace, with colorful local welcoming traditions such as the hanging of Persian carpets from windows, symbolizing the wish of the local populace for a safe and successful journey.

ABOVE: **Mozaffar ad-Din Shah with his three-wheeled tricycle.** *(Golestan Palace)*

RIGHT: **Mozaffar ad-Din Shah in Russia.** *(irdc.ir)*

OPPOSITE TOP: **Saad od-Dowleh, Iranian Ambassador to Belgium, standing beside a Gardner-Serpollet 10 hp in Belgium. It was to be the first car to ever arrive in Iran.** *(Borzou Sepasi)*

---

[1] *Fakhr ol Molk, "Mozaffar ad-Din Shah Qajar – First and Second European Travel Diaries," Darbar, Tehran, 1902*

Chapter 1: Iran enters the Automotive Age ~ The Qajar Dynasty

Fit for a King ~ The Royal Garage of the Shah of Iran

From Tabriz, the Shah and his delegation entered Russia and traveled by sea and train through Germany and Switzerland, eventually arriving in the French city of Contrexéville for the first of two royal visits, one to take place on an unofficial basis to be followed by a second official state occasion.

It was not uncommon for Persian Monarchs to undertake two state visits. The first, "unofficial" visit, with the Shah and his retinue taking up quarters at the health resort of Contrexéville, would allow the King to see the sights and sounds of the country he was visiting without the burden of protocol and the pomp and circumstance inherent in an official tour. The trip was the first exposure of the Shah to life outside Iran and his diaries reflect that he was continuously amazed by what he saw and experienced. In particular, the timing of the trip coincided with the shift of transportation from the horse and carriage to the automobile. Not surprisingly, it did not take long for the

Chapter 1: Iran enters the Automotive Age ~ The Qajar Dynasty

Shah to order his aides to find and purchase an automobile for his personal use.

Coincidently, Ketabchi Khan, the son of the head of the Iranian Customs Organization, paid his respects to the King. He was accompanying his father to oversee the Iranian pavilion at the 1900 Paris *"Exposition Universelle"* (World Fair), and drove to his appointment in a steam-powered Gardner-Serpollet 8 hp Victoria, immediately catching the eye of the Monarch.

The company founder, Leon Serpollet, had launched his first car in 1887 and gradually increased production until, faced with a financial crisis, was obliged to take on an American businessman by the name of Frank Gardner as a partner which resulted in the renaming of the company as Gardner-Serpollet.

The Shah, after sitting in the car and curiously checking all its details, expressed an initial interest in making a purchase before inexplicably changing his mind and claiming that it was too much like a "wheelbarrow" and that he had seen better automobiles. Nonetheless, sitting in the passenger seat, he still asked the young Ketabchi Khan to drive him around.

In the midst of the visit to France, the Shah and his entourage made a short detour to Russia and Germany, before travelling to Paris on board the luxurious French Presidential train. Upon arrival, the Shah was warmly welcomed by the President and a who's who of French officialdom. Also in attendance were the Iranian Ambassadors to France and Belgium and, of course, both the younger and elder Ketabchi Khans.

Notwithstanding all the pomp and circumstance, the sixth day of the state visit was marred by a strange turn of events. Whilst preparing to board his carriage to attend a reception arranged by the French foreign minister at the Palace of Versailles, Saad od-Dowleh, the Iranian Ambassador in Belgium informed the Monarch that a new car had been found for possible purchase and was ready for his inspection. The automobile was another Gardner-Serpollet, a 10 hp version, slightly larger than the 8 hp model presented by Ketabchi Khan. It caught the immediate attention of the Shah, as it not only came with closed coachwork enabling it to accommodate four passengers, but also was a landaulet having a retractable roof in the rear.

LEFT: **Mozaffar ad-Din Shah and his entourage standing next to the second Gardner-Serpollet, an 8 hp version.** *(Golestan Palace)*

OVERLEAF: **The third Gardner-Serpollet ordered by Mozaffar ad-Din Shah, also an 8 hp version, waiting for the Shah at the Palace steps.** *(Golestan Palace)*

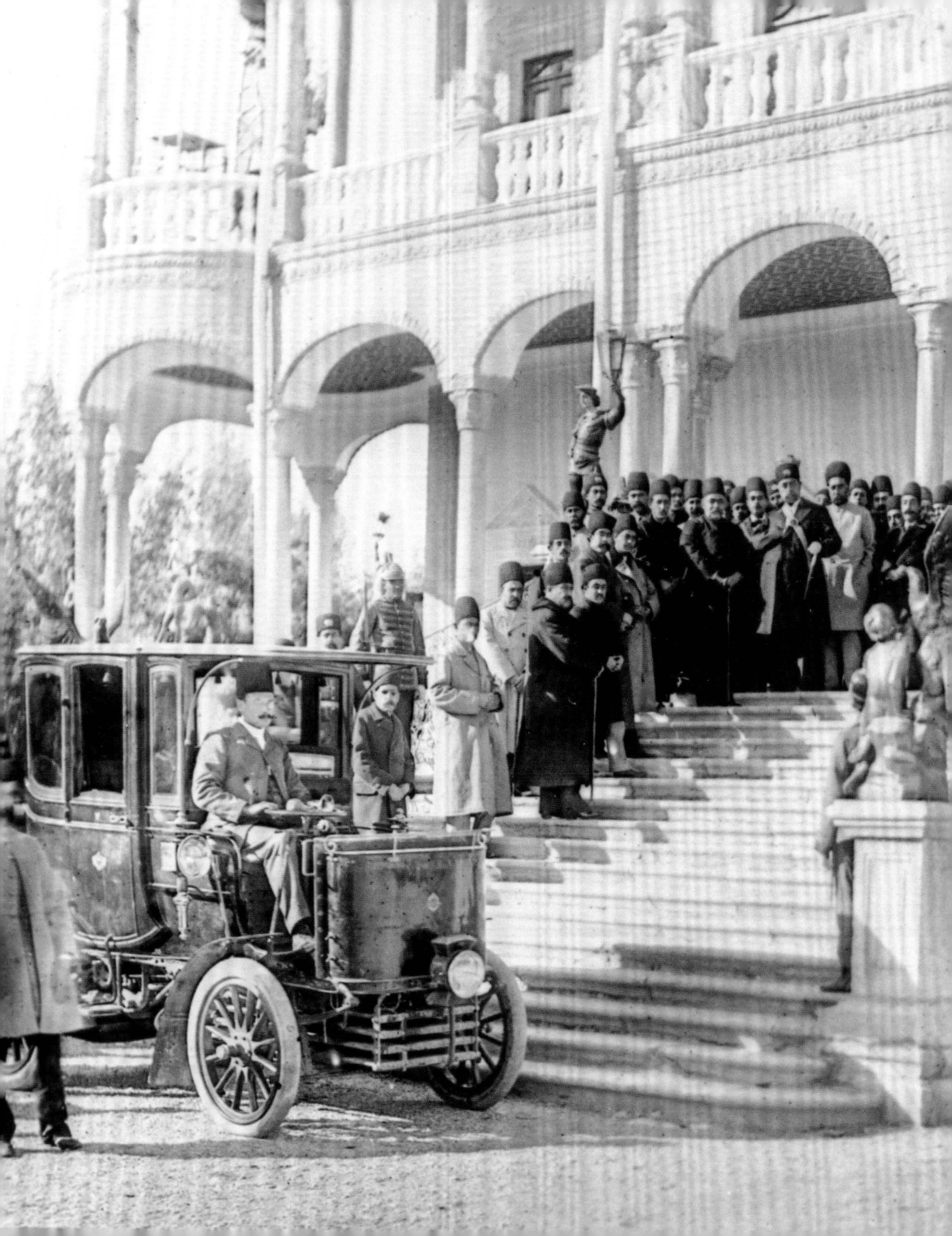

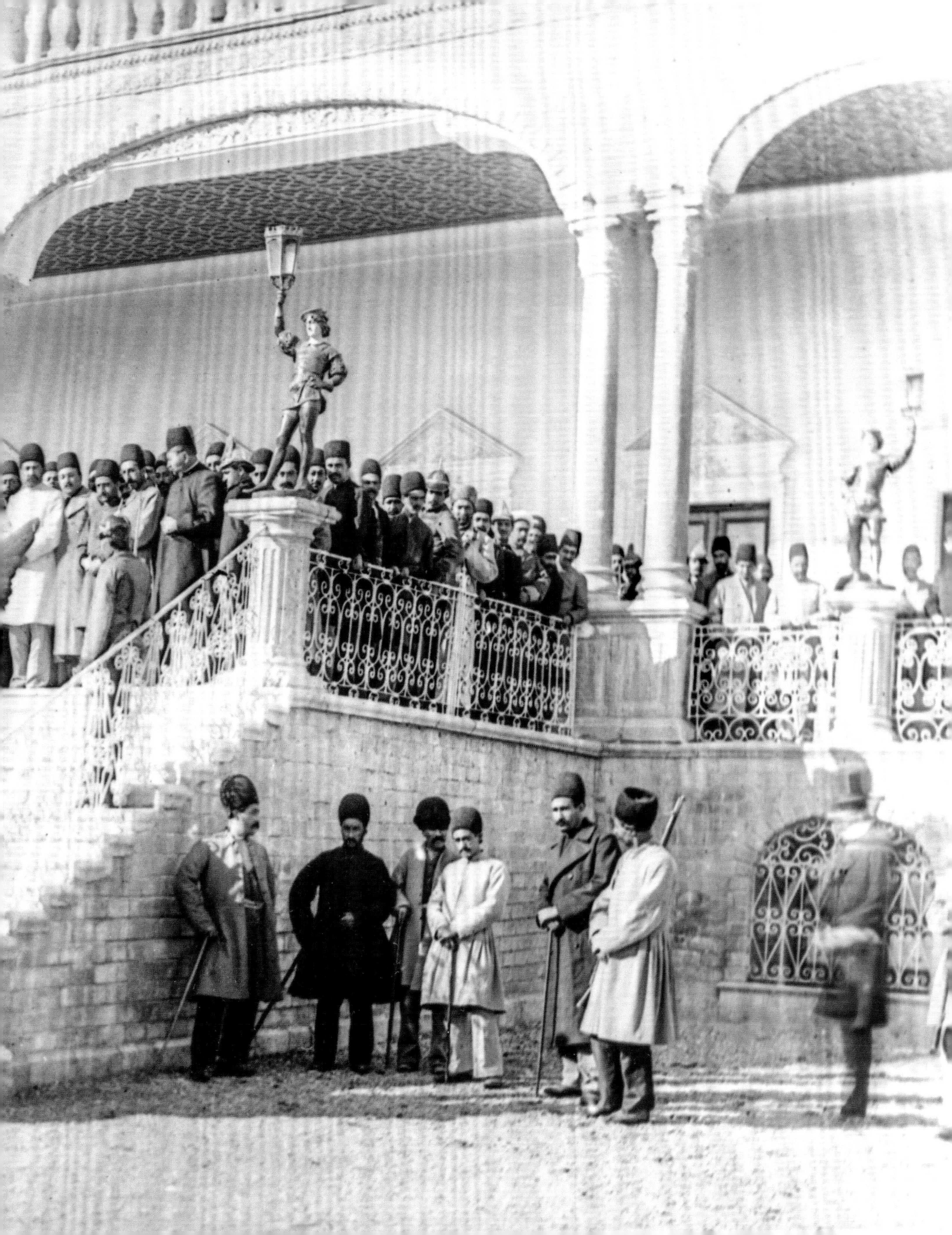

Fit for a King ~ The Royal Garage of the Shah of Iran

After spending several minutes examining the vehicle, the Shah made an on-the-spot decision to make the purchase. Simultaneously, the Shah's Minister of Royal Affairs suddenly shouted a warning prompting the Shah to turn around and see that the minister was grappling with a pistol-wielding assassin. After a short struggle, the police arrived and arrested the would-be assassin, a French anarchist. It was a strange twist of history that the decision to purchase the first car for import to Iran would be almost concomitant with the first assassination attempt on the Shah.

After the assassination attempt, the Shah then entered his carriage to sightsee in Paris and the newly-purchased Gardner-Serpollet 10 hp joined the procession, enabling him to ride in both the car and carriage, and to compare them. The car was then shipped to Iran through Eastern Europe and Russia, eventually reaching the Iranian Caspian Sea port of Anzali.

With the first automobile to be imported into Iran en route, the Shah continued his journey, visiting a number of other European countries before returning home.

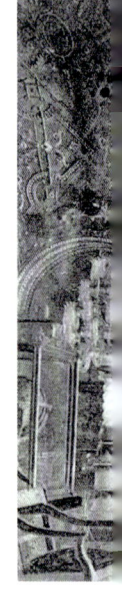

Chapter 1: Iran enters the Automotive Age ~ The Qajar Dynasty

OPPOSITE: The Golestan Palace as it stands today.

LEFT: Shams ol-Emareh (Palace of the Sun), located in the Golestan Palace compound providing a panoramic view of Tehran for the Shah. *(Golestan Palace)*

TOP LEFT: Reception Hall of Golestan Palace. *(Golestan Palace)*

ABOVE: An oil on canvas of the Mirror Hall of the Golestan Palace by famed Iranian painter Kamal-ol-Molk.

He met his new car in the city of Qazvin, 150 miles northwest of the capital of Tehran and he decided use it to complete his journey. Being that the automobile was a new phenomenon in Iran and there was no one qualified to drive one, the Shah, thinking ahead, had hired a French chauffeur, a Monsieur Marnay who, fortuitously, was with the royal retinue. With the Shah in the passenger seat, the chauffeur left the royal entourage "in the proverbial dust" as the two sped to Tehran.

The Shah, perhaps not used to such speeds, asked Monsieur Marnay to slow down, under the guise of allowing the rest of the royal procession to keep up. Three days later near Tehran in "Kan" province, the car began experiencing mechanical problems forcing the Shah to revert to riding his carriage to the capital. The car was subsequently transported to Tehran and repaired in the Golestan Palace, a Safavid-era (1501-1736) royal compound which the Qajars had rebuilt and once again had become the royal seat. It was there that not only the Gardner-Serpollet but also Monsieur Marnay and his wife made their new home in Tehran. Monsieur Marnay stayed on for years as the royal chauffeur and, with his wife, went on to establish the first European cuisine restaurant in the capital of Iran.

It would seem that the creations of Gardner-Serpollet left a lasting impression on the Shah, as less than one year after his return from Europe, he ordered two more new Gardner-Serpollets, these being of the 8 hp fixed head model.

Mozaffar ad-Din Shah's second trip to Europe

The spring of 1903 marked the eighth year of Mozaffar ad-Din Shah's rule. Assisted by a new 10 million Ruble loan from a Russian bank, the Shah set off on his second trip to Europe. On April 11, he started his journey in one of the two new Gardner-Serpollet 8 hp, heading for the Iranian border. When they were near Qazvin, the boiler screw in the car came apart with an explosion of steam. Fortunately, the Shah had already decided to switch to his accompanying carriage, and the car was towed back to Tehran by two horses.

As with the preceding trip, the Shah traveled first to Contrexéville, visiting the natural spa there, as well as riding horses and hunting. He expressed his desire to meet the creator of his cars and Leon Serpollet arrived with his most state-of-the-art product, the Gardner-Serpollet "Easter Egg," a streamlined two-seater racing car. Serpollet, who was both an inventor and a manufacturer, having been credited with inventing the "flash" boiler, had also set the land speed record of 120 km/h in the same car in 1902. At the meeting, Serpollet discussed his company and the new models he had in the pipeline. It was then that Mozaffar ad-Din Shah ordered a new 50 hp *landaulet de voyage*, which was shipped to Tehran, a few months later. The body was yellow and the upholstery in blue satin. The rear seat was large and comfortable, and the Shah was so pleased with that new car that he promptly ordered a second 50 hp from the company, this time in black.

Chapter 1: Iran enters the Automotive Age ~ The Qajar Dynasty

BELOW: Mozaffar ad-Din Shah in his yellow Gardner-Serpollet 50 hp in the outskirts of Tehran. *(Golestan Palace)*

RIGHT: The second Gardner-Serpollet 50 hp, in black paint, with a damaged tire on the road to Karaj, the largest suburb on the outskirts of Tehran. *(Golestan Palace)*

OPPOSITE: Monsieur Marnay behind the wheel of the Gardner-Serpollet 50 hp. *(Leo McAllam, prewarcar.com)*

23

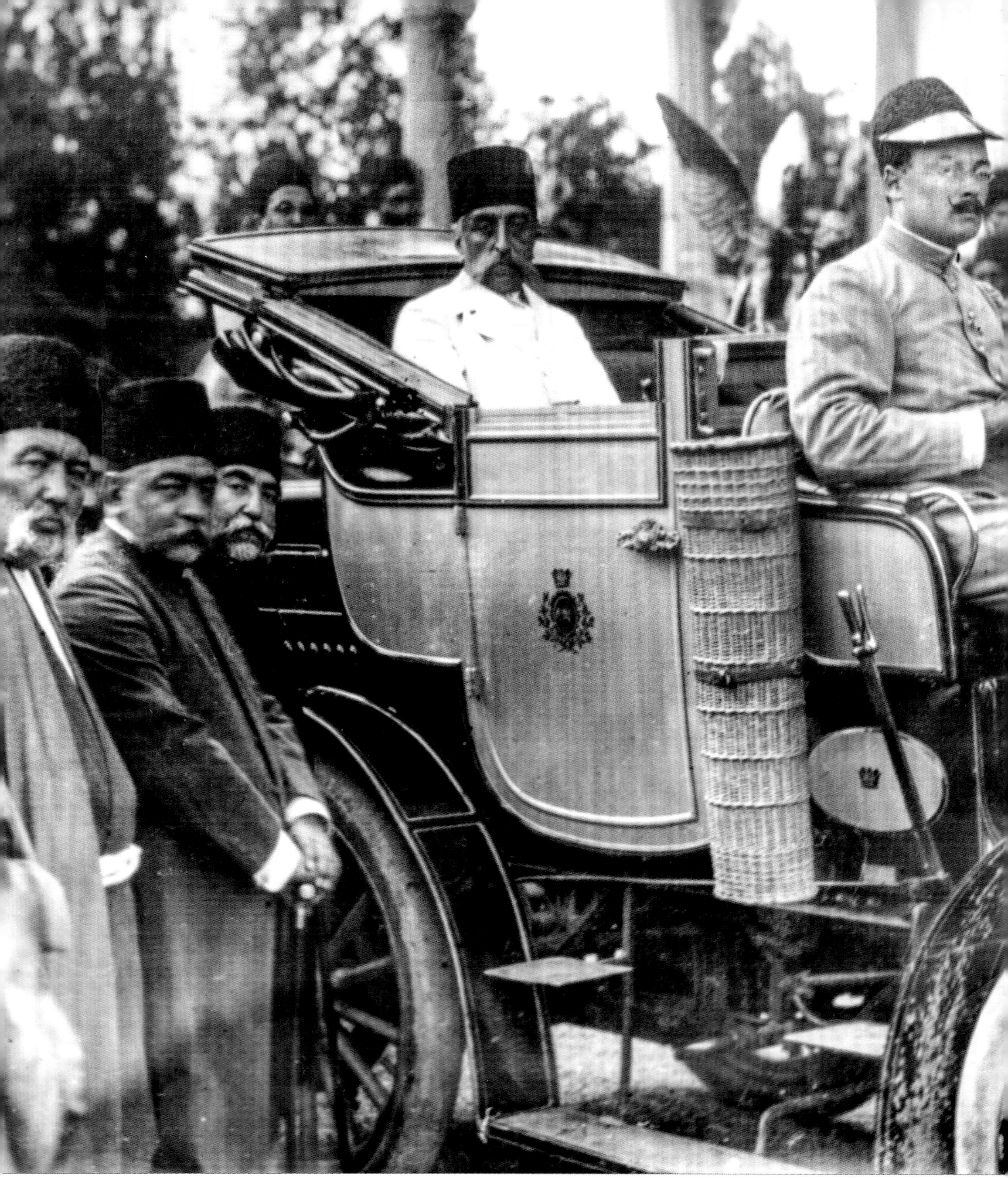

Mozaffar ad-Din Shah reigned for a total of eleven years and, despite his faults and propensity to put Iran into debt and grant monopolistic concessions to foreign powers, was nonetheless regarded as one of the more progressive Shahs of the Qajar dynasty. History has judged him positively for his success in introducing Iranians to various aspects of modern life, including cinematography, a pursuit that remained his lifelong passion. Perhaps the primary legacy of Mozaffar ad-Din Shah was the establishment of a national Parliament and endorsement of a Constitution, which, after two millennia of monarchical rule, for the first time transferred a portion of the powers vested in the Shah to parliamentary rule. No less than forty days after this monumental event, on January 3, 1907, 53-year-old Mozaffar ad-Din Shah suffered a fatal heart attack.

The Progeny: Mohammad Ali Shah and his father's cars

With the passing of Mozaffar ad-Din Shah in 1907, his cars were inherited by his son and successor, Mohammad Ali Shah Qajar. The new Shah promptly took steps to overturn and undo all his father's reforms, including the new Constitution, and went so far as to dissolve the fledgling Parliament, taking the unprecedented step of bombarding the Parliament building with artillery fire when protests broke out.

Despite, Mohammad Ali Shah Qajar's efforts to prove that he was not his father's son when it came to reforms, these feelings were not parlayed when inheriting and enjoying his father's collection of Gardner-Serpollet automobiles and the new Shah used them frequently.

Sharing the common thread between father and son for taste in cars was the macabre coincidence that the Gardner-Serpollet automobile seems to also have been a magnet for assassination attempts.

Surrounded by the crowds, Mozaffar ad-Din Shah greets his subjects in the first Gardner-Serpollet 50 hp with an open top.
(Golestan Palace)

Mohammad Ali Shah Qajar was to have a similar experience with the black 50 hp Gardner-Serpollet. On February 27, 1908, the new Shah had planned an excursion from the Golestan Palace to Dowshan Tappeh located in the east of Tehran. However, on this date, there were rumors of a conspiracy to assassinate him. As a result, and as per daily routine, the driver brought the car around to the main entrance of the Palace so that the Shah could board.

However, instead, staff from the royal court quickly sat in the car in his place and drew the curtains to disguise that the Shah was not inside. The driver was then instructed to leave without the Shah who would then follow in his carriage approximately fifty meters behind. When the car reached Avenue Bagh-e Vahsh (Zoo Street), the car was attacked, when two hand bombs were thrown towards the vehicle. The Shah, upon hearing the explosion, quickly disembarked from his carriage, took refuge in the nearest building and returned to the safety of the Golestan Palace. Unfortunately, on the next day, two street sweepers cleaning up the debris came accross another bomb hidden in the trash, which detonated killing them both.

Chapter 1: Iran enters the Automotive Age ~ The Qajar Dynasty

Eventually, the would-be assassins were identified and arrested. Upon investigation, it became clear that they were constitutional activists affiliated with the nascent Iranian Communist Party.

OPPOSITE TOP: **Mohammad Ali Shah Qajar.** *(Golestan Palace)*

OPPOSITE BOTTOM: **The second Gardner-Serpollet 50 hp outside Tehran.** *(Golestan Palace)*

THIS PAGE: **The second Gardner-Serpollet 50 hp after the failed assassination attempt, with the bomb damage clearly visible.** *(Borzou Sepasi)*

27

The Ahmad Shah era and the end of the Qajar dynasty

Mohammad Ali Shah Qajar had five sons and two daughters from two wives. His second son and first born from his second wife Malekeh Jahan was Ahmad Shah, the designated Crown Prince of Persia. Born in January 1898, the Crown Prince was known to be smart, inquisitive and, unlike his ancestors, had a keen interest in education, in particular the subjects of history and law. During his early education, the Crown Prince studied international law and, with the help of a French teacher, became fluent in the French language. The Monarch in waiting spent most of his early youth reading scientific books and engaging in intellectual discourse with people usually much older than himself.

In 1909, the pro-constitution movement came to a head and its supporters marched from across Iran to congregate in Tehran, forcing Mohammad Ali Shah to flee into exile and leading to the successful reinstitution of the Constitution. After an unsuccessful attempt to retake his throne in 1911, Mohammad Ali Shah died in exile in San Remo, Italy in 1925.

On July 16, 1909, the resurrected Parliament voted to place the 11-year-old Ahmad Shah on the throne. Due to his young age, a regent, who was also his uncle, became his guardian and handled his affairs. Upon reaching the age of majority in 1914, Ahmad Shah's coronation was ominously held, coincidently with the start of World War I.

As the United Kingdom and Russia entered into the war, a front was opened against the Ottoman Empire, leading to the effective occupation of Iran to use it as a springboard for attacking Ottoman territories, impugning Iranian sovereignty and involving Iran in a war, which it could neither afford nor had the will to fight.

This state of affairs was further exacerbated in 1917 with the collapse of Tsarist Russia and Great Britain's attempt to attack Russia from Iranian territory in order to reverse the course of Russia's fledgling revolution. An enraged Bolshevik government took steps to exact revenge on the Iranian government, attacking and annexing large portions of Iran and incorporating this territory into the newly formed Soviet Union. Concomitantly, the Bolsheviks then extracted large and humiliating economic concessions from Iran.

All these events were a sad situation for a Monarch who, unlike his predecessors, not only supported constitutional rule, but was also well-educated, erudite and preferred to eschew the luxurious trappings of royal life. Nevertheless, by 1921, Ahmad Shah was the ruler of a greatly weakened Iran, severely affected by the corruption of his court and the rivalry between Russia and Great Britain for control and influence.

Chapter 1: Iran enters the Automotive Age ~ The Qajar Dynasty

Large portions of his kingdom had been occupied by the Russian Red Army on the one hand, whilst some areas still remained controlled by the English, whose increasing demands led to a virtual stranglehold on the Iranian economy.

Such a state of affairs culminated in a military coup led by Reza Khan, the head of the Iranian Cossack Brigades, a cavalry unit modeled after the Caucasian Cossack regiments of the Imperial Russian Army. He was the strongest and most organized military leader in Iran and sensing the vacuum left by Ahmad Shah's greatly weakened state, on February 21, 1921, he marched 2,500 of his troops into Tehran, facing no opposition whatsoever. Ahmad Shah asked Reza Shah to form a new government, which he duly carried out, yet, instead of assuming the position of Prime Minister, he became Minister of War, also referred to as *Sardar-Sepah* (Commander of the Army). The pro-British Seyyed Ziaeddin Tabatabaee became Prime Minister. This coup would change the face of the Iranian political landscape, and the course of history.

In October 1923, Reza Khan assumed the post of Prime Minister following a royal decree by Ahmad Shah. At this point, coming to the realization that he was nothing more than a figurehead who had been effectively stripped of all his powers, and under the guise of health issues, Ahmad Shah left Iran for an extended European visit. In 1925, with Ahmad Shah still "on vacation" Reza Khan declared the end of the Qajar dynasty and became the new Shah of Iran. Taking the name Reza Shah Pahlavi (the Middle Persian language of pre-Islamic era), Reza Khan's ascendancy to the throne was subsequently ratified by Iran's constitutional assembly and Ahmad Shah's vacation became a permanent exile. He died in France less than five years later at the age of 32.

The simplicity of his lifestyle and the eschewing of the luxurious trappings afforded by the royal court can be exemplified by the fact Ahmad Shah often preferred the use of carriages, versus the automobile. It was not until several years into his rule that he finally made the decision to purchase his first car, a 1918 Cadillac Type 57. Many pundits have speculated that the decision to purchase a Cadillac was not only to spite the British who held a stranglehold on Iran's economy, but also a nod to the growing role of America as a symbol of democracy.

However, Ahmad Shah did eventually purchase a new Rolls-Royce Silver Ghost in 1922, but in light of the events that took place leading to his exile, he had no opportunity to use the vehicle, a void that his successor Reza Shah Pahlavi would more than make up for.

OPPOSITE: **The young Ahmad Shah Qajar.** *(iichs.ir)*

RIGHT: **Ahmad Shah leaning against the 1918 Cadillac Type 57.** *(iichs.ir)*

CHAPTER 2

The Sheikh Khazal Rebellion and the Rise of the Pahlavi Dynasty

Chapter 2: The Sheikh Khazal Rebellion and the Rise of the Pahlavi Dynasty

The discovery of oil and the evolution of the automobile in Iran

Despite being readily visible and even bubbling up to the surface in certain areas from time immemorial, May 26, 1908 is the date when oil was officially "discovered" in Iran, as symbolized by the first gusher rising from what was recorded as Oil Well Number 1.

This event changed the history of the country forever, and its automotive landscape. The discovery, which took place in the southern city of Masjed Soleyman, also led to the further tightening of British control over the Iranian economy, as the "discoverer", William Knox D'Arcy, had already secured an exclusive sixty-year concession for Iranian oil from Mozaffar ad-Din Shah. The pittance that was paid as royalties was squandered on the lavish spending of the Qajar court.

An interesting automotive footnote is that the search and discovery for oil was initiated by General Ketabchi Khan, the same man whose son was instrumental in introducing the first automobile to Iran by way of the Gardner-Serpollet to Mozaffar ad-Din Shah. A firm believer in the prospects for Iranian oil, the General succeeded in persuading D'Arcy to negotiate the concession for securing the rights for the oil and played a direct role in its subsequent execution.

Following the first gusher, D'Arcy sold most of his rights to the Burmah Oil Company, which in turn on April 14, 1909 established the Anglo-Persian Oil Company (APOC). The first mass-market products launched by the APOC were petrol and other petroleum-based products, packaged and marketed with the BP logo. In a stroke of marketing genius, the BP trademark was designed with the intent of having two very separate and distinct meanings. For the Iranian market, it stood for *Benzene Pars*, meaning the benzene of the Parsian (Persian) people, a marketing ploy with the objective of circumventing growing anti-British sentiment in Iran. Outside Iran, BP was marketed as an acronym for British Petroleum. So, a simple wordplay on two initials catering to two separate markets led to the growth and recognition of what would eventually become one of the most iconic and recognized brands in the world.

The expanding activities of the APOC influenced the automotive landscape in Iran as well, as more and more vehicles were imported and put in service by the company. Some of the most remarkable of these vehicles were the Straussler tanker trucks. These eight-wheeled trucks, painted in black with APOC logos on their tanks, were equipped with massive 7.2-liter V8 engines, which developed in excess of 150bhp, and their size and power left a lasting impression wherever they were used.

At the same time, the APOC staff also used a fleet of Ford Model Ts in both pickup and passenger car configurations. While automobiles had been used on a limited scale by the Iranian elite, the entry into the country of the mass-market Model T by APOC created awareness for the Iranian middle class that perhaps they too could have access to automobiles. Soon thereafter, the Ford Model T and other vehicles began to have a growing presence in Iran with one specific Model T playing a role in the suppression of a major rebellion and paving the way for the coming into power of a new royal dynasty.

The Pahlavis takeover

Reza Khan was born in the village of Alasht in northern Iran. He spent his childhood in poverty and in his teenage years he joined the army, advancing rapidly through the ranks. Upon becoming War Minister, he was successful in forming an integrated and unified armed force, replacing the previous hodgepodge of separate brigades. His reforms included securing better and more modern equipment for the armed forces, among which was a Ford Model T as his personal military staff car, a vehicle that would play a role in the changing political dynamics of Iran. With his reorganized troops Reza Khan set his sights on unifying the country by retrieving control of vast swathes of land from a litany of tribes with rulers who, taking advantage of the weak central government,

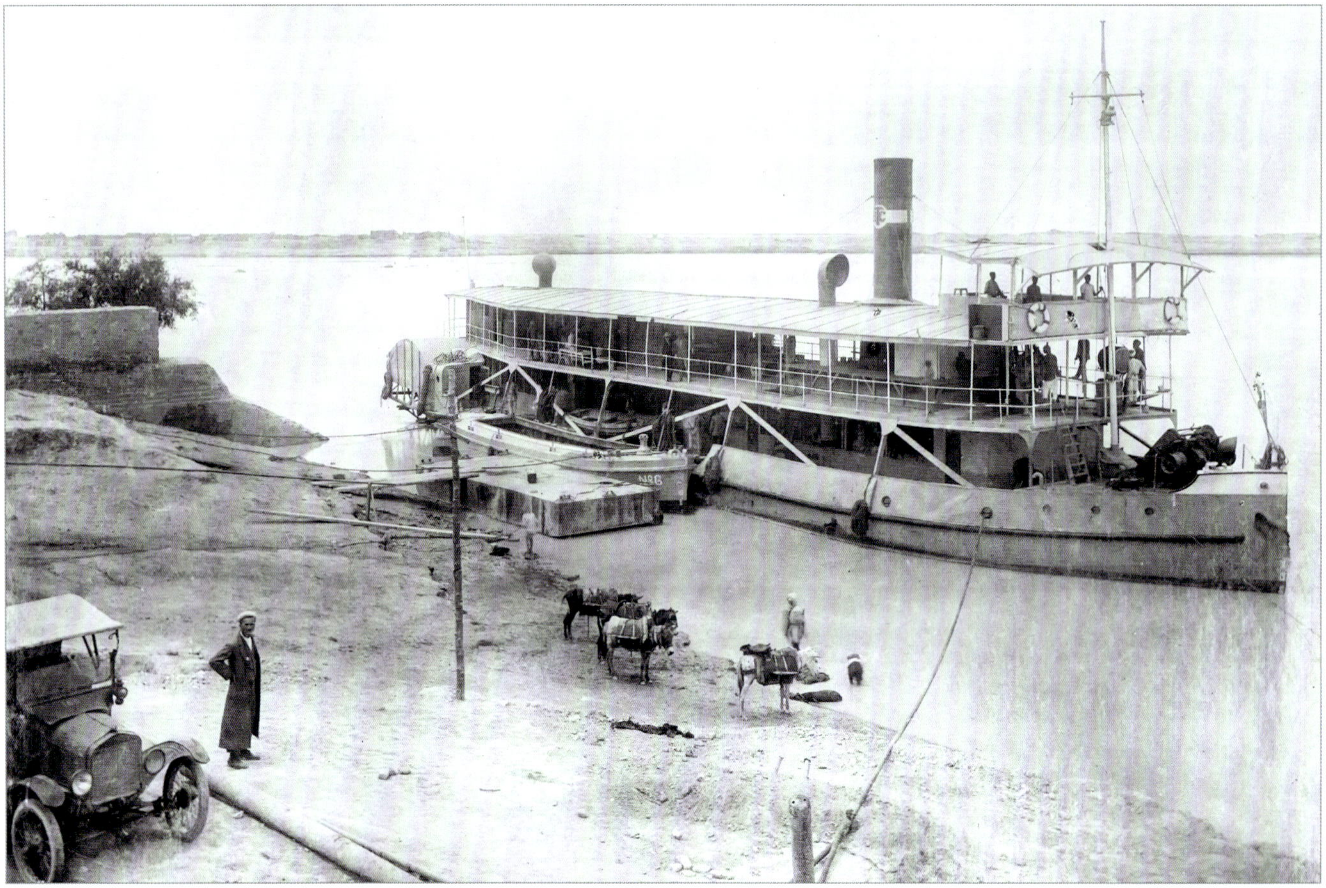

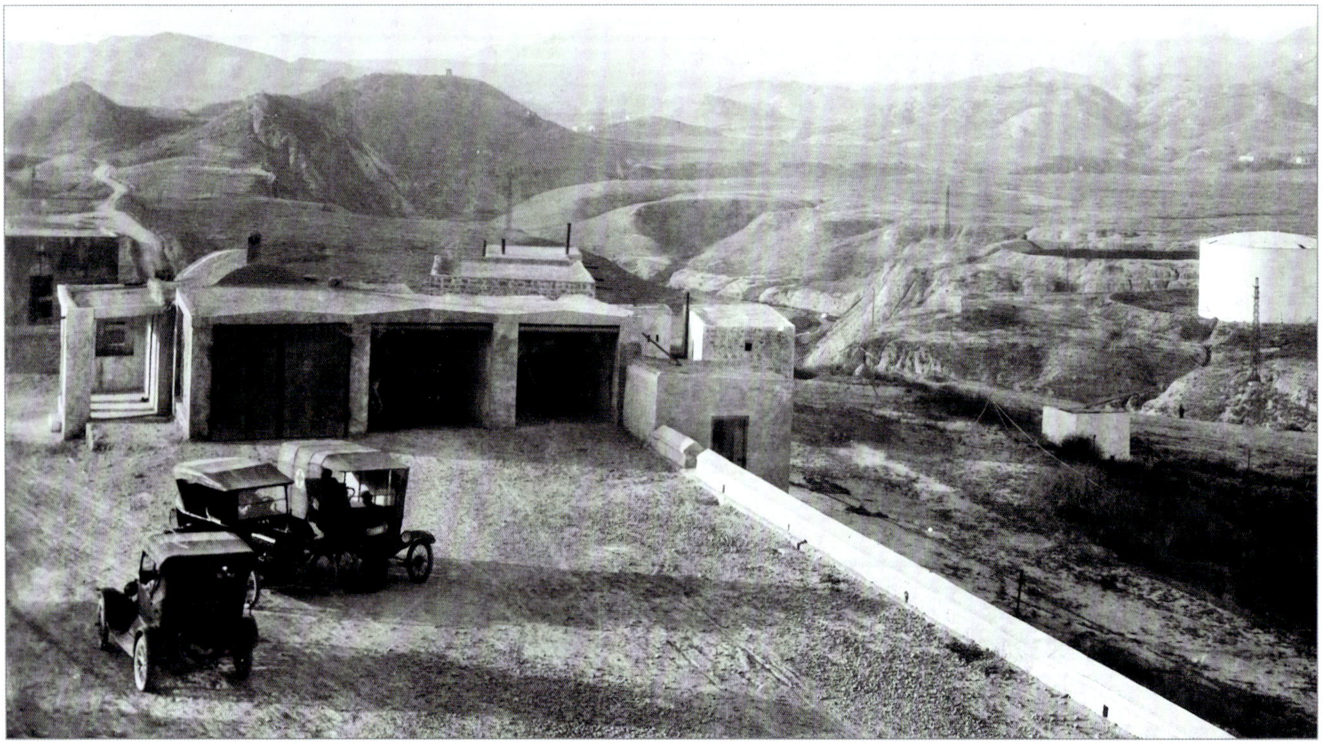

Chapter 2: The Sheikh Khazal Rebellion and the Rise of the Pahlavi Dynasty

had set up their own autonomous governments. Having re-asserted control over these areas, he then concentrated on bringing back law and order to the roads and railways connecting the Iranian provinces that had been overtaken by gangs of bandits. Upon his appointment as Prime Minister in 1923, Reza Khan focused his attention on one of the last remaining territories that was still operating independently of the Iranian central government, the region of Mohammareh, which today is known as the province of Khuzestan. It was here that Reza Khan's Ford Model T played a role in quelling the Sheikh Khazal Rebellion.

In 1897, Khazal bin Jabir bin Merdaw al Kabi, the tribal leader of the Banu Kaab tribe assumed his position as the Sheikh of Mohammareh, one of the largest and most oil-rich regions of Iran. Khazal immediately appointed his sons to governorships of different areas, establishing de facto autonomous control over large swathes of southwest Iran. The British, whose oil concessions fell within these territories found it more convenient to deal directly with the Sheikh instead of the central government and by various means worked to cultivate him as a key ally. By way of example, APOC purchased a large tract of land from him to establish what would eventually become the world's largest oil refinery in the city of Abadan. The Sheikh was also the main beneficiary of a number of lucrative contracts to provide protection to APOC and its installations.

Taking on Sheikh Khazal posed risks for Reza Khan, as the Sheikh was a foe to be reckoned with. He not only had vast wealth at his disposal, but also strong alliances with local and regional tribal leaders as well as the tacit backing of the British government. He became the leader of an Arab separatist uprising, appealing to the League of Nations to gain recognition for his cause. Undeterred, Reza Khan set out for the province of Khuzestan in November 1924, using his 1919 Ford Model T staff car for the 1,000 km journey.

Accounts as to how the Sheikh Khazal Rebellion was defeated by Reza Khan are somewhat varied. However, during the course of the research for this book, the author was fortunate to discover a rare, published account by Reza Khan of his journey to Khuzestan and the events that took place on the way. Following is a

ABOVE: **Sheikh Khazal.**

TOP RIGHT: **V8-powered Straussler trucks used for transporting oil before the building of pipelines.** *(NIOC)*

OPPOSITE TOP: **One of the many Ford Model Ts widely used by the APOC in the south of Iran.** *(iichs.ir)*

OPPOSITE BOTTOM: **The Masjed Soleyman oil fields.** *(iichs.ir)*

Fit for a King ~ The Royal Garage of the Shah of Iran

ABOVE: One of the first gas stations built by the Anglo-Iranian Oil Company, themed on Islamic architecture. *(BP)*

RIGHT: Five Iranian Army Citroën P2 Half-Tracks, chassis numbers unknown, in a 1924 parade in Isfahan. *("The Great Reza Shah, Travel Account of Khuzestan" book)*

OPPOSITE TOP: Citroën P2 Half-Tracks undergoing testing by the Iranian Army. *(Borzou Sepasi)*

Chapter 2: The Sheikh Khazal Rebellion and the Rise of the Pahlavi Dynasty

summary of that diary, including some pictures from the travelog.

According to Reza Khan's travelog, *The Great Reza Shah, Travel Account of Khuzestan*,[1] one of the most important layovers on the way to Khuzestan was at the ancient city of Isfahan, the former capital of Iran. It was there that the British Ambassador contacted Reza Khan in an effort to deter him from proceeding. Whilst the message was ostensibly meant to convey the British concern for Reza Khan's personal safety, the implication was that the British were not happy that their regional ally was under threat.

During Reza Khan's stay in Isfahan, a military parade was arranged for him in the historical Shah Square. On display was the latest military equipment that had been procured by Reza Khan during his tenure as Minister of War, including five Citroën P2 Half-Tracks. These unique vehicles were equipped with straight-four 1452cc engines developing 20 hp and were capable of towing heavy armaments such as heavy artillery. Using a Citroën Type B2 chassis, the P2 Half-Tracks were the brainchild of Adolphe Kégresse, inventor of the half-track and dual clutch transmission.

Before joining Citroën, Kégresse had served as the technical director of the royal garage of the Russian Czar Nicholas II in St. Petersburg. During his tenure there, he had not only served as the Tsar's personal chauffeur, but in order to improve the mobility of the Imperial fleet during Russia's deep winter snows, he had modified a number of cars into Half-Tracks, including the Czar's Rolls-Royce Silver Ghost. The P2 Half-Tracks had gained worldwide fame and media attention having successfully achieved the first motorized expedition and crossing of the Sahara Desert in 1922.

Reza Khan traveled next to Shiraz and from there to the port city of Bushehr where he had hoped to witness the arrival of a new warship, which he had ordered from Germany for the now rejuvenated Iranian Navy. When it became apparent that the ship had not yet arrived, he

---

[1] Farajollah Bahrami, "The Great Reza Shah, Travel Account of Khuzestan," Pahlavi Political Culture Research and Publication Center, Tehran, 1976

Chapter 2: The Sheikh Khazal Rebellion and the Rise of the Pahlavi Dynasty

traveled to the city of Ahvaz. Despite being in the heart of Sheikh Khazal's home turf, large crowds turned out to welcome him at the city entrance which he entered riding in his Model T. Sheikh Khazal's son and eight local tribal leaders were amongst the crowds, though Khazal himself was not present, and his home had been prepared to be used as Reza Khan's residence. Despite the fact that the residence was surrounded by armed guards with some of them roaming the halls, Reza Khan was not deterred, entering Ahvaz ahead of his troops fully determined to put an end to Sheikh Khazal's activities once and for all.

During the first two days of the visit, Sheikh Khazal stayed on his personal yacht while Reza Khan used his residence, but on the third day, Sheikh Khazal ventured out to meet Reza Khan face-to-face. Reza Khan was taking a stroll on the south porch when they bumped into one another. Against all expectations, Sheikh

OPPOSITE: **Reza Khan leaving Sheikh Khazal's home in Ahvaz.** *("The Great Reza Shah, Travel Account of Khuzestan" book)*

TOP: **The Palace of Sheikh Khazal.**

ABOVE: **Sheikh Khazal's yacht.** *("The Great Reza Shah, Travel Account of Khuzestan" book)*

Khazal fell to his knees attempting to kiss Reza Khan's hand. Reza Khan raised the Sheikh to his feet and said to him, "Be sure that I do not have the greed to take your property and I do not want to take your life and I want to respect you. But to do so, there is but one condition, from now you have to consider yourself an Iranian citizen and obey the government in Tehran." More ominously, he then warned the Sheikh, "If you continue with the previous behavior, your punishment will be death."[2] In a matter of minutes, Sheikh Khazal had capitulated.

After quelling the Sheikh Khazal uprising, Reza Khan used the opportunity to visit the other cities of Khuzestan province with his Ford Model T. On the way to the city of Dezful, he crossed a river, transporting the Ford on a small raft-like vessel. Reza Khan was aware that the rainy season was quickly approaching which would invariably make travel by road most difficult. Near the city of Shush, the seasonal rains started, and the Prime Minister and his retinue had to take shelter at the homes of local villagers.

As soon as the weather cleared up enough, Reza Khan crossed the border from Iran to Iraq to make a pilgrimage to Shia Muslim shrines and then returned to Tehran as a national hero. Near the outskirts of the city, Reza Khan's Model T was escorted by a procession of cars, which had come to welcome him, and military aircraft appeared in the sky dropping bouquets of flowers and confetti. When the Ford entered Tehran, large crowds were in the streets and in Sepah Square, symbolically where the military barracks were located that had housed this once lowly soldier who had now risen to become Prime Minister.

When the Model T could no longer pass through the throngs of people, Reza Khan was obliged to stand and address the crowd, and was finally only able to escape when a soldier managed to bring Reza Khan a horse, which he rode back to his home. After this incident, Reza Khan's star was on the rise and was a prelude of things to come.

Pahlavi Rising: The Last Royal Car of the Qajar dynasty

In 1922, Ahmad Shah took delivery of a new Rolls-Royce Silver Ghost, chassis number 38PG. With a beautiful convertible body by Hooper, his enjoyment of this vehicle was short-lived, because in 1923, ostensibly for health reasons, but in reality for lifelong exile, Ahmad Shah left for Europe. Shortly thereafter, on December 15, 1925, in his capacity as Prime Minister, Reza Khan initiated a coup by instructing Parliament to depose Ahmad Shah and declare himself as Monarch. This event was followed by a coronation ceremony on April 25, 1926. One of his first acts after becoming the new Monarch was to commandeer the ownership of this Rolls-Royce.

---

[2] *Farajollah Bahrami, "The Great Reza Shah, Travel Account of Khuzestan," Pahlavi Political Culture Research and Publication Center, Tehran, 1976, p. 147*

LEFT: **Reza Khan in Band-e-Mizan after quelling the Khazal Rebellion.** *("The Great Reza Shah, Travel Account of Khuzestan" book)*

OPPOSITE TOP: **The royal carriage built by Carl Marius of Austria at Reza Shah's coronation, April 25, 1926.** *(iichs.ir)*

OPPOSITE BOTTOM: **Reza Shah in his royal carriage in Toopkhaneh Square. (April 25, 1926)** *(iichs.ir)*

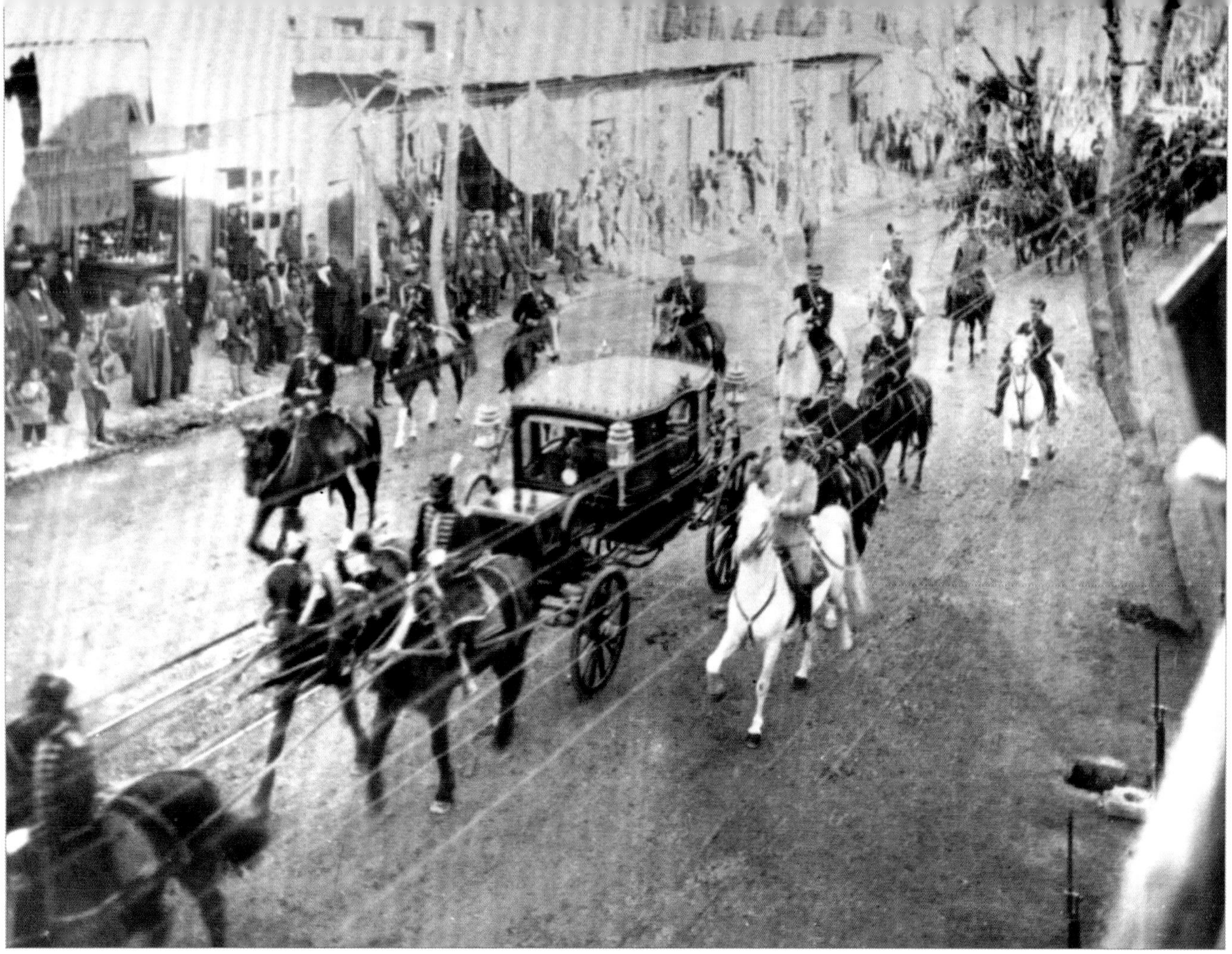

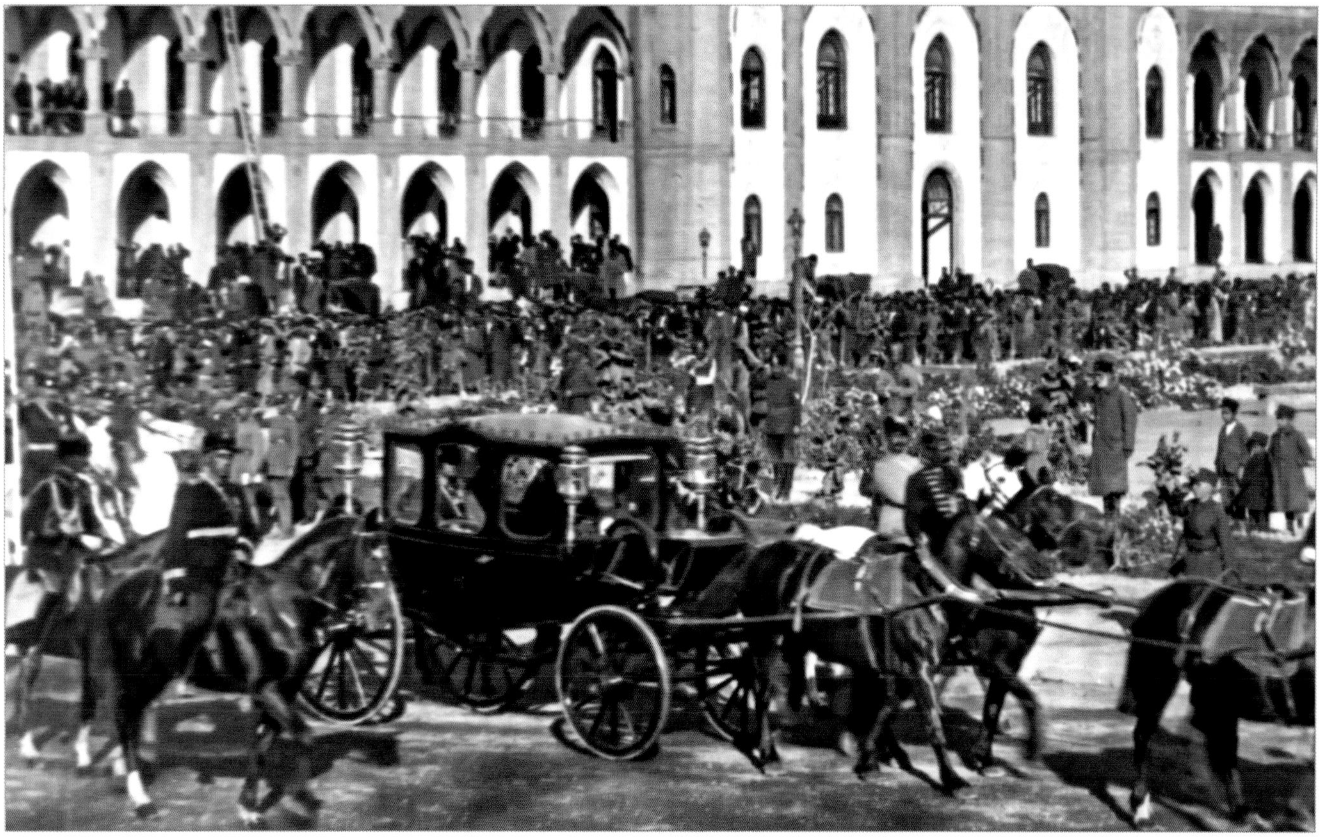

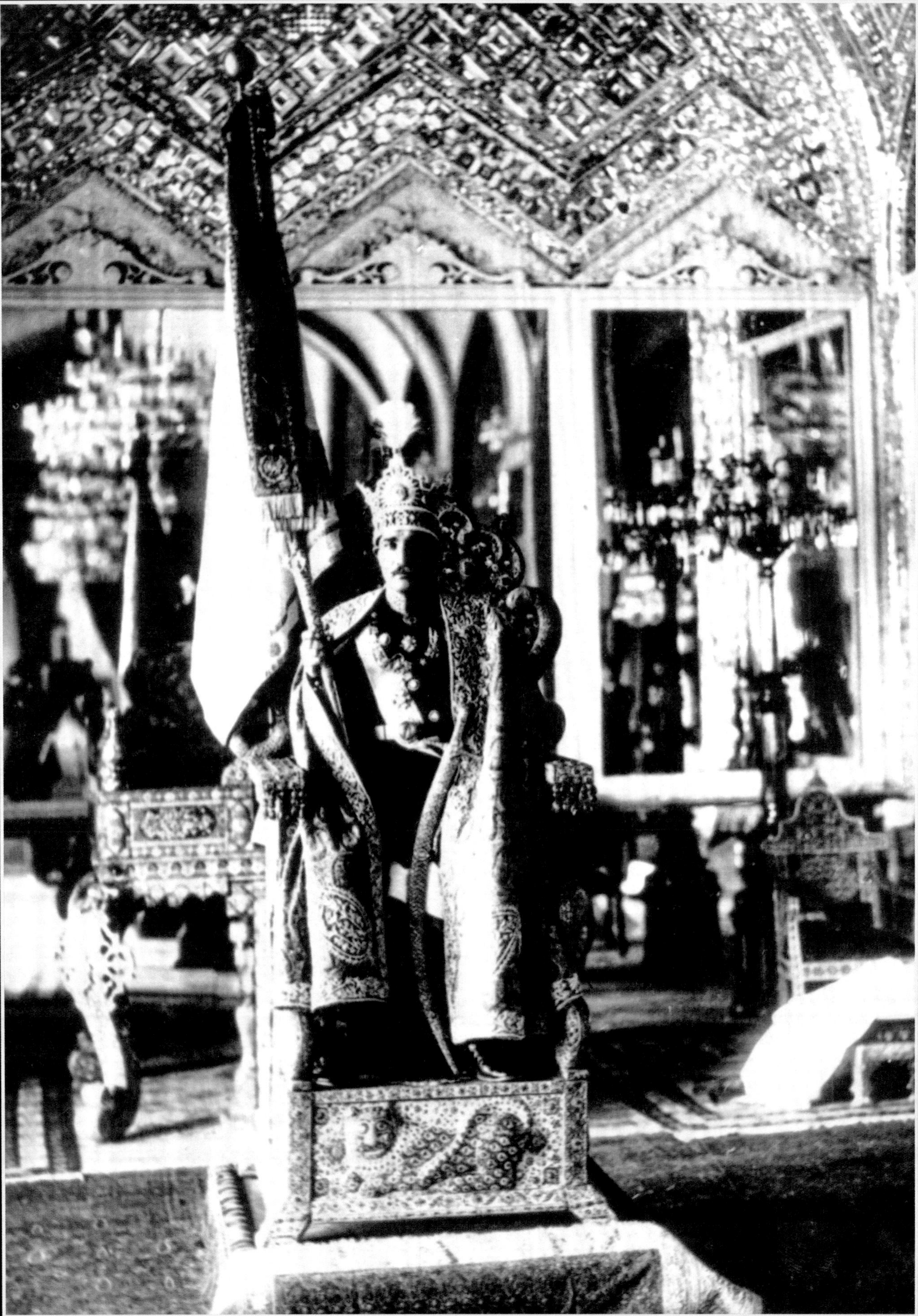

Chapter 2: The Sheikh Khazal Rebellion and the Rise of the Pahlavi Dynasty

OPPOSITE: Reza Shah on the day of his coronation, April 25, 1926.

RIGHT: Inaugurating the "Beseem Pahlavi" (Pahlavi Wireless Center) in the Rolls-Royce Silver Ghost on April 27, 1926. *(Tehran Telegraph Office)*

BELOW: The official visit of King Faisal I of Iraq to Iran in 1932. Reza Shah and the Iraqi King are passing along Sepah Avenue on their way to the Golestan Palace in the Rolls-Royce Silver Ghost, chassis number 38PG, bodied by Hooper. *(Borzou Sepasi)*

The royal Silver Ghost was used mostly during the summer season because of its convertible roof, especially during the visits of foreign legations. It is documented that such foreign dignitaries as King Faisal I of Iraq, Prince Gustaf VI of Sweden, Lev Karakhan, Deputy People's Commissar of Foreign Affairs of the Soviet Union, Hjalmar Schacht, the Reich Minister of Economics, and Prince Faisal, Viceroy of Hejaz, were all passengers in this car at different times.

The Rolls-Royces of the Imperial Army

Rolls-Royces were not only pressed into duty for royal use, but also for military purposes. During his tenure as Minister of War, in 1923 Reza Khan ordered four armored Rolls-Royce Silver Ghosts for the Iranian Army, which emerged as the symbol of a new, organized modern army.

Rolls-Royce had a history of producing armored vehicles, with the first being launched in 1914 with the start of World War I. The first series utilized a Silver Ghost chassis, which were subsequently modernized in 1920 under the moniker Rolls-Royce 1920 Pattern and again in 1924 referred to as the Rolls-Royce 1924 Pattern. The models, which were procured for the Iranian Army were Silver Ghosts referred to as the 'Indian Pattern'. This series was derived from the 1920 Pattern but had extended hull armor to provide more space and a domed turret with four ball mounts for a Vickers 303 machine gun.

The Iranian Army Silver Ghosts had the chassis numbers 266WO, 267WO, 268WO and 269WO and were painted in a leopard camouflage color at the time of delivery but were later repainted in black and each car was given a Farsi name.

TOP (BOTH): **Armored Rolls-Royce Silver Ghosts, chassis numbers 266WO, 267WO, 268WO and 269WO of the Imperial Army shortly after delivery to Iran.** *(Borzou Sepasi)*

RIGHT: **At an army parade, Reza Shah inspecting the black armored Rolls-Royce Silver Ghosts.** *(Borzou Sepasi)*

Chapter 2: The Sheikh Khazal Rebellion and the Rise of the Pahlavi Dynasty

The Rolls-Royces of the Qajar and early Pahlavi era ~ from bribes to coups

During this era, the affinity for Rolls-Royce cars did not just extend to the monarchy. Aristocrats and politicians also took a liking. Notable among them were Vossug ed Dowleh and Prince Nosrat-ed Dowleh Firouz, the first being a twice-serving Prime Minister and the second a foreign minister. Their ownership of Rolls-Royce cars intertwined with the fates of their political careers.

Vossug ed Dowleh owned a 1921 Rolls-Royce Silver Ghost Touring Phaeton by Hooper, chassis number 11LG, and is believed to have purchased his vehicle with funds earned by less than orthodox means. Apparently, in 1919, during his second tenure as Prime Minister, Vossug ed Dowleh was a lead player in negotiations with the British over the Anglo-Persian Agreement, which, according to pundits would have virtually reduced Persia to a protectorate. The agreement was so controversial in its scope that it led to an outcry from the United States. Eventually, it became public knowledge that Vossug ed Dowleh had been bribed in return for signing the agreement, and his Rolls-Royce was believed to be the result of these ill-gotten gains. Despite repeated denials and offers to pay back the sum in question, the public outcry was so high that he was eventually forced to leave Iran. Years later, after self-imposed exile, Vossug ed Dowleh returned to Iran and was able to regain the trust of Reza Shah, resuming his public service until his eventual death in Tehran in 1951.

Prince Nosrat-ed Dowleh Firouz, another signatory to the Anglo-Persian Agreement, had a less fortunate fate. Prince Firouz had served as the Minister of Foreign Affairs during the Anglo-Persian Agreement negotiations. He was also tainted by allegations of

Vossug ed Dowleh leaning against his 1921 Rolls-Royce Silver Ghost Touring Phaeton, chassis number 11LG, bodied by Hooper. (Borzou Sepasi)

Chapter 2: The Sheikh Khazal Rebellion and the Rise of the Pahlavi Dynasty

bribery, forcing him to leave for exile in Paris. A *bon vivant*, Prince Firouz lived a life of luxury, driving around Paris in a 1914 Rolls-Royce Silver Ghost with license plate number FN 2792. In 1921, after hearing of the nascent coup by Reza Shah and with hopes of succeeding Ahmad Shah, Prince Firouz Mirza jumped into his Rolls-Royce and rushed to Tehran, driving straight from Paris, apparently in such a hurry that he did not have the time to remove his original license plates.

As fate would have it, following his entry into Iran and somewhere between Qazvin and Tehran, he ran into an army battalion that was on its way to join forces with the coup. Any hope of Prince Firouz becoming the next King of Iran quickly vanished as he watched helplessly while his Rolls-Royce was confiscated by the rebellious

Chapter 2: The Sheikh Khazal Rebellion and the Rise of the Pahlavi Dynasty

troops for use by Reza Khan in Tehran. Shortly thereafter, Prince Firouz himself was arrested and sent to prison. During his three-month incarceration, he translated Oscar Wilde's *De Profundis*. He then returned to public service again only to be subsequently re-arrested for bribery in 1930, after which he was sent to exile in Semnan where he died under mysterious circumstances.

Prince Firouz's Rolls-Royce is unique in that this vehicle was commandeered by the armed forces of a country not once, but twice in its history. Chassis 50AB was bodied in Paris by the Coachbuilder Lachlaverie & Gaches and delivered by the French Rolls-Royce dealer, Via Autos, where it was then sold to a T. Buxareo. With the start of World War I, the vehicle was commandeered in 1914 from its unfortunate owner by British forces stationed in Paris and used for both official and ceremonial use, including a troop review by King George V.

With the end of World War I, the vehicle was decommissioned and ended up in the hands of Prince Firouz. Some pundits view this as a simple coincidence, whilst others take the more cynical view that the

OPPOSITE (BOTH): **Rolls-Royce Silver Ghost Torpedo, chassis number 50AB, bodied by Lachlaverie & Gaches, that between 1914-19 was used by the English Military Authorities in Paris, here seen with King George V in the back. After 1919 the car was owned by Prince Nosrat-ed Dowleh Firouz.** *(Ben Erickson)*

BELOW: **The Imperial Bank of Persia in Toopkhaneh Square where the J. McMurray Rolls-Royce Silver Ghost, bodied by Cunard Motor and Carriage was delivered.** *(Antoin Sevruguin)*

Fit for a King ~ The Royal Garage of the Shah of Iran

Chapter 2: The Sheikh Khazal Rebellion and the Rise of the Pahlavi Dynasty

vehicle was given to him as a bribe by the British for the positions taken by Prince Firouz in the Anglo-Persian Agreement, citing that the approximate time of delivery of the vehicle to Prince Firouz from the British Army, coincides with the date of the Agreement.

It was not only the Iranian elite who used Rolls-Royces as their personal transportation. In 1899, based on one of the many concessions granted to the British, the Imperial Bank of Persia was founded. It not only emerged as the leading commercial bank in Iran, but also became the de facto state bank. In 1920, the bank's chief officer, J. McMurray, took delivery of a Silver Ghost bodied by Cunard Motor and Carriage Company. After delivery, the car virtually disappeared only to pop up again in 1976 when it was displayed in an exhibition commemorating the Pahlavi dynasty, where it was presented as one of Reza Shah's personal cars. It is not clear when this vehicle became a part of the royal garage, but given the bodywork and stature of this vehicle, it may have at some time been acquired for use by the royal court.

Reza Khan posing in front of Nosrat-ed Dowleh Firouz's confiscated Rolls-Royce Silver Ghost Torpedo, chassis number 50AB, bodied by Lachlaverie & Gaches, upon his triumphant march into Tehran. Note the license plate. *(Borzou Sepasi)*

CHAPTER 3

The Pahlavi Garage Comes of Age

Chapter 3: The Pahlavi Garage Comes of Age

A new arrival: 1930 Pierce-Arrow Model A Town Car ~ "Something Different"

By 1929, the royal garage had expanded into a fleet of automobiles including the leading brands of the period. As Reza Shah consolidated power, his taste in vehicles gravitating away from the standard offerings of the manufacturers of the day to specially ordered, one-off vehicles, which both literally and figuratively would be "fit for a Shah."

In this vein, on December 11, 1925, Reza Shah ordered his first custom-built car, a Rolls-Royce Phantom I. This replacement for the Silver Ghost, the former mainstay of the royal garage, was put into production with chassis number 72DC and then sent to the coachbuilding company, Hooper, which produced the body with the serial number 8556. However, from this point on, things took a different turn. Reza Shah personally ordered modifications and additions such as gold-plated body trim, pale golden-tinted windows, and the painting of the Pahlavi crests on the doors. The finished car was delivered to the Palace in September 1926, and it was put into duty for various events and ceremonies.

Reza Shah's custom-built Rolls-Royce Phantom I, chassis number 72DC, bodied by Hooper in front of Mar-Mar (Marble) Palace. *(Borzou Sepasi)*

Fit for a King ~ The Royal Garage of the Shah of Iran

Following this experience, Reza Shah explored the possibility of ordering something more unique. During this period, in an age when concepts such as *compliance* and *conflict of interest* were in their infancy, the Shah's private banker, Colonel Khan Amir Khosravi, head of the Pahlavi Bank, also held the agency for Pierce-Arrow, and Reza Shah Pahlavi himself became his largest customer. In 1929, not satisfied with his custom-ordered Phantom I, the Shah requested Colonel Khosravi to order a special car for him, one that had to be different.[1] It should then be of no surprise that this order went to the Pierce-Arrow Company.

During this era, Pierce-Arrow had three models in production, namely the A, B, and C. Of these, the most luxurious and expensive version was the Model A, which would become the basis of the "different" vehicle which was to be proverbially fit for a Shah. Based on the order received from Colonel Khosravi, acting as agent, and paid for by Colonel Khosravi, as private banker, the company processed the order by first producing the rolling chassis numbered 3025354, and then sending the chassis to the coachbuilding company Brunn & Company.

During those years, Herman Andrew Brunn was a renowned custom auto designer and coachbuilder, having designed and built cars for such notable luminaries such as Katharine Hepburn, J.P. Morgan, and Irving Berlin,

[1] *Mohammad Gholi Majd, "August 1941: The Anglo-Russian Occupation of Iran and Change of Shahs", University Press of America, Lanham, Maryland, 2012, p. 326*

TOP: The Phantom I and other vehicles from the royal garage being dispatched by train to serve as transportation during a royal visit outside Tehran in 1932. *(irdc.ir)*

ABOVE: Reza Shah entering the National Assembly. (March 14, 1933) *(Borzou Sepasi)*

OPPOSITE: Reza Shah stepping into his Pierce-Arrow Model A, chassis number 3025354, bodied by Brunn & Company. *(Borzou Sepasi)*

not to mention royalty such as King Carol of Romania and King George of Greece. Based on the Model A platform, a special body was designed by George Woodfield and hidden from public view. The vehicle was almost entirely built by hand and registered by Brunn in the company archives as design number 2330 and body number 1. Painted in a luminous white, the exterior metal parts such as bumpers, front windshield frame, door handles, and wheel covers were gold-plated. The same theme was carried over to the windshield and glass, which had a unique pale gold hue. The interior was upholstered in champagne-colored silk, the motif of which was a gold wreath. The cigarette case was made of solid gold. Uniquely, this car did not have the famous Pierce-Arrow helmeted archer hood ornament, having in its place, two small Pahlavi crowns mounted on the front lights and on the rear doors. The car was powered by an in-line eight-cylinder engine with 6306cc displacement making 132 horsepower.

When the car made its debut in April 1930 in Manhattan, New York, it became known as the most expensive car in the world. Though the price was never announced officially, it was estimated at the time that the finished cost was in the vicinity of $30,000. In the obituary of Herman Brunn, published in the *New York Times* on September 23, 1941, the car, referred to as that of the "Shah of Persia," was specifically mentioned and stated that Brunn's life work was "climaxed by his design of a partly gold-plated, diamond studded auto for the Shah of Persia, now Iran."

The Pierce-Arrow arrived in Tehran in 1931 whereupon Reza Shah promptly ordered it repainted to dark blue. However, the modifications did not end there. He ordered the installation of side mount spare tires with gold-plated covers and demanded the removal of the small royal crowns on the front lights. The car joined the rest of the fleet in the royal garage, being used for various ceremonies and royal outings, eventually, becoming part of many historical moments during the reign of Reza Shah such as the opening sessions of the ninth through the twelfth National Assembly (Parliament) meetings in 1933, 1935, 1937, and 1939.

ABOVE & BELOW: The royal Pierce-Arrow Model A, chassis number 3025354 and bodied by Brunn & Company, was displayed in Manhattan, New York prior to delivery to Iran. *(Pierce-Arrow Museum, Buffalo, New York)*

RIGHT: Gold-plated Pahlavi crown found on the rear doors. *(Borzou Sepasi)*

OPPOSITE TOP LEFT: The plate of the coachbuilder, Brunn & Company, affixed to the Pierce-Arrow. *(Borzou Sepasi)*

OPPOSITE TOP RIGHT: The chassis number plate. *(Borzou Sepasi)*

OPPOSITE BOTTOM: The champagne-colored silk upholstery, inlaid satin wood trim, and wolfhound fur rugs on the floor of the Pierce-Arrow Model A. *(Borzou Sepasi)*

Chapter 3: The Pahlavi Garage Comes of Age

Fit for a King ~ The Royal Garage of the Shah of Iran

LEFT: The 1934 Harley-Davidson RLs which served as the motorcade escorts of the Shah. (Mid 1930s) *(Borzou Sepasi)*

BELOW: Reza Shah getting out of the Pierce-Arrow Model A on the opening day of the National Assembly in front of the Parliament building on Baharestan Square. (March 14, 1933) *(Borzou Sepasi)*

Chapter 3: The Pahlavi Garage Comes of Age

RIGHT: Sepahsalar Mosque and the National Assembly entrance gate. (Late 1920s) *(irdc.ir)*

BELOW RIGHT: National Assembly building on Baharestan Square with a Ford Model A parked in front. (Late 1930s) *(irdc.ir)*

CHAPTER 4

In his Father's Footsteps

Chapter 4: In his Father's Footsteps

1931 Hispano-Suiza J12 Saoutchik~ a different car for a chosen son

Whilst Reza Shah was consolidating power and ordering his unique and different car, Reza Shah's eldest son, Crown Prince Mohammad Reza Pahlavi, had been sent to Switzerland in 1931 to complete his high school education at the prestigious Institut Le Rosey boarding school. The elite school, with the progeny of some of the world's leading families, exposed the future King to a new world, wholly different from growing up in a Palace under the shadow of a stern disciplinarian father.

Throughout his life, Mohammad Reza Pahlavi was a known car aficionado, and as will be seen, he eventually owned some of the most unique cars in the world. At first, in Switzerland, he was too young to have a driver's license, so this blossoming love of cars initially manifested itself by driving Iranian Embassy cars inside the compound.

Within time however, and on the eve of the start of his attendance at Le Rosey, the Crown Prince asked his father to buy a car for him. He followed in his father's footsteps, searching for something unique. After reviewing sales catalogs and other literature, he discovered Hispano-Suiza. The Swiss Hispano-Suiza agent paid a personal visit to the Crown Prince and exhibited photographs of available Hispano-Suiza models with the Crown Prince eventually selecting the J12 model. It is interesting to note than when the price of the J12 was stated to be a then extraordinary amount of 70,000 Swiss Francs, the court representatives tried to cut the cost by circumventing the Swiss dealer and approaching the factory directly. They were offered the most beautiful car available in the company at the time, a yellow J12 with chassis number 13010 and engine number 321013, which carried a hand-crafted body built by the famous coachbuilder Saoutchik. This car, which served as a showcase of the company, made its

Crown Prince Mohammad Reza Pahlavi (pictured) first learned to drive at the age of ten in a 1929 Chrysler 75, before leaving Iran for Switzerland. *(Borzou Sepasi)*

Fit for a King ~ The Royal Garage of the Shah of Iran

debut at the 1931 Paris Salon and was also subsequently displayed at the 1932 London and Geneva Motor Shows. It featured a 9425cc V12 engine, developing 220bhp.

After a great deal of correspondence between the Iranian Embassy in Switzerland and Hispano-Suiza, haggling over the price, the car was finally sold to the Crown Prince at a price of 55,000 Swiss Francs. On October 30, 1932, four days after his 13th birthday, the car was delivered to him in Geneva. Accompanying the car was Jacques Saoutchik, the founder and owner of the coachbuilder J. Saoutchik, who traveled to meet with the Crown Prince and personally introduce him to the car and its features.

After registering the car, a chauffeur was hired and the royal Hispano-Suiza was sent to Lausanne where Le Rosey was located. When laying his eyes on the car, the Crown Prince is said to have exclaimed, "This is the car that I wanted, and I don't want anything else!"

Arriving on the first day of school in the canary yellow Hispano-Suiza, accompanied by his chauffeur, valet, footman, and a "spectacularly handsome, silver-haired old gentleman who was… a Persian diplomat of high rank, what came to be called the *Affair Pahlavi* took place".

As the Crown Prince descended from the vehicle, he looked at his peers "with a stare that he must have intended to be regal". According to pundits, this attempt to put on royal airs for his classmates was an abject failure, as the Crown Prince was outshined by his own Hispano-Suiza. The Crown Prince's classmates, like himself no doubt, were also attracted to fancy cars and were "oblivious to his royalty, but were instead busy examining the snake-like chrome tubes that coiled out of the hood of this car".[1]

---

[1] *Abbas Milani, "The Shah," Palgrave Macmillan, New York, 2011, p. 45*

ABOVE: Hispano-Suiza J12, chassis number 13010, bodied by Saoutchik in Paris Salon 1931. *(Nethercutt Museum, the Jules Heumann Collection)*

OPPOSITE TOP: The Hispano-Suiza stand at the Geneva Auto Salon in 1932. The royal Hispano-Suiza J12 was on prominent display. *(Hervé Pannier)*

OPPOSITE BOTTOM: A ten years-old Crown Prince Mohammad Reza Pahlavi at the wheel of a 1929 Pierce-Arrow 133, equipped with the optional package of bracket-mounted headlights. *(Borzou Sepasi)*

OVERLEAF: Reza Shah welcoming the Crown Prince in Tehran after his arrival from Switzerland in a 1929 Pierce-Arrow 133. (1936) *(Borzou Sepasi)*

Chapter 4: In his Father's Footsteps

Used as the Crown Prince's daily transportation to school, the vehicle was involved in a fender bender, requiring it to be sent back to the factory for repair. Eventually, the Crown Prince grew so fond of this car that when he finished his education and returned to Iran, he took this car with him. The future Shah used this car daily, usually driving it himself with an open top and going to his usual hangouts such as Stadium No. 1 for a quick game of football. People eventually recognized the car as that of the Crown Prince and would wave to him as he drove by while drivers in the streets would try to clear the way for him to pass.

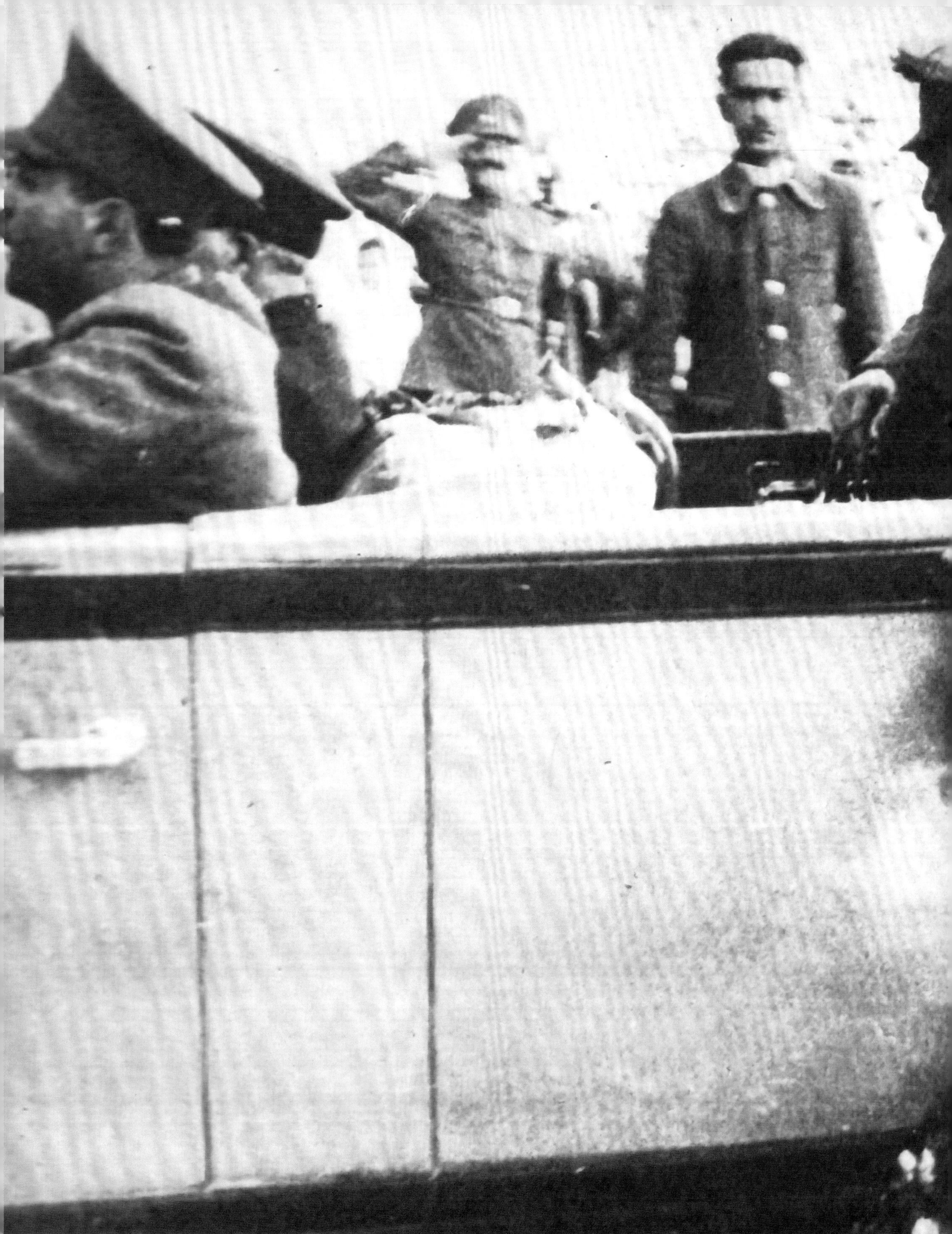

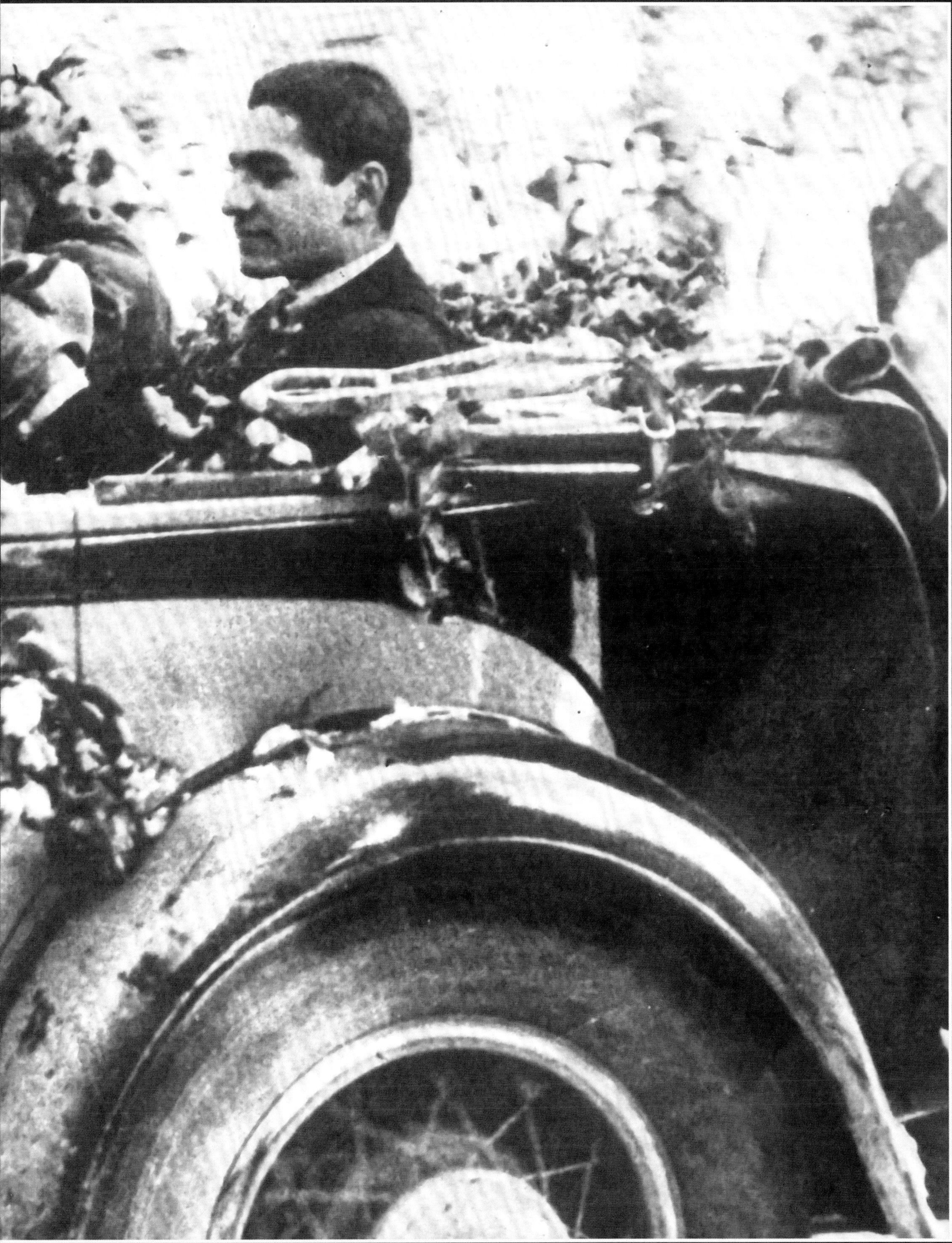

CHAPTER 5

A new Modern Iran begins to Emerge, 1925 to 1936

Chapter 5: A new Modern Iran begins to Emerge, 1925 to 1936

The rule of Reza Shah was marked by many social upheavals and changes as he unflinchingly attempted to transform a feudal society into a modern nation state. In 1926, Iran was a country primarily of peasant villages, tribes and small towns with little industry, a weak and ineffectual army and a population of less than twelve million. Reza Shah set out to make the country strong and united and to develop it so that it could be truly independent with an effective army to resist foreign intervention and impose internal order.

Looking back on this period, most Iranians credit Reza Shah for unifying their country and bringing about law and order. Major strides were made in industrialization, education, infrastructure development and the emancipation of women. Many of the historical events that took place during this period are uniquely intertwined with the vehicles in the royal garage. For example, there was the Model T which he used on his journey traveling across Iran to unite Iran's disparate (and usually warring) tribes under one flag, the opening of a re-invigorated parliamentary session in his one-off Pierce-Arrow or the 1922 Rolls-Royce Silver Ghost which was used to mark the emancipation of women from the veil.

Kashf-e hijab ~ the unveiling

During this period of Reza Shah's rule, no event influenced Iranian society more than the mandatory banning of the use of the veil by Iranian women. Following in the footsteps of Kemal Ataturk of Turkey, Reza Shah adopted the view that to successfully make the transition to a modern society, the manner of dress of Iranians would have to be modernized. As a result, men were mandated to wear suits and ties, topped off by a cap that was popularly known as the "Pahlavi Hat." Even more controversial was the elimination of the "Chador" for Iranian women, a full-body-length shroud-like garment which covered women from head to toe, which put Reza Shah on a collision course with Iran's powerful clergy and more conservative elements in Iranian society.

ABOVE & FOLLOWING PAGE: Reza Shah entering the women's primary college ceremony with the Rolls-Royce Silver Ghost, chassis number 38PG, bodied by Hooper. (January 8, 1936) *(Borzou Sepasi)*

For the announcement of this decree, Reza Shah chose to have an official ceremony on January 8, 1936 and to set an example by having his wife and daughters appear in a primary college ceremony without their veils. Oddly, the vehicle of choice for this controversial "coming out" was the black 1922 Rolls-Royce Silver Ghost, chassis number 38PG. Many found it strange that at a time when there existed more modern and luxurious cars in his garage, Reza Shah would resort to the use of this fourteen-year-old vehicle. Some pundits have raised the theory that since this vehicle was one of the automobiles that coincided with and symbolized the period of Reza Shah's rise to power, it was a reminder to all, including himself, of where he had started. Others have surmised that by using an older, if not simpler looking car (when compared to the newer models in the royal garage) he would seem less ostentatious on such a controversial day.

The Renaissance of the Imperial Iranian Army

Concomitant with this period of social change, as a dyed in wool military man, it was no surprise that Reza Shah would also direct his attention at modernizing the Iranian armed forces. Steps taken during this period ranged from sending his officers to the best military academies across the world, to procuring some of the most modern equipment available. The Iranian Air Force became fully operational with its first cadre of British-trained pilots. Iran's newborn Air Force had many planes of European origin such as: Junkers W33 (1927), de Havilland Tiger Moth (1932), Polikarpov R-5 (1933), Hawker Fury (1933), Hawker Persian Audax (1933), Hawker Hind (1938), Airspeed Oxford (1940) and Hawker Hurricane (1940).

Chapter 5: A new Modern Iran begins to Emerge, 1925 to 1936

THIS PAGE: **Junkers F13 entered the fleet of the Iranian Royal Army in 1924.** *(iichs.ir)*

Fit for a King ~ The Royal Garage of the Shah of Iran

Many historians have overlooked the fact that parallel to the founding of the Iranian Air Force, Reza Shah also set up a fledgling aeronautics industry with the establishment of the "Shahbaz" company which secured the right to assemble a bevy of planes such as the de Havilland Tiger Moth, Hawker Hind and Hawker Audax. Accordingly, by 1936, Iran became the first country in the Middle East to have an aeronautics industry, no small feat when less than two decades earlier the country was suffering from famine, internal strife and instability. Unfortunately, with the start of World War II, the activities of the Shahbaz Company ended.

The Iranian Air force was not the only branch of the armed forces to attract Reza Shah's attention. During this period, the Iranian Navy was equipped with new warships, which were mostly procured from Italy. Concomitantly, the ground forces were supplied with the latest tanks, armored vehicles and artillery, the majority of which were purchased from European countries.

THESE TWO PAGES: A review of the troops by the Crown Prince in a Rolls-Royce Phantom I, chassis number 72DC, bodied by Hooper. (Late 1930s) *(Borzou Sepasi)*

Chapter 5: A new Modern Iran begins to Emerge, 1925 to 1936

Fit for a King ~ The Royal Garage of the Shah of Iran

ABOVE: Reza Shah and Crown Prince Mohammad Reza Pahlavi visiting a de Havilland Dragon Rapide in Qaleh Morghi Airport. This plane was bought by the army for transporting mail on behalf of the Iranian Post Office. (1936) *(Saad Abad Palace)*

LEFT: Reza Shah and the Crown Prince visiting the Shahbaz Airplane Manufacturing Company. (July 21, 1938) *(Saad Abad Palace)*

OPPOSITE TOP: Hawker Hind assembled by the Shahbaz Aeronautics Factory. (1938) *(Saad Abad Palace)*

OPPOSITE BOTTOM: The "Palang" warship was delivered to the Iranian Army in 1931. It was made in Italy and had two Fiat engines, outputting 1,500 hp. *(History of Iranian Modern Army)*

Chapter 5: A new Modern Iran begins to Emerge, 1925 to 1936

Fit for a King ~ The Royal Garage of the Shah of Iran

Chapter 5: A new Modern Iran begins to Emerge, 1925 to 1936

ABOVE: Reza Shah in his Rolls-Royce Phantom I, chassis number 72DC, in Jalaliyeh Square for the military parade on February 22, 1936. *(Borzou Sepasi)*

OPPOSITE TOP: The Czech Republic delivered TNHP tanks to Iran during the years from 1935 to 1937. (Early 1940s)

LEFT: Iranian Army soldiers with modern equipment. (Late 1920s) *(Saad Abad Palace)*

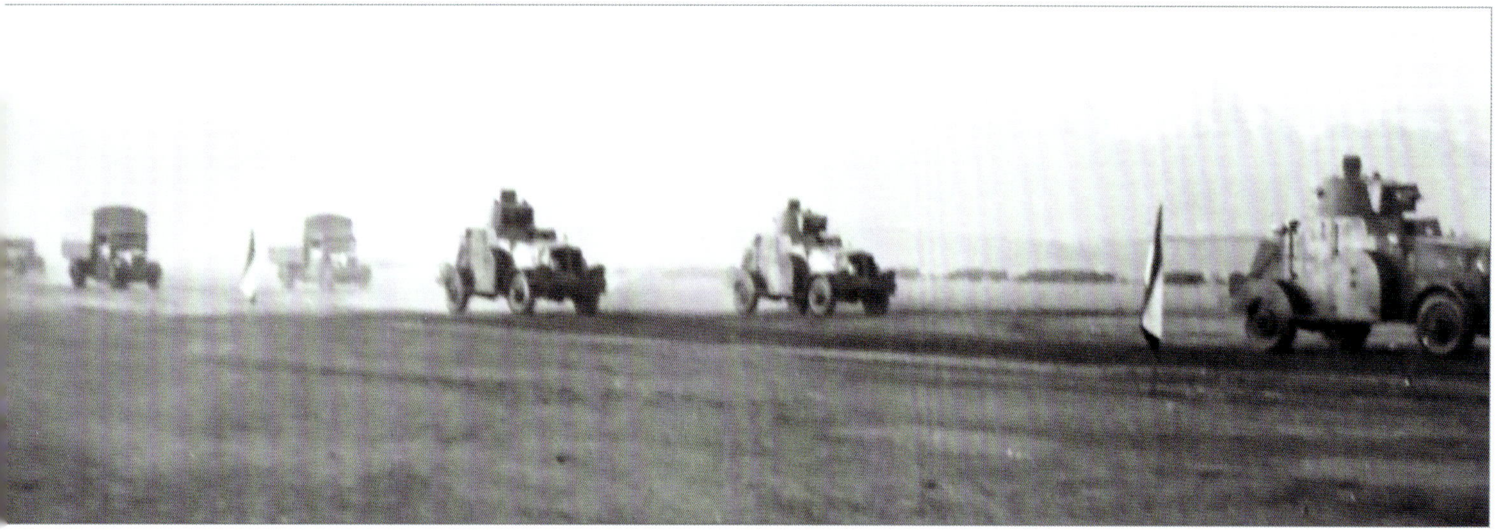

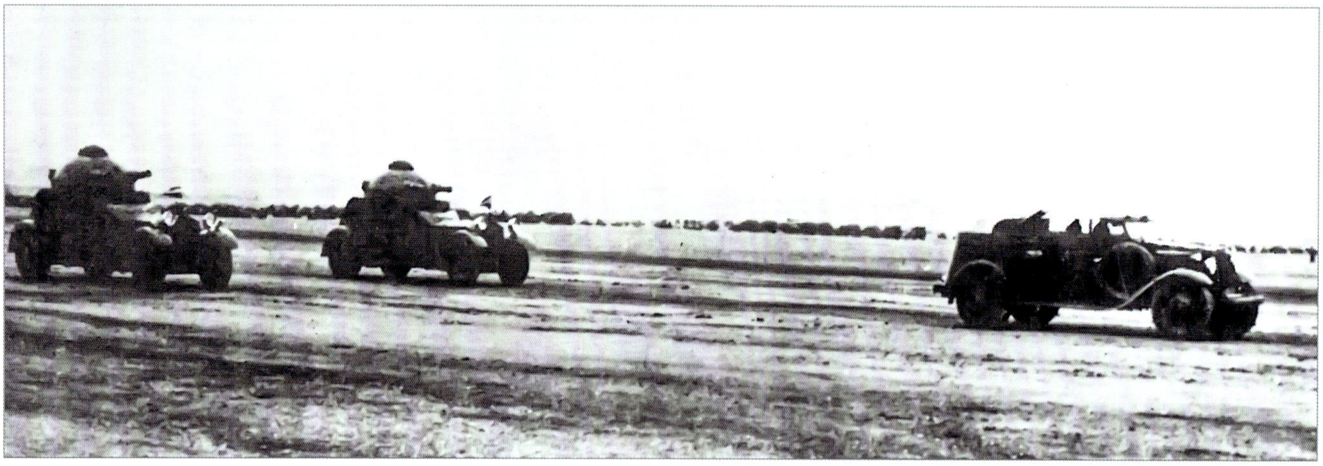

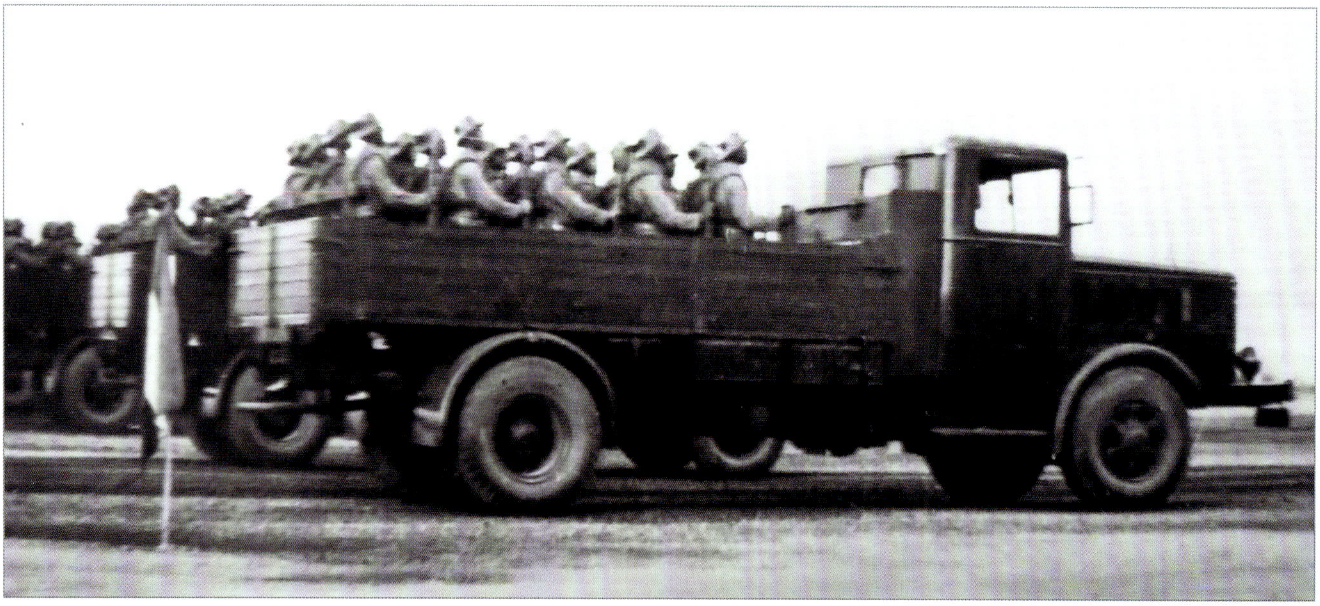

Chapter 5: A new Modern Iran begins to Emerge, 1925 to 1936

ABOVE: Reza Shah viewing a flyover at the parade. *(iichs.ir)*

RIGHT & OVERLEAF: Reza Shah with his Rolls-Royce Phantom I, chassis 72DC, at Jalaliyeh Square after the parade. *(Borzou Sepasi)*

OPPOSITE TOP: Marmon-Herrington armored vehicles on parade. *(Borzou Sepasi)*

OPPOSITE MIDDLE: Armored Rolls-Royce Silver Ghosts, chassis numbers 266WO, 267WO, 268WO and 269WO, of the Iranian Army following a Marmon-Herrington A7 Scout. *(Borzou Sepasi)*

OPPOSITE BOTTOM: Büssing trucks of the Iranian Army. *(Borzou Sepasi)*

Fit for a King ~ The Royal Garage of the Shah of Iran

Chapter 5: A new Modern Iran begins to Emerge, 1925 to 1936

For many, February 22, 1936 is known as the date on which the modern Iranian Army came of age and is marked as one of the most important days in Reza Shah's reign. The fully modernized army made its national debut with a massive parade, putting all its wares and capabilities on display in Tehran's Jalaliyeh Square. Reza Shah attended this ceremony to the salutation of huge crowds, arriving in a vehicle, which would symbolize the grandiosity of the day, namely a Rolls-Royce Phantom I. This vehicle, chassis number 72DC, was paraded in front of the crowds before being parked, with Reza Shah and his retinue disembarking to the cheers of the crowds and the salutes of the troops and officers.

"Made in Iran"

"Made in Iran" was Reza Shah's dream and mantra. Under the Qajars, whose ineffective rule he detested, cheap European products, especially textiles, were imported with low or virtually no tariffs, undercutting domestic craftsmen and destroying their livelihoods. As a result, in addition to setting up a nascent military industrial complex to support the modernization of the Iranian armed forces, Reza Shah also encouraged budding entrepreneurs in establishing new factories and implemented import substitution policies. These efforts were buoyed by a number of directives to help the newly established factories achieve economies of scale, including an official mandate that all government employees should wear Iranian-made clothes to work, including the Imperial Army whose uniforms had to be procured locally. This directive created a boom for the Iranian textile industry. However, since many of these factories were located in scattered cities, Reza Shah realized that he had to also create the required infrastructure to enable Iran's new factories to bring their goods to market in an economic and timely fashion.

During the Qajar dynasty, many of the few roads in Iran had fallen into a state of disrepair. When first assuming the post of Prime Minister before his takeover of the throne, Reza Shah established the first Ministry of Roads to focus on developing a road network to link all four corners of Iran. Of these, one of the most important was the road corridor between the capital city of Tehran to the Caspian Sea.

This road came to symbolize one of the greatest achievements of Reza Shah's rule. During the winter months, because of the heavy snows and other impediments, access between Tehran and the Caspian region was virtually impossible. As a result, Iran's largest and longest tunnel was bored through the Alborz Mountains at a height of 2,700 meters. With construction commencing in 1935, the opening ceremony, attended by Reza Shah, of the new Kandovan Tunnel took place three years later on May 17, 1938. Even today, it is viewed as a major feat of engineering. His car of choice on this day of crowning achievement was a 1934 Cadillac 355 Imperial Sedan. It is interesting to note that this Cadillac was used primarily for the inauguration of and visits to infrastructure and public works projects. Some surmise that since many of these projects constituted visits to outlying areas with underdeveloped road networks, the comfort and robustness of the Cadillac made it the vehicle of choice. Another Cadillac was also procured for the royal garage during this period, but for a completely different purpose. The second Cadillac, a 1937 Series 60 Convertible Coupe was bought for the speed-loving Crown Prince Mohammad Reza, who subsequently became famous for his high-speed jaunts to the Caspian along the road and through the tunnel built by his father.

BELOW: **A visit to the city of Shiraz with the Cadillac 355 Imperial Sedan. (1937)** *(Borzou Sepasi)*

OPPOSITE: **Reza Shah and the Crown Prince at the opening ceremony of the Kandovan Tunnel on Chalus Road with the Cadillac 355 Imperial Sedan. (May 17, 1938)** *(Borzou Sepasi)*

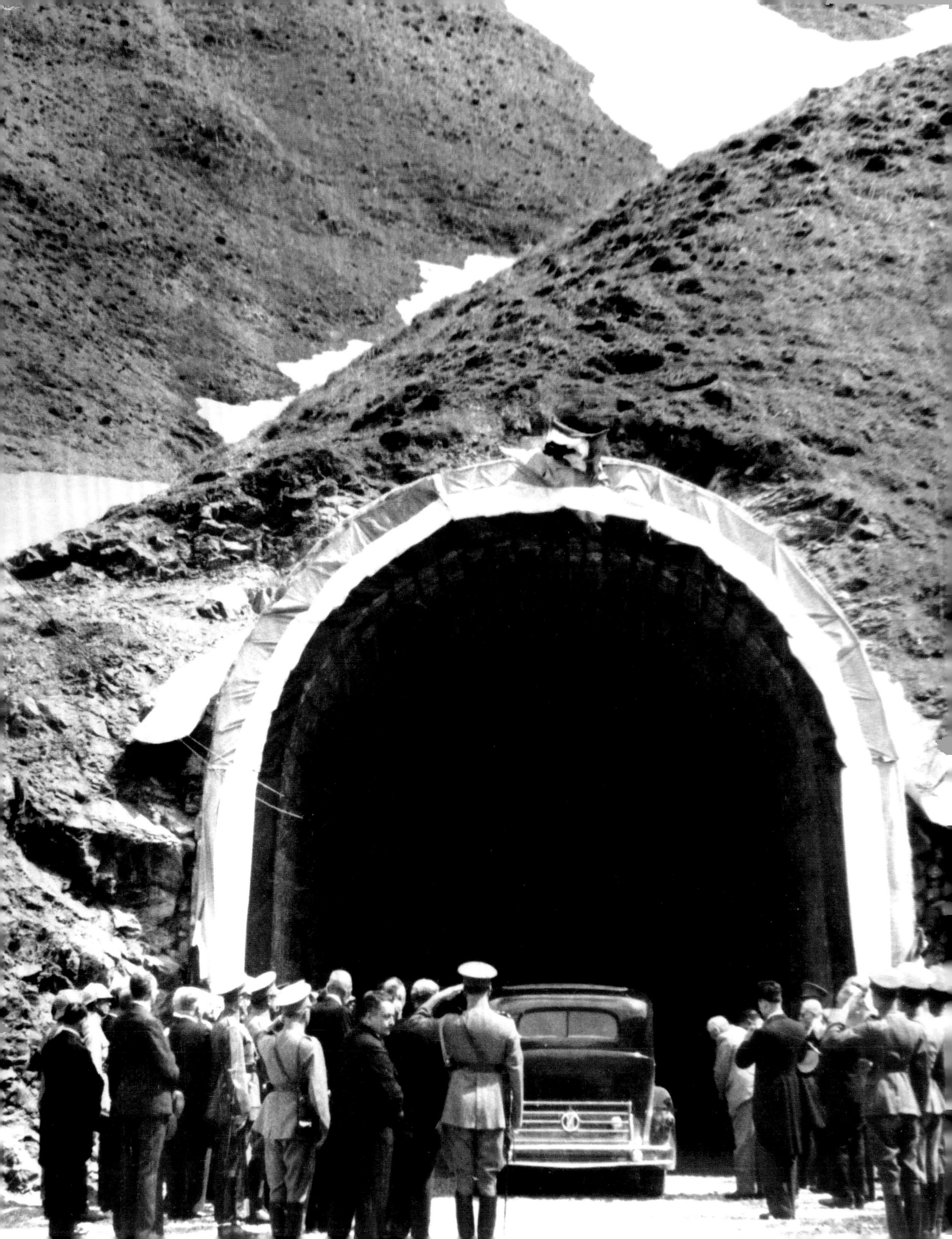

Fit for a King ~ The Royal Garage of the Shah of Iran

During Reza Shah's reign, over fifty factories related to knitwear, spinning yarn and wool were launched, as well as eight large sugar factories, seven for manufacturing leather goods, six match factories, twenty-eight soap-making plants and forty-five cotton cleaning facilities. Additionally, factories for the manufacture and processing of tobacco, tea, paper, copper smelting and crystal products were established, with many of them commissioned in the presence of Reza Shah, and all of these events were notable for his use of a bevy of Lincolns, Chevrolets and Packards.

On April 11, 1936, Reza Shah visited a "Made in Iran" products exhibition, which was held in front of Bagh-e Melli (National Garden) Gate. This landmark, formerly referred to as the Parade Square, was used as a military shooting range during the Qajar period before being converted by Reza Shah into a public park. The exhibition was held to celebrate Reza Shah's years of efforts to build up local industry via his unique brand of state-directed industrialization and economic development. The vehicle of choice this time was the Rolls-Royce Phantom I, which was used to celebrate his other crowning achievement, the modern Iranian military.

BELOW: **Reza Shah and the Crown Prince in Mazandaran province with the Cadillac 355 Imperial Sedan. (1938)** *(Borzou Sepasi)*

OPPOSITE (BOTH): **The Crown Prince in his Cadillac Series 60 Convertible Coupe. (Early 1940s)** *(Borzou Sepasi)*

Chapter 5: A new Modern Iran begins to Emerge, 1925 to 1936

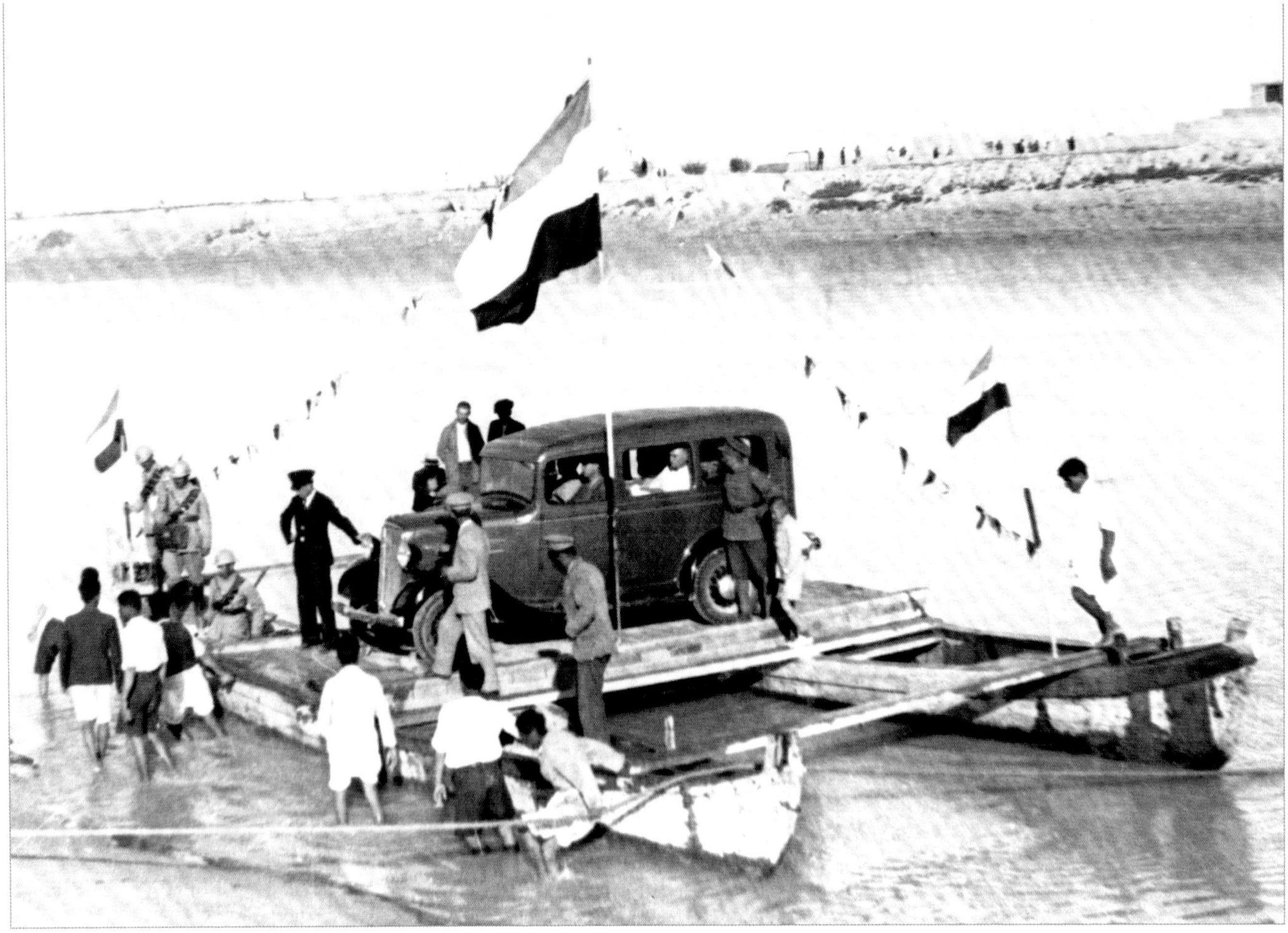

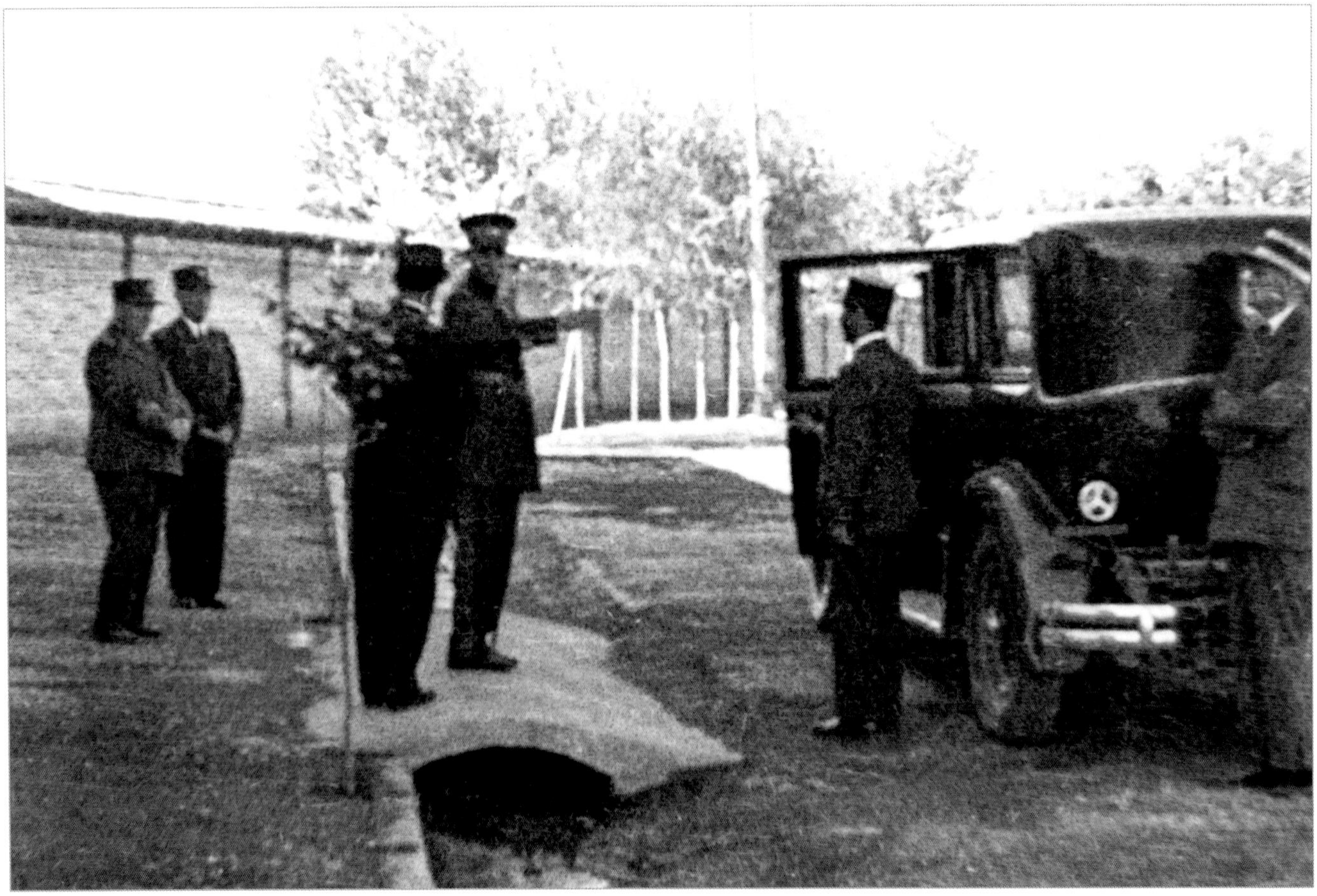

Chapter 5: A new Modern Iran begins to Emerge, 1925 to 1936

ABOVE: Visit to the city of Borujerd with Cadillac 355 Imperial Sedan. (1936) *(Borzou Sepasi)*

RIGHT: Reza Shah and his Lincoln L in the north of Iran. (Early 1930s) *(irdc.ir)*

OPPOSITE TOP: Reza Shah in a Chevrolet Carryall Suburban on the banks of the Karoon River being transported by barge. (Mid 1930s) *(irdc.ir)*

OPPOSITE BOTTOM: Reza Shah visiting a sugar factory in Kahrizak in his Lincoln L. (Early 1930s) *(irdc.ir)*

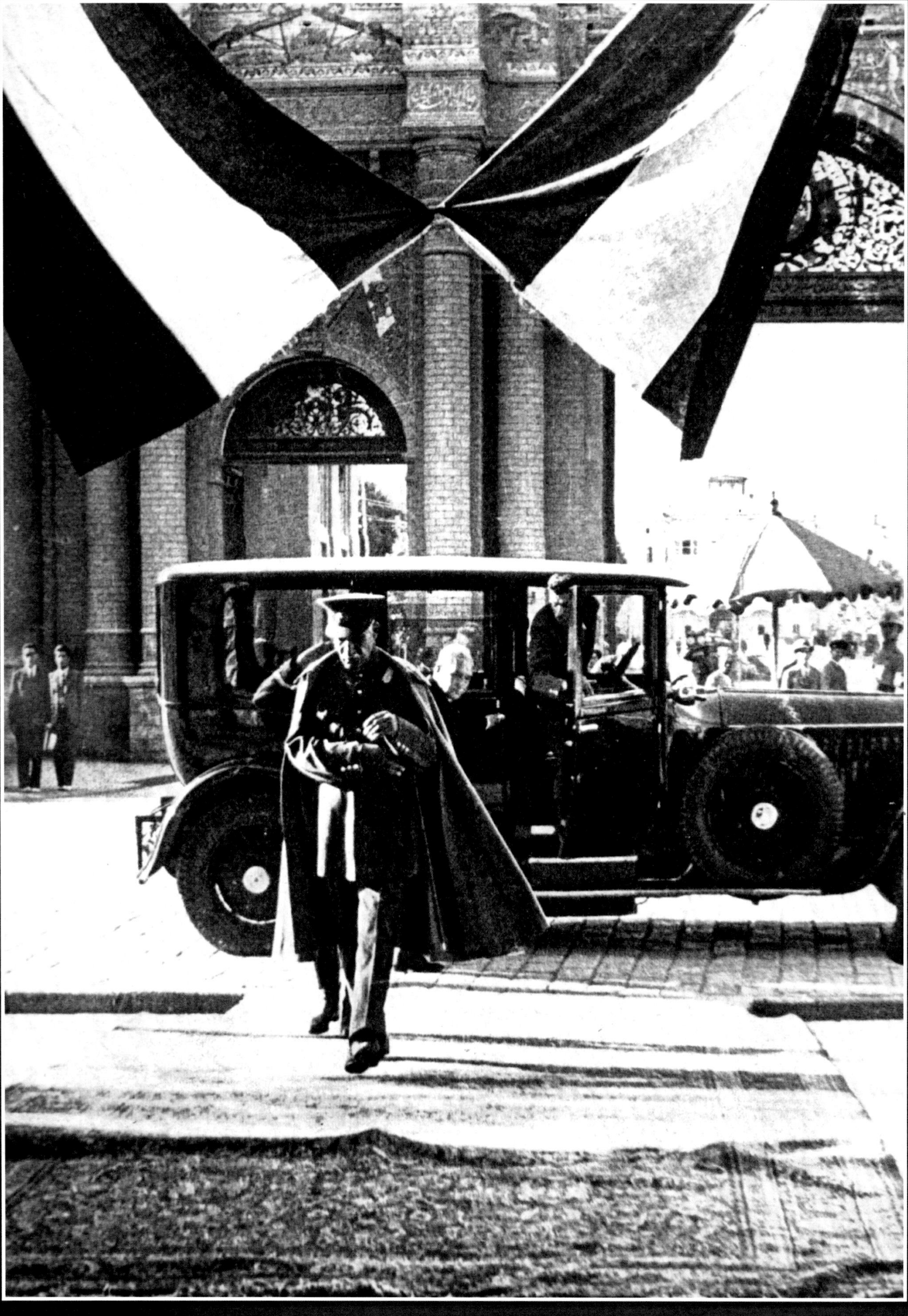

Chapter 5: A new Modern Iran begins to Emerge, 1925 to 1936

ABOVE: Reza Shah entering the "Made in Iran" products exhibition. (April 11, 1936)
(Borzou Sepasi)

RIGHT: Bagh-e Melli (National Garden) Gate. (1970s)

OPPOSITE: At the entrance of the "Made in Iran" exhibition with Rolls-Royce Phantom I, chassis number 72DC. (April 11, 1936)
(Borzou Sepasi)

85

Fit for a King ~ The Royal Garage of the Shah of Iran

LEFT: The Cadillac 355 Imperial Sedan during a visit to the province of Mazandaran. *(Borzou Sepasi)*

BELOW: Reza Shah and the Crown Prince at the southern Iranian port of Bushehr with the Cadillac 355 Imperial Sedan. (April 1937) *(Borzou Sepasi)*

The Trans-Iranian Railway

On May 29, 1925, the Iranian Parliament enacted legislation levying taxes on the consumption of sugar and other goods to subsidize a massive expansion of the Iranian rail network. Reza Shah saw the development of a national railway linking all four corners of Iran as the linchpin to his development plans. Shortly thereafter, the Trans-Iranian Railway Plan was approved by the Parliament, the National Railway Organization of Iran was established, and immediately twelve foreign engineers were hired. In the beginning, the project suffered from a lack of trained personnel. However, with the dispatch of Iranian students to Europe for training complemented by "train the trainer" courses for local employees, this impediment was eventually overcome. During this period, the route map of the railway was prepared, and the necessary construction equipment procured.

On October 15, 1927, Reza Shah visited the site of what was to become the Grand Central train station of Tehran and symbolically ordered the official start of construction of this massive project to link Tehran with the Persian Gulf to the south and the Caspian Sea to the north with connections to the east and west of Iran. Construction was started from three separate points, in the north, center and south of the country with the objective that they would link together at different stages. Meanwhile, the Iranian Railways Organization ordered several locomotives from European manufacturers, including sixteen from NOHAB of Sweden. Luxury carriages were also bought in 1935 from NOHAB to be used for transporting Reza Shah when he traveled to supervise the pace and progress of construction and to inaugurate those portions of the project which were completed. These black and cream-colored carriages trimmed in wood had separate quarters with every room having two beds, a WC and a ceiling fan that used the air flow from the carriage roof.

Due to the frequency of his visits, Reza Shah concluded that he needed special carriages which, like his Pierce-Arrow, were built in accordance with his exact preference and precise specifications. The order went to the German company Linke-Hofmann-Werke, and, after several months, the company completed four carriages, all of which were painted in blue and cream, and delivered them to Tehran in 1936. The first, to be used by Reza Shah exclusively, had two Pahlavi crowns on each side and included a large dining hall, which was linked to the living room with two sliding doors. It included a luxury bedroom, toilet facilities, bath and a crew room. The second carriage had one royal crest on the body and was for use by the Queen Mother (Reza Shah's wife) and had a different floor plan with a dining room, sitting room, bedroom and servants' quarters as well as a small kitchen. The third had a large conference room and accommodations for members of the royal entourage and the fourth served as a kitchen and storage area for baggage.

Working continuously under the direct supervision of Reza Shah, the Trans-Iranian Railway was completed on August 25, 1938 and was marked by an official opening ceremony held at the Fawzia Station, named in honor of the Crown Prince's Egyptian wife. Having started with a lowly few kilometers of railway, this huge project had expanded the Iranian rail network to 1,700 km and linked the key geographic corridors of the country together for the first time in its history. Throughout the years of the execution of this project, Reza Shah's vehicle of choice for supervising its progress all across Iran, was a 1927 Lincoln L, apparently chosen for its ruggedness, as many of the site visits mandated driving through rough terrain.

Chapter 5: A new Modern Iran begins to Emerge, 1925 to 1936

OPPOSITE: Reza Shah uses a Draisine to supervise the progress of the construction of the Trans-Iranian Railway. (Mid 1930s) *(iichs.ir)*

TOP LEFT: Reza Shah at the opening of the Tabriz Train Station with his Lincoln L. (Mid 1930s)

TOP RIGHT: Arrival of the first train at Tehran Station. (1937) *(iichs.ir)*

MIDDLE LEFT: The NOHAB carriages prior to their delivery to Iran. (1935)

MIDDLE RIGHT: The NOHAB carriages being unloaded in the Shah Port in southern Iran. (1935) *(Borzou Sepasi)*

ABOVE: The NOHAB production plate.

RIGHT: Reza Shah in the Linke-Hofmann-Werke royal carriage at Tehran Station. (1937) *(irdc.ir)*

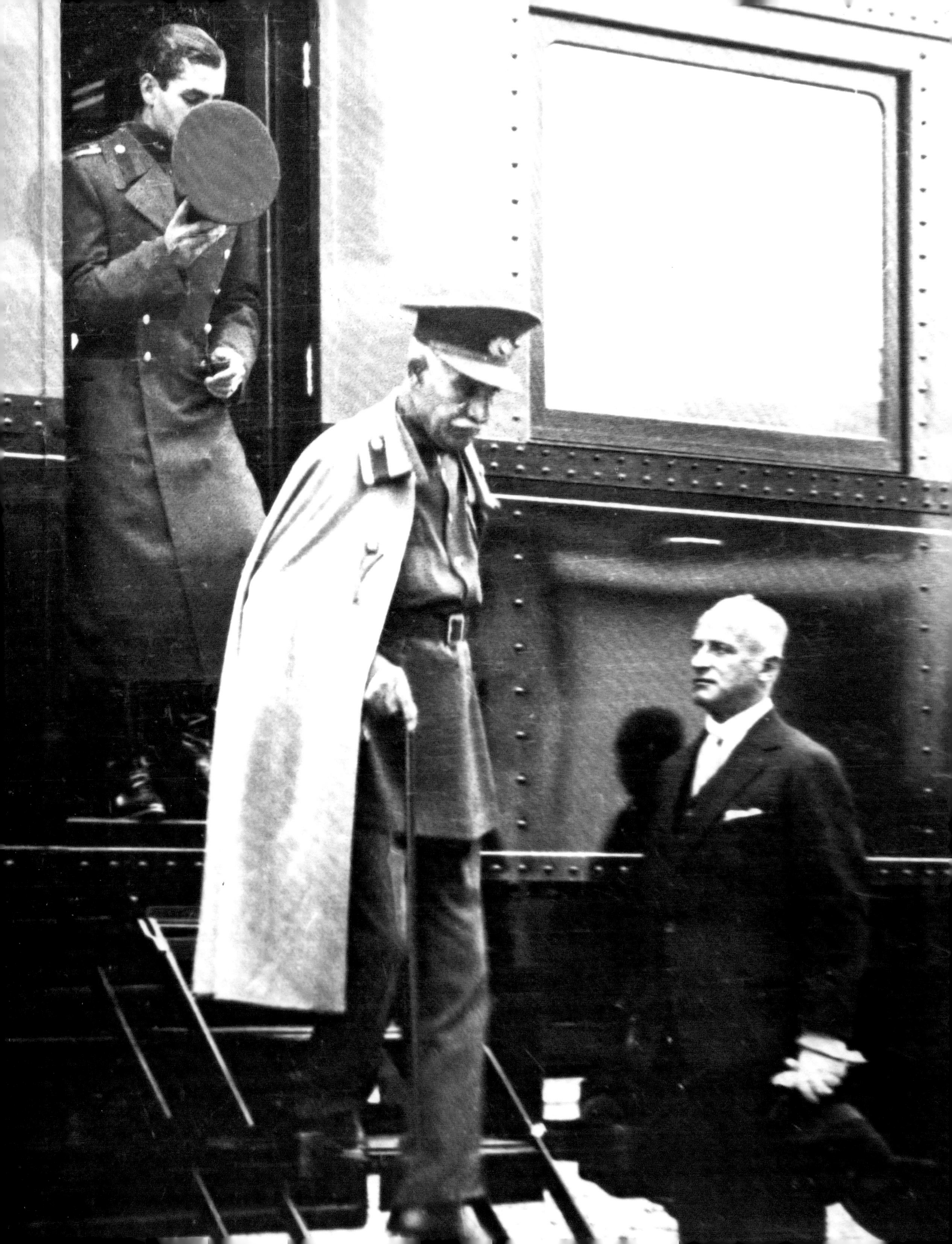

Chapter 5: A new Modern Iran begins to Emerge, 1925 to 1936

ABOVE: The NOHAB carriage during the visit of Reza Shah to Abbas Abad Station. (1936) *(iichs.ir)*

RIGHT: Crown Prince Mohammad Reza Pahlavi in the Linke-Hofmann-Werke carriage. (1937) *(irdc.ir)*

OPPOSITE: Reza Shah and the Crown Prince disembarking from the NOHAB carriage at the Dorood Station opening ceremony. (1936) *(irdc.ir)*

THESE TWO PAGES: Recent images of the Linke-Hofmann-Werke royal carriage details. *(Borzou Sepasi)*

93

CHAPTER 6

The Winds of War and a Special Gift from the Third Reich

Chapter 6: The Winds of War and a Special Gift from the Third Reich

The 1936 Mercedes-Benz 500K Autobahnkurier

After the accession of Reza Shah to power, relations between Iran and Germany improved markedly. Reza Shah acted to balance Britain's extensive influence in the country, and throughout the 1930s, many German technicians and engineers arrived in Iran to work on the expanding number of projects underway. In turn, with looming winds of war, the Germans and the Allies saw Iran as a key to wartime victory with both camps launching charm offensives to endear themselves to Reza Shah.

Germany began ingratiating itself with Reza Shah by offering, among other things, to construct a steel mill, a project he greatly coveted.[1] Other developments included the founding of the first air transport service between Iran and Germany in 1927, operated by the German company Junkers, transferring passengers and mail. In turn, Iran reciprocated by increasing its purchases from Germany, including military items, infrastructure projects and commercial goods. German motorcycles such as BMW were popular in Iran and were used by the army as well.

The Iranian media extensively covered the latest news from Germany, with a particular focus on the latest technical innovations, as well as the victories of both Mercedes and Auto Union in different races. Without fail, on the eve of every Iranian New Year, *Nowruz*, (March 21), Reza Shah would receive congratulatory messages from Adolf Hitler. Relations between the two countries improved to the level that when in 1935 Germany's new Ambassador arrived in Tehran and was to proceed to Sa'dabad Palace to present his credentials, Reza Shah sent his personal driver and coveted Pierce-Arrow to pick him up and bring him to the ceremony. As a result of these expanding relations, Germany's rank as a trading partner with Iran rose from fourth place in 1932 to first place by 1941.

During this period, Reza Shah and Hitler also exchanged gifts to commemorate various occasions. Reza Shah sent a

---

[1] Abbas Milani, "The Shah", Palgrave Macmillan, New York, 2011, p. 68

TOP: A Junkers F13 flying over Tehran.

ABOVE: In 1928, the Tehran municipality of Baladiyeh procured several Mercedes-Benz L45 fire engines from Germany. *(Tehran Fire Department)*

105-square meter hand-woven Persian carpet for Hitler's conference room. This unique carpet was constructed over a period of eight years by Iranian weavers. In turn, Hitler, who made it a practice of sending gifts to governments who enjoyed good relations with the Nazi regime, usually sent cars as examples of Germany's technical prowess.

It was during this era when King Farouk of Egypt received a Mercedes 540K as a wedding gift, and Hitler bequeathed a Mercedes-Benz G4 to the King of Spain. Knowing that the Crown Prince of Iran had a proclivity for sports cars and with a hint towards the future when he would succeed his father, Hitler set out to bestow a special car on that would win over the Crown Prince's sympathies to Germany.

Fit for a King ~ The Royal Garage of the Shah of Iran

96

Chapter 6: The Winds of War and a Special Gift from the Third Reich

OPPOSITE TOP (BOTH): In the 1930s, Iranian newspapers constantly provided extensive coverage of German innovations, especially those pertaining to the automotive industry. The left photograph shows the 1935 French Grand Prix, which Rudolf Caracciola won driving a Mercedes-Benz W25B. The photograph to the right introduces the 1935 Mercedes-Benz LO3500 stromlinien bus. *(Ettelaat Newspaper, August 24, 1935)*

OPPOSITE BOTTOM: The Mercedes-Benz 500K Autobahnkurier, chassis number 130898, prior to delivery to Iran. (1936) *(Carl Benz, Lebensfahrt eines deutschen Erfinders book)*

TOP RIGHT: The prototype 5.4-liter Mercedes-Benz 500K Autobahnkurier engine.

MIDDLE RIGHT: Crown Prince Mohammad Reza Pahlavi driving his Mercedes-Benz 500K Autobahnkurier on the recently built Pahlavi Road, which, when completed, was the longest road in the Middle East. (1938) *(Borzou Sepasi)*

BOTTOM RIGHT: ID plate of the Mercedes-Benz 500K Autobahnkurier. *(Borzou Sepasi)*

BELOW: The Prince playing football. The Mercedes-Benz 500K Autobahnkurier is just visible next to the football field. (1938) *(Borzou Sepasi)*

Fit for a King ~ The Royal Garage of the Shah of Iran

For this purpose, Hitler consulted with the management of Mercedes-Benz who came up with the proposal of providing a Mercedes-Benz 500K Autobahnkurier. This exceptional model was styled by the senior designer of the company, Hermann Ahrens, and made its debut at the 1934 Berlin Motor Show. It was designed to maximize airflow and to minimize drag, and the result was a streamlined, aerodynamic body. The name Autobahnkurier arose from the fact that the vehicle was purpose-built to suit the newly constructed *Autobahn* roadway. With a green light from Hitler, the production process was started. First, the rolling chassis number 130898 from the 500K series was made. During this period, Mercedes-Benz engineers were working on increasing the capacity of 5-liter 500K engines to 5.4 liters, and they installed one of the 5.4-liter prototype engines on the chassis. The body was based on the 1934 Berlin Motor Show car with some minor differences. In the interior, everything was covered with green velvet, the window frames had a wooden frame and the dashboard was covered with marble. The body was cream with green fenders. Autobahnkurier number 130898 was manufactured in 1936, and the total production of this model was limited to four 500Ks and two 540Ks.

The car was delivered to Tehran in 1937, and the speed-loving Crown Prince now had one of the fastest cars in the world in his possession. The speed and proverbial "flash" of the car caused quite a stir whenever the vehicle was driven, which took place frequently, with many gazing in awe as the Crown Prince, without his bodyguards, sped across Tehran.

Chapter 6: The Winds of War and a Special Gift from the Third Reich

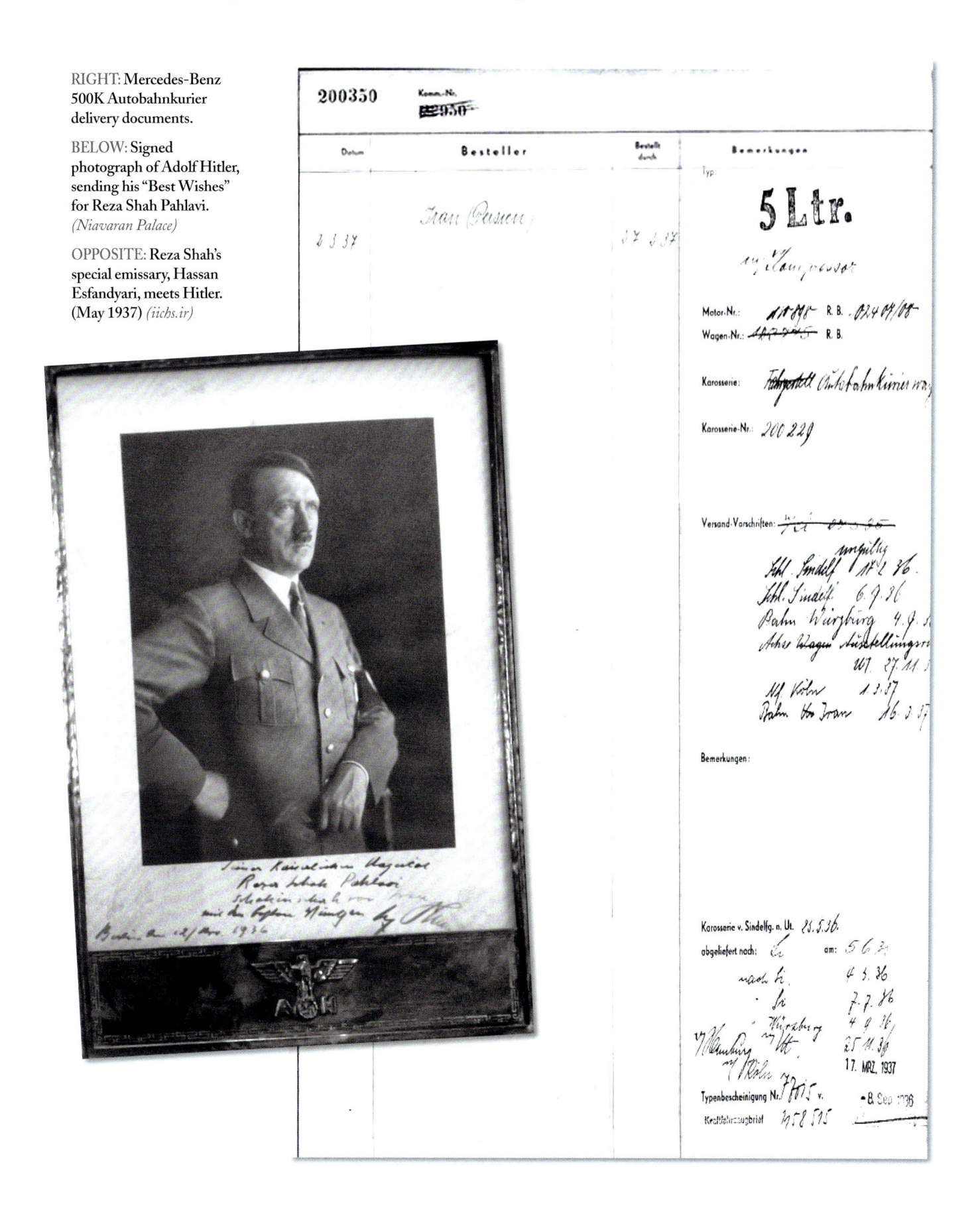

RIGHT: Mercedes-Benz 500K Autobahnkurier delivery documents.

BELOW: Signed photograph of Adolf Hitler, sending his "Best Wishes" for Reza Shah Pahlavi. *(Niavaran Palace)*

OPPOSITE: Reza Shah's special emissary, Hassan Esfandyari, meets Hitler. (May 1937) *(iichs.ir)*

Tehran, the Automotive Capital of the Middle East

With the progress stimulated by Reza Shah's economic and development policies came wealth, triggered by a new class of entrepreneurs who founded and ran Iran's new industries and a new class of doctors and other professionals who were granted scholarships to attend the best universities in the West and who set up successful practices upon their return to Iran.

As a result, while the Crown Prince and the Autobahnkurier may have caused a stir speeding across Tehran, this *nouveau riche* class, primarily Western-educated Iranians began to seek and purchase some of the best automobiles available at the time. It was not an anomaly to see in Tehran on any given day everything ranging from a Chrysler Airflow on one end of the spectrum to a record-setting Rolland-Pilain Type C23 with a Kelsch body on the other end, earning Tehran the moniker of the "Automotive Capital of the Middle East".

Tehran had been chosen as the capital of Iran by Agha Mohammad Khan Qajar in 1796 in order to remain within reach of Iran's territories in the Caucasus region and to keep a close eye on possible enemies in the former Iranian capitals of Shiraz and Isfahan. During the Qajar monarchy, Tehran was fortified by walls with several entry gates. This all ended when Reza Shah, having consolidated power and bringing peace and stability, saw the walls as a symbol of a tumultuous past and had them knocked down.

During his rule, Reza Shah constructed Pahlavi Road in Tehran, which, with a span of near 20 km, was and remains to this day, the longest street in the Middle East. The road starts at the train station in the south of Tehran and reaches to Tajrish at the northernmost point of the city, and no doubt provided a unique driving environment for the automotive exotica that was being imported. It was not uncommon to see showrooms for cars and motorcycles for manufacturers as diverse as Pierce-Arrow, Auburn, Packard, Cord, Lincoln, Chrysler, Harley-Davidson, and BMW. Most of these showrooms were located in Saadi and Cheragh Bargh, which were near the Tehran Grand Bazaar and the Golestan Palace, two areas with concentrations of wealth. With such a broad array of vehicles driving across Tehran, it is not surprising that an early version of

LEFT: Rolland-Pilain Type C23 with a Kelsch body which set many world records in Montlhéry and 24 Hours of Le Mans in 1924, 1925 and 1926 and was subsequently imported to Iran. *(Borzou Sepasi)*

TOP: Tehran daily newsletter *Ettelaat* announcing the debut of the Cord 810, soon after its introduction at the Salon de l'Automobile in Paris 1936 and the fact that it would soon be available to Iranian customers by Cord's local agent Shahinian Trading House. (February 1937) *(Borzou Sepasi)*

OPPOSITE (ALL): A sample of advertisements for the Lincoln Zephyr, as well as Chrysler and Packard cars. (Late 1930s) *(Borzou Sepasi)*

پاکارد جدید

PACKARD

ساختمان دقیق - در تمام صنعت اتومبیل سازی هیچ کارخانه مانند کارخانه پاکارد در مصالح ساختمان و دقیق بودن مدل سازی اهتمام نورزیده . ادعای برتری با کارد بعث تعجبی نیست که مهندسین عالی مقام کارخانه در ظرف ۳۵ سال مطالعات عمیق بدست آورده و شعار آنها همیشه روی تهیه جنس درجه اول بوده است .

اختصاصی که از سایه پاکارد مطالعه بخوبی می دانند سازنده آن همه ساله در استحکام و راحتی و در عین حال قشنگی آن کوشش نموده و هیچگاه به تقلید از دیگران ارزانی قیمت کالا که مستلزم انتخاب مصالح بی دوام است منظور اساسی خود قرار نداده است .

پاکارد ۱۲۰ - مخصوصا مدل ۳۶ همان اندازه قوی ، مجهم، مرتب ساخته شده است . سایر ارقام با پاکارد

مدل ۳۶ - دارای ۱۲۰ اسب قوه یعنی ده اسب قوی تر از مدل ۳۵ و مصرف ۱۵ از لحاظ بنزین و روغن در ده درصد کمتر

بعلاوه و فوق العاده نرم - بی صدا - فرمانبردار - وسیع - راحت - مجلل و بی تکان است

دستگاه های مخصوصی که در چرخ و عقب ماشین برای جلو بردن راحتی و میزان...

دستگاه ترمز در تمام خط سیر خود با اوله...

با ترمز دستی ...

بعلاوه پاکارد ۱۲۰ نسبت به سایر اتومبیلها از زمین ارتفاع زیادی دارد مخصوصا...

نمانید به هر نقطه و لو خارج از جاده...

دارای سرعت فوق العاده ...

برادران - خیابان سعدی (شیخ صدوق)

Chrysler Airstream 6-8

اتومبیلهای سواری دارای کرایسلر دارای...
ومخصوصا است که به عبد اختیار آن بخارائی آباد...
این مزایا در نتیجه تجربیات مدت هندسین فراهم شده است ...

کرایسلر موسوم به ۸ و ۶ ابرامزام ۳۶ در سال ۱۹۳۶ قدم پر معانی نهاد . کذارنده تشلیل سالیان دراز مساعدت در تبریز ناشناس و طراحان کارخانه کرایسلر بمیاهنده ارزش دقیقی برای کرایسلر پیدا نمود - سبک جدید و اسلوب و ابل و تکور اتومبیلهای جدید کرایسلر نظر هر شخصی را جلب خواهد کرد .

نماینده انحصاری اتومبیلهای دوج و کرایسلر در ایران
ف . آ . کتانه

شرکت سهامی تجارتی کازادما محدود

نماینده کل در ایران

لینکلن زفیر که یکی از معجزات صنعت اتومبیل بشمار میرود در نمایشگاه فروش این شرکت بزودی بمعرض نمایش گذارده خواهد شد

میدان مخبر الدوله شرکت کازادما تلفن ۱۵۳۸

سرویس تعمیرات بیرون دروازه دولت تلفن ۱۳۸۶

Fit for a King ~ The Royal Garage of the Shah of Iran

automotive cruising would take place in Tehran's Laleh-Zar Street where enthusiasts and poseurs alike cruised around showing off their latest cars. Laleh-Zar was the symbol of a new and modern Iran where artisans, actors, and intellectuals congregated to enjoy the multitude of restaurants, theaters, cinemas, cabarets, as well as the famous Grand Hotel.

With the start of World War II and the Anglo-Soviet invasion of Iran, this golden age ended and many cars were either destroyed or exported from Iran.

TOP RIGHT: Benz 10/30 PS Tourenwagen surrounded by onlookers outside the Old Gate of Tehran. The moat around the city and Gate Bridge are visible in the photograph. Tehran had twelve gates and all of them where built with Islamic architectural motifs and covered with hand-painted tiles and bricks. (1918)

RIGHT: An advertisement for a Voisin for sale in Tehran. (April 1928) *(Borzou Sepasi)*

BELOW: A Packard caught in traffic caused by street festivities on the occasion of the termination of the D'Arcy concession in 1933. *(iichs.ir)*

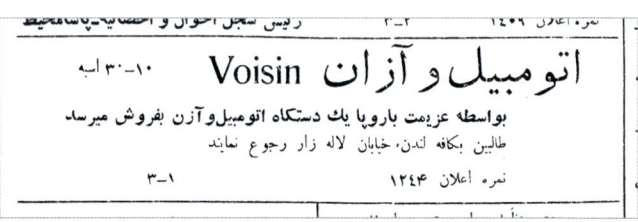

Chapter 6: The Winds of War and a Special Gift from the Third Reich

TOP: A 1935 Chrysler Airflow in Ferdowsi Street, Tehran. (1938) *(Borzou Sepasi)*

ABOVE LEFT: A Horch 853 Cabriolet by Glaser parked beside the Marble Palace main entrance. The car has a registration plate, meaning that it had a private owner and was not owned by the Shah. (Early 1940s) *(Borzou Sepasi)*

ABOVE RIGHT: An Isotta Fraschini Tipo 8A owned by Anushiravan Sepahbody, an Iranian diplomat pictured with his family. (1935)

CHAPTER 7

The Royal Wedding ~ an Egyptian Princess fit for an Iranian Prince

Chapter 7: The Royal Wedding ~ an Egyptian Princess fit for an Iranian Prince

In 1938, apparently without the knowledge of the 20-year-old Crown Prince, Reza Shah set out to find a bride, and future Queen for him.[1] Athletic, and cutting a dashing figure, crisscrossing Tehran in the Autobahnkurier, many of Iran's leading families hoped to give away their daughter to the man who someday would be the Shah of Iran.

However, Reza Shah had something else in mind, as he was seeking a daughter-in-law "well-versed in the ways of royalty".[2] After a search of eligible candidates from royal families across the world, 18-year-old Princess Fawzia of Egypt, the sister of King Farouk, was selected and negotiations for an Egyptian-Iranian marital union commenced. On May 26, 1938, the Iranian and Egyptian royal courts simultaneously announced the engagement of Crown Prince Reza of Iran to Princess Fawzia of Egypt. When Reza Shah was asked why he had chosen Fawzia to be his future daughter-in-law, he responded by stating that he wanted someone from a good family and to connect the Pahlavi's to another royal family.[3]

[1] *Abbas Milani, "The Shah," Palgrave Macmillan, New York, 2011, p. 62*

[2] *ibid*

[3] *ibid*

Reza Shah bids farewell to the Crown Prince next to the Cadillac 355 Imperial Sedan as he prepares to travel to Egypt. (February 24, 1939) *(Iran National library)*

Fit for a King ~ The Royal Garage of the Shah of Iran

ABOVE: The Crown Prince arrives in Baghdad escorted by King Ghazi's representative, Amir Zeyd in King Ghazi's Mercedes-Benz 770K Voll & Ruhrbeck Cabriolet Limousine as they make their way to Al-Belad Palace to meet King Ghazi. (February 26, 1939) *("Ettelaat, the Crown Prince Wedding Memorial" book)*

LEFT: King Ghazi also owned an Isotta Fraschini 8B with a Carrozzeria Touring Dual Cowl Phaeton body. The car is pictured before its delivery to Baghdad in the Piazza Santarosa in Milan. (1935) *(Carrozzeria Touring)*

OPPOSITE BOTTOM: King Ghazi's 1935 Mercedes-Benz 500K, chassis number 123732, bodied by Erdmann & Rossi. *("Mercedes-Benz, The Supercharged 8 Cylinder Cars of the 1930s, Vol. 2" book)*

OPPOSITE TOP: The Iranian Crown Prince and Iraqi King Ghazi enjoying tea at the Royal Iranian Embassy in Baghdad. (February 27, 1939) *("Ettelaat, the Crown Prince Wedding Memorial" book)*

Chapter 7: The Royal Wedding ~ an Egyptian Princess fit for an Iranian Prince

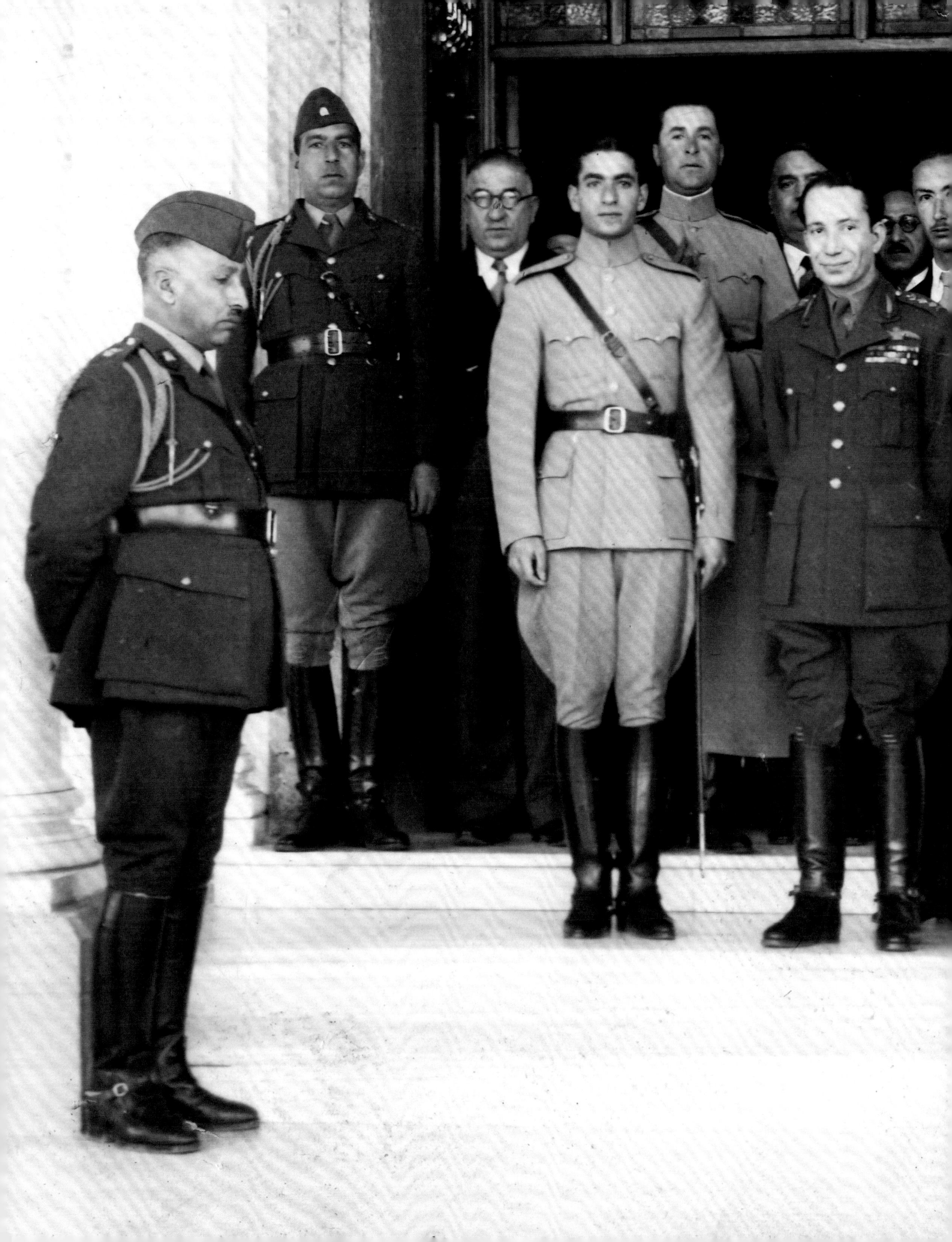

It was decided that there would be two wedding ceremonies. The first to be held in Egypt, followed by another in Iran. On the morning of February 24, 1939, Crown Prince Mohammad Reza and his entourage bade farewell to the Iranian royal family and traveled to Egypt by way of Iraq, Syria and Lebanon. In Iraq, the Crown Prince was welcomed by King Ghazi with whom he shared a passion for fast and exotic cars. King Ghazi bought his first car, a Vauxhall 30/98 Sport with wooden body, when he was just 14 years old. He also had a Mercedes-Benz 500K, but his car had a Special Roadster body made by the coachbuilder Erdmann & Rossi. King Ghazi was also the first Monarch in the Middle East to pilot a plane and owned a Miles M.14 Magister. The Crown Prince arrived in Alexandria on March 2. After a formal introduction to the Eqyptian royal family, he was, for the first time, able to lay eyes on his future wife. The wedding took place on March 15, officiated by Sheikh Mohammad Mustafa Al-Maraghi, from the Sheikh of Al-Azhar, one of the leading theological institutions of the Muslim world. The conclusion of the ceremony was commemorated by a 41-gun salute in Cairo, and the Egyptian Air Force enacted a spectacular fly-over.

ABOVE: On his journey to Egypt to meet his bride-to-be, the Crown Prince Mohammad Reza Pahlavi used this Fageol truck which was unique for that period as it was effectively an air-conditioned motorhome. The truck was used primarily to cross the Iraqi desert and earned the nickname "the Train". Some are of the view that it was loaned to the Crown Prince for use by King Ghazi of Iraq, while others surmise that it was gifted by the United States in anticipation of the Crown Prince's forthcoming nuptials. *(Borzou Sepasi)*

LEFT: King Ghazi (right) and Mohammad Reza Pahlavi (left) at King Ghazi's Palace. (February 27, 1939) *(iichs.ir)*

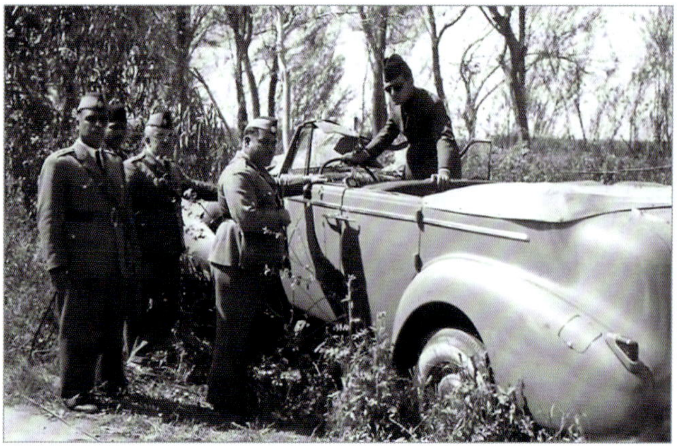

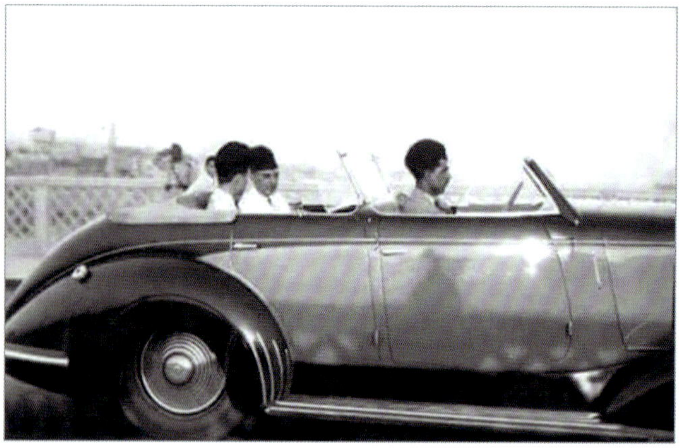

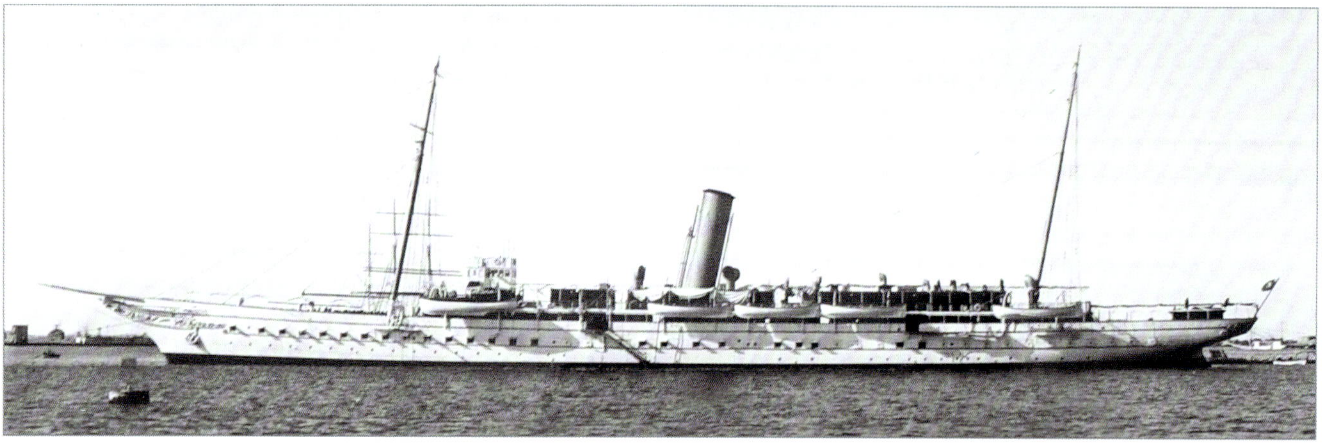

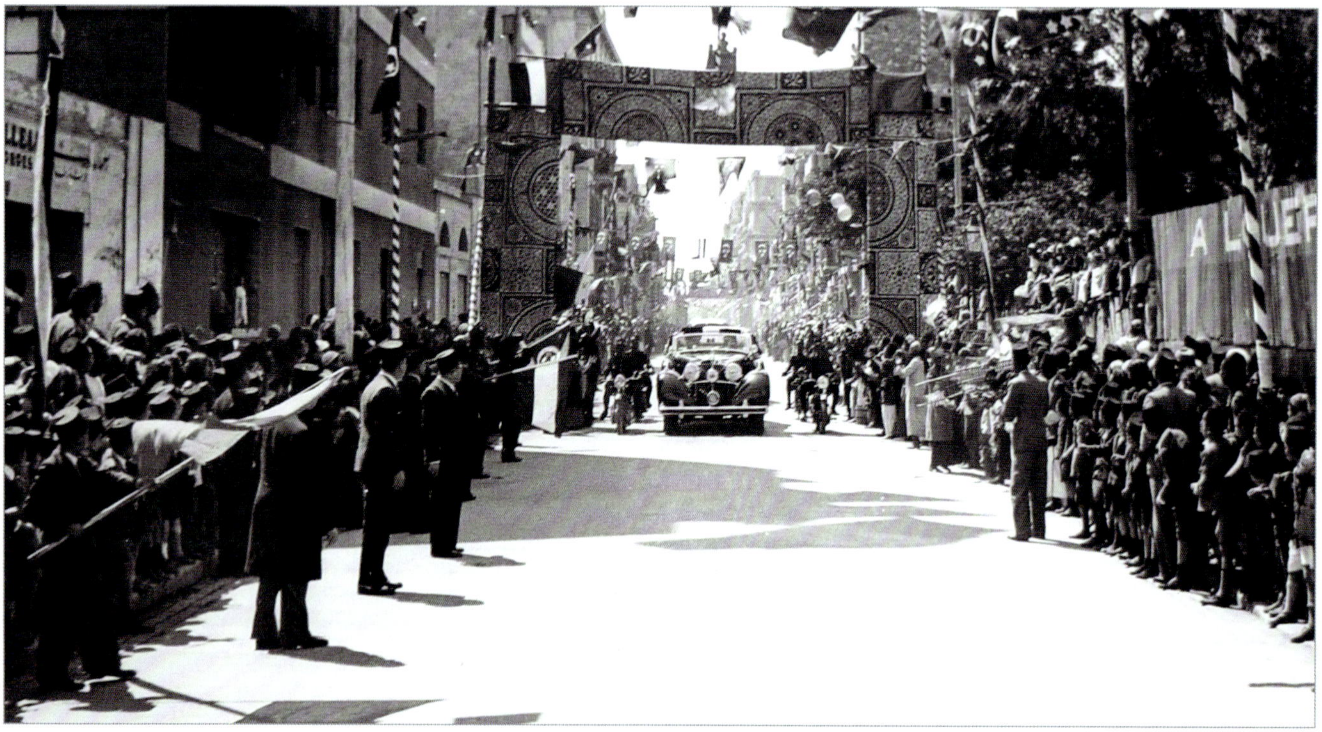

Chapter 7: The Royal Wedding ~ an Egyptian Princess fit for an Iranian Prince

OPPOSITE TOP LEFT: King Ghazi died in a car accident just a month and a half after his meeting with the Crown Prince. He was driving this brand-new 1939 Buick Roadmaster Convertible Sedan when he lost control and was thrown from the car. (April 4, 1939) *(non14.net)*

OPPOSITE TOP RIGHT: After King Ghazi's death, his Isotta Fraschini 8B with Carrozzeria Touring Dual Cowl Phaeton body was used by "Abd al-Ilah" his first cousin and brother-in-law who served as regent for King Ghazi's son, King Faisal II from April 4, 1939 to May 23, 1953, when Faisal came of age. The car is believed to have been destroyed in the coup d'état of July 14, 1958 when the Iraqi royal family was slaughtered and the monarchy in Iraq ended. (1940s) *(Borzou Sepasi)*

OPPOSITE MIDDLE: The Egyptian royal yacht "Mahrouseh". (March 3, 1939) *(Saad Abad Palace)*

THIS PAGE & OPPOSITE BOTTOM: The Crown Prince of Iran riding in King Farouk's Mercedes-Benz 770 during his visit to the Malek Fuad I Hospital. (March, 1939) *(Saad Abad Palace)*

Fit for a King ~ The Royal Garage of the Shah of Iran

LEFT: King Farouk and Mohammad Reza Pahlavi visiting the Pyramids. (March 1939) *(Saad Abad Palace)*

BELOW: King Farouk's 1921 Rolls-Royce Silver Ghost, chassis number 2UE, previously owned by his father and upgraded in 1935, transporting the King and Iranian Crown Prince. (March 1939) *(Saad Abad Palace)*

ABOVE: Group photograph of Mohammad Reza Pahlavi and Princess Fawzia with the Egyptian royal family on their wedding day at Abdeen Palace. (March 15, 1939) *(Saad Abad Palace)*

RIGHT & OVERLEAF: Mohammad Reza and Fawzia. (March 15, 1939) *(Saad Abad Palace)*

BELOW: The insignia of the intertwined Iranian and Egyptian flags which was printed on all the wedding invitations.

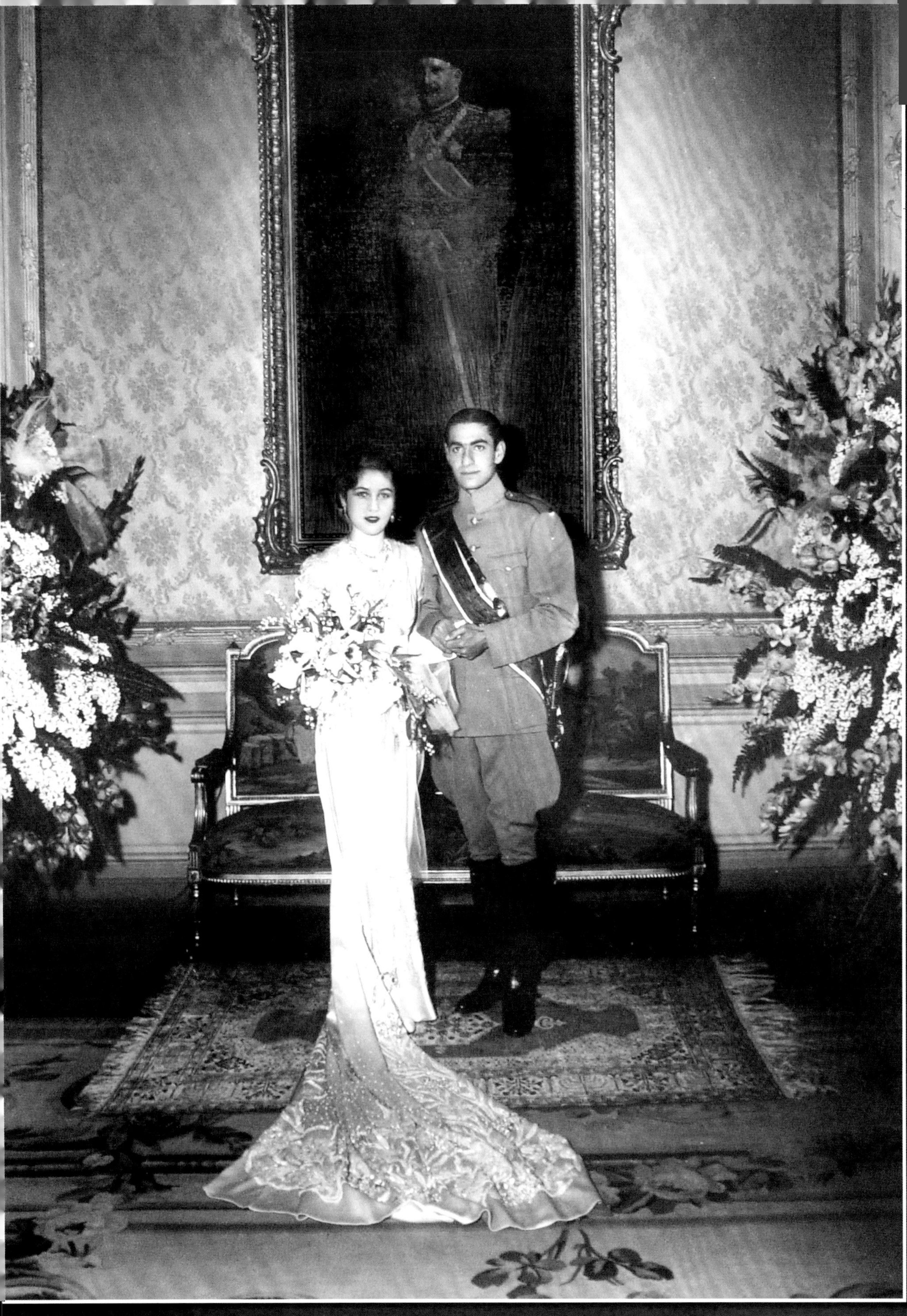

Chapter 7: The Royal Wedding ~ an Egyptian Princess fit for an Iranian Prince

city's landmarks such as the Grand Al-Azhar Mosque, the newlyweds traveled back to Iran by sea passing through the Suez Canal, the Red Sea and the Persian Gulf, arriving at the Iranian port of Shahpour, in Southern Iran. The Iranian Queen Mother was there to welcome Fawzia and her mother Queen Nazli. From the port, the two royal families boarded the royal train built by Linke-Hofmann-Werke, for the final leg of the journey to Tehran.

To commemorate the arrival of Crown Prince Mohammad Reza Pahlavi and his new bride, Tehran was lit up with fireworks and other celebratory displays. When the train arrived in Tehran on April 16, many of Iran's highest-ranking officials had gathered inside the station to welcome the couple, while outside throngs of people had congregated. Reza Shah chose his Rolls-Royce Silver Ghost for the occasion, and the Iranian Royal Air Force staged a fly-over above the station, dropping colored confetti.

The procession proceeded to the Golestan Palace, with twenty-three convertible cars following. Reza Shah and Queen Nazli sat in the first car, the Rolls-Royce Silver Ghost. The second car, a 1937 Packard 1502 Convertible Sedan 'Dietrich', was used to transport the Queen Mother and the new bride, Fawzia, followed by the groom and Princess Faiza, the sister of the bride, in his prized Hispano-Suiza.

On April 22, the second wedding ceremony was held at the Golestan Palace. In addition to members of the Iranian royal court, the guest list also included foreign delegations. Each ambassador presented a wedding gift for the royal couple during the ceremony.

The American Ambassador presented a furnished air-conditioned trailer similar to a mobile home. The French sent a large delegation led by General Maxime Weygand, in his capacity as the French military Commander for the Orient Region, and presented a Bugatti Type 57C, chassis number 57808, with a special one-off body made

The Queen Mother of Iran and Queen Nazli of Egypt at the Tehran railway station alongside the royal train. (April 16, 1939) *("Ettelaat, the Crown Prince Wedding Memorial" book)*

Fit for a King ~ The Royal Garage of the Shah of Iran

THIS PAGE: The lead car of the procession, a Rolls-Royce Silver Ghost, chassis number 38PG, body by Hooper with Reza Shah and Queen Nazli on board. (April 16, 1939) *(Borzou Sepasi)*

Chapter 7: The Royal Wedding ~ an Egyptian Princess fit for an Iranian Prince

THIS PAGE: The fifth car in the procession was a Buick Series 80 Roadmaster Convertible Phaeton with Princess Ashraf Pahlavi (Mohammad Reza Pahlavi's twin sister) and Princess Fathia (Fawzia's other sister). *(Borzou Sepasi)*

Fit for a King ~ The Royal Garage of the Shah of Iran

Chapter 7: The Royal Wedding ~ an Egyptian Princess fit for an Iranian Prince

OPPOSITE: **Crown Prince Mohammad Reza Pahlavi and his new bride on one of their first outings as a couple visiting a "Made in Iran" Exhibition with a Chrysler C-24 Imperial. (April 1939)** *(irdc.ir)*

TOP: **The two royal families visit a Parade in "Jalaliyeh Square". As before they traveled in several separate cars including this 1938 Packard. (April 25, 1939)** *(Borzou Sepasi)*

ABOVE: **Commemorative Medallion of the marriage of Crown Prince Mohammad Reza Pahlavi and Princess Fawzia of Egypt.** *(Niavaran Palace)*

by the coachbuilder Vanvooren. The body design was very similar to the famous Figoni et Falaschi designs and had sweeping curves, with the fenders covering the wheels. The Type 57C featured a 160bhp supercharged in-line 8-cylinder engine. The Bugatti was never on public view before being sent from France, and even during shipment it was hidden in a container.

The British government's gift was a black 1939 Rolls-Royce Phantom III, which had been delivered by ship on April 22. This car, chassis number 3DL138, came with a streamlined sweeping body by Park Ward and was powered by an aluminum-alloy V12 engine having a displacement of 7.33 liters. Because of the design and color of this vehicle, this car was used by the royal couple for both private and official functions.

Not to be outdone, the Third Reich also commissioned a car from Mercedes-Benz. As it was to be "unique", it was the most luxurious car in the Mercedes portfolio, the "770", with chassis number 429319 also known as the *Großer Mercedes* (Grand Mercedes). This one-off car, with a specially designed "Cabriolet B" body was never sent to Iran due to the onset of World War II and instead was delivered to a German customer.

Fit for a King ~ The Royal Garage of the Shah of Iran

LEFT: **General Maxime Weygand, head of the French delegation to the royal wedding.** *("Ettelaat, the Crown Prince Wedding Memorial" book)*

BELOW: **General Weygand and the French Ambassador with the rest of the French delegation.** *("Ettelaat, the Crown Prince Wedding Memorial" book)*

OPPOSITE TOP LEFT: **The Crown Prince behind the wheel of the Bugatti Type 57C. (Early 1940s)**

OPPOSITE TOP RIGHT: **Mohammad Reza Pahlavi beside his new Bugatti Type 57C, chassis number 57808, bodied by Vanvooren. (Early 1940s)**

OPPOSITE BOTTOM: **Mohammad Reza and his wife Fawzia alighting from the British government's wedding gift, the Rolls-Royce Phantom III, chassis number 3DL138, bodied by Park Ward. (1942)** *(Borzou Sepasi)*

Chapter 7: The Royal Wedding ~ an Egyptian Princess fit for an Iranian Prince

The Czechoslovakian and Polish governments outdid the UK and Germany when the Czechs presented a Praga E-114 (Air Baby) construction number 108 aircraft, later registered EP-ACA in Iran, while the Poles gave a DWL RWD-13 registered SP-BNY, serial number 285.

Fit for a King ~ The Royal Garage of the Shah of Iran

THESE TWO PAGES: The Phantom III, chassis number 3DL138, transporting the Crown Prince and Princess Fawzia to an official visit. **(Late 1940s)** *(Borzou Sepasi)*

Chapter 7: The Royal Wedding ~ an Egyptian Princess fit for an Iranian Prince

Fit for a King ~ The Royal Garage of the Shah of Iran

Chapter 7: The Royal Wedding ~ an Egyptian Princess fit for an Iranian Prince

Fit for a King ~ The Royal Garage of the Shah of Iran

PREVIOUS TWO PAGES, ABOVE & OPPOSITE BOTTOM: The 1940 Mercedes-Benz Type 770 Cabriolet B (W 150), chassis number 429319, the one-off built for the wedding of the Crown Prince of Iran which due to the start of World War II could not be delivered to Iran and was instead sold off to a German customer. After the war, the car was moved to the Soviet Union. *(Media.Daimler.com)*

OPPOSITE TOP (BOTH): The RWD-13 serial number 285, the wedding gift of the government of Poland to Mohammad Reza Pahlavi photographed prior to delivery to Iran in Warsaw. (April 1939) *(Narodowe Archiwum Cyfrowe, Polish National)*

Chapter 7: The Royal Wedding ~ an Egyptian Princess fit for an Iranian Prince

129

CHAPTER 8

Iran and the Second World War

Chapter 8: Iran and the Second World War

Reza Shah began to feel like a "helpless pawn upon the slippery chess board of power politics".[1]

As the world was slowly edging to the brink of World War II, Iran was not immune from these developments. While in Iran itself people were abuzz from the news of the wedding of the Crown Prince and Fawzia, the more affluent Iranians were increasingly concerned with the news garnered from a new phenomenon in Iran, the radio.

While Poland was under invasion, in Iran, the people celebrated the birth of Princess Shahnaz, the first child of the royal couple on October 27, 1940. However, this tranquility and immunity from global developments was not to last as Iran was slowly dragged into a global conflict, which it was trying desperately to avoid.

When Britain and the Soviet Union were thrown into an alliance in June 1941 by Hitler's invasion of Russia, the writing was on the wall for Iran. The country had officially declared its neutrality in the war, but such an act only prompted the British government to accuse Iran of siding with the Axis powers. The British objective of undermining Iran's neutrality had a hidden agenda, knowing full well that gaining control over Iran's oil resources, and in particular, the Abadan refinery, the largest in the world at that time, could change the course of the war. Iran's warm water ports in the Persian Gulf, combined with the Trans-Iranian Railway, which Reza Shah had striven to construct, now served as a gateway for sending supplies and support to Russia as it faced the threat of a Nazi invasion.

As a result, and without warning, on August 25, 1941 in a military operation named 'Countenance', the Soviet, British and other Allied forces launched an invasion of Iran with the aim of occupying the country, especially the strategic north and south corridors. Caught off guard, Reza Shah's vaunted armed forces, which he had worked so hard to build into an effective force, crumbled as it faced invasions from both the north

---

[1] *Abbas Milani, "The Shah," Palgrave Macmillan, New York, 2011, p. 67*

The Iranian warship *Babr* following its sinking by British naval forces during the invasion of Iran. *(Raaz-e-Payandegi)*

by Soviet forces and in the south spearheaded by the British. As expected, the British immediately occupied Iran's southern oil fields whilst the Soviets took over northern Iran, propagating pro-Soviet propaganda and supporting pro-Soviet sympathizers.

The Trans-Iranian Railway was taken over and used to send supplies to Soviet forces whilst Iran's armory was confiscated for use by the British. The effects of the invasion were profound on the Iranian people as they faced a national humiliation. The open presence of Allied forces, acting as occupiers also led to food shortages and economic disruption as it was not uncommon for the occupiers to expropriate resources for themselves. Notwithstanding these events, the royal compounds were left intact, ensuring the survival of the cars in the royal garage.

Fit for a King ~ The Royal Garage of the Shah of Iran

OPPOSITE TOP: A pontoon bridge fortified and supported by boats as used by British troops to cross the Karoon River in the south of Iran during the invasion. (August 1941)
(Raaz-e-Payandegi)

OPPOSITE BOTTOM LEFT: A Soviet BA-10 armored vehicle in Iran during the Russian invasion. (August 1941)
(Raaz-e-Payandegi)

OPPOSITE BOTTOM RIGHT: British and Soviet officers greet each other at the city of Sahneh after the invading forces met from the northern and southern corridors. (August 1941)
(Raaz-e-Payandegi)

ABOVE: Tehran under occupation. (1941) *(Raaz-e-Payandegi)*

RIGHT: Transporting supplies from the Persian Gulf across Iran to the Soviet Union using trucks from the recently established company, UKCC. (1941) *(Raaz-e-Payandegi)*

Abdication and the Exile of Reza Shah

Twenty days after the invasion, the Iranian National Consultative Assembly (Parliament) announced that Reza Shah had abdicated from the monarchy, and on September 15, 1941, Crown Prince Mohammad Reza Pahlavi went there to take the oath in succession to his father. On this historical day, the new Shah, chose his black Packard Eight 1405 Limousine, driving past throngs of supporters. Whilst his son was addressing Parliament, Reza Shah was being driven into exile by his personal driver Sadegh Khan, in what was described as a nondescript car (believed to have been a Buick) to avoid attracting undue attention from Allied soldiers manning checkpoints across Iran. Before him eleven members of the royal family had already left Tehran in what was also believed to have been a Buick. The car went to Isfahan and Kerman, arriving at Bandar Abbas in the Persian Gulf coast.

There, Reza Shah and his family boarded the ship *Bandra*, heading for an uncertain future. Virtually a prisoner of war of the British, Reza Shah had been promised safe passage to the United States but was soon to learn that the government of Britain had arranged for his exile in the island of Mauritius. The first port of landing was Bombay, India, where the once proud King was not allowed to set foot. Reza Shah and his family were then transferred to a second ship, the *Burma*, and after a nine-day journey, arrived in the British Colony of Mauritius. As the climate was not compatible with Reza Shah's health, and after extensive lobbying by the new Shah, the British government relented and Reza Shah and his family were moved to Johannesburg, South Africa. He lived in exile there until his death on July 26, 1944, of what doctors termed a heart attack, and what his family believed was heartbreak.

A number of cars were shipped from the royal garage in Tehran to Mauritius for use by the royal family during their exile. Among them was a Mercedes-Benz 540K Cabriolet A and a Lincoln Zephyr. The cars were mostly used by the younger members of the family, including Mohammad Reza's brother Ali Reza Pahlavi and his half-brother Gholam Reza Pahlavi. When the family moved to Johannesburg the cars were sent there too.

Meanwhile, between November 28 and December 1, 1943, Iran played host to a summit of Allied leaders presided over by Winston Churchill, Franklin D. Roosevelt and Joseph Stalin. The conference, held in the Soviet Embassy in Tehran, was the first meeting of the "Big Three" and its goal was to plan the strategy for victory against Nazi Germany and the other Axis

LEFT: **The ship *Bandra* which was used to transport Reza Shah to exile.** *(Borzou Sepasi)*

TOP: **An Iranian Bayer-Peacock Garratt locomotive on the Veresk Bridge. This famous bridge, a major engineering feat, was constructed during the reign of Reza Shah prior to World War II by the Austrian engineer Walter Aigner. It is located in Mazandaran province in north Iran. During the war, it was known as the "Bridge of Victory". (1940s)** *(iichs.ir)*

Chapter 8: Iran and the Second World War

LEFT: Arrival of Crown Prince Mohammad Reza Pahlavi at the National Assembly for his swearing-in ceremony as the new Shah of Iran, in his 1936 Packard Eight 1405 Limousine. (September 16, 1941) *(Raaz-e-Payandegi)*

BELOW: Mohammad Reza Pahlavi disembarks from the Packard Eight 1405 Limousine and salutes, while standing next to Mohammad Ali Forooghi, the Prime Minister, as he prepares to enter the National Assembly building. (September 16, 1941) *(Raaz-e-Payandegi)*

Mohammad Reza Pahlavi reads his oath of office. (September 16, 1941) *(Raaz-e-Payandegi)*

Chapter 8: Iran and the Second World War

forces, in particular the final alignment for the launch of Operation Overlord, the code name for the Battle of Normandy, and one of the turning points of World War II. For Iranians, the key outcome of the meeting was a commitment from the Allies to withdraw from Iran after the war and recognize the country's independence.

During the war years, the newly-crowned Shah visited different locales across Iran to better familiarize himself with his kingdom. As an enthusiast, he had put together a collection of unique cars, which he used in his travels. Before the start of the war, he had bought a 1938 Cadillac Series 90 V16 Town Sedan which was a good choice for his sojourns into the provinces due to its comfort and powerful engine. However, the Shah also liked to use Buicks, Packards and Oldsmobiles. In 1943, during an official visit to the province of Khorasan in northeastern Iran the itinerary included visits to different factories and governmental organizations for which he chose his Cadillac, but as this car was a closed roof sedan, he switched to his Buick Roadmaster Convertible when greeting crowds.

TOP: **The Packard Eight 1405 as it leaves the gates of the National Assembly building transporting the new Shah of Iran back to his Palace shortly after the swearing-in ceremony. (September 16, 1941)** *(Raaz-e-Payandegi)*

MIDDLE: **Reza Shah and his children on the first leg of his exile in Mauritius. Shortly, after finding the weather not to his liking, Reza Shah traveled to his permanent exile in Johannesburg, South Africa. Reza Shah is pictured with Princess Shams, her then-husband Fereydoun Djam, Prince Gholam Reza, Prince Ahmad Reza, Prince Abdol Reza and Prince Mahmood Reza Pahlavi at their residence in Mauritius. (1941)** *(iichs.ir)*

RIGHT: **Mohammad Reza Pahlavi with his wife Fawzia and their daughter Shahnaz Pahlavi on the Palace grounds of Saad Abad. (1941)** *(iichs.ir)*

Fit for a King ~ The Royal Garage of the Shah of Iran

LEFT: Prince Gholam Reza Pahlavi and Prince Ali Reza Pahlavi ride in a Mercedes-Benz 540K Cabriolet A in Mauritius. Sitting in the rear is the Chief of Staff of Reza Shah, Ali Izadi. It is believed that this car was a wedding present from Adolf Hitler to Crown Prince Mohammad Reza Pahlavi. It was shipped to Mauritius, and then South Africa, to be used by Reza Shah during his exile. (1941) *(Borzou Sepasi)*

BELOW: The Shah inspecting soldiers at the National Assembly. His Cadillac 355 Imperial Sedan can be seen parked outside of the National Assembly gate. The gate had "Lion and Sun" emblems on each side which represent the pre-1979 revolution emblem of the Iranian flag. *(Borzou Sepasi)*

Chapter 8: Iran and the Second World War

THIS PAGE: Visiting the Red Lion and Sun Society building in the city of Mashhad located in northeast Iran. The Shah had his 1938 Cadillac Series 90 V16 Town Sedan transported by train from Tehran. The Red Lion and Sun Society was a charity established in 1922 which was admitted to the International Red Cross and Red Crescent Society in 1923. (October 1943) *(Borzou Sepasi)*

Fit for a King ~ The Royal Garage of the Shah of Iran

Chapter 8: Iran and the Second World War

OPPOSITE TOP: Visiting a sugar factory in the city of Abkooh during the trip to Mashhad with the 1938 Cadillac Series 90 V16 Town Sedan and a 1937 Buick Roadmaster Convertible, which was also transported from Tehran. (October 1943) *(Saad Abad Palace)*

OPPOSITE BOTTOM: The Shah riding in the Buick Roadmaster Convertible during the visit to Mashhad. (October 1943) *(Saad Abad Palace)*

LEFT: The "Big Three" at the Tehran Conference. Left to right: Joseph Stalin, Franklin D. Roosevelt and Winston Churchill. (1943) *(irdc.ir)*

BELOW: Mohammad Reza Shah Pahlavi and Queen Fawzia Pahlavi alighting from their Cadillac Series 90 V16 Town Sedan on a visit to an American military base in Tehran established for assisting the Soviet Union during World War II. (1944) *(Borzou Sepasi)*

CHAPTER 9

The Shah adjusts to a New World

Chapter 9: The Shah adjusts to a New World

With the end of World War II, the British and Russians slowly withdrew their forces and Iran ceased to be under occupation. At the same time, in May 1945, Queen Fawzia left Iran for her Egyptian homeland to seek a divorce. This divorce while initially not recognized by the Iranian royal court, was officially announced on November 17, 1948. Fawzia's brother King Farouk, also divorced his first wife, Queen Farida, at the same time.

The now single Mohammad Reza Pahlavi, indulged in his passion for sports, speed and adventure. An all round athlete, he enjoyed skiing in the winter, swimming in the summer and hunting year-round. With automobile production ramping up in the immediate post-war years, he bought two new Buick Supers, using them more and more in place of his aging Hispano-Suiza and other cars in the royal garage. Not being satisfied with high-speed jaunts to the Caspian Sea, the Shah decided to earn a pilot's license, even stating in one of his speeches that, "in a country like Iran where distances are long, lots of development is needed in the air transport industry to travel inside the country and to make better relations with other countries."[1]

Pursuant to this speech, whether to set an example, or more cynically, as an excuse to draw funds from the treasury to buy a personal plane, a de Havilland Tiger Moth plane was secured to train the young King. After 132 days, on October 17, 1946, he completed his pilot training course, culminating in a solo flight from Qaleh Morghi Airport to Dowshan Tape Airport, and officially earned his wings. His pilot's license was handed over by the most experienced pilot in the Imperial Iranian Air Force, Major General Ahmad Nakhjavan. From then on, when making visits to different areas and provinces across Iran, it was not uncommon for the Shah to pilot the plane himself. With the same passion that he had for

---

1 Hooshang Ansari, "Raaz-e-Payandegi", *Pahlavi Political Culture Research and Publishing Center, Tehran, 1969, p. 417*

The Shah traveling on the outskirts of Tehran with a 1938 Buick Limited Series 90. *(Niavaran Palace)*

fast cars, the Shah tested and flew many different types of planes, with his favorite being the Hawker Hurricane.

On most of the trips by plane, the Shah made a point to drive to the airport in one of his high-speed cars, such as the Mercedes-Benz 500K Autobahnkurier, the Cadillac Series 60 or the Bugatti Type 57C. He made it a game to outpace his motor escort leaving his bodyguards trailing behind. It was not uncommon that by the time they caught up with him, he was already in the air. On one particular jaunt, after taking a curve at a high speed, the Shah looked behind in his rear-view mirror to see that one of the two motorcycle escorts that was trying its best to keep up, was missing. Turning back, he found that the escort had lost control and had gone off the road. After making sure that the rider was unhurt, he continued.

LEFT (BOTH): **Mohammad Reza Shah flying a de Havilland Tiger Moth. (June 25, 1946)** *(Raaz-e-Payandegi)*

BELOW: **The Shah receiving his pilot license from Iran's most famous pilot, Major General Ahmad Nakhjavan.** *(Raaz-e-Payandegi)*

TOP: **Preparing to fly a Hawker Hurricane. (1946)** *(Raaz-e-Payandegi)*

ABOVE LEFT: **The Shah standing in front of his Hawker Hurricane. (Late 1940s)** *(irdc.ir)*

ABOVE RIGHT: **On a trip back from the province of Azerbaijan with the Hispano-Suiza J12, chassis number 13010, bodied by Saoutchik. (1947)** *(Borzou Sepasi)*

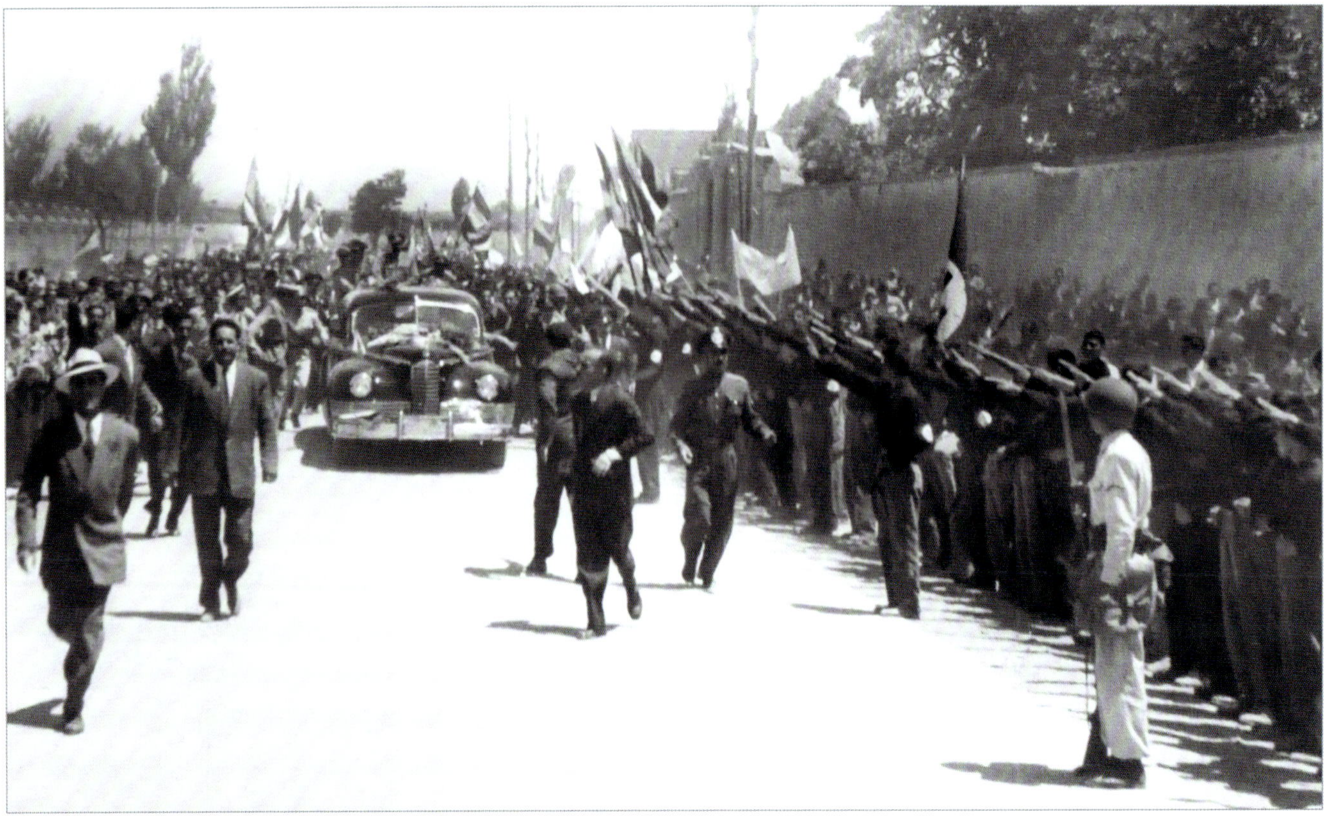

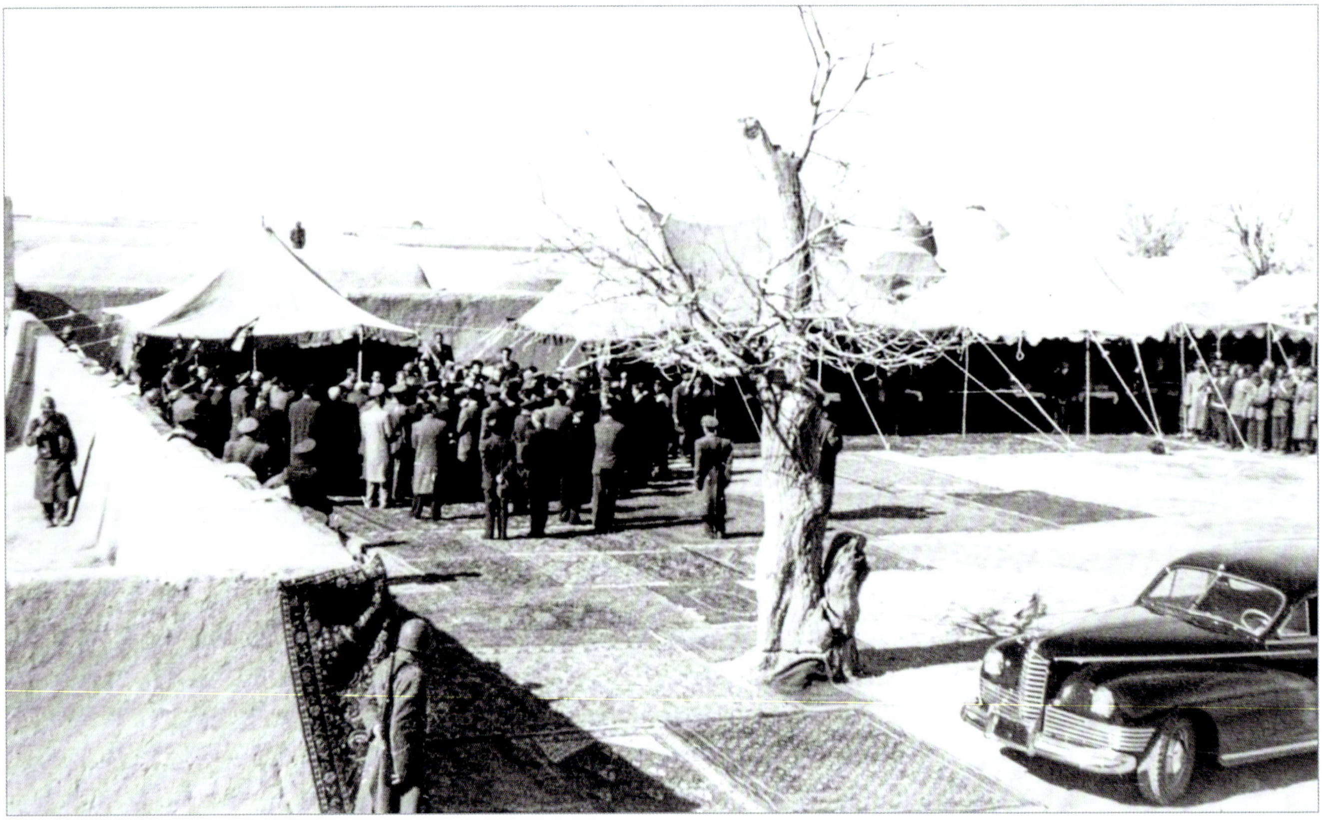

Chapter 9: The Shah adjusts to a New World

OPPOSITE TOP: Greeting crowds while driving the Packard Custom Super Clipper. *(Niavaran Palace)*

OPPOSITE BOTTOM: The Packard is used in a visit to the provinces. (Late 1940s) *(Saad Abad Palace)*

ABOVE LEFT: The Shah and his brother Prince Ali Reza Pahlavi at target practice in the outskirts of Tehran. The Buick Super is visible. (Late 1940s) *(irdc.ir)*

ABOVE RIGHT: Leaning against his Lincoln Cosmopolitan at the Lashgarak Ski Resort, the Shah is with his Swiss boyhood friend, private secretary and confidant Ernest Perron. (February 1950) *(irdc.ir)*

LEFT: Driving past the crowds in a 1946 Buick Super on a visit to Khuzestan province in 1952. *(Raaz-e-Payandegi)*

The end of global hostilities and the growing availability of new products also led the Shah to seek a new luxury car for ceremonial use, eventually settling on a 1947 Packard Custom Super Clipper. The new car was used extensively for official ceremonies and for visits to small cities and villages, even those without paved roads.

The Shah makes a Royal Visit to the United Kingdom and France

On July 17, 1948, the Shah, in a radio address to the Iranian nation, announced his forthcoming state visit to the United Kingdom following an official invitation from King George VI. The Shah met with King George at Buckingham Palace, visited the House of Commons, Oxford University, the Goodwood horse racetrack, the Royal Air Force, the British Museum, and inaugurated the wireless telephone line between Tehran and London.

Fit for a King ~ The Royal Garage of the Shah of Iran

On July 29, he accompanied George VI and Queen Elizabeth for the opening ceremony of the 1948 London Olympics.

He also toured the Bristol Aeroplane Company and the Frazer-Nash Company. *Motor* magazine reported: "During his recent visit to England, HIH The Shah of Iran visited the Frazer-Nash works at Isleworth, and after a demonstration run, placed an order for one of the post-war 'High Speed' models."[2] The Frazer-Nash selected by the Shah was a two-seater car with chassis number 421/E2. This particular vehicle was assembled in 1947, and then prepared for a press presentation.

---

[2] Motor *magazine, September 8, 1948*

RIGHT: In the quadrangle of Buckingham Palace with King George VI. *(iichs.ir)*

BELOW, OPPOSITE & FOLLOWING PAGE: **Frazer-Nash,** chassis number 421/E2, bodied by Carrozzeria Touring Superleggera, following its completion in Milan in the winter of 1947. The picture was taken in Milan's famed Santorre di Santarosa Square, near the Touring factory located at Via de Breme 95. *(Bianchi Anderloni Family)*

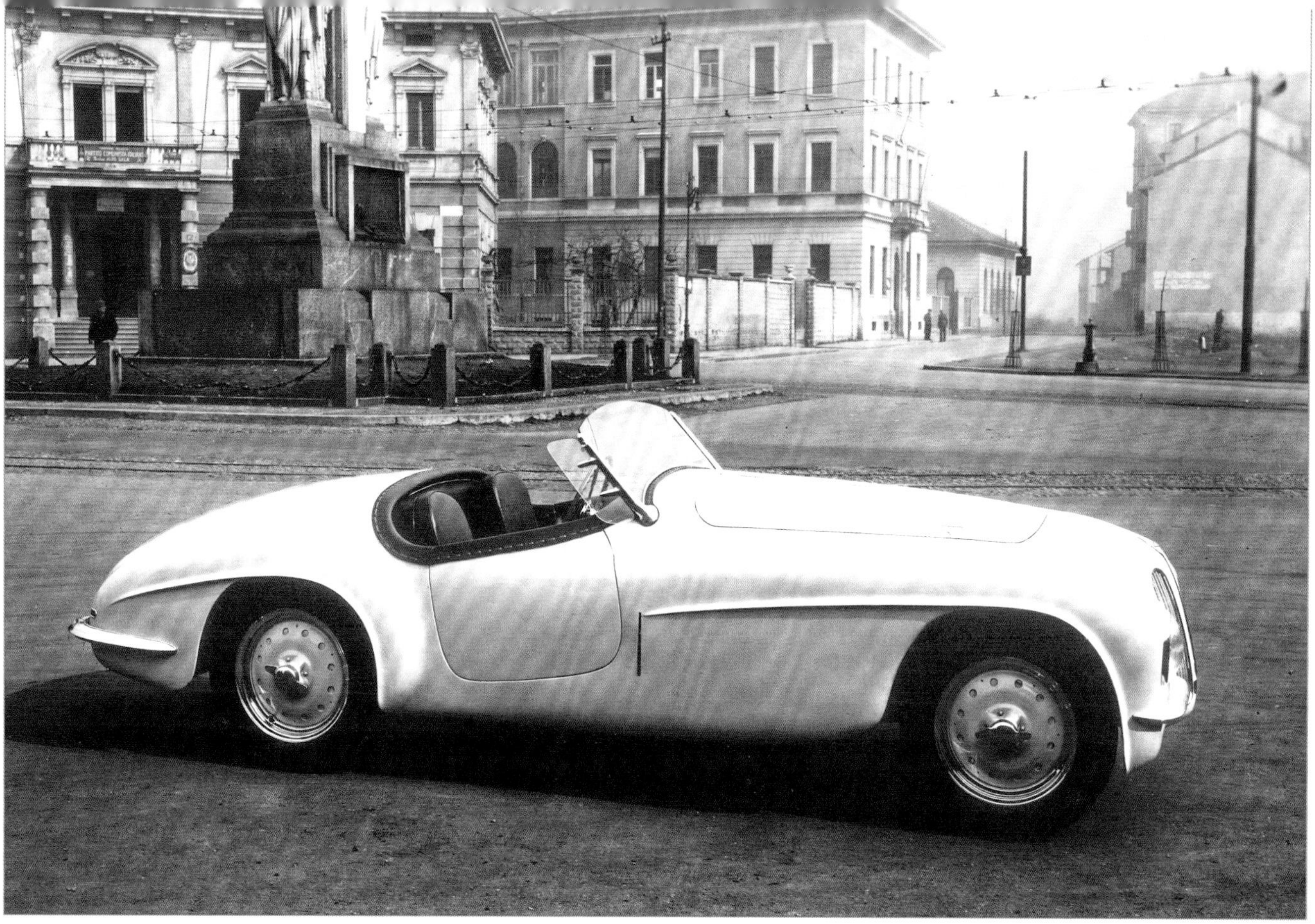

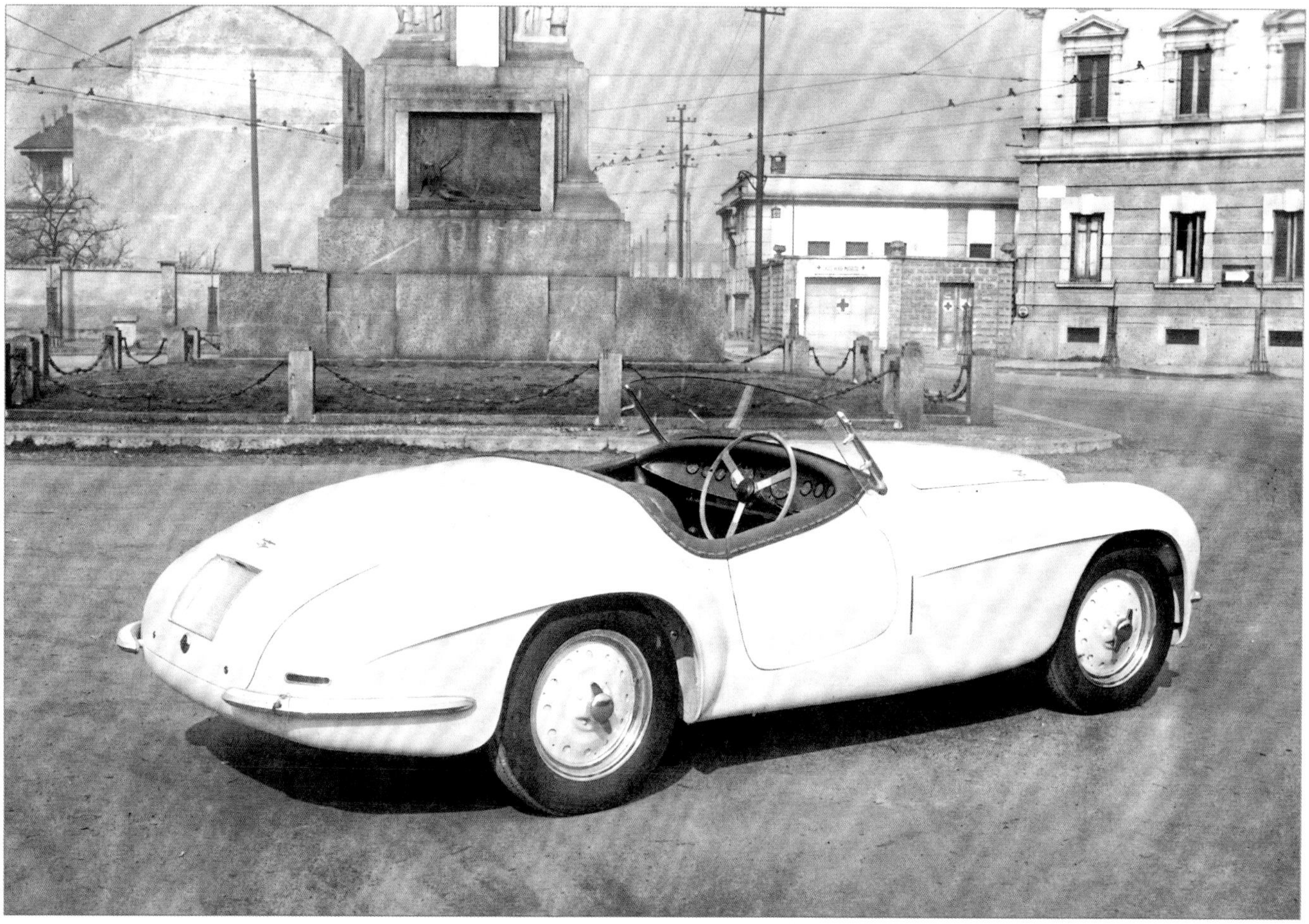

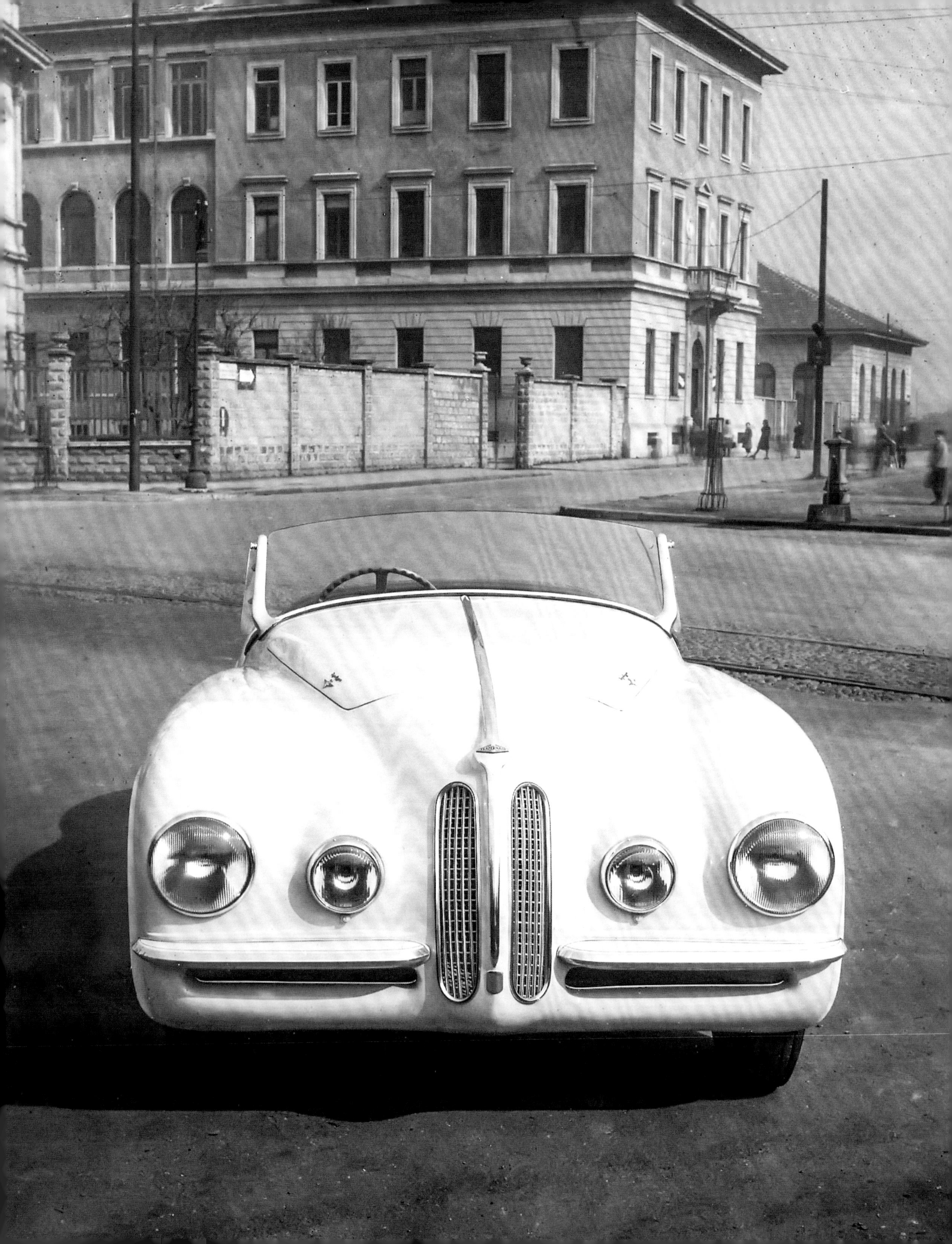

THIS PAGE: The Frazer-Nash won the Roma Pincio Concours d'Elegance held at the end of May 1948. The above photographs show the car in the Pincio Terrace in Rome. *(Bianchi Anderloni Family)*

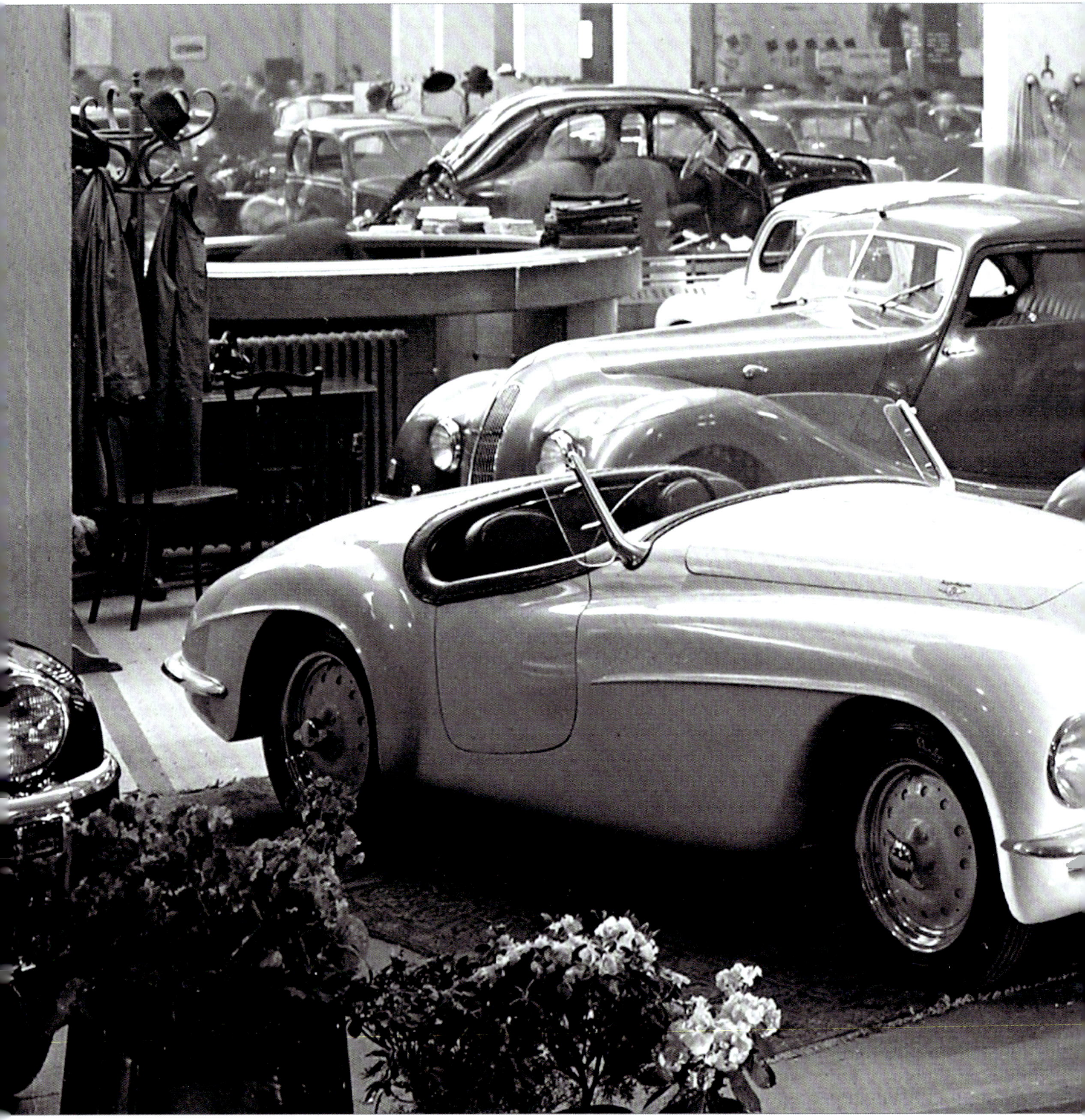

Chapter 9: The Shah adjusts to a New World

The car received extensive media coverage in the British motoring press with details, photographs and drawings published in the January 23, 1948, edition of *Autocar* magazine and the January 23 and February 4 editions of *Motor* magazine. It was subsequently sent to Carrozzeria Touring Superleggera of Milan to be fitted with a body derived from an early version of a design used by Touring on several Alfa Romeo 2500 chassis during the late 1940s, with a BMW-style grille similar to that used by Touring on its Bristol saloons. The Frazer-Nash accompanied by two other Superleggera Bristol saloons, were put on display at the Geneva Motor Show from March 11-21, 1948, and then shipped to Tehran in October, arriving just in time for the Shah's 29th birthday.

From Britain, the Shah and his entourage traveled to France, also as an official state visit. He participated in a number of ceremonies, including laying a wreath at the Tomb of the Unknown Soldier beneath the Arc de Triomphe and holding a meeting with the French President, Vincent Auriol.

During this seven-day visit, the Shah selected another car to complement the Frazer-Nash, a Delahaye 135M, with exceptional styling by Ghia. During this period, Luigi Segre and Mario Boano were in charge of design at Ghia and three Delahaye 135s were produced by them: a cabriolet, chassis number 800488, bodied by Ghia Aigle (the company originally operating as a subsidiary of Carrozzeria Ghia in Aigle, Switzerland) and exhibited at the 1948 Geneva Motor Show, a coupé, chassis number 800573 also by Ghia Aigle, and the car ordered by the Shah, a coupé, chassis number 800514 bodied by Ghia Turin. This coupé was fitted with Delahaye's 3557cc in-line six-cylinder engine, with triple carburetors, developing 152bhp.

The Frazer-Nash on display at the Geneva Motor Show in March 1948. *(The Frazer-Nash Archives)*

Fit for a King ~ The Royal Garage of the Shah of Iran

Chapter 9: The Shah adjusts to a New World

OPPOSITE TOP: Making the final adjustments to the Frazer-Nash at the factory before delivery. *(Bianchi Anderloni Family)*

OPPOSITE BOTTOM & BELOW: The Frazer-Nash at the factory in October 1948 being readied for shipment to the royal garage in Tehran. *(Bianchi Anderloni Family)*

RIGHT: *The Daily Mirror* newspaper published an article on September 1, 1948 about the Shah's new Frazer-Nash. *(Bianchi Anderloni Family)*

Shah's car During his recent visit to Britain the Shah of Iran bought this high-speed British Frazer-Nash sports car, capable of 118 m.p.h. With Treasury permission it was sent to Milan, Italy, to have its streamlined body fitted. Yesterday it was back at Isleworth (Middlesex) for testing. Total cost of the Shah's car was £2,500. It has no luxury fittings; both chassis and body are standard types.

State Visits and Equipping the Iranian Military

In July 1949, King Abdullah I of Jordan arrived in Tehran for a state visit, and the Shah welcomed him at the airport in his Packard Super Clipper. The two leaders visited different sites such as a sport festival at the Lashgarak Army garrison in this car. In November 1949, Faisal II the Regent of Iraq also visited Iran and the official car was again the Packard. During the years 1948 to 1950, the Packard served as the Shah's vehicle of choice for most state ceremonies, including a visit to the northwestern regions of Iran in 1950.

It was during this period that the Imperial Iranian Army also ordered new multi-purpose vehicles. When the new Land Rover was launched in 1948, the Iranian Army became one of its first customers with the Shah personally being involved in the decision, even going so far as to specially ordering one for his own use from its sales representative in Tehran, the Bidar company. The Shah's personal Land Rover was used at the ceremony of the 27th graduating class of the Royal Army Cadet University on September 30, 1950. In April 1950, Mohammad Zahir Shah, the King of Afghanistan, made an official visit to Iran. The Shah and the Afghan King traveled to a number of local sites together in the Land Rover, including Tehran University, Golestan Palace and the depository of royal jewels in Melli Bank. They also inspected the Imperial Guard regiment, saluting the troops, whilst standing at the rear of the car.

In parallel to Land Rover, the American company Willys-Overland also successfully sold its Jeep CJ-3A to the Iranian Royal Army through its official representative in Tehran, Sherkate Sahami Automobile.

Chapter 9: The Shah adjusts to a New World

THESE TWO PAGES: King Abdullah I of Jordan and the Shah of Iran in Tehran. (1949) *(Saad Abad Palace)*

Fit for a King ~ The Royal Garage of the Shah of Iran

THIS PAGE: **King Abdullah I of Jordan visits an Iranian Royal Army unit.** *(Saad Abad Palace)*

OPPOSITE TOP: **King Faisal II of Iraq is welcomed at Mehrabad Airport. (November 1949)** *(Saad Abad Palace)*

OPPOSITE BOTTOM: **The Shah personally drives King Faisal II in a Willys-Overland Jeep CJ-3A during a troop review. The Willys-Overland Company supplied large numbers of Jeeps to the Iranian Royal Army through its official representative in Tehran, Sherkate Sahami Automobile Jeep. (November 1949)** *(Saad Abad Palace)*

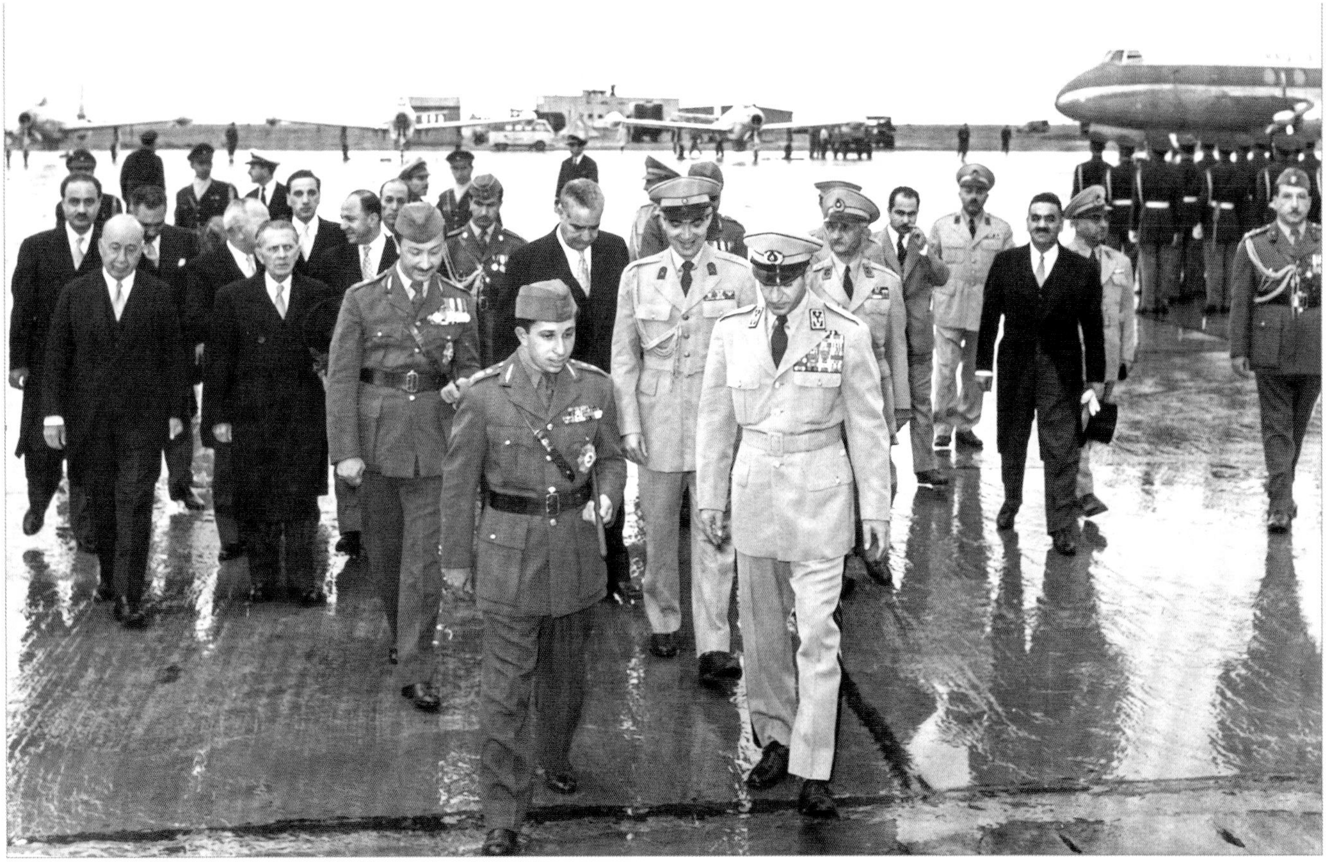

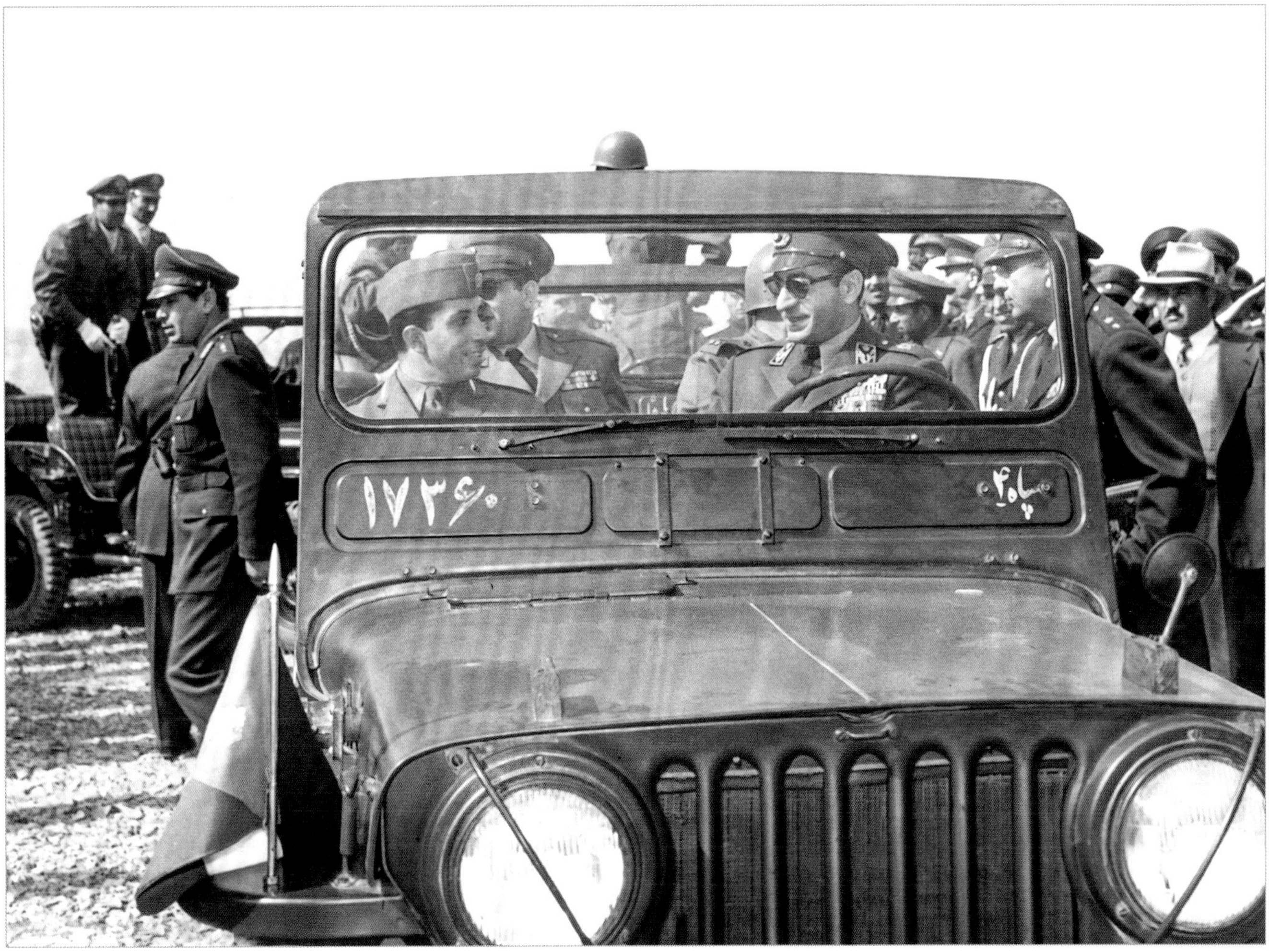
۱۷۳۶۰

Fit for a King ~ The Royal Garage of the Shah of Iran

LEFT: Driving a Jeep CJ-3A during a troop review. (Late 1940s) *(irdc.ir)*

BELOW & OPPOSITE: The Shah undertaking troop reviews with a Land Rover, chassis number unknown. (Early 1950s) *(Borzou Sepasi)*

Chapter 9: The Shah adjusts to a New World

Fit for a King ~ The Royal Garage of the Shah of Iran

Chapter 9: The Shah adjusts to a New World

LEFT & TOP: The Shah and King Mohammad Zahir Shah of Afghanistan saluting the troops during his state visit to Iran. The Iranian Army also used Land Rovers extensively alongside their fleet of Jeeps. (1950) *(Borzou Sepasi)*

ABOVE: Attending the graduation ceremonies of the twenty-seventh class of the Royal Army Cadet University. *(1950) (Ettelaat Newspaper)*

The Shah's personal Boeing B-17G Superfortress

In April 1947, Trans World Airlines (TWA) gifted a Boeing B-17G Superfortress to the Shah. This plane, with serial number 44-85728, had originally been delivered new to the United States Air Force in May 1945. With the end of World War II many of the planes used for the war effort became surplus and were snapped up by airlines who had begun the process of gearing up for normal civilian operations. TWA was one such airline and in 1946 its President, Jack Frye and his team selected this plane to join its fleet. At Boeing Field, it was deconstructed, all its military hardware was removed and in place extensive soundproofing and comfortable cabin appointments were added. Additional windows were installed in the fuselage and upgraded avionics, engines, and propellers were incorporated.

In 1946, TWA was awarded a five-year contract to manage Iran's fledgling national airline Iran Air and TWA took a 10% ownership stake in the company. Subsequently, in April 1947, TWA's luxuriously appointed B-17 was presented to the Shah of Iran as a "deal sweetener" and re-registered as EP-HIM (His Imperial Majesty) and flown by TWA crews.

Two years later, following a restructuring of Iran Air, TWA saw its contract terminated and, in 1952, the B-17 was sold to the IGN (Institute Geographique National) as F-BGOE for scientific and global mapping survey flights.[3] The IGN used the B-17 until around 1967 before it was scrapped in 1972, an unfortunate end for the only "Royal" B-17.

---

[3] *Aeroplane Monthly, June 2010, Volume 38, Number 6. "The Flying Fortress Airliner: The Original Stratofortress?" by Marshall Wainwright, p. 56-59*

THESE TWO PAGES: **The Shah's Boeing B-17G, serial number 44-85728, prior to delivery to Iran with TWA markings.** *(TWA)*

OPPOSITE BOTTOM LEFT: **The Imperial emblem on the B-17 fuselage, serial number 44-85728.**

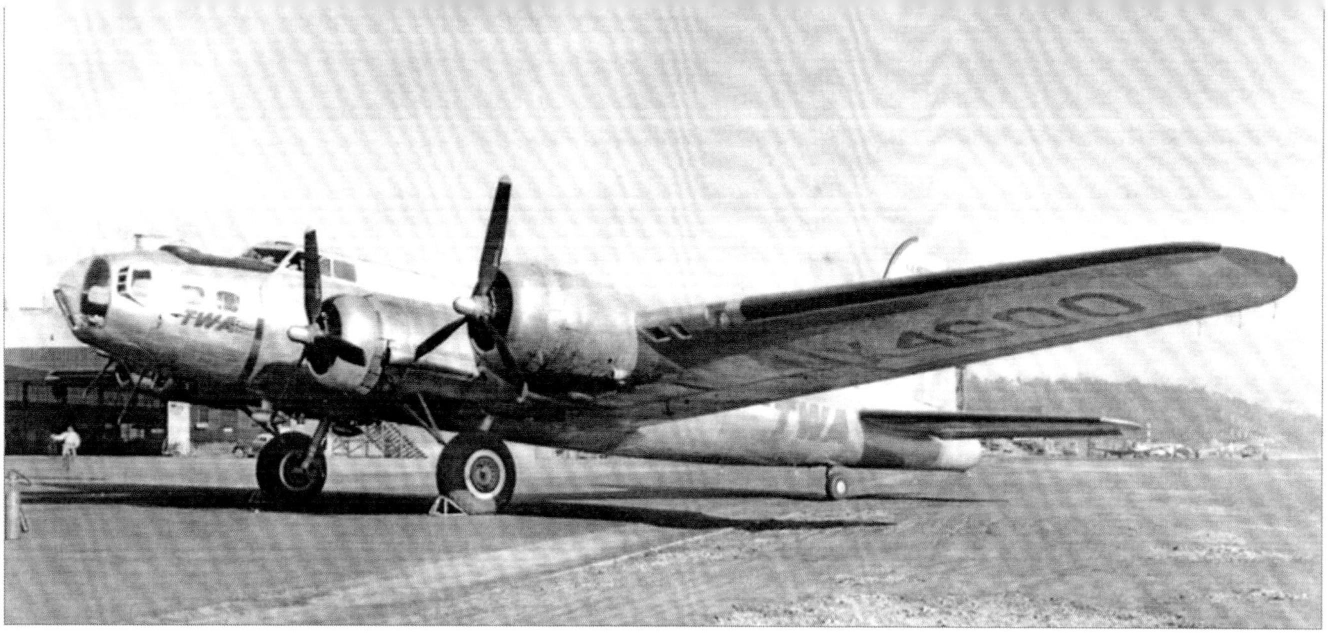
TWA

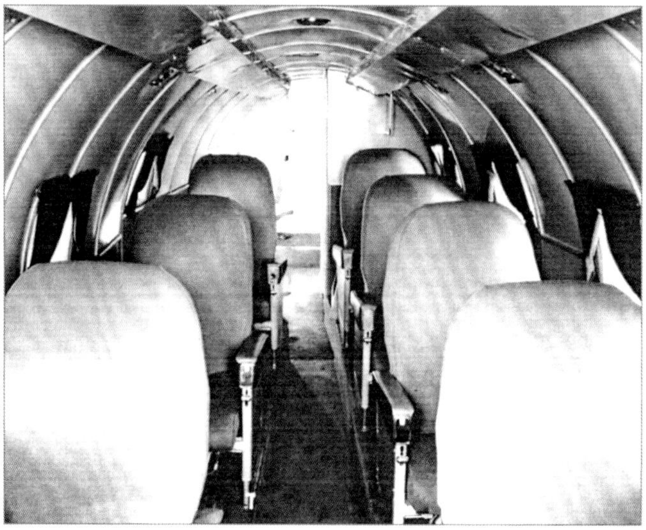

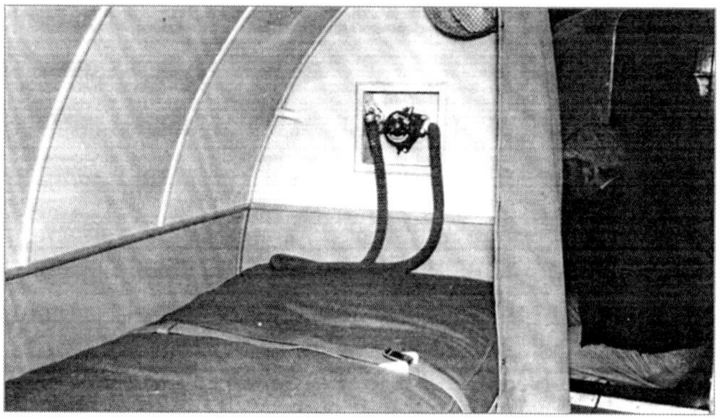

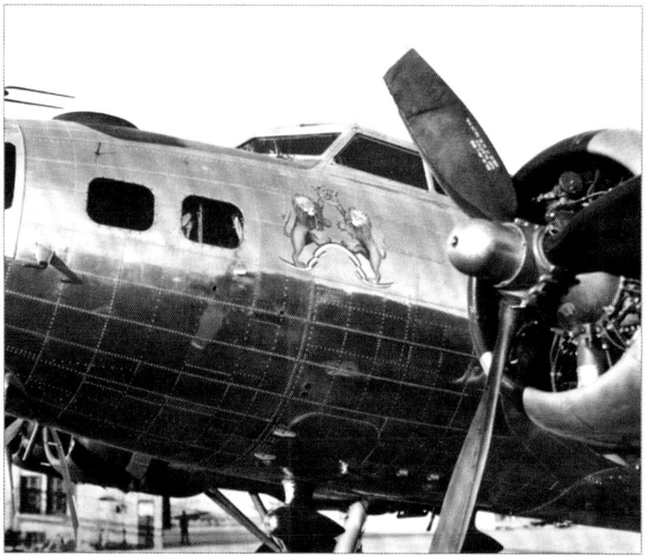

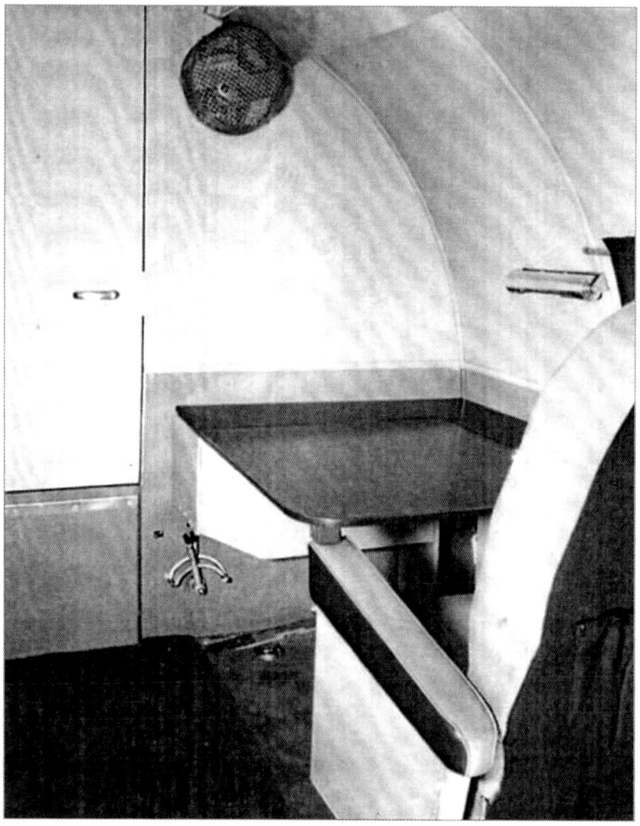

CHAPTER 10

Reza Shah returns Home

Chapter 10: Reza Shah returns Home

With the death of the exiled Reza Shah in South Africa on July 22, 1944, Mohammad Reza Shah faced a conundrum. As Iran was under occupation and Mohammad Reza's own position as Shah during this period was, at best, precarious, the transfer of his father's remains back to Iran bore many risks. Instead, the body was mummified by the famous Russian expert Dr. Boulgacov, and temporarily interred in Egypt until the situation in Iran became more stable, and it could be transported back to Iran.

With the end of World War II and the withdrawal of Allied forces from Iran, Mohammad Reza Shah made plans to have his father's body returned home, and in 1947, ordered the construction of a mausoleum to serve as his father's final resting place.

In April 1950, the mummified body of Reza Shah was transported to Mecca for various religious rites and from there it was taken to the southern Iranian city of Ahvaz. The remains were then transferred from the airport to the Ahvaz train station by a Ford truck and then taken

THIS PAGE: Mohammad Reza Shah arrives to check the progress of the construction of Reza Shah's Mausoleum in his 1946 Cadillac Series 62 Convertible Coupe. (November 6, 1948) *(Saad Abad Palace)*

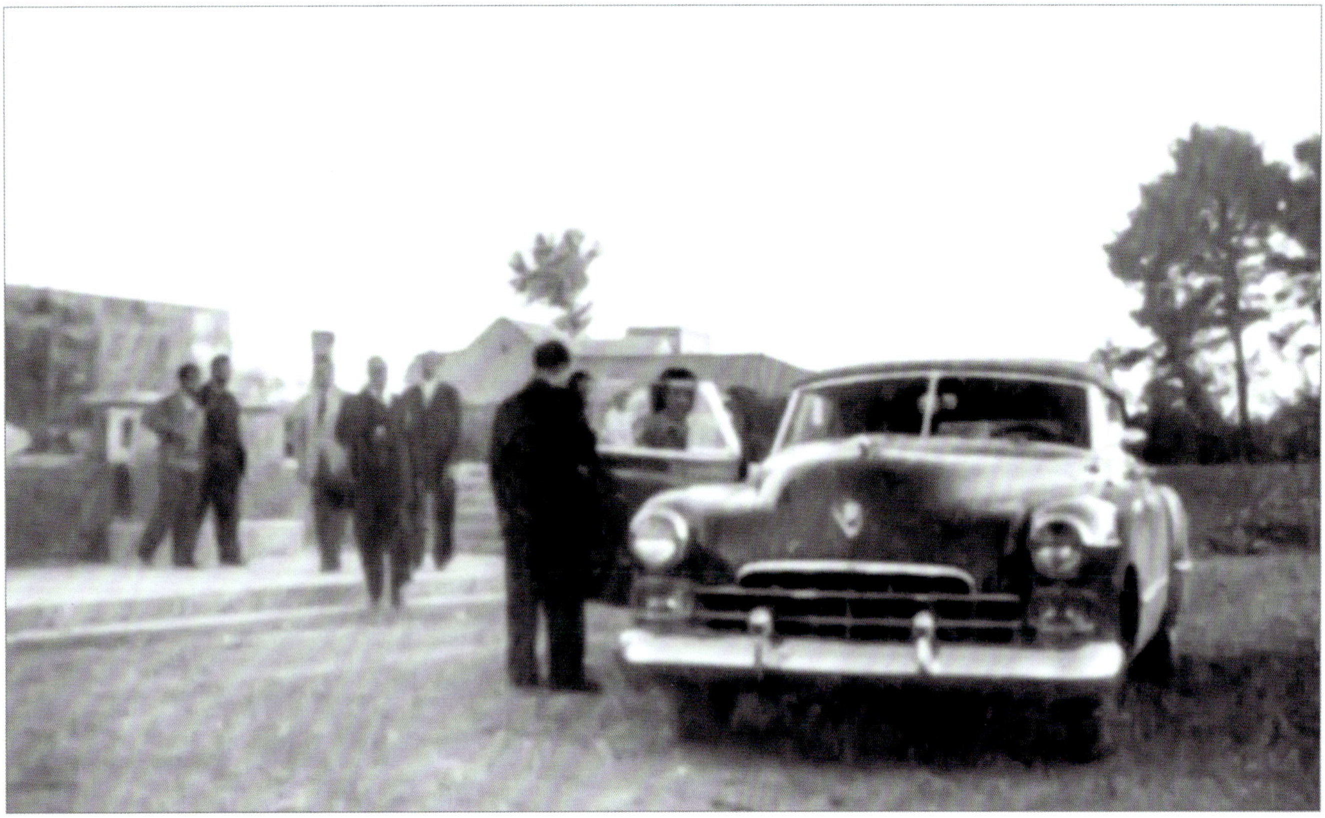

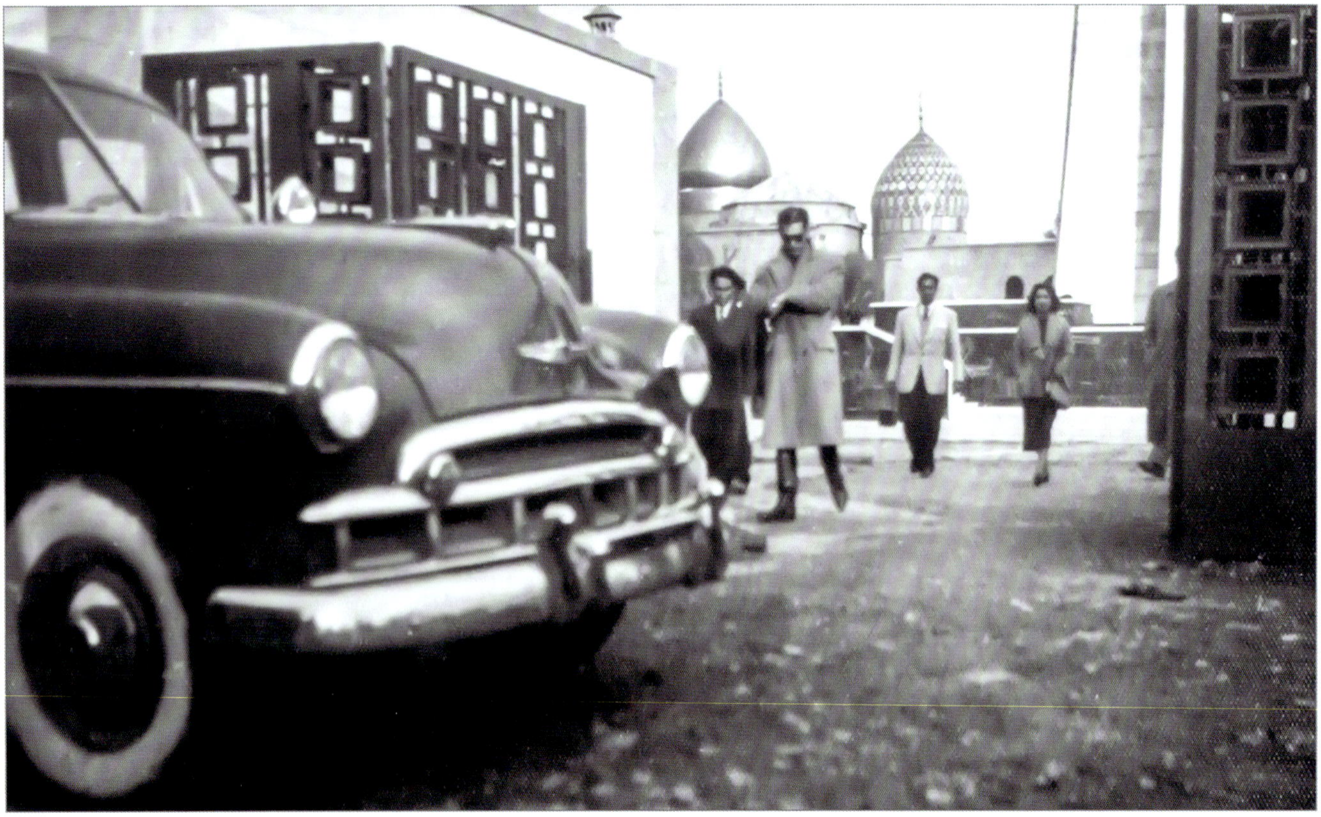

Chapter 10: Reza Shah returns Home

OPPOSITE TOP: **Princess Ashraf Pahlavi, the Shah's twin sister, leaves after visiting the construction site of Reza Shah's Mausoleum in her Cadillac Series 62 Convertible Coupe. (November 2, 1948)** *(Saad Abad Palace)*

OPPOSITE BOTTOM: **The Shah returning to his Chevrolet Styleline DeLuxe after a visit to the same site. (1948)** *(Saad Abad Palace)*

ABOVE: **The Reza Shah Mausoleum. (1950)** *(iichs.ir)*

to Tehran symbolically on the late Reza Shah's crowning achievement, the Trans-Iranian Railway. They were loaded on to a luxurious black carriage, decorated with Quranic verses and laurel wreaths painted in gold. The train made its first stop at the holy city of Qom and from there the remains were transferred by a GMC truck to the Fatima Masumeh holy shrine for a religious funeral.

Fit for a King ~ The Royal Garage of the Shah of Iran

Both the GMC and Ford trucks were specially modified for this somber occasion. The trucks had been adapted to be used as hearses whilst the railway carriage was converted into a funeral trolley car. All the modifications had been carried out by the employees of the Iranian railways, who used this occasion as an opportunity to pay tribute to Reza Shah for his role in the construction of the railways.

On the top of the two trucks and carriage, a gold-plated Pahlavi crown was installed. However, the modifications to the two trucks had some differences. The Ford truck, which was used in Ahvaz had a closed container and the coffin was not visible from outside, whilst the GMC truck used in Qom had an open sided container and was ringed by guards. On the driver doors of both trucks laurel wreaths figured prominently.

On May 7, 1950 the funeral procession arrived in Tehran. The royal coffin was unloaded from the funeral carriage, placed on a Bofors cannon and towed by a Marmon-Herrington truck with chassis number A-30-6-1216. The rear of the truck was loaded with wreaths and bouquets. In the final leg of the funeral procession towards the mausoleum, the truck and cannon were placed in front, followed by Mohammad Reza Shah in his father's special Pierce-Arrow. Following arrival at the mausoleum, the coffin was unloaded and in a special ceremony, after years of exile in both life and death, Reza Shah was laid in his final resting place, back in his homeland. As Reza Shah's mausoleum was located close to the Ab-dol-Azim Shrine, the mausoleum became a popular place to visit by pilgrims

Chapter 10: Reza Shah returns Home

OPPOSITE: Reza Shah's coffin is unloaded from the plane during a stop in Mecca, Saudi Arabia to carry out religious rituals before being transferred to Iran. (May 5, 1950) *(iichs.ir)*

THIS PAGE: The Ford truck, which had been converted into a hearse, pictured in Ahvaz. (May 5, 1950) *(iichs.ir)*

Fit for a King ~ The Royal Garage of the Shah of Iran

Chapter 10: Reza Shah returns Home

TOP LEFT: The Bofors cannon selected to support Reza Shah's coffin. (1950) *(Borzou Sepasi)*

TOP RIGHT: The Pierce-Arrow Model A, chassis number 3025354, bodied by Brunn & Company was protected by an armed escort during the funeral ceremony. (May 7, 1950) *(Borzou Sepasi)*

MIDDLE LEFT: Postal stamp commemorating Reza Shah's mausoleum. (1950)

ABOVE: Covered in flowers, the Marmon-Herrington truck, chassis number A-30-6-1216, which towed the cannon and coffin in the ceremony. (May 7, 1950) *(irdc.ir)*

BOTTOM LEFT: Mohammad Reza Shah Pahlavi in the Pierce-Arrow Model A following behind Reza Shah's coffin on the last day of the funeral ceremony in Tehran. (May 7, 1950) *("Old Photos of Tehran, Vol. 1" book)*

OPPOSITE TOP (BOTH) & MIDDLE LEFT: The second hearse, a converted GMC truck, here pictured in the holy city of Qom. (May 6, 1950) *(iichs.ir)*

OPPOSITE MIDDLE RIGHT: The GMC hearse as it crosses the ceremonial gate in Qom. (May 6, 1950) *(iichs.ir)*

OPPOSITE BOTTOM LEFT: Funeral train locomotive. (May 6, 1950) *(iichs.ir)*

OPPOSITE BOTTOM RIGHT: The funeral carriage constructed by the Iranian State Railway. (1950) *(iichs.ir)*

CHAPTER 11

The 1950s ~ a New Decade, a New Era, a New Queen

Chapter 11: The 1950s ~ a New Decade, a New Era, a New Queen

As Iran entered the 1950s the country was undergoing fundamental changes. The effects of the Allied occupation were fading, and the economy was in recovery with the purchasing power of Iranians improving, and the local distributors of global automotive brands started to once again import and sell the latest models.

Following his divorce from Fawzia, the Shah became known as one of the world's most eligible bachelors. Speculation followed him everywhere as to who would be selected as the next Queen of Iran, and in 1950, the court began the search for a suitable candidate. The Shah's sister Shams Pahlavi found a photograph of a young teenager named Soraya Esfandiary, the daughter of Khalil Bakhtiari Esfandiary, a nobleman from the powerful Bakhtiari tribe and his German wife Eva Karl. Born on June 22, 1932 in Isfahan, Soraya was raised in Berlin and Isfahan, and educated in London and Switzerland.

Stunned by Soraya's beauty and also her right lineage, linked to one of Iran's most powerful tribes, made her an ideal candidate. Shams lost no time in tracking Soraya down, and as fate would have it, there was little searching to do as both were in London at the time. A meeting was arranged, and the two hit it off almost immediately. Princess Shams arranged for Soraya to travel back with her to Tehran. Shortly after their arrival, the Shah and Soraya met for the first time at the Palace of the Queen Mother, and the Shah was said to have been completely smitten by her.

A royal engagement ceremony followed shortly thereafter, on December 27, 1950 in the fabled Mirror Hall of Golestan Palace, and the wedding followed on February 12, 1951. On that day, the Pierce-Arrow picked up the bride and drove through the snow-covered streets of

LEFT: **Soraya Esfandiary.** *(bakhtiarifamily.com)*

TOP: **The soon-to-be-Queen Soraya in her wedding dress as she leaves the Pierce-Arrow Model A.** (February 12, 1951)

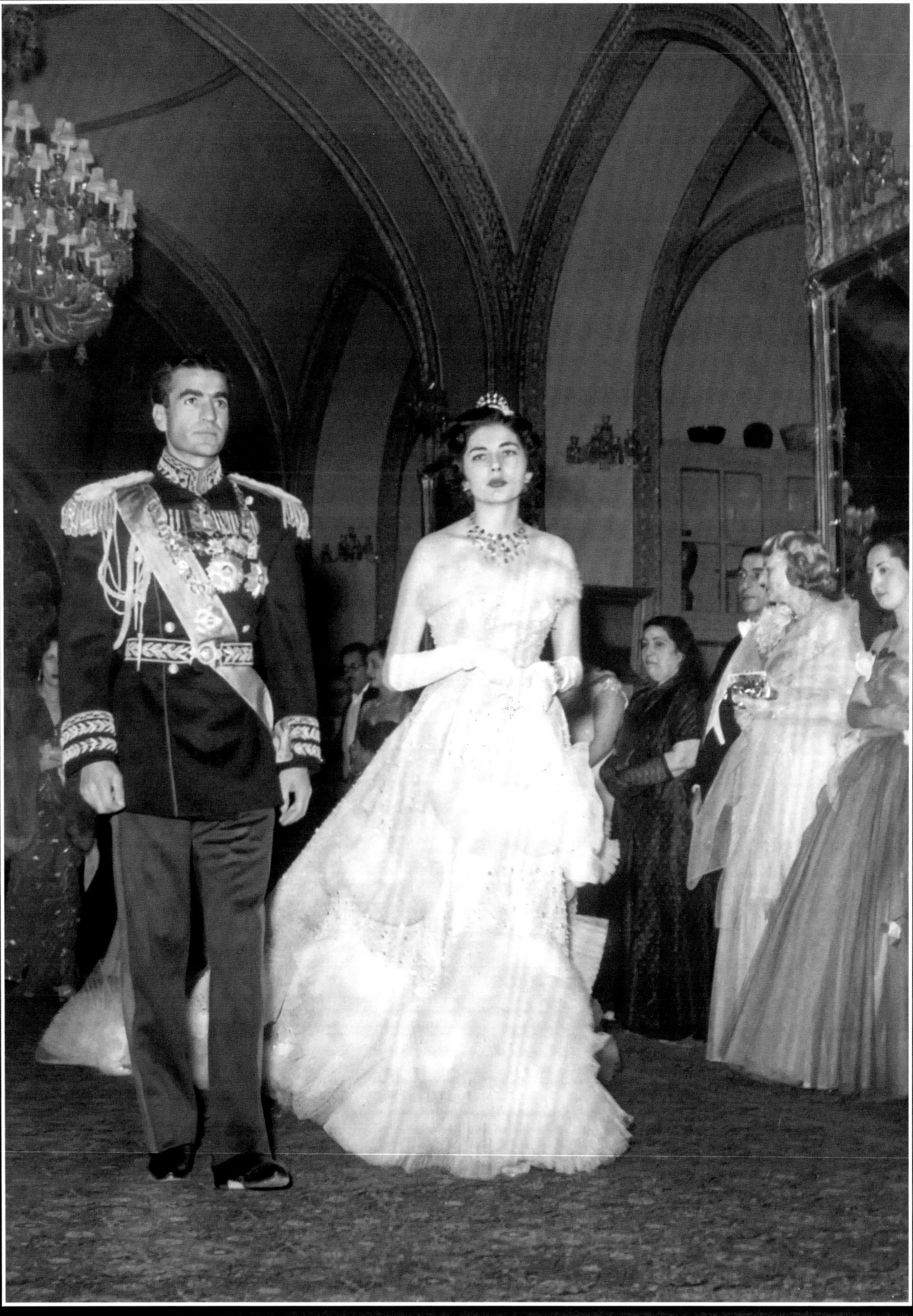

Chapter 11: The 1950s ~ a New Decade, a New Era, a New Queen

Tehran. Notwithstanding the extremely cold weather and heavy snow, crowds lined the streets with a hope of getting a glimpse of their new Queen. The official wedding ceremony was followed by a large reception where guests, dignitaries and foreign ambassadors alike paid their respects and bestowed gifts on the royal couple.

Before his second marriage to Soraya, the Shah, combining his automotive enthusiasm with a virtually unlimited access to funds, was able to purchase some of the most unique and exotic vehicles available, with Rolls-Royces being a particular favorite. In 1948, Rolls-Royce launched the Phantom IV with the first being ordered for use by the Queen of England and the second by the Shah of Iran. Being single, and not envisioning any major events in the coming years requiring a large limousine for protocol purposes, the Shah ordered the car as a two-door drophead coupe.

Upon receiving the order from Iran, Rolls-Royce Limited commenced the manufacture of the Phantom IV rolling chassis (numbered 4AF6), powered by a 5675cc in-line eight-cylinder engine, (numbered P3A). The chassis was then sent to the coachbuilder H. J. Mulliner where its designers constructed an extraordinary body, combining tradition and modernity. Perhaps the most spectacular

OPPOSITE: **Shah and his new Queen Soraya at the Golestan Palace. (February 12, 1951)** *(Archives of the Iran National Library)*

ABOVE: **Soraya signing her marriage certificate.** *(Archives of the Iran National Library)*

Fit for a King ~ The Royal Garage of the Shah of Iran

part of the design was the Silver Dawn-type headlamps, which were never used on any other Phantom IV. The huge drophead coupe body was finished in a light metallic blue with white leather upholstery, and, as a finishing touch, two small Iranian royal coat of arms were added on the doors. This one-off Rolls-Royce, however, had several completion issues, and only after a two-year delay was it finally delivered to the Shah on the eve of his wedding to Soraya. As a result, the 'sporty' Rolls-Royce, which the Shah ordered for his personal use, instead ended up becoming a wedding gift from him to his new Queen. Nevertheless, in almost all photographs, the Shah himself, and not Queen Soraya, is seen driving this car.

ABOVE: The Shah's Rolls-Royce Phantom IV Drophead Coupe, chassis number 4AF6, bodied by H. J. Mulliner prior to delivery to Iran. *("Rolls-Royce" The Complete Works, Mike Fox & Steve Smith)*

LEFT: Mohammad Reza and Soraya in the Rolls-Royce Phantom IV Drophead Coupe. *(Borzou Sepasi)*

OPPOSITE TOP: The Shah at the wheel of the Rolls-Royce Phantom IV Drophead Coupe. Floor mats made of exquisite Persian carpets are clearly visible behind the front seat. (Early 1950s) *(Borzou Sepasi)*

Chapter 11: The 1950s ~ a New Decade, a New Era, a New Queen

BELOW: Soraya at the wheel of a Packard 250 Convertible. Emblems of the Pahlavi crown are clearly visible on the doors. *(Borzou Sepasi)*

BOTTOM: The Shah and Queen Soraya in a 1953 Chrysler New Yorker Convertible in front of the Ramsar Hotel located near the Caspian Sea. This hotel was built during the reign of Reza Shah and was one of the most luxurious and modern hotels in Iran. Ramsar is famous for its lush forests and rice fields, providing a magnificent view from the hotel. The Shah had a private Palace close to the hotel, yet during their visits to the Palace, the couple preferred to dine at the hotel for lunch and dinner. *(Borzou Sepasi)*

Fit for a King ~ The Royal Garage of the Shah of Iran

Chapter 11: The 1950s ~ a New Decade, a New Era, a New Queen

THESE TWO PAGES: The Shah's trip to the city of Cannes. This photograph is taken in front of the Carlton Hotel. (1953) *(Edward Quinn)*

ABOVE: **The Shah and Queen Soraya riding horses in front of the Shah's Palace in Kelardasht. A 1951 Chrysler Imperial and the 1952 Packard 250 Convertible are parked in front of the building.** *(Borzou Sepasi)*

BELOW: **The Ramsar Hotel. (1960s)**

TOP RIGHT: **The Shah and Queen Soraya arriving in Khuzestan province by the royal train. (December 1952)** *(Borzou Sepasi)*

After their marriage, the royal couple visited parts of Iran using various vehicles depending on the nature of the visit. In December 1952, they took a trip to Khuzestan province by train, and as it was an official trip, the Shah rode in a 1952 Buick Roadmaster Convertible owned by the Khuzestan Province Governorate. The Shah usually preferred to use convertible cars on his official visits to the provinces during warmer weather. In Khuzestan province, at the entrance of the city of Abadan, The Shah and Queen Soraya drove the Buick in the midst of the crowds, who were gathered on both sides of the road. The goal of this trip was primarily to visit the Abadan refinery and the oil facilities, which at that time were under the control of the Anglo-Iranian Oil Company, a trip that was a foreshadowing of events to come in Iranian history. They also visited different development projects, using the Buick but the Packard Custom Super Clipper was also often used.

Chapter 11: The 1950s ~ a New Decade, a New Era, a New Queen

TOP (BOTH): The Shah visiting the Abadan Oil Refinery. (December 1952)

MIDDLE (BOTH): The Shah used his Packard Custom Super Clipper for the visit to Khuzestan Province. (December 1952) *(Borzou Sepasi)*

RIGHT: On April 26, 1952, the Shah opened the 17th National Assembly. He traveled to this ceremony in the Pierce-Arrow Model A, followed by his 1949 Cadillac Fleetwood Series 75 and an escort of a number of Buicks. *(Borzou Sepasi)*

CHAPTER 12

1953 ~ the Year of the Coup and Drophead Coupe

Chapter 12: 1953 ~ the Year of the Coup and Drophead Coupe

Dr. Mohammad Mossadegh has a legacy in Iran as one of the most renowned politicians in its modern history. With a doctorate in law from the prestigious Institut d'Etudes Politiques de Paris, for over a quarter of a century, Dr. Mossadegh was at the forefront of Iranian politics during a period marking some of the greatest upheavals of the era.

He first came to prominence in 1925 when, as a Parliamentarian, he stood out as one of the few politicians who was brave enough to attempt to block Reza Shah's ascension to the throne. He even went as far as voting against legislation introduced by Reza Shah's supporters to dissolve the Qajar dynasty and declare Reza Shah the new Monarch of Persia. As a result, with the subsequent accession of Reza Shah to the throne, it was no surprise that Mossadegh, after a period of imprisonment, would withdraw from political life.

With Reza Shah's exile in 1941, Dr. Mossadegh made a political comeback and successfully won back his Parliamentary seat by a landslide in the 14th Parliament. The elections, the first held under the reign of Mohammad Reza Shah, were also the first that were held while Iran was under virtual occupation by the Allies and Russia. As a result, Dr. Mossadegh's nationalist policies, combined with his reputation for honesty and integrity, held wide appeal across Iran, launching him to the forefront of Iranian politics.

On April 28, 1951, the wave of popularity enjoyed by Dr. Mossadegh led to his appointment by Mohammad Reza Shah as Prime Minister. Once in office, one of Dr. Mossadegh's first acts was to shut down the activities of the Anglo-Iranian Oil Company, replacing it with the National Iranian Oil Company. The crowning achievement of his career as a Parliamentarian came when he successfully authored legislation nationalizing the Iranian oil industry, ending the lop-sided concessions held by the British. In retaliation, the British government, the primary shareholder of the Anglo-Iranian Oil Company, organized a global embargo against Iranian oil, and submitted a claim against Iran in the International Court of Justice in which an Iranian legal team, headed by Dr. Mossadegh himself, emerged victorious in getting the case dismissed.

Having lost one of its most lucrative concessions, the British government then made efforts to undermine Mossadegh's government, and, acting in conjunction with the United States, which had a fear of the infiltration of communism into Iran, to stage a coup against Dr. Mossadegh.

Dr. Mossadegh, who at the time was at the zenith of his popularity, was hinting at transforming Iran from a monarchy to a republic. This prompted the Shah to appeal to the British and the Americans to save his throne and he colluded with them on August 15,

Dr. Mohammad Mossadegh.

Fit for a King ~ The Royal Garage of the Shah of Iran

1953 in the first attempt at a coup. This was soundly defeated by Mossadegh's forces, prompting the Shah and Queen Soraya to flee Iran by Beechcraft C-45H plane, serial number A525, first to Baghdad and from there to Rome. Upon their arrival, the couple was met with a lukewarm reception as many had written off the Shah, and, even the Iranian Ambassador, an ardent Mossadegh supporter, failed to show up at the airport. Having fled Iran with literally only the clothes on their backs, many of the expenses of the royal couple were covered by a sympathetic Iranian businessman staying in Italy, including the use of his own personal Cadillac.[1]

ABOVE (BOTH) & TOP RIGHT: Pro-Shah demonstrators on the day of the coup. (August 1953) *(iichs.ir)*

RIGHT: The Beechcraft C-45H, serial number A525 with EP-HIH registration, which was used by the royal couple to flee Iran after the failure of the first coup against Dr. Mossadegh. *(iichs.ir)*

---

[1] *Abbas Milani, "The Shah," Palgrave Macmillan, New York, 2011, p. 188*

Chapter 12: 1953 ~ the Year of the Coup and Drophead Coupe

ABOVE: The Shah and Queen Soraya during their temporary exile in Rome. (August 1953) *(iichs.ir)*

TOP RIGHT: The Shah at the wheel of the Rolls-Royce Phantom IV Drophead Coupe in Rome. (August 1953) *(Khandaniha magazine)*

ABOVE RIGHT: The Shah entering his Rolls-Royce Phantom IV Drophead Coupe after his return to Tehran. *(British Pathe film)*

On an earlier visit to Italy, Queen Soraya had sent her wedding present, the Rolls-Royce Phantom IV Drophead Coupe to Rome for her use and had left it behind in the care of the Iranian Embassy. When the royal couple contacted the Embassy to have the car handed over, the Iranian Ambassador Nazem Noori, already feigning a trip to excuse his lack of attendance at the airport, refused to hand over the keys of the Rolls-Royce. Finally, after a sympathetic Embassy staffer surreptitiously pried the keys away from the Ambassador, the Shah personally went to the Embassy and drove the car away. The Shah and Queen Soraya used the Rolls-Royce to visit the sights and sounds of Rome during the day and dining outside their hotel at night.

On August 19, the Shah was handed a news bulletin by a reporter from the Associated Press News agency, informing him that a second coup had taken place, and one of his trusted officers, General Fazollah Zahedi had successfully ousted Dr. Mossadegh and taken over the government. Once assured that his throne was safe, the Shah arranged the transportation of the Drophead Coupe back to Tehran, and chartered a flight for his return, accompanied by an entourage of reporters. Upon arrival in Tehran, the Shah was greeted by a large crowd of supporters, with the Drophead Coupe parked at the steps of the plane to transport him to his Palace.

After the coup, General Zahedi was appointed by the Shah as Prime Minister and Dr. Mossadegh was arrested and sentenced to three years' imprisonment by a military court. After finishing his sentence, he was sent to exile in the village of Ahmad Abad on the outskirts of Tehran, where he lived out his years until his death in 1967.

CHAPTER 13

Surviving the Coup

Chapter 13: Surviving the Coup

Shortly after the coup and with the country settling back to relative normalcy, the Shah ordered a new car. His choice was a white Mercedes-Benz 300S Roadster which, at the time, was one of the most expensive cars in the world. The order was processed through the official Mercedes-Benz importer to Iran, Merrikh Co. Following suit, the Shah's twin sister, Princess Ashraf Pahlavi, also ordered a 300S, but in green, which she used mainly during her frequent trips to the south of France. The 300S Roadster is considered one of the rarest models produced by Daimler-Benz as only 141 cars were produced between 1951 to 1955, with two of them being owned by the Pahlavi siblings.

THIS PAGE: **The Shah and Queen Soraya beside their Mercedes-Benz 300S Roadster. (Mid 1950s)** *(Borzou Sepasi)*

THIS PAGE: **Princess Ashraf, twin sister of the Shah alongside her 300S, chassis number 188.012.00301.53, in front of the Carlton Hotel in Cannes in 1953.** *(Edward Quinn)*

190

With his throne now secure, the Shah began to travel across Iran with greater frequency to raise his profile. In May 1954, during a visit to the city of Hamedan, accompanied by Queen Soraya, he inaugurated a mausoleum dedicated to Avicenna, the renowned Persian polymath who is regarded as one of the most significant physicians, astronomers, thinkers and writers of his age. It was designed by the Iranian architect Hooshang Seyhoun, who, starting with the modernization policies of Reza Shah, was one of the wave of students sent to study in the West; in the case of Seyhoun, at the École Nationale Superieure des Beaux Arts in Paris. Seyhoun, who was also a sculptor, painter, scholar, as well as professor, has left a widespread architectural legacy across Iran.

During this visit, a growing affinity by the Shah for American cars can be seen, especially for those manufactured by Chrysler. In Hamedan, despite having brought his Packard Custom Super Clipper, the Shah chose to forego this car and use the personal transport of the local Governor, a 1953 Chrysler New Yorker Convertible.

This growing affinity for Chrysler cars was clear as the Shah started to use them even for his own personal use.

ABOVE: **The Avicenna Mausoleum and as pictured on an Iranian ten Rial bill.**

BELOW: **The royal 1947 Packard Custom Super Clipper during his visit to Hamedan.** *(Niavaran Palace)*

FOLLOWING PAGE: **The Shah in a 1953 Chrysler New Yorker Convertible while visiting the city of Hamedan.** *(Saad Abad Palace)*

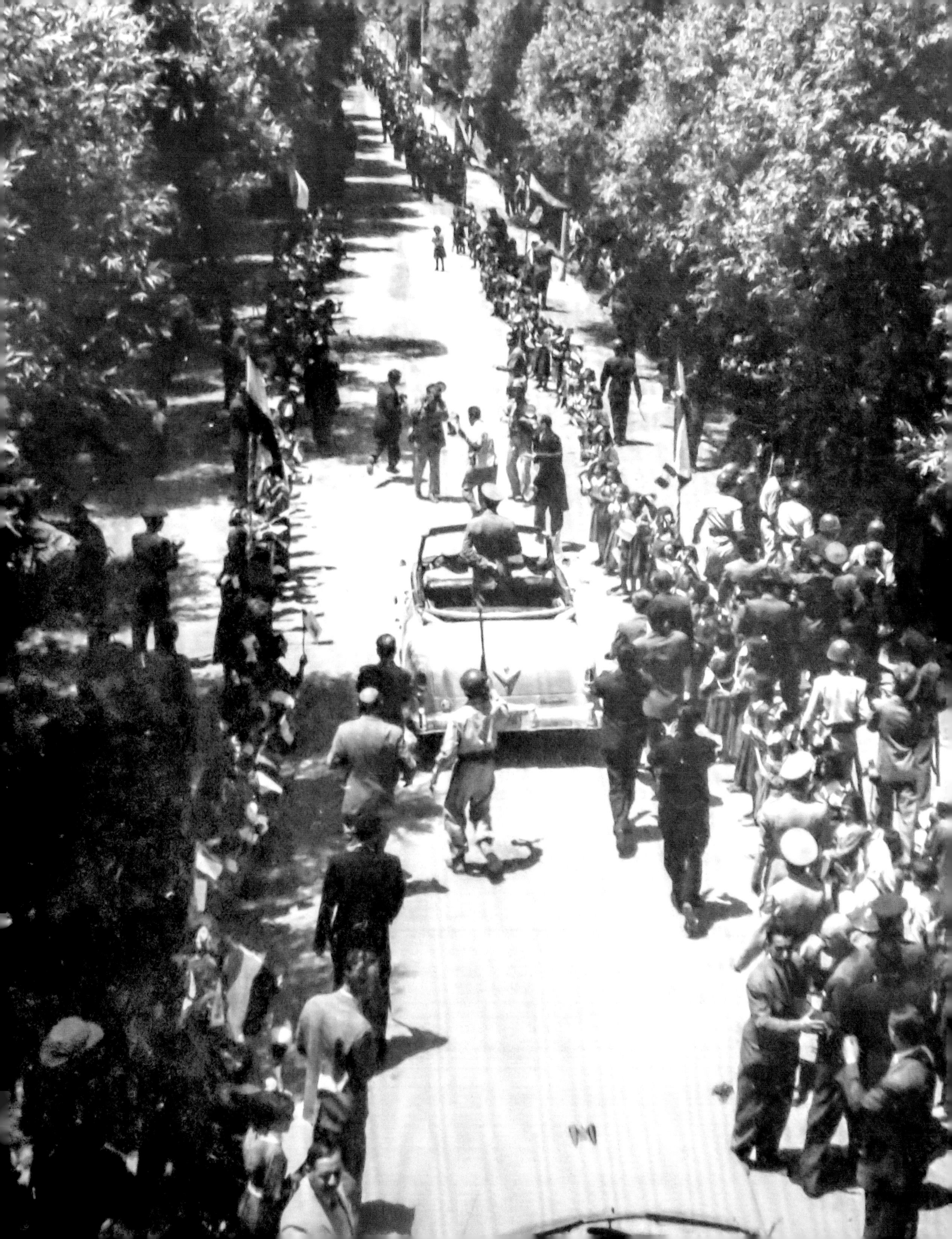

For example, in the waning days of 1954, Tehran and the surrounding areas were covered in unseasonably heavy snow, and the royal couple took a ski trip to one of the well-known slopes known as Ab-Ali, located 70 km outside Tehran in the Alborz mountains. On the way, they made impromptu stops at some of the villages, and, at Rudehen, they visited the homes of some of the villagers. The vehicle of choice for this excursion was a 1951 Chrysler Imperial, which, as would be seen in the coming years, exemplified a growing fondness for American cars and products.

THIS PAGE: The Shah and Queen Soraya in their 1951 Chrysler Imperial making a surprise visit to a small village of Rudehen. *(irdc.ir)*

193

This growing fondness for all things American culminated in a semi-private visit on December 5, 1954. The visit to the United States was slated primarily for rest and recreation and only a handful of days were dedicated to official events.[2]

The royal couple and their entourage traveled across the United States in what has been described as a "star-studded trek",[3] meeting with celebrities such as Humphry Bogart and Grace Kelly, and socializing with the American elite such as media magnate William Randolph Hearst, at his palatial mansion known as Xanadu.

On January 15, 1955, they arrived in Miami, Florida. After an official welcome attended by local luminaries including the Governor of Florida, the Mayor of Miami and several senior officials, the couple were presented with a key to the city. As this was an unofficial visit, the Shah had arranged for the shipment of his beloved Rolls-Royce Phantom IV Drophead Coupe to the United States, with the car receiving a special license plate, so as to be able to traverse the American roads. To forget the stressful events of 1953, the royal couple made the most of their holiday, putting aside all pomp and circumstance, in favor of some personal time at the beach as well as for playing tennis and water skiing. The military uniforms and the glamorous gowns were replaced by casual clothes and sandals.

However, no matter how hard they tried to blend in and be inauspicious, their efforts would come to naught whenever they drove the Drophead Coupe, its flamboyant and unique body style drawing attention everywhere they went. Usually driven with its top down, the car would cause a stir everywhere. After the first few days of their stay in Miami, the Shah mixed some official duties with his vacation and partook in some official and semi-official visits. This included meeting with local business community leaders, Iranian students studying in Florida, a visit to the airport and participating in a Grand Parade as an honored guest of the Mayor of Miami.

---

[2] *Abbas Milani, "The Shah," Palgrave Macmillan, New York, 2011, p. 199*

[3] *ibid*

TOP: **The Shah and the Queen taking a casual stroll in Miami.** *(Getty images)*

MIDDLE: **The hotel room with the door embellished with the "Lion and Sun" of the Iranian flag.** *(Getty images)*

ABOVE: **The Shah water skiing.**

Chapter 13: Surviving the Coup

LEFT: The royal couple taking a sail in the boat named, somewhat non-royally, the *Chick*. *(Getty images)*

BELOW & BOTTOM: The Rolls-Royce Phantom IV Drophead Coupe with its top up parked in front of the Sans Souci Hotel. *(Getty images)*

195

THIS PAGE: The royal family taking a leisurely drive in Miami. The Shah is behind the wheel of Rolls-Royce Phantom IV Drophead Coupe. *(Getty images)*

Chapter 13: Surviving the Coup

Whilst visiting the United States, the Shah's affinity for Chrysler cars reached a new high with the purchase of one of the most unique Chryslers of this period, a one-off Chrysler K-300 Ghia Special, with chassis number 3N551511.

The genesis of this car took shape when in 1949, designer Virgil J. Exner started his new position as the head of the Chrysler Corporation Advanced Styling Studio and commenced a joint cooperation with Luigi Segre of Carrozzeria Ghia S.p.A in Italy. The

THIS PAGE: A Ghia Studio design rendering of the Chrysler K-300. *(Ghia)*

Fit for a King ~ The Royal Garage of the Shah of Iran

198

Chapter 13: Surviving the Coup

result was a series of Chrysler concept cars, with the first debuting in 1954, the Chrysler K-310, followed by the Chrysler K-200, the Chrysler D'Elegance and the Special. In late 1954, a new K-300 chassis was sent from Chrysler, prompting Ghia to make a rendering, based on the chassis, which caught the eye of the Shah. Out of the rendering evolved a one-off, ultra-luxurious, two-door coupe, badged as the K-300 Ghia Special. It was equipped with a bevy of options including leather interior, a wooden dashboard with gold-plated trim, a state-of-the-art Highway Hi-Fi Phonograph, and even a refrigerator behind the seats. Gold-plated Pahlavi emblems were embossed onto the doors.

In late 1955, the K-300 was delivered to the royal garage in a large wooden pallet. When it was unpacked, Ahmad, the Shah's head chauffeur, unable to start the car immediately sent it to the Chrysler central workshop in Tehran where a young mechanic, Reza Dardashti, worked on the engine ordering a number of new parts from the factory. When the car was running satisfactorily, the workshop manager instructed Dardashti to refrain from delivering it until he was absolutely sure that all the mechanical issues had been sorted out since they did not want to risk further embarrassment, and having to deal with possible fallout should the Shah of Iran be stranded on the side of the road. The car was test-driven extensively

OPPOSITE TOP LEFT: **The workers of the Carrozzeria Ghia S.p.A car body factory in Turin applying the finishing touches to the Shah's Chrysler K-300 Ghia Special, chassis number 3N551511. Among the special options are a radio, telephone, refrigerator, long-playing gramophone, and air conditioning.** *(Autocar, April 1956)*

OPPOSITE TOP RIGHT, MIDDLE & BOTTOM: **The Shah's 1955 Chrysler K-300 Ghia Special prior to delivery to the royal garage.** *(Ghia)*

BELOW: **1955 Chrysler K-300 Ghia Special.** *(Borzou Sepasi)*

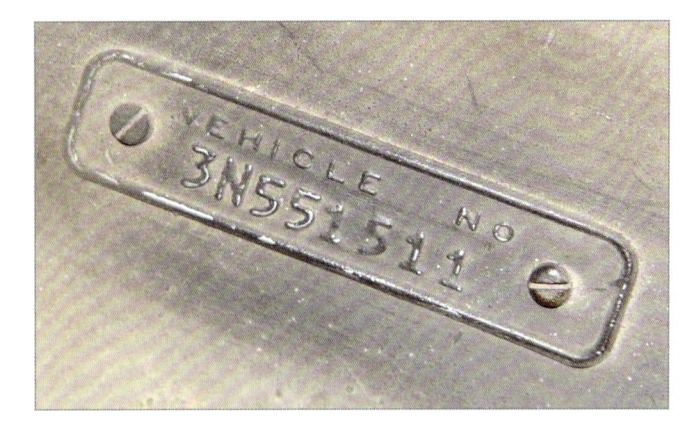

Fit for a King ~ The Royal Garage of the Shah of Iran

TOP LEFT: The Chrysler K-300, chassis number 3N551511, bodied by Ghia. *(Borzou Sepasi)*

ABOVE: The Shah also had a standard 1955 Chrysler Windsor Deluxe. *(Borzou Sepasi)*

MIDDLE LEFT: There were also a few Chrysler Ghias exported to other Middle Eastern countries like this 1952 Special which was sold new to Saudi Arabia. *(Borzou Sepasi)*

LEFT: One unique example of the Chrysler Special was a 1955 Corsair, bodied by Boano belonging to Prince Moulay Hassan of Morocco. He had been exiled to Corsica and then Madagascar by the French authorities in 1953, together with his father, Sultan Mohammad V. Mohammad V and his family returned from exile on November 16, 1955 and Sultan Mohammad specially ordered this car from Boano as a gift to his son in return for his loyalty and service during their exile. After receiving the car, Moulay Hassan traveled with it to several countries in the Middle East. *(Borzou Sepasi)*

Chapter 13: Surviving the Coup

around Tehran, and the local residents, expecting to get a glimpse of the Shah trying out his latest toy, were taken aback to see a young mechanic in overalls.[4]

---

[4] *Interview by Sam Noroozi with Reza Dardashti, Summer 2014*

TOP (BOTH): The 1955 Chrysler Nardi Boano Corsair II of Prince Moulay Hassan prior to delivery to Morocco.

ABOVE (BOTH): Another Ghia-bodied car which was exported to Morocco was this 1954 De Soto Adventurer II, chassis number 14093762, that was sold to Mohammad V, King of Morocco.

BOTTOM LEFT: The Shah and Queen Soraya as guests of the Queen at Buckingham Palace. From left to right, the Duke of Edinburgh, Queen Soraya, the Shah and the Queen of England. (February 1955)

After giving the green light to his superiors, the car was returned to the royal garage. Over the years, Reza Dardashti, because of his mechanical skills, was closely associated with many of the cars that are the subject of this book.

From the United States, the royal couple headed to the United Kingdom, setting sail on the HMS Queen Mary on February 12, 1955, for an official visit. Always the enthusiast, the Shah satisfied his love of special cars by ordering a Bentley R-Type Continental, which, at

Fit for a King ~ The Royal Garage of the Shah of Iran

the time, was considered to be the fastest four-seater production car in the world. The Shah's car was built with chassis number BC73D and engine number BCD72 and then sent for road testing on March 5, 1955. After completion of all tests, the vehicle was delivered directly to the Iranian Embassy in London on March 18, 1955 and, from there, was transported to Tehran. The body of the R-Type was made by H. J. Mulliner and painted in Circassian Blue with gray upholstery and the doors had the royal Iranian crest inscribed on them.

LEFT: Winston Churchill and the royal couple. (February 1955)

BELOW: The Shah's 1955 Bentley R-Type Continental, chassis number BC73D, bodied by H. J. Mulliner. *(Giles Crickmay, Frank Dale & Stepsons, London)*

Chapter 13: Surviving the Coup

On the last leg of their trip, the royal couple traveled to Germany, arriving in Hamburg, on February 24, 1955. For Queen Soraya, whose mother was German, it was in some ways a homecoming. They were welcomed by the German Chancellor, Konrad Adenauer, and President Theodore Heuss and the Shah and Queen Soraya joined the Chancellor in his Mercedes-Benz 300 limousine. Once again, the Shah found time to indulge his passion for cars and arranged a visit to the Mercedes-Benz Sindelfingen factory in Stuttgart on March 4. At that time, Iran was one of the largest export markets for Mercedes-Benz products in Asia, a boon for the carmaker, which was emerging from the devastation of World War II. The Iranian Mercedes-Benz exclusive agent, Merrikh Co., had a booming business, with the sale of the two 300S Roadsters to the Shah and his twin sister, just a small part of the sales being generated. Furthermore, Daimler-Benz management were no doubt aware that the Shah had already purchased two vehicles during his visit to the United States and the United Kingdom, and, in order not be left out, pulled out all the stops during the factory visit, providing an unprecedented "royal" welcome.

In the first part of the factory tour, the Shah and the Queen visited the Ponton and 300 series production lines. From there they were taken to inspect the commercial vehicle and bus factories where an artificial fire was staged to show the capabilities of Mercedes-Benz fire trucks in putting out blazes since at the time Iran was also one of the largest markets for Mercedes-Benz firefighting trucks.

While visiting the bus production line, the Shah and the Queen became familiar with the latest production models. Iran's state-controlled bus fleet primarily used the Mercedes-Benz O3500 which was used for public transportation in Tehran, competing with privately-owned older American models. There is no doubt that this visit had an impact, as the Iranian bus fleet was soon modernized with the all-new O321 bus, in *both* the public and private sectors.

Saving the best for last, the Shah and the Queen were then taken to the motorsport section of the factory, where they saw firsthand the famed W-196 racing cars, which had been successfully campaigned throughout the 1954 and 1955 race seasons. From there, the couple were taken to see the complete 1955 model line-up, with a Mercedes 300SL Gullwing parked at the very end. The Gullwing, which had only recently made its debut and was the highlight of the display, was positioned on an elevated platform to showcase its design and the gullwing doors. The Shah was immediately smitten by the car and placed an order on the spot. That very same night, the Shah's 300SL Gullwing was readied, and delivered to him with German Export registration plates. Upon delivery, the Shah sat behind the wheel and, after a Daimler-Benz representative explained the car's features, the Shah drove off into the night. Shortly thereafter, the vehicle was shipped to the royal garage in Iran. The Shah's Gullwing featured the chassis number 198.040.55.00111, and its engine number was 1989805500070.

The Shah, Queen Soraya and President Theodore Heuss of Germany. (February 1955) *(iichs.ir)*

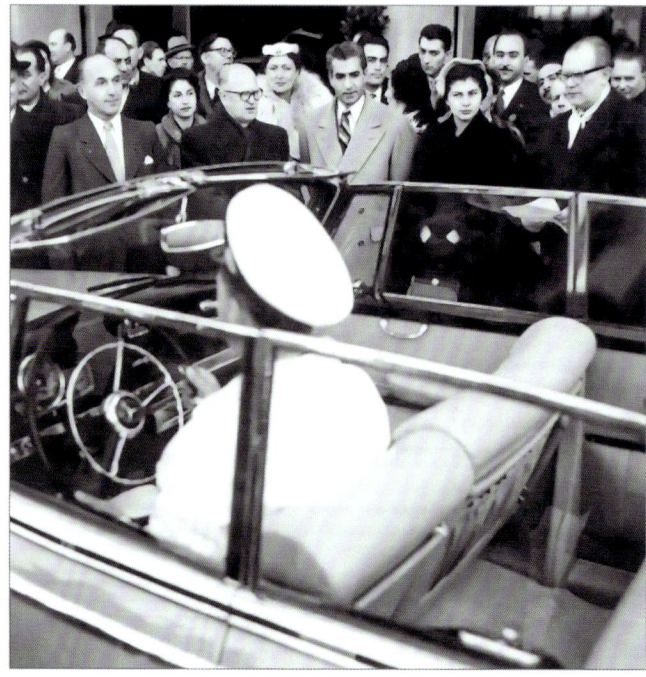

Fit for a King ~ The Royal Garage of the Shah of Iran

OPPOSITE TOP: The Shah arriving at the Mercedes-Benz factory. *(Saad Abad Palace)*

OPPOSITE BOTTOM (BOTH) & THIS PAGE: The 1955 Mercedes-Benz model lineup on display for the Shah's review. All these vehicles were available in Iran through the Iranian Mercedes agent Merrikh Company. *(Saad Abad Palace)*

Fit for a King ~ The Royal Garage of the Shah of Iran

Chapter 13: Surviving the Coup

THESE TWO PAGES: The royal couple take delivery of 300SL, chassis number 198.040.55.00111, while a Mercedes-Benz official explains the features of the car. *(Saad Abad Palace)*

TOP: The Shah peers closely at the interior of a W-196 race car. This car had nine wins in Formula One races between 1954 and 1955. *(Saad Abad Palace)*

ABOVE: The Shah and Queen Soraya pictured visiting the historic vehicle section of the Mercedes-Benz factory. *(Saad Abad Palace)*

LEFT: Visiting the commercial vehicle division of the Mercedes factory. *(Saad Abad Palace)*

OPPOSITE: The Shah at the wheel of his 300SL Gullwing, chassis number 198.040.55.00111, on the night of delivery. *(Borzou Sepasi)*

Chapter 13: Surviving the Coup

209

ABOVE: A Mercedes-Benz LAF3500 fire engine in use in Tehran. Some had locally manufactured equipment from the company, Arj. *(irdc.ir)*

RIGHT & BELOW (BOTH): The Shah also bought a Porsche 356 Speedster on his trip to Germany, taking delivery at the factory as the management of Porsche look on. *(Borzou Sepasi)*

Chapter 13: Surviving the Coup

Any visit to the state of Baden-Wurttemberg would not be complete for a car aficionado like the Shah without paying a visit to Porsche. As with Mercedes-Benz, the management at Porsche were no doubt just as excited to receive a visit from a customer of such royal pedigree, as well as the enthusiasm and deep pockets as the Shah of Iran. Porsche also put out a grand welcome and at the end of the day, the Shah did not disappoint, placing an order for a Porsche 356 Speedster, with the 1.5-liter engine, receiving his Porsche in the presence of the senior management of the company.

THIS PAGE: The Shah and Queen Soraya used the DB V-200 001 Prototype locomotive to travel from Cologne to Baden-Baden. The locomotive had two V12 diesel engines, with a combined total of 1972 horsepower. *(Niavaran Palace)*

CHAPTER 14

The Rise of Shah Mohammad Reza Pahlavi

Chapter 14: The Rise of Shah Mohammad Reza Pahlavi

Newly energized from their long three-month trip overseas, the couple threw themselves into a whirlwind of royal duties. In May 1955, the Shah and Queen Soraya traveled to the historic city of Shiraz, a bastion of Iranian culture and history. On the first day of their three-day visit, they took in a sporting event and from there the Shah departed to inspect the Shiraz garrison of the Army using an Iranian Army Land Rover Series I as his transportation. On the following day, commandeering the same Land Rover, Queen Soraya joined the Shah, and the couple took a break from royal duties to go hunting on the outskirts of the city. On the third, and last day, the couple attended several inaugural ceremonies, including what was to become over time, one of Iran's most recognized hospitals, the Namazi Hospital.

With his throne secure, and the days of the coup long past, foreign leaders and dignitaries began to make official visits to Iran in increasing numbers. On August 8, 1955, King Saud of Saudi Arabia, accompanied by a large delegation of Saudi royal family members and ministers, traveled to Iran by way of a Saudi Arabian Airlines (SAA) Lockheed Constellation plane.

The Shah went to Tehran's Mehrabad International Airport to greet his royal counterpart using, perhaps surprisingly, given the car's age, a black 1949 Cadillac Fleetwood Series 75, which was accompanied by a large contingent of ceremonial cars and motorcycle escorts. From the airport, the Shah and his guest proceeded to the Saheb Gharaniyeh Palace, the former Palace of the Qajar dynasty.

The Shah during a troop review in Shiraz, riding in a Land Rover Series I. (May 1955) *(Borzou Sepasi)*

Fit for a King ~ The Royal Garage of the Shah of Iran

The itinerary for the Saudi delegation included the National Jewelry Museum located at the Central Bank of Iran, a munitions factory of the Iranian Army, a swimming competition (where the Shah personally drove the Saudi King in a Jeep) and Tehran University. Throughout the visit, the Series 75 Cadillac was used as transport, including through the mountainous roads leading to the shores of the Caspian Sea, via Iran's famed Chalus Road when the Saudi King was taken to visit the Caspian region.

BELOW: **The Shah behind the wheel of an Iranian Army Jeep while visiting a swimming competition with King Saud. (August 1955)** *(iichs.ir)*

OPPOSITE TOP LEFT: **The Shah and King Saud beside the Shah's 1949 Cadillac Fleetwood Series 75. This Cadillac, powered by a 331 cubic inch V8, was quite exclusive, with just 595 produced. (August 1955)** *(iichs.ir)*

OPPOSITE TOP RIGHT & INSET: **The mass circulation newspaper *Kayhan* covered in detail King Saud's arrival in Iran. In a photograph published on the cover page, the Shah's 1949 Cadillac Fleetwood Series 75 is seen passing Ferdowsi Square in downtown Tehran whilst a camel was being sacrificed in honor of the two kings. (August 9, 1955)**

OPPOSITE BOTTOM LEFT: **The Shah's 1949 Cadillac Fleetwood Series 75 parked in front of the White Palace of the Saad Abad Palace Complex, the Shah's primary residence.** *(Ma Vie, Soraya Esfandiary, 1963)*

Chapter 14: The Rise of Shah Mohammad Reza Pahlavi

215

Fit for a King ~ The Royal Garage of the Shah of Iran

Following on the heels of King Saud, on September 18, 1955, Celâl Bayar, the President of Turkey arrived in Tehran. The road leading from Tehran's Mehrabad International Airport to the city was decorated with the flags of Iran and Turkey and the municipality of Tehran built a number of ceremonial gates along the route for the procession to pass under. As relations between Iran and Turkey were very strategic, the Shah provided the ultimate compliment by sending his own car, a yellow 1955 Cadillac Eldorado Convertible to transport the Turkish President to the Saheb Qaranie Palace, where he welcomed President Bayar to Iran. During this seven-day trip, ceremonial visits took place, including troop reviews and a significant number of economic agreements were executed, including rail links, an increase in the number of flights between the capitals of the two countries, and the creation of a wireless telephone network.

THESE TWO PAGES: The Shah and Queen Soraya pictured next to their 1955 Cadillac Eldorado Convertible while traveling to the southern Iranian city of Abadan. *(Saad Abad Palace)*

Chapter 14: The Rise of Shah Mohammad Reza Pahlavi

The Shah's 1955 Eldorado was also used a few months later during an official visit of the Shah and Queen Soraya to the southern city of Abadan, the heartland of Iran's oil production. The Shah took the wheel of his Cadillac, where the highlight of the trip was the re-naming of the Anglo-Iranian Oil Company (AIOC) to the National Iranian Oil Company (NIOC). The royal couple then traveled to the provincial cities of Ahvaz, Masjed Soleyman, Haftgol and the port of Mahshoor, by plane, with the Shah personally piloting the aircraft.

The Shah also owned a second Cadillac Eldorado Biarritz Convertible, a blue 1956 model, which was kept in the Iranian Embassy in Switzerland, for the use of the Shah and his immediate family members, during their visits to Switzerland.

Despite his growing fondness for American cars, during this period the Shah ordered a second Phantom IV to be dedicated solely for ceremonial use. An order was processed through the Iranian Embassy in London, despite the fact that production (albeit limited) of this model was winding down. In 1955, the factory commenced work on the Shah's Phantom IV. With chassis number 4CS6 and a straight-eight engine of 6515cc, it was sent to Hooper & Co Ltd, for the design

THIS PAGE: **Rolls-Royce Phantom IV Limousine, chassis number 4CS6 and bodied by Hooper, prior to delivery to Iran.**

OPPOSITE: **The Shah attending the "Atom for Peace" exhibition at Tehran University in his Rolls-Royce Phantom IV, chassis number 4CS6. (1957)** *(Borzou Sepasi)*

Chapter 14: The Rise of Shah Mohammad Reza Pahlavi

and handcrafting of the black body, with the design number of 8425. Hooper charged £4200 for the work, which, when combined with the rolling chassis price of £3950, amounted to £8150. In comparison, a Silver Cloud at that time was priced at £3385. With the completion of the car, promotional photographs were taken on the premises of the Hooper Company before it left England.

The second Phantom IV arrived in Iran on December 10, 1956, two months after completion. It became the primary ceremonial vehicle of the Shah and, from then on, can be seen in use in almost all major ceremonies attended by the Shah in Iran throughout the 1950s, 1960s and the early 1970s. Noteworthy is the fact that despite a six-year production run, just 18 Phantom IVs were produced, making this Rolls-Royce not only a car with a unique history, but also one of the rarest.

The Phantom IV made its public "debut" on March 5, 1957, at an exhibition in Tehran, inaugurated by the Shah called "Atoms for Peace". The exhibition received widespread media coverage starting with the Shah's arrival, in his new Phantom IV, as he disembarked in front of the main entrance of the Faculty of Sciences of the University of Tehran.

Ilyushin IL-14M, serial number 147001241, a gift from Nikolai Alexandrovich Bulganin, Chairman of the Council of Ministers of the Soviet Union, landed at Mehrabad Airport in March 1957. After arrival, the EP-HMI registration was applied for it, however it was never known to have been flown with the Shah onboard.

Perhaps, as a foreshadowing of events that were to take place decades later, after his rule, the Shah went to the podium to make public the signing of a bilateral cooperation agreement for atomic energy with the United States. The agreement had been signed a day earlier at the US State Department, by the Iranian Ambassador, Dr. Ali Amini, who would later go on to serve as Prime Minister under the Shah. Following the Shah's speech, the American Ambassador to Iran took to the podium and spoke for a few minutes. Then the Shah went on to visit the exhibition guided by Iran's most renowned academic, Dr. Mahmoud Hesabi, head of the Faculty of Sciences of the University. From there, the Shah headed back to his Palace in the Phantom IV. Looking back some six decades later, this event would be an inauspicious debut for a car at an event, which would have major implications for Iran's relations with the world in the years to come.

Reciprocating the visit of the King of Saudi Arabia to Iran, the Shah traveled to Saudi Arabia on March 11, 1957. On the first night of his stay, the Shah attended a

Chapter 14: The Rise of Shah Mohammad Reza Pahlavi

banquet in his honor and the following morning, together with the Saudi King, he attended military drills by the Saudi Army and from there traveled on to the capital Riyadh. On March 14, the Shah made a pilgrimage to the holy city of Mecca to perform the Hajj ritual and then moved on to the holy city of Medina. Following the state visit and accompanying pilgrimage, the two nations issued a joint communique reaffirming their ties.

Of note during this visit were the two cars used by the Saudi King to ferry the Shah from place to place, a Cadillac Series 75 Convertible Ghia Special and an Imperial Crown Limousine Ghia Special. In 1953, the Saudi King due to the excessive heat of the country, had ordered two coachbuilt convertible Cadillac limousines. The first car, sourced out to the famous Italian coachbuilder Ghia, was based on a 1953 Series 75 Fleetwood. Ghia removed the roof and re-designed

THESE TWO PAGES: King Saud and his guest, the Shah in his one-off Cadillac Series 75 Convertible Ghia Special. (1957) *(Borzou Sepasi)*

portions of the body. The car was then equipped with modified rear fins and retractable running boards and assist handles at the A- and B-pillars for security guards. In the front, the standard Cadillac grille was untouched, but the bumper "bullets" were removed and replaced with extra road lamps.

A second Cadillac delivered to the Saudi court was manufactured by the French coachbuilder Saoutchik and had a completely different body style. This vehicle was not used during the visit of the Shah, but, as will be seen elsewhere in this book, it would cross paths with the Shah in the years to come.

During this period the Saudi court emerged as a major customer for Ghia. In 1956, another three Ghia vehicles were ordered, comprising of a Ghia Imperial limousine and two Mercedes-Benzes. The first Mercedes was a four-door convertible, named Allungata and the second one was a closed roof version of the same model named Sedan Allungata. Both cars were based on the 300c (W186) chassis and had air conditioning, car-phone and a bulletproof divider window. The Imperial Crown Limousine Ghia Special was based on the 1956 Imperial C-70 chassis, however, the body was completely redesigned and derived from the 1951 Chrysler K-310

ABOVE: The Iranian entertainment magazine *Khandaniha* published a short article on King Al Saud's Cadillac Series 75 Convertible Ghia Special.

RIGHT: The Shah and the Saudi King ride together in a 1956 Imperial Crown Limousine Ghia Special. (1957) *(Borzou Sepasi)*

THIS PAGE: **The customized Imperial of the Saudi court prior to delivery to Saudi Arabia.** *(www.coachbuild.com)*

ABOVE: **Mercedes 300 Allungata Ghia.** *(Carrozzeria Ghia)*

LEFT: **Mercedes 300 Allungata Ghia design rendering.** *(Carrozzeria Ghia)*

BOTTOM: **The Shah and General Franco visiting the Alcázar of Toledo.**

Concept, designed by Virgil Exner and hand-built in Ghia. After delivery to the Saudi court, this car was painted black, and put into use for ceremonial occasions.

In May 1957, the Shah and Queen Soraya traveled to Spain at the invitation of General Francisco Franco, the Spanish ruler. Their itinerary included cultural activities interspersed with official functions and diplomatic meetings. The vehicles used to transport the Shah and Queen Soraya were a Mercedes-Benz 300 Cabriolet D and General Franco's two Rolls-Royce Phantom IVs, chassis numbers 4AF14 and 4AF16.

During this visit, the Spanish government not only presented the Shah with its highest national honor, and no doubt taking a cue from other countries trying to curry favor with oil-rich Iran, appealed to the petrolhead part of the Shah, gifting him with a Pegaso Z-102 Berlinetta Touring Prototipo. Powered by a 2.8-liter V8

Chapter 14: The Rise of Shah Mohammad Reza Pahlavi

ABOVE (BOTH): Two Rolls-Royce Phantom IVs, chassis numbers 4AF14 and 4AF16, served as the official cars during the Shah of Iran's visit in Spain. The photograph on the right was taken in Gunnersbury Park in south-west London soon after the car's completion at the nearby coachworks of H. J. Mulliner & Co. *(left: Getty images, right: Martin Bennett)*

RIGHT: The Shah and Queen Soraya in Madrid, in a Mercedes-Benz 300 Cabriolet D, chassis number unknown. *(Getty images)*

BELOW: The Shah taking delivery of his new Pegaso Z-102 Berlinetta Touring Prototipo, chassis number 0102.150.0119. *(pieldetoro.net)*

Fit for a King ~ The Royal Garage of the Shah of Iran

THIS PAGE: The Shah's 1952 Pegaso Z-102 Berlinetta Touring Prototipo in both black and white and a colorized version. *(pieldetoro.net)*

Chapter 14: The Rise of Shah Mohammad Reza Pahlavi

engine, the Pegaso's chassis number was 0102.150.0119 and the engine number was 0102.017.0119. This car was already five-years old, as it was the 1953 New York Motor Show show car and had subsequently been pressed into service for two years in the United States as a press car and demonstrator, all the while using the temporary registration number of B-104-440. Most notably, in November 1954, it had been driven from New York City to Los Angeles as part of a road test, and from there it was entered into the Carrera Panamericana Race in Mexico.

In late 1955, the Pegaso was returned to Spain, where it underwent a complete restoration and all the interior parts were plated in gold, in preparation for being given to the Shah. After receiving the car, the Shah drove it to the city of Seville and upon wrapping up his visit to Spain, had it shipped to the royal garage in Tehran.

The Shah and Queen Soraya were very fond of aquatic sports and each summer they traveled to the shores of the Caspian Sea and stayed at the Nowshahr Palace in northern Iran where the Shah kept several yachts, and

The Shah and Queen Soraya in front of the royal yacht *Shahsavar* with their 300SL Roadster, chassis number 198.042.75.00462. (Antibes 1958)
(Edward Quinn)

other luxurious aquatic vehicles, mainly of Italian origin. To reach the Palace, the couple had to drive the Chalus Road, the legacy of the Shah's father which even today is viewed by many enthusiasts as among the best driving roads in the world. One of the Shah's favorite pastimes was tackling this challenging road at top speed. With the arrival of the 175bhp Pegaso, this car quickly became his vehicle of choice for the high-speed runs to the Caspian and back, usually with Queen Soraya at his side, and, if the pundits are to be believed, scared her out of her wits.

As much as he enjoyed his Pegaso, the Shah exhibited a keen fondness for his 1955 Mercedes-Benz 300SL Gullwing, and, when becoming aware in 1957 that

The Shah and Queen Soraya at Nice Airport in France alongside the Mercedes-Benz 300SL Roadster. (1957) *(Edward Quinn)*

Chapter 14: The Rise of Shah Mohammad Reza Pahlavi

ABOVE & RIGHT (BOTH): The Shah at the wheel of his Mercedes-Benz 300SL Roadster in Nice in 1958, and in Italy in 1964. *(Edward Quinn)*

BELOW: The 300SL beside the Iranian royal yacht *Shahsavar* in Nice. (1957) *(Edward Quinn)*

229

Mercedes was launching a Roadster version, immediately ordered one. The chassis number of this Roadster was 198.042.75.00082, one of the earliest built, and was painted in blue with a white convertible top. Enamored of this car, the Shah then ordered a second with chassis number 198.042.75.00462 painted in light gray and with a white top, which was immediately delivered to the Iranian Embassy in Switzerland. He used this car during his frequent European trips and could be spotted driving it in destinations as varied as southern France, Italy, and Switzerland.

The Shah's Morane-Saulnier MS-760 "Fleuret II"

In 1957, the Shah visited the Paris Air Show where he was invited to witness the demonstration flight of the new Mirage fighter jet. While there, a small jet caught his eye and upon closer inspection he was told it was a Morane-Saulnier MS-760 prototype called Fleuret II. Intrigued, the Shah asked if he could fly it to Capri, Italy at the end of the show to which the company reacted favorably. A trainer was provided whereby the Shah familiarized himself with the airplane and took some practice flights in the vicinity of Paris. Once fully acquainted with the plane, he flew to Capri with Queen Soraya in tow.

At the end of the trip, the Shah finalized his order for this airplane and construction number 2 was prepared with delivery taking place in Tehran in May 1958 with and registered as EP-HIM (His Imperial Majesty).

The Royal Divorce

After what many termed a 'fairytale' marriage, on March 14, 1958 Iranians were shocked to learn of the announcement of the divorce of The Shah and Queen Soraya. Though it is widely agreed that the couple loved and cared for each other deeply, her inability to bear an heir doomed their marriage and the Shah requested a divorce so as to ensure an heir and the continuation of the Pahlavi dynasty. Soraya, who received the news while visiting her parents in Germany, took it in stride, stating that she would make any sacrifice necessary to ensure the future of the monarchy.

On November 27, 1958, Mohammad Reza Shah made a state visit to Italy. Arriving at Ciampino Airport in Rome, the Shah was welcomed by the Italian President, Giovanni Gronchi and transported by presidential limousine, a Fiat 2800 Torpedo Farina, in the presence of throngs of crowds lining the road, to the Quirinal Palace. The importance placed on this trip by the Italian government was such that the next day, postal stamps were issued in commemoration. The Shah went on to visit Rome to unveil the statue of the epic Persian poet Ferdowsi in Villa Borghese Park. The statue was made by the Iranian artist Abolhassan Sadiqi, whose statues of Ferdowsi in the Ferdowsi Square in Tehran, the statue of Nader Shah in his mausoleum in Mashhad, and the portrait of Avicenna are examples of his iconic and internationally recognized works.

The trip to Rome was followed by a visit to the Italian Naval Academy in Livorno, where the Shah met Iranian naval cadets dispatched for training by the Italian Navy, and from there, on December 1, he arrived at the Vatican for an audience with the Pope. Next, the Shah headed to Milan to meet with Italian oil industry executives, and after conversing with Iranian expatriates, he ordered the opening of an Iranian Consulate in the city.

The Shah's Morane-Saulnier MS-760, serial number 2. (May 2, 1966) *(Jim Cain)*

Chapter 14: The Rise of Shah Mohammad Reza Pahlavi

THIS PAGE: The Shah and Italian President Giovanni Gronchi riding together in the Presidential car, a Fiat 2800 Torpedo Farina, one of six built. (November 1958) *(Borzou Sepasi)*

Fit for a King ~ The Royal Garage of the Shah of Iran

As with his other state visits, the car enthusiast side of the Shah took over, and the next stop was Turin, where he toured the Fiat works. From there, though now officially divorced, former Queen Soraya, who was vacationing separately in Madrid, flew over and joined the Shah for a visit to the Ferrari factory in Maranello. They were welcomed by Enzo Ferrari himself, and given a tour of the factory where the Shah is said to have taken a very personal interest in Ferrari's racing cars, in particular the 801 model. At the end of the visit, the Shah was handed the keys of a new Ferrari 410 Superamerica Series II, with chassis number 0717SA, from Enzo Ferrari. He had ordered his Ferrari prior to the state visit and in July 1957, the chassis had been sent to Pininfarina, where a beautiful body painted in Grigio Metalizzato silver with a red roof and red leather interior was installed. After completion, the Shah's car was exhibited at the Paris Salon in October of that year, followed by the Brussels Expo.

When informed that the Ferrari was ready for delivery to Iran, the Shah insisted that he would rather take delivery personally at the factory, and it was left in storage for a few months. It was only after being delivered to the

ABOVE: Ferrari 410 Superamerica Series II, chassis number 0717SA, bodied by Pininfarina on display at the Paris Salon in 1957. *(www.classiccarcatalogue.com)*

RIGHT (BOTH): Enzo Ferrari personally accompanies the Shah and former Queen Soraya during their visit to the Ferrari works. *(IranSupercars.blogspot.com)*

OPPOSITE TOP: The Ferrari 410 Superamerica Series II, chassis number 0717SA, bodied by Pininfarina. *(Alex Marks)*

232

Chapter 14: The Rise of Shah Mohammad Reza Pahlavi

Lore has it that this car was bequeathed to the former Queen Soraya, whose only association with it would be that she was present when the Shah took delivery. However, documentary and photographic evidence shows that after the car was shipped to Iran, it was used frequently by the Shah, including visits to various sites such as the mausoleum of his late father Reza Shah, and, as the next chapter will show, even to go on dates with Farah Diba, who would shortly emerge as his future Queen. Given the fact that Soraya was never to again set foot in Iran, and that the Ferrari was still in use even after the Shah had married his next Queen, evidence would seem to show unequivocally that this car was never owned by Soraya.

Shah, and most probably being driven at high speeds in the back roads of Modena, that the Ferrari was shipped to the royal garage. The 410 Superamerica, had a production run from 1955 to 1959 in three different series. The Shah's car was from the second series, with a short chassis, of which only six were manufactured, all powered by a 4949cc V12, developing 340bhp. Today the vehicle is not only recognized for its beauty, but also its rarity.

Following the delivery of his Ferrari 410 Superamerica, the Shah turned his attention from Maranello to Livorno, where he visited the Maserati works. He was particularly impressed with the performance of the Maserati 3500 GT after being taken for a drive by Maserati's test driver Guerrino Bertocchi. While at the factory and glancing through some of the Maserati factory brochures for the 3500GT series, the Shah spotted an advertisement for a "retired" Maserati 450S race car with a 5-liter V8

The Shah's Maserati 5000GT, chassis number AM103.002, bodied by Carrozzeria Touring Superleggera prior to delivery to Iran. *(Giovanni Bianchi Anderloni)*

engine with four Weber carburetors and an output of 340bhp. He pulled out a sales sheet on the 450S and stated, "I want a car using this as a basis. I'd like to have something special I can use on the street". [1] After setting out the cars parameters with the Shah, Engineer Giulio Alfieri commenced the project by reinforcing a 3500 GT chassis to handle the larger and more powerful 450S engine, as well as modifying other key areas such as the suspension and brakes.

---

[1] *Winston Goodfellow, "Maserati 5000GT", Magneto Magazine, Issue 4, Winter 2019, p. 106*

In fact, the Shah's car with chassis number 103-002 was sent to Carrozzeria Touring Superleggera and a new superleggera tubing and aluminum body was developed for it. What emerged from the Shah's 'proposal' was to become one of the most iconic cars of the period and became known as the Maserati 5000GT "Scia di Persia" (Shah of Persia). The Shah's car was shipped from Livorno to the royal garage on August 21, 1959, where it joined the rest of its high-performance stablemates.

With a top speed in excess of 170mph, the combination of the beauty and performance of the Shah's car triggered a production run of a further 34 5000GTs. It is not surprising that the Shah, who had emerged, once

Chapter 14: The Rise of Shah Mohammad Reza Pahlavi

THESE TWO PAGES: More views of the Shah's Maserati 5000GT, chassis number AM103.002, bodied by Carrozzeria Touring Superleggera prior to delivery to Iran. *(Giovanni Bianchi Anderloni)*

دربار شاهنشاهی

اداره کل گمرک

یکدستگاه اتومبیل مازارتی از نوع ۵۰۰۰ - تی جی موتور شماره ۱۰۳-۰۰۲ میباشد از طریق گمرک مهرآباد با هواپیمای ارتش جهت تعمیر بطور موقت ارسال گردیده ـ دستور فرمائید برای اتومبیل نامبرده گمرک مهرآباد پروانه خروج صادر نماید تا پس از مراجعت اتومبیل پروانه نامبرده باطل شود . از طرف وزیر دربار شاهنشاهی

رونوشت برای اقدام به گمرک مهرآباد ارسال میشود .
از طرف وزیر دربار شاهنشاهی

۳۰

رونوشت در پاسخ نامه شماره ۱۲۵/فد - ۴۵/۳/۶ برای اطلاع آقای کامبیز آتابای ارسال میشود .
از طرف وزیر دربار شاهنشاهی

Documentation from the royal garage archives dated May 27, 1966 pertaining to the transport by air of the Maserati 5000GT to the Maserati works for servicing. *(Borzou Sepasi)*

Chapter 14: The Rise of Shah Mohammad Reza Pahlavi

again, as one of the world's most eligible bachelors and was a prominent member of the "jet set" was followed by many of his peers in the same social circles, becoming owners of the Maserati model he helped create. This included Giovanni Agnelli, Prince Agha Khan, Briggs Cunningham, the American actor Stewart Granger, even the President of Mexico, Adolfo Lopez Mateos. Unlike the Shah however, they set out to differentiate their vehicles, and had their cars bodied by Italy's best coachbuilders, such as Monterosa, Pininfarina, Allemano, Michelotti, Ghia, Frua and Bertone.

On May 13, 1958, the Shah left Tehran for an official visit to the Far East at the invitation of both Chiang Kai-shek, President of the Republic of China (Taiwan) and Emperor Hirohito of Japan. On the way, he had short stop over in Karachi, Pakistan and a meeting with the Pakistani President and then proceeded on to Taipei, the capital of Taiwan. During this trip, the offical car was a 1956 Mercury Montclair Convertible belonging to the government of the Republic of China.

The Shah's next stop was in Tokyo, Japan where he was welcomed at the airport by Emperor Hirohito, the Japanese Prime Minister and other ranking government officials, and, was transported to the Palace in the Emperor's 1935 Mercedes-Benz 770 Grand Mercedes Pullman Limousine. On the second day of the State

ABOVE & FOLLOWING PAGE: **The Shah and Chiang Kai-shek in a Presidential 1956 Mercury Montclair Cabriolet while visiting a navy yard.** *(Saad Abad Palace)*

Chiang Kai-shek welcoming the Shah. *(Saad Abad Palace)*

The Shah on his official visit in Taipei. *(Saad Abad Palace)*

Chapter 14: The Rise of Shah Mohammad Reza Pahlavi

visit, the Shah paid a call on Emperor Hirohito by way of a Japanese royal carriage. After carrying out all royal protocol activities, the Shah then visited the Toyota Motor Company, a Japanese entertainment company, the factories of Canon and Toshiba, Tōdai-ji (a Buddhist temple complex) and an exhibition about Iranian History which was being held at the National Museum of Japan. It was during this time that the "Asian Games" commenced in Tokyo and the Shah and Emperor Hirohito participated together in its opening ceremony.

As the 1950s, with all its turbulence and change, began to wind down, the Shah commenced his final overseas state visit of the decade. On November 2, 1959, at the invitation of King Hussein, who, in the years to come, would become a trusted friend and fellow connoisseur of

ABOVE: The Shah and the Emperor ride together in the Japanese royal car, a Mercedes-Benz 770 Grand Mercedes Pullman Limousine, as they leave Haneda Airport. *(Borzou Sepasi)*

BELOW: The Shah arriving at Haneda International Airport in Tokyo welcomed by Emperor Hirohito. *(Borzou Sepasi)*

Fit for a King ~ The Royal Garage of the Shah of Iran

240

Chapter 14: The Rise of Shah Mohammad Reza Pahlavi

OPPOSITE TOP (BOTH): **The Shah in a Japanese royal carriage.** *(Borzou Sepasi)*

OPPOSITE MIDDLE LEFT: **Arrival at the Toyota Motor Company.** *(Saad Abad Palace)*

OPPOSITE MIDDLE RIGHT: **Visiting the Toyopet Crown production line.** *(Saad Abad Palace)*

OPPOSITE BOTTOM (BOTH): **Inspecting the 1958 Toyota models lineup.** *(Saad Abad Palace)*

TOP LEFT: **The Shah in a Japanese Imperial carriage.** *(Borzou Sepasi)*

TOP RIGHT: **Meeting with Nobusuke Kishi the Japanese Prime minister.** *(Borzou Sepasi)*

cars, the Shah made his first state visit to Jordan. After a short layover in Kuwait, the Shah and his entourage arrived in Amman where he was greeted with army parades and other military displays. On the second day, the two royals traveled together to Jerusalem visiting the Al-Aqsa Mosque where a key to the city, made of olive wood, was given to the Shah.

The car used to transport the Shah from ceremony to ceremony was the 1953 Cadillac Convertible with a Saoutchik body, ordered by King Saud of Saudi Arabia. This 24-foot-long car was originally painted in green and

The Saoutchik Cadillac prior to delivery to King Saud, the photograph was taken in rue Jacques Dulud in Paris in front of the Saoutchik office. (September 1953) *(Peter Larsen)*

Fit for a King ~ The Royal Garage of the Shah of Iran

Chapter 14: The Rise of Shah Mohammad Reza Pahlavi

white, with a silver- and gold-plated palm and scimitar on the grille, reflecting the colors and symbols of the Saudi flag, and had a power-operated top. At some point, the car was repainted black, the Saudi Arabian emblems removed from the grille, and the car was given to King Hussein of Jordan as a gift.

Little more than a month after his return from Jordan, the Shah was to host his most important guest of the decade, General Dwight D. Eisenhower, President of the United States. The visit, which took place on

THESE TWO PAGES: Mohammad Reza Shah Pahlavi and King Hussein partaking in a Jordanian Army Parade in the black Saoutchik Cadillac. (November 3, 1959) *(Borzou Sepasi)*

Fit for a King ~ The Royal Garage of the Shah of Iran

December 13, 1959 and lasted no longer than a half a day, was marked by major ceremonies across Tehran. Notwithstanding an unprecedented snowfall, the Tehran municipality, working night and day, was able to clear the snow from the parade and ceremonial routes in time for the arrival of the American President.

Eisenhower arrived on a Boeing 707 (Code VC-137) landing at 8:45am in Tehran's Mehrabad International Airport, where he was greeted by the Shah. After the welcoming ceremony, the pair traveled together to the Marble Palace, riding in a light blue 1958 Cadillac Eldorado Biarritz Convertible. With the top down and escorted by a motorcade of Harley-Davidson police motorcycles and security vehicles, they were greeted by cheering crowds lining the route.

The two leaders met face-to-face for a little over two hours to discuss the latest situation in the Middle East and the Cold War maneuverings of the Soviet Union in the region. At the end of the meeting, a valuable hand-woven Persian carpet was given to the American President by the Shah. President Eisenhower, in turn, expressed his thanks, as well as his appreciation of the Persian carpet. This appreciation was all the more evident when, having noticed that the motorcade was driving over a number of Persian carpets laid on the route as a measure of respect, he protested for fear that these beautiful artifacts would be damaged.

The same Cadillac was used by the Shah, during the visit of the President of Pakistan, Muhammad Ayub Khan on November 9, 1959.

THIS & FOLLOWING PAGE: **The Shah and President Eisenhower make their way to the Marble Palace.** *(Borzou Sepasi)*

Chapter 14: The Rise of Shah Mohammad Reza Pahlavi

Fit for a King ~ The Royal Garage of the Shah of Iran

ABOVE (BOTH): On the route from the airport to the Palace some streets were covered by Persian carpets. *(Borzou Sepasi)*

CHAPTER 15

House cleaning in the Royal Garage

Chapter 15: House cleaning in the Royal Garage

In the post-war years, the entry of newer and more modern cars to the royal garage combined with a growing lack of space and the relative obsolescence of the older vehicles, prompted the Shah to unload some of his cars. As a result, many of the cars from the 1930s and 1940s were sold off, mostly to people who had ties to the court.

Among the more notable cars disposed of were the Hispano-Suiza J12, the Bugatti Type 57C, the Mercedes-Benz 500K Autobahnkurier, the Frazer-Nash Spyder, as well as a number of Packards, Cadillacs and Chryslers. Quite a few of the pre-war cars had seen little use, and consequently had very low mileage, surviving unscathed the occupation of Iran in 1941, and the 1953 coup d'état. Nevertheless, the Shah saw to it that cars with historical significance and/or personal value were retained, including, his father's Pierce-Arrow Model A and several of the Rolls-Royces.

The subsequent fate of some of these cars are worth noting. The Bugatti Type 57C Vanvooren was sold on April 22, 1957 to a Houshang Jalili, with a "scrapped" title. Even so, the new owner was able to register the car and received the license plate 20011 - Tehran 38. Thus, unsurprisingly, he began using it as his daily driver. The Bugatti was next sold to Salim Bahary, who took the car out of Iran, traveling across Europe in it. At the time, he was a resident of the Netherlands and soon became

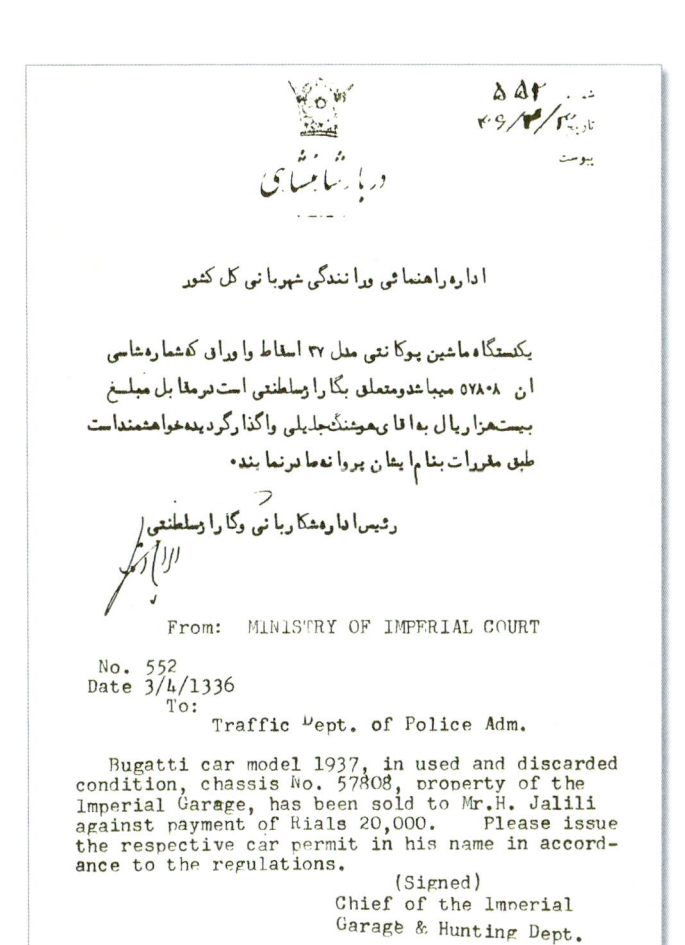

TOP: The sales document for the Bugatti Type 57C, chassis number 57808, bodied by Vanvooren issued by the royal garage. The car was sold for 20,000 Rials equal to $275 to Mr. H. Jalili. *(Jack Braam Ruben/www.fineautomobiles.nl)*

ABOVE: The car in Tehran with the wheel covers. *(Borzou Sepasi)*

LEFT: The Bugatti Type 57C in Tehran with an Iranian registration plate before being driven out of the country. *(Jack Braam Ruben/www.fineautomobiles.nl)*

known in Holland for his flamboyant lifestyle, his wealth and, of course, his Bugatti. He used the car frequently until it suffered an engine failure and, after replacing the original engine with a Packard unit, sold the car in Rotterdam to its third owner, an American. The new owner was able to secure an original Bugatti Type 57C engine (with supercharger) and had it installed in the car by the Dutch Bugatti agent van Ramshorst. Over the years, the car changed hands several times.

Chapter 15: House cleaning in the Royal Garage

OPPOSITE TOP LEFT: Salim Bahary in his new car outside Tehran. *(Jack Braam Ruben/www.fineautomobiles.nl)*

OPPOSITE BOTTOM LEFT: Salim Bahary and his Bugatti Type 57C in Europe. *(Oscar Davis)*

OPPOSITE RIGHT (ALL) & THIS PAGE: The Bugatti Type 57C in The Netherlands. *(Jack Braam Ruben/www.fineautomobiles.nl)*

251

Fit for a King ~ The Royal Garage of the Shah of Iran

The other unique car that the royal garage sold was the Hispano-Suiza J12, which was also acquired by Salim Bahary. He kept the car for several years and then sold it to an American by the name Ortenburger, via an advertisement in *Road & Track* magazine in 1965.

Years after production had stopped, and for unknown reasons but perhaps for spares, a second Hispano-Suiza J12, chassis number 13031 had also been shipped to Iran by air, via Air France in 1948. As of this writing (2021), the fate of this car remains unknown.

TOP RIGHT: **Hispano-Suiza J12, chassis number 13010, bodied by Saoutchik in the royal garage before being auctioned.** *(Lawrence Southward)*

BELOW: **The photograph of the Shah's Hispano-Suiza J12 printed on a "Boulder Bank and Trust Company" card. (1966)** *(Nethercutt Museum, the Jules Heumann Collection)*

252

ARTIC-AUTOS

SOCIÉTÉ A RESPONSABILITÉ LIMITÉE AU CAPITAL DE 17.000 NF.

ATELIER DE RÉPARATIONS AUTOMOBILES

36, RUE AUGUSTE-BLANCHE PUTEAUX (SEINE)

TÉL. : LONGCHAMP 30-67   R. C. SEINE 57 B 823

HISPANO-SUIZA
BUGATTI
VOITURES AMÉRICAINES
ET ANGLAISES

27 Février 63

PAR AVION

Mr SALIM BAHARY
P.O. Box 1257
TEL - AVIV   Israel.

Cher Monsieur,

    Merci pour votre lettre du 21 Février. La voiture HISPANO SUIZA No 13010 - 12 cylindres a été livrée à H.I.M. the SHAH d'IRAN en SUISSE le 31 Octobre 1932.

    Elle comportait alors une carrosserie SAOUTCHICK. Je me suis occupé personnellement de cette affaire et j'étais allé en SUISSE regler la question avec l'Ambassade d'IRAN à l'époque.

    Il est difficile de fixer une valeur pour ce type de voiture, car elle dépend de son état mécanique, des pneus etc... On peut cependant dire que cette valeur varie de $ 3000 à $ 6000.

    Restant à votre disposition pour tous renseignements complémentaires dont vous pourriez avoir besoin, je vous prie d'agréer, Monsieur l'expression de mes sentiments distingués.

H. MOREAU

The letter of "Artic Autos" dated February 27, 1963 in reply to Salim Bahary's price inquiry for the Hispano-Suiza J12. The estimated price was $3,000 to $6,000 based on the car's location. At that time Mr. Bahary was living in Tel Aviv/Israel. *(Lawrence Southward)*

1951 ROLLS-ROYCE. With what must be considered the rarest Post War convertible Phantom IV coachwork, this enormous motor car was designed by request for the late Shah of Persia and has been featured in many editorials, offers invited in the region of **£85,000**

The Rolls-Royce Phantom IV Drophead Coupe, chassis number 4AF6, bodied by H. J. Mulliner, once a favorite of the Shah, met a more ominous fate. In 1959, it was shipped back to the Rolls-Royce factory, neither for sale nor refurbishment, but apparently to be scrapped. The strange fate of this car mirrors the turbulence the Shah faced during the 1950s. After surviving everything from a coup to an unwanted divorce, some pundits surmise that he was trying to put behind him anything that could be a reminder of the political and personal problems that he faced, by arranging the destruction of the vehicle that most symbolized his life during this period. After delivery to the Rolls-Royce factory, though the car was dismantled, the original body and engine are known to have survived and were sold to private collectors, and according to a number of sources, the chassis was destroyed.

TOP: The Shah's Rolls-Royce Phantom IV, chassis number 4AF6 with its Drophead Coupe body. *(Borzou Sepasi)*

ABOVE LEFT: The advertisement is from *Thoroughbred & Classic Cars*, Laurence Kayne in London. (1987) *(Coachbuild.com)*

ABOVE: Data sheet for Rolls-Royce Phantom IV Drophead Coupe, chassis number 4AF6, bodied by H. J. Mulliner. *(Rolls-Royce Foundation)*

Chapter 15: House cleaning in the Royal Garage

The Mercedes-Benz 500K Autobahnkurier had a luckier fate. At some point, while still in the royal garage, it had developed engine problems and had been languishing, without use for several years. It is believed to have been subsequently sold to a buyer with the last name Tabatabaie and, in 1962, it was spotted in the central Mercedes-Benz workshop of the dealer Merrikh Co. in Saadi Street in Tehran by Fuad Majzub, one of Iran's most noted automobile collectors. With only 10,000 km on the odometer, Majzub bought the car immediately. As the original engine was missing, he bought a second-hand Cadillac engine and had it installed and registered the car, receiving the license plate number 63934/Tehran-A. The Autobahnkurier became a frequent mode of transport for Majzub and it was not uncommon to see the car on the streets of Tehran. Some years later, in the early 1970s, Majzub paid a visit to Mercedes-Benz in Stuttgart where he shared photographs of the car. Seeing the photographs of one of their most unique creations that had been considered lost by the factory for more than four decades came as a great surprise and Daimler-Benz tried to purchase the vehicle from Majzub for its museum. Majzub refused the German giant, pointing out that the car belonged to Iran.

ABOVE: **The 500K Autobahnkurier, chassis number 130898 with Iranian registration plate, photographed at Fuad Majzub's home. (1960s)** *("The Complete Automobile Encyclopedia of Cars in Iran" book)*

BELOW: **The photograph that Fuad Majzub showed to Mercedes-Benz during his visit.** *("Mercedes-Benz, The Supercharged 8 Cylinder Cars of the 1930s, Vol. 2" book)*

INSET: **After its sale from the royal garage, the 500K Autobahnkurier was registered by the new owner and received the Iranian license plate, 63934 Tehran-A.** *(Borzou Sepasi)*

BOTTOM LEFT: **It is believed that for a certain period in the late 1950s/early 1960s, the Mercedes-Benz 500K Autobahnkurier was owned by a family with last name Tabatabaie as evidenced by this family photograph shared with the author.** *(Borzou Sepasi)*

255

Unlike the other cars of the royal garage, the fate of the Frazer-Nash is less clear. Local lore has it that the car was involved in a serious accident after its sale and written off whilst others claim that the car is still extant.

With the sale of the earlier cars, the Shah then turned his attention to clearing out some of the relatively newer models.

In 1957, the 1949 Delahaye 135M, chassis number 800514, bodied by Ghia was sold to a Dutch KLM pilot who exported the car to the Netherlands. In 1964, he sold the Delahaye to a Mr. Wiltschut, the owner of a bakery business in Hilversum. The presence of this car in Holland garnered much attention, even culminating in the publishing of a comprehensive article in the Dutch car magazine *De Auto* on January 15, 1965. The article gave the sales price of the Delahaye at 60,000 Dutch Florins, which, at the time, was almost the price of a new Ferrari 330GT.

The Shah's Mercedes-Benz 300SL Gullwing, chassis number 198.040.55.00111, was given to his personal physician in appreciation for his services. Subsequently, the car was exported to Australia and then it was sold to a buyer in the Middle East.

At some point in the early 1960s, the Shah also decided to let go of the 1952 Pegaso Z-102 Berlinetta Touring Prototipo. The buyer, Eduard Khachikyan, an Iranian Armenian, received the car with some delay as the royal garage replaced the gold-plated switches and handles with brass ones. Khachikyan repainted the car in red and changed the interior to black, and subsequently sold it to an expatriate American geologist named Cheldon Gershmam, working in Iran at the Iranian National Oil Company. Gershman sent the car by air to Hamburg and then to Enasa in Spain by truck for a complete restoration.

LEFT: This photograph of the Delahaye 135M by Ghia was published in the Dutch car magazine *De Auto* on January 15, 1965. The person in the photograph is the owner at the time in the Netherlands, a Mr. Wiltschut, who lived in Hilversum. *(Dr. Vincent van der Vinne)*

ABOVE: The Shah's 1952 Pegaso Z-102 Berlinetta Touring Prototipo after its return to Europe. *(Pieldetoro.net)*

RIGHT: The future Queen of Iran disembarking from an Austin Princess, chassis number unknown. *(Saad Abad Palace)*

Chapter 15: House cleaning in the Royal Garage

CHAPTER 16

Farah Diba,
the new Queen of Iran

Chapter 16: Farah Diba, the new Queen of Iran

Farah Diba was born on October 14, 1938 in Tehran, to an upper-class family. She was the only child of Army Captain Sohrab Diba and his wife, Farideh Ghotbi. Her father's unexpected death in 1948 deeply affected her family and they were faced with financial difficulties, forcing her widowed mother to move her family from a spacious villa in northern Tehran into a shared apartment with one of her brothers.

The young Farah Diba began her education at Tehran's Italian School, subsequently transferring to the French language Jeanne d'Arc School where she remained until the age of 16, and then to the bi-lingual (French and Farsi) Lycée Razi, from where she completed her high school. She then pursued her interest in architecture at the École Spéciale d'Architecture in Paris.

Many Iranian students who were studying abroad at this time were dependent on scholarships from the government. Therefore, when the Shah, as head of state, made official visits to foreign countries, he frequently met with groups of Iranian students studying abroad. It was during such a meeting in 1959 at the Iranian Embassy in Paris that Farah Diba met face-to-face with Mohammad Reza Pahlavi, which was the first spark in their relationship. After returning to Tehran in the summer of 1959, the Shah and Farah Diba began a carefully choreographed courtship, orchestrated in part by the Shah's daughter from his first marriage to Queen Fawzia, Princess Shahnaz.

The couple announced their engagement on November 23, 1959. As a diehard car enthusiast, if there were ever a sign as to just how smitten the Shah was with his young new fiancé, it could be symbolized by the fact that when their engagement was official, he proceeded to bequeath her with his favorite car. This was the blue Mercedes-Benz 300SL Roadster, chassis number 198.042.75.00082. During this period, Farah Diba was staying at her uncle's villa in Tehran's tony Darroos street. When journalists from *Paris Match* and *LIFE* magazine traveled to Tehran to photograph and interview the future Queen of Iran, they could see the

Farah Diba. *(Alamy photo)*

transformation of the young architecture student into a future Queen, as evidenced by her latest *haute couture*, as well as her drives in the Mercedes, followed by three security vehicles, serving as escort.

The future Queen of Iran, along with three members of her family, flew to Paris to order a wedding dress from Yves Saint Laurent. Upon landing at Orly Airport, she was greeted by a swarm of reporters, forcing the police to form a protective ring around her. Eventually, the police and her bodyguards were able to reach the waiting car of the Iranian Embassy in France, a Jaguar Mark I, chassis number unknown, with the diplomatic registration plate of CD75 IT 8832.

Even when Farah Diba and her entourage were finally able to get into the Jaguar and shut the doors, the press continued to surround the car, and, with great difficulty the Embassy driver was able to finally escape the crowd. Even then, the Jaguar continued to be chased by the reporters all the way to Paris' famous Hotel de Crillon, were Farah was to stay during her visit. The next morning, the headlines of almost all the newspapers in France and many across the globe published the news of the arrival of the future Queen of Iran to Paris on

A photograph on the front page of the Tehran daily newspaper, *Kayhan*, showing the French Iranian Embassy's Jaguar Mark I driving down the Champs-Elysee whisking the future Queen Farah away as the car is chased by the paparazzi. *(Kayhan newspaper)*

Chapter 16: Farah Diba, the new Queen of Iran

their front page, with the Jaguar of the Iranian Embassy featuring prominently.

On November 28, 1959, back in Iran, the Shah and Farah Diba paid homage to the Tomb of Reza Shah, with the Shah selecting his Ferrari 410 Superamerica for

LEFT: The Jaguar Mark I of the Embassy surrounded by the paparazzi at Orly Airport. *(Youtube.com)*

BELOW: On December 1, 1959, the Tehran daily newspaper *Kayhan* published an article about the future Queen of Iran. The front page prominently displays Farah Diba and her 300SL Roadster, chassis number 198.042.75.00082 given to her by her fiancé the Shah, parked in front of her uncle's villa in the "Darroos" neighborhood of Tehran. *(Kayhan newspaper)*

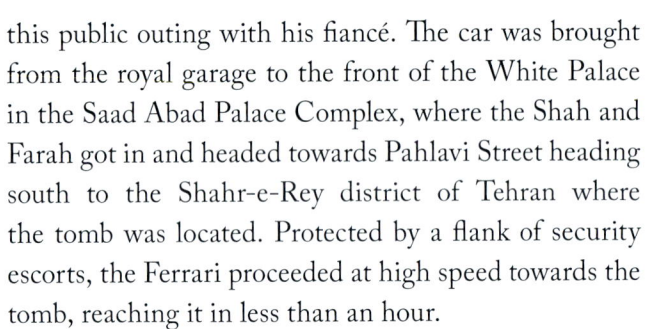

Fit for a King ~ The Royal Garage of the Shah of Iran

this public outing with his fiancé. The car was brought from the royal garage to the front of the White Palace in the Saad Abad Palace Complex, where the Shah and Farah got in and headed towards Pahlavi Street heading south to the Shahr-e-Rey district of Tehran where the tomb was located. Protected by a flank of security escorts, the Ferrari proceeded at high speed towards the tomb, reaching it in less than an hour.

Upon arrival, the Ferrari was parked at the entrance. The Shah and Farah entered the building and placed a wreath on the grave of Reza Shah. The purpose of the visit was, in effect, a tribute from the future new Queen of Iran to the founder of the Pahlavi dynasty. From there, the couple proceeded to visit the grave of Ali Reza Pahlavi, the Shah's younger brother who had died several years earlier in a plane crash. Photographers were allowed from a distance during this personal visit.

The Shah and Farah's wedding was scheduled to be held on December 20, 1959. As per tradition, the bride was to travel from her house to the ceremony accompanied by a motorcade of family and friends (as well as security personnel). The route from the bride's residence (her uncle's house, located at 11, Ariana Street, Marvdasht Street), to the Marble Palace, where the ceremony was to be held, covered a considerable distance and required extensive preparations, which began a week before the wedding. Even as early as 6am the morning of the wedding, the workers of Tehran's municipality were still frantically sweeping and decorating the streets and hanging Iranian flags on both sides of the route to the wedding ceremony.

From early morning, the bride's house was filled with family, friends and courtiers of the court. Across Iran, while Iranians waited for news of the ceremony, the soon-to-be-Queen bride was being readied for her royal debut, with her bridal bouquet arriving directly by plane from the Netherlands, and her hairdressers beginning "work" on the bride, near noon. Farah's tiara, which was designed by Harry Winston, arrived shortly after lunch, followed by her wedding gown, which, after her fitment during her visit to Paris, was delivered from Yves Saint Laurent, arriving by plane from France in a large garment bag, then delivered by truck at the villa. The garment bag, holding the dress, was covered in a green velvet, and this was carefully taken to the house. The whole package including the wedding dress, shoes and underpants weighed 84kgs, and was valued at 23 million French Francs. Yves Saint Laurent's tailors spent over one month sewing the dress. When the dress was flown to Tehran, because of its importance, it was not kept in the cargo hold, but in the cockpit under the watchful eyes of the crew.

TOP LEFT: The Shah and Farah Diba on their way to the Tomb of Reza Shah in the Shah's Ferrari 410 Superamerica Series II, chassis number 0717SA, bodied by Pininfarina. (November 28, 1959) *(Getty Images)*

TOP RIGHT: The royal couple returning from the Tomb of Reza Shah back to the Saad Abad Palace in the 410 Superamerica. (November 28, 1959) *(Borzou Sepasi)*

OPPOSITE: The Shah and Farah disembarking from the 410 Superamerica, in front of the Tomb of Reza Shah. (November 28, 1959)

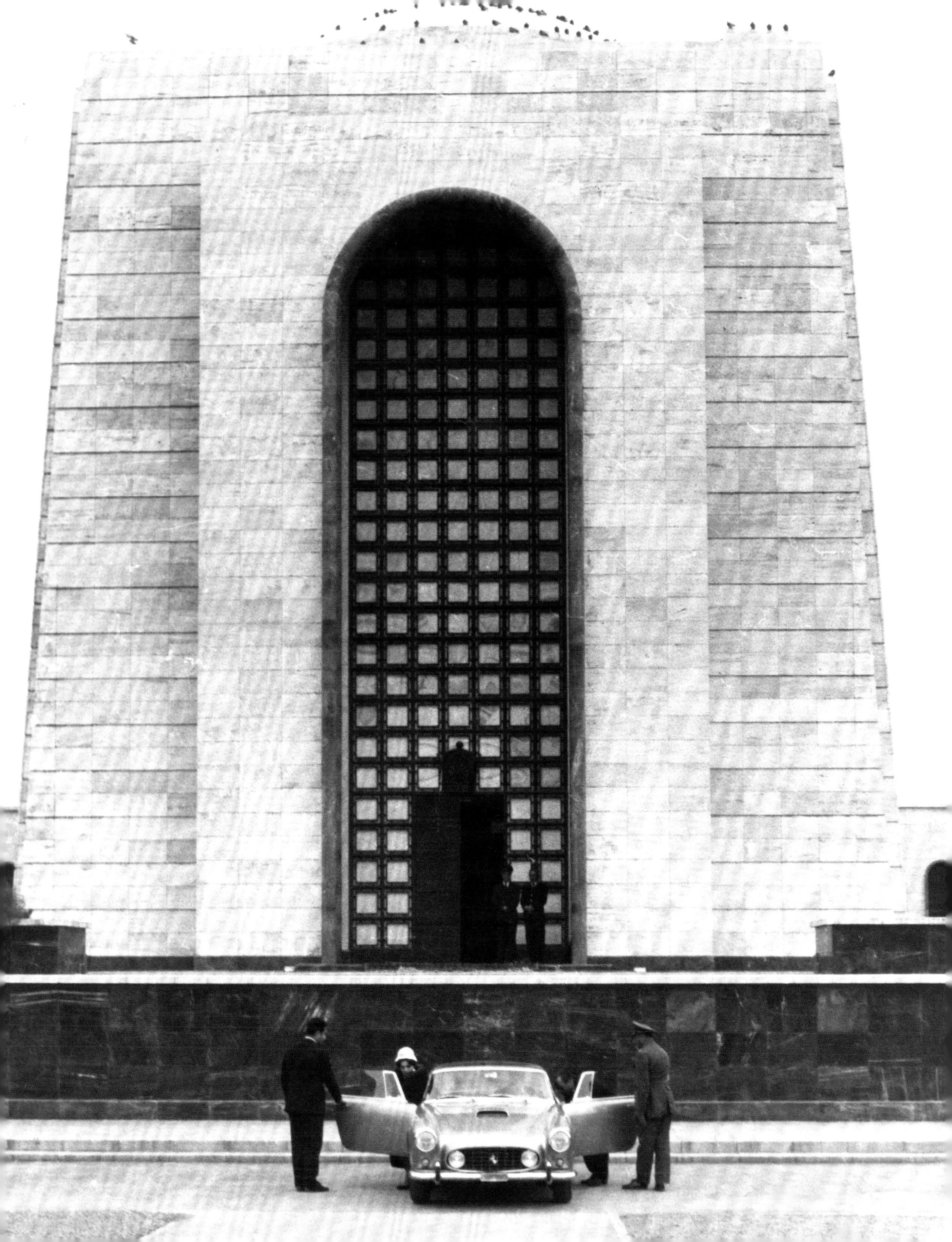

Fit for a King ~ The Royal Garage of the Shah of Iran

At 2:20pm, workers began to lay down beautiful Persian ornamental carpets leading from the hallway up to the limousine that was due to pick up Farah. One of the foreign journalists asked the gardener of the villa as to why the car would park on the carpets, to which he was told, "to avoid any risk of soiling the wedding dress when Farah would board her car."[1] Shortly thereafter, a car arrived at the front door of the villa and unloaded a large cage with a number of nightingales inside the yard. This was followed by the sound of the sirens announcing the imminent arrival of Farah's motorcade.

A few moments later, the motorcade arrived at the villa. The motorcade was led by a black Austin Princess, which was the vehicle designated to transport the soon-to-be-Queen to the ceremony. The Austin was parked at the main entrance of the villa. The Shah's daughter, Shahnaz Pahlavi, got out and entered the villa, followed by the Iranian Prime Minister and his wife. Finally, after a few minutes, at exactly 3:12pm, the future Queen of Iran appeared at the top of the stairs, startled by the flashbulbs of the multitude of photographers shooting the wedding. Making things worse, the nightingales which had been brought to the villa earlier, were released almost simultaneously, and with the flash of the cameras, instead of flying in formation, scattered in confusion, with one of them even taking refuge under the wedding dress of Farah.

Despite such chaos, Farah quickly gathered herself up, and, as per tradition, passed under a copy of the Holy Quran held above her head and boarded the Austin Princess heading towards the ceremony at the Marble Palace.

Unlike the frenzy at her uncle's villa, there was relative calm at the Marble Palace as everything had been readied in advance in anticipation of the soon-to-be Queen's arrival.

As per Iranian tradition, an elaborate floor spread (known as the *sofre aghd* or the "wedding table") was laid out with several kinds of foods and decorations in the famous hall of mirrors in the Marble Palace. A multitude of reporters from around the world had gathered and were stationed on the second floor. Guests from the local elite and international nobility gradually entered the Palace. At precisely 16:50, the groom, wearing a black military uniform, entered the Palace in the Rolls-Royce Phantom IV, chassis number 4CS6, and some minutes later, the soon-to-be Queen's Austin Princess arrived through the main door of the Palace. After getting out of the Austin, Farah entered the Palace and gradually walked up the stairs. Surrounding her were nine bridesmaids, with one in the front holding a bouquet of flowers and the rest following behind her. In a separate hall, with the presence of all the members of the royal family, the cabinet, parliamentarians and members of the senate, the chief justice and the attorney general, as well as members of the court, Farah's immediate family and other dignitaries and functionaries.

The royal couple proceeded to exchange vows. The newlyweds then proceeded to drive to the Golestan Palace in the Rolls-Royce Phantom IV.

At the Golestan Palace, thousands of guests were waiting to greet the Shah and Farah. A splendid ceremony was held at the Palace in honor of the bride and groom, but what caught the most attention of the pundits of the period were the wedding gifts that were proffered to the couple. A broad array of gifts, from countries across the world, stood out due to their variety and extravagance. The Italian government sent a make-up box covered in snakeskin and the French government sent a Baccarat Crystal Service. Pakistani President Ayub Khan gave a large silver tray. Queen Elizabeth of England sent a golden tea pot, the German government sent a very exquisite tea and dinner service, and the Indian government provided the replica of a ship carved entirely out of ivory. The Soviet Union gave an antique chest pertaining to the Tsarist era. Complementing these items, were gifts from corporations, banks ministries and other organizations. Later that evening, with the end of the ceremonies, the Shah and Farah boarded the Rolls-Royce Phantom IV Limousine, retiring to the Saad Abad Palace.

---

[1] Keyhan *newspaper*, December 21, 1959.

The Shah and Farah Pahlavi at their wedding ceremony. (December 20, 1959) *(Alamy photo)*

Fit for a King ~ The Royal Garage of the Shah of Iran

Following the wedding, on December 29, 1959, the Shah and the new Queen, Farah Pahlavi, traveled to the Caspian Sea for their honeymoon. On the day of the trip, at 9am sharp, the royal couple left the Saad Abad Palace in their brand-new 1959 Lincoln Continental Mark IV and headed for the Tehran Train Station in southern Tehran. The route to the rail station had already been announced publicly in advance and as a result, crowds lined the route to the station hoping to catch a glimpse of the royal newlyweds, in particular, their new Queen.

An hour later, the couple arrived at the rail station, where they were welcomed by other members of the royal family. In particular, the Shah's daughter from his marriage to Queen Fawzia, Princess Shahnaz and her husband, the Iranian diplomat, Ardeshir Zahedi who

Chapter 16: Farah Diba, the new Queen of Iran

had played a key role as matchmakers between the Shah and Farah, Queen Farah's mother, the Shah's sister Princess Shams and the Shah's twin sister, Princess Ashraf Pahlavi, all had gathered at the station, as they were to join the newlyweds on their honeymoon.

Together they all boarded the royal train, which had been specially ordered by the Shah and had been delivered in

OPPOSITE: **The Shah and Farah Pahlavi at the wedding ceremony with Farah being followed by her bridesmaids.** (December 20, 1959)

ABOVE: **The royal couple inside the Wegmann & Co. Kassel royal carriage, at the beginning of their honeymoon.** *(iichs.ir)*

time for the honeymoon trip to the Caspian and embarked on the six-hour trip to the lush forests and beaches of the Caspian Sea. The Lincoln, which was the Shah's choice of transportation for his honeymoon was also loaded into the train and fastened in one of the carriages.

The train had been custom ordered by the Shah from the German company Wegmann & Co. Kassel, and included four carriages as well as the locomotive. The last carriage of the train had sleeping quarters and a very luxurious living room. The living room, which was placed exactly at the most far end of the train included a lounge with windows that provided a 180-degree

THIS PAGE: The royal train built by Wegmann & Co. Kassel (production number of 5179), prior to delivery to Iran. *(Borzou Sepasi)*

Chapter 16: Farah Diba, the new Queen of Iran

view of the surrounding landscapes. The carriage was decorated with the most expensive of materials, amongst other things, light fixtures embedded with gems. The Shah was known to have particularly enjoyed relaxing in this carriage and listening to his favorite records on his gramophone, watching the beautiful scenery of the route to the Caspian. This carriage also had two large and luxurious bedrooms. As with Reza Shah's Linke-Hofmann-Werke carriages, this carriage, which was for the exclusive use of the Shah, followed the same motif, with two prominent Pahlavi crowns on each side.

The next carriage was a dedicated conference room, and, in the middle, was a large hall used for private gatherings, featuring a rectangular table and 16 chairs. At the head of the table, the chair dedicated to the Shah, was engraved with a large royal Insignia of Iran. There was a simple rest room in front of the hall. The third carriage was dedicated to the kitchen, the wireless communication room and the guards and crew coupes. The fourth carriage was directly connected to the locomotive, and was a carriage for carrying up to three automobiles for the Shah's use, and as well as the generators used to provide electricity for the train.

The royal couple arrived at their honeymoon retreat, on the Caspian, at exactly 4pm, when the train entered the city of Shahi. The royal couple and their accompanying entourage disembarked from the train, and the Lincoln was waiting at exit of the station. With the Shah behind the wheel, his new Queen next to him, he proceeded to drive off towards the royal Palace in the city of Babol, with other members of the royal family members following in a Chrysler New Yorker Convertible.

The Shah and Farah Pahlavi, trying out a Vespa 150, on their honeymoon in Ramsar with the royal Lincoln Continental Mark IV. *(Borzou Sepasi)*

Fit for a King ~ The Royal Garage of the Shah of Iran

THESE TWO PAGES: **The Shah at the wheel of his Lincoln Continental Mark IV in Lahijan city.** *(Borzou Sepasi)*

In Babol, as part of a tradition, the streets were lined with ornamental carpets for the Lincoln to drive over and even some local residents, as per local tradition, sacrificed sheep and cows to protect the royal couple from evil. After several idyllic days of engaging in different activities from water sports to impromptu local visits, the royal couple then continued their journey to the province of Gilan, known for its lush green scenery and which is Iran's largest tea and rice producing province. Notwithstanding a heavy rainstorm, the Shah and Farah visited the local tea organization in the city of Lahijan, and then proceeded to visit the fields of tea of the area.

On the last day of the trip, they entered Ramsar and drove through the city, later paying surprise visits to several rural villages where the residents, after recovering from their initial shock, proceeded to welcome the royal couple into their homes. The next day, the royal couple and their retinue returned to the train station in the city of Shahi, loaded the Lincoln back on the train, and proceeded back to Tehran.

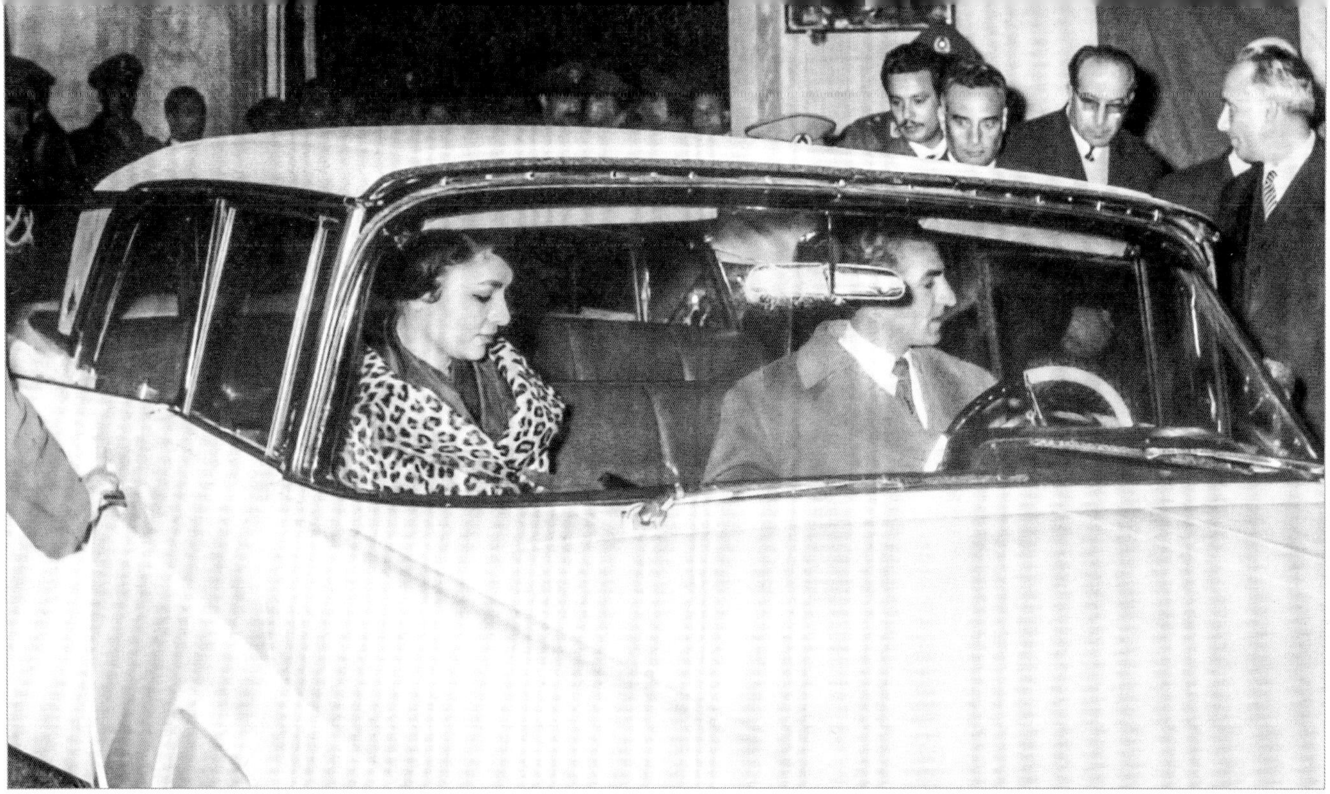

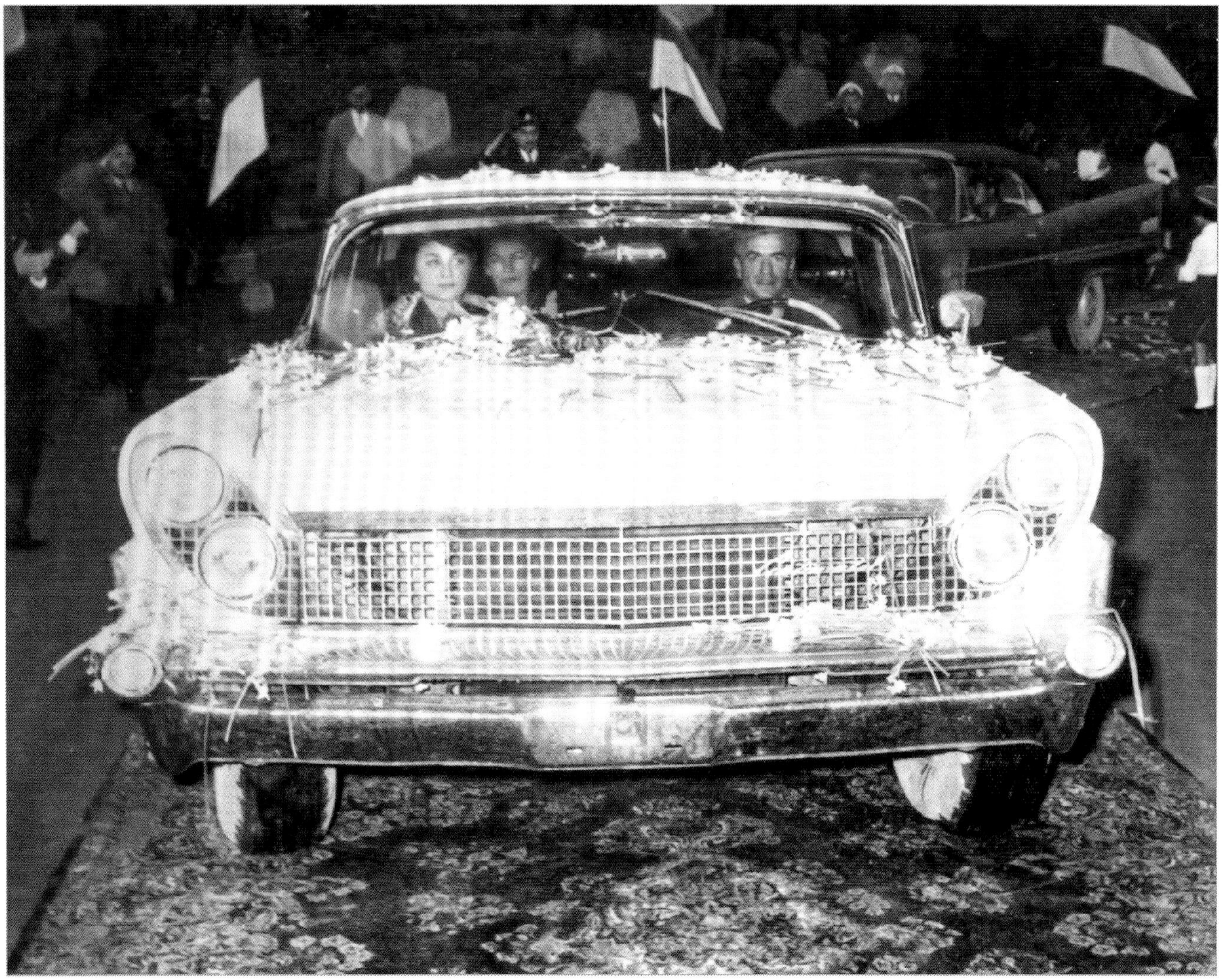

CHAPTER 17

Farah bears
a Crown Prince

Chapter 17: Farah bears a Crown Prince

Queen Farah was able to provide the Shah what his two previous wives were unable to do, namely a male heir to the throne. The doctors had predicted that the Crown Prince would be born on October 25, 1960, which was just a day before the Shah's own birthday. For this reason, a large number of journalists and ordinary people alike gathered around the "Hemayat Madaran" maternity hospital from the night before in anticipation of the news of the birth. They stayed until midnight waiting for the Queen's arrival, but she did not come. The next day, the Shah celebrated his 42nd birthday. The royal garage had prepared a Rolls-Royce Phantom V to be used to whisk the Queen off to the hospital as soon as the Queen went into labor. The Phantom V had been a relatively new entry to the royal garage, coming right off its market launch by Rolls-Royce in 1959. This new Rolls-Royce, chassis number 5LAS39, was built with a hand-crafted body by the coachbuilder Park Ward and was now pressed into duty for this special event.

The road leading up to the maternity hospital was, as per tradition, laid out in ornate Persian carpets in preparation for the arrival of the Queen. This was quite a contrast, as the hospital was located near the slums of southern Tehran. The fact that this hospital was chosen for the birth of the future Crown Prince reflected the new Queen's attempt to connect with Iranians of all walks of life, whether rich or poor.

At the top of the entry gate to the hospital, a large ornate tray was placed with a copy of the Holy Quran wrapped in a green satin cloth, clearly visible. Again, as per tradition, this was done to protect the Queen and her

The Rolls-Royce Phantom V, chassis number 5LAS39, bodied by Park Ward which was used to transport Queen Farah and the Shah to the hospital when she went into labor. (Borzou Sepasi)

Fit for a King ~ The Royal Garage of the Shah of Iran

THIS PAGE: The Shah and Queen Farah arriving at the hospital in the Phantom V, as she begins to go into labor. (October 31, 1960) *(Borzou Sepasi)*

OPPOSITE: The Rolls-Royce Phantom V pictured on the front page of the daily newspaper Kayhan, one of the highest circulation papers at the time. The headline reads "The Crown Prince of Iran was born this Morning." (October 31, 1960) *(Borzou Sepasi)*

در میان هیجان و شادی فوق العاده مردم ایران

ولیعهد ایران صبح امروز پا بعرصه وجود گذاشت

فوق العاده کیهان بلافاصله در تهران و سراسر کشور انتشار یافت

۲ شنبه ۹ آبان ۱۳۳۹ - شماره ۵۲۰۰

کیهان

دولت در سراسر کشور سه روز شادی عمومی اعلام کرد
بمناسبت تولد نوزاد فردا سراسر کشور تعطیل عمومی است و مدارس دو روز تعطیل خواهند بود

اعلامیه دربار شاهنشاهی
«وزیر دربار شاهنشاهی بانهایت مسرت باطلاع عموم میرساند که خداوند متعال در روز دوشنبه نهم آبانماه ۱۳۳۹ ساعت یازده و پنجاه دقیقه بأعلیحضرت همایون شاهنشاه وعلیاحضرت ملکه پسری عنایت نموده است»

نوزاد سلطنتی
امروز نوزاد سلطنتی دقیقه ای بعد از وضع حمل بدنیا آمد اورا میکشیدند و مرتبش کردند این نوزاد همانطوریکه چندین روز بلکه چندین هفته انتظار ورود
بقیه در صفحه ۱۶

مصاحبه اختصاصی خبرنگار کیهان با علیاحضرت ملکه فرح

خبرنگار کیهان اولین خبرنگار جهان بوده که توانست قبل از تشریف فرمائی علیاحضرت ملکه به زایشگاه مصاحبه اختصاصی با معظم لها انجام دهد

علیاحضرت فرمودند:
باحتمال زیاد موقع وضع حمل بیهوش خواهم بود، اگر بیهوش نبودم یک نفس راحت کشیده بدرگاه احدیت شکر خواهم کرد

متن فرمایشات شاهنشاه، خبرنگار مخصوص کیهان و همچنین مصاحبه های اختصاصی با علیاحضرت ملکه پهلوی و والاحضرت شاهدخت شهناز و والاحضرت شمس و اشرف پهلوی و خانم فریده دیبا و آقای قطبی دائی علیاحضرت ملکه فرح پهلوی
در صفحه ۱۶ چاپ شده است

علیاحضرت ملکه مادر بانفاق والاحضرت شاهدخت شمس پهلوی و آقای بهبد بلافاصله در بیمارستان حضور یافتند

شاهنشاه پس از اطلاع از پسر بودن نوزاد بسیار شادمان بودند و در این عکس به ابراز احساسات مردم پاسخ میدهند

شاهنشاه در بیمارستان بازوی علیاحضرت ملکه را گرفته بودند و ایشان را اهدایت میفرمودند

ساعت ۹ صبح امروز علیاحضرت ملکه فرح پهلوی در حالیکه شاهنشاه معظم لها همراهی میفرمودند با اتومبیل مخصوص بدون خبر به زایشگاه بنگاه حمایت مادران تشریف فرما شدند و در ساعت یازده و ۵۰ دقیقه صبح علیاحضرت ملکه وضع حمل فرمودند و خداوند پسری به اعلیحضرت همایونی و علیاحضرت ملکه عطا فرمود بلافاصله پس از تولد نوزاد سلطنتی، اعلامیه دربار شاهنشاهی منتشر گردید
در صفحه ۲

از کاخ شاهنشاه
متقین صورت نامزد های انتخابات را به نخست وزیر میدادند
وقتی به مصدق پیشنهاد نخست وزیری کردم گفت بشرط موافقت انگلیسها با من همکاری خواهم کرد

جمهوریت چی برای کشور
* وقتی که از مصدق پرسیدم چرا مجلس را از اکثریت میاندازد
گفت روسها با نخست وزیر وقت موافق نیستند
بقیه در صفحه ۲

کاباره دانسینک شکوفه نو
مولد مسعود نوزاد سلطنتی را بعموم همیمهنی گرامی از صمیم قلب تبریک میگوید
ش ۹۷۷۹

فوق العاده کیهان
ساعت یازده و پنجاه دقیقه امروز علیاحضرت ملکه فرح در زایشگاه بنگاه حمایت مادران وضع حمل فرمودند و ساعت ۱۲ و نیم درست ۵ دقیقه بعد از میلادمسعود ولیعهد دربار شاهنشاهی فوق العاده روزنامه کیهان با ساعتهائی که (پ. ازلوله نوزاد) شاهنشاه و علیاحضرت ملکه مادر والاحضرت شاهدخت شهناز پهلوی والاحضرت شاهدخت اشرف و والاحضرت شمس و خانم فریده دیبا و آقای قطبی قابل انتظار بود یافت
انتشار فوق العاده کیهان چند لحظه پس از تولد نوزاد سلطنتی با استقبال و توجه مردم مواجه شد بطوریکه در مدتی کوتاه نسخه های آن تمام شد و چاپخانه کیهان مجدد فوق العاده روزنامه کیهان را چاپ میگرداند
در آغاز میکرد
فوق العاده جدید شامل اعلامیه دربار مبارک شاهنشاهی بمناسبت تولد نوزاد سلطنتی و بقیه مطالب آن از شماره اول روزنامه ارجعه میگردد

۵ پسر و دو دختر مقارن وضع حمل مولود سلطنتی در زایشگاه حمایت مادران متولد شدند

مولد مسعود ولیعهد والاحضرت را به شاهنشاه بزرگ ومکرم سوگوار ومالک ایرانی ما تبریک میگویم
خانواده های افسران زندانی

کشاف منصفی ضمن عرض تبریک مولد مسعود مژده میدهد که از امروز تا سه روز
بکلیه مشتریان کشاف منصفی یک مانتوی نوزاد و تخفیف ۲۸ درصد روی کلیه اجناس کافی السابق ادامه دارد
کشاف منصفی - خیابان شاه آباد

اتومبیل رولز رویس مخصوصی که علیاحضرت ملکه فرح باتفاق اعلیحضرت همایونی بوسیله آن بزایشگاه تشریف فرما شدند

کیهان ورزشی روزهای شنبه منتشر میشود

کشورهای جدید آفریقائی و انجمن پیوستگی مردم آفریقا و آسیا

RIALCO

کاناداد رای

Fit for a King ~ The Royal Garage of the Shah of Iran

This was then followed by the Shah addressing the press and expressing his joy at the birth of the Crown Prince. Tehran Radio immediately announced the news, which was met with great elation among the populace. That afternoon, when the Shah intended to return to the Palace from the hospital, a large crowd of hospital staff and other well-wishers surrounded his car, prompting the Shah to get out of the car and greet them.

On that same day, the Shah traveled to the Tomb of Reza Shah in celebration of the birth of the next heir to the Pahlavi dynasty and, from there, returned to the Saad Abad Palace. Upon arrival at the Palace, the Shah began to receive congratulatory messages from leaders and dignitaries around the world, including the Pope, Queen Elizabeth II, President Eisenhower, German Chancellor Adenauer, the King of Belgium, Marshal Ayub Khan of Pakistan and the President of Hungary.

That night the Shah traveled back to the hospital and had dinner with the Queen. Returning back the next morning, the Shah arrived at the hospital with the Mercedes-Benz 300SL Roadster and, on that day, the press was provided their first access to the newborn Crown Prince where he was photographed extensively. For this opportunity, the Crown Prince was placed on a small bed and wrapped in a bedsheet, with only his head visible. The baby's doctors, nurses and French nanny were all on hand.

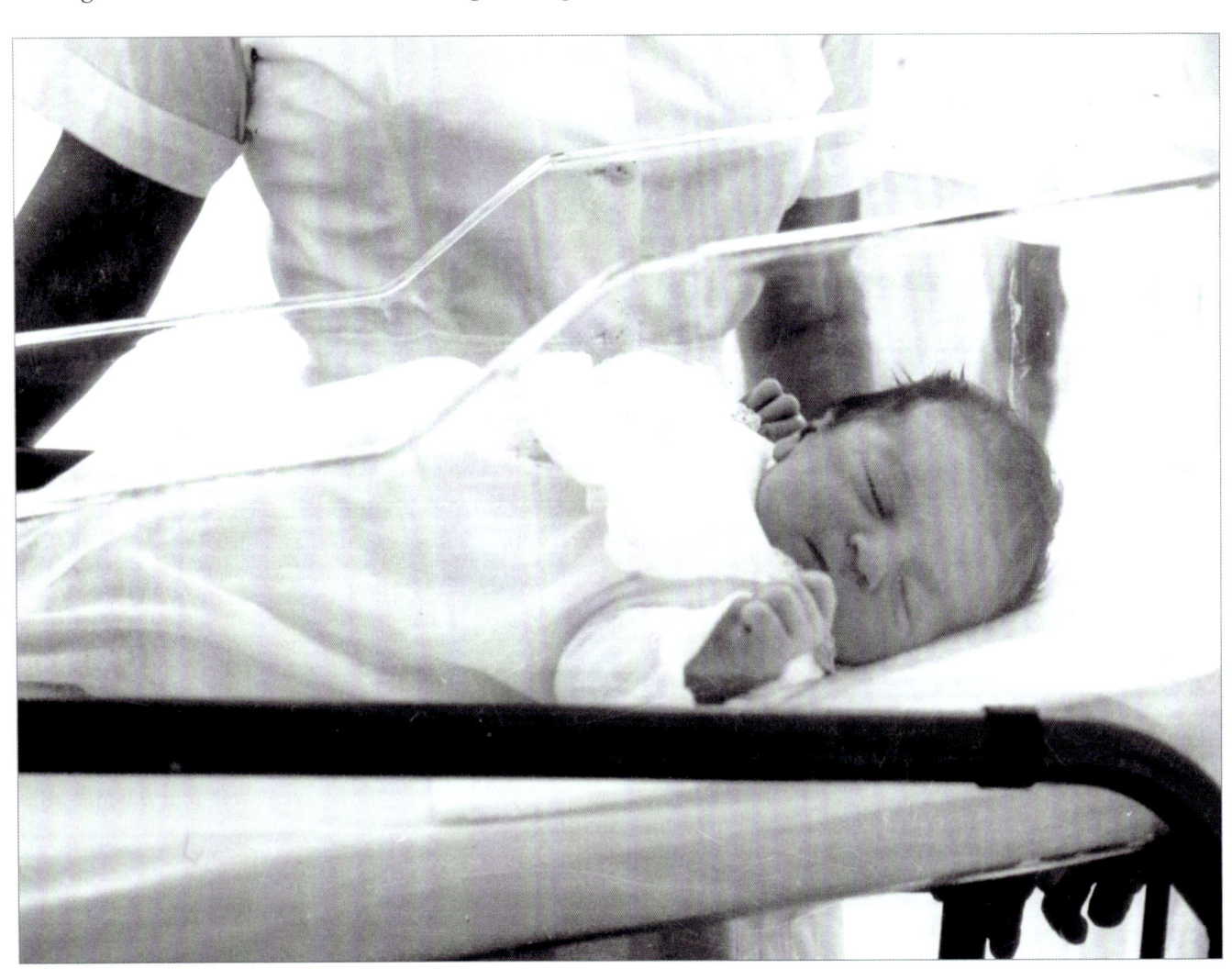

The royal baby "Reza" being introduced to the press. *(iichs.ir)*

The Shah and Farah Pahlavi, with the newborn Crown Prince, leaving the maternity hospital and boarding the Rolls-Royce Phantom IV, chassis number 4CS6. *(Borzou Sepasi)*

Later that afternoon, several members of the royal family arrived at the hospital. Over the next few days, the Shah would take a few hours off from his busy schedule to spend several hours of his day at the hospital with the Queen and the Crown Prince. On November 3, the naming ceremony was carried out and, in honor of his grandfather Reza Shah, the Crown Prince was named Reza, and his birth certificate was issued. That night, Prince Bernhard (spouse of Queen Juliana of the Netherlands) who at the time was on a visit to Iran, went to the hospital and visited the royal couple and their newborn.

On Saturday, November 4, was the day that the newborn Crown Prince was to be brought home, to the Palace. In preparation for this day, and, as the Phantom V had been left at the hospital on standby, the Shah's black Rolls-Royce Phantom IV Limousine, chassis number 4CS6, was readied and parked in front of the Palace in preparation to transport the Shah to the hospital to pick up the Queen and Crown Prince. In anticipation of the precious package that it would be transporting, the Phantom IV was even subjected to a rigorous servicing by factory technicians dispatched from Crewe.

At 10am, Mohammad Reza Shah, wearing a cream-colored military uniform, descended from the Palace stairs and boarded the Phantom IV. Initially, on the route the crowd was sparse, but as the Rolls-Royce made its way towards the hospital and the populace got wind of the Shah's trip, throngs of people made their way towards the hospital, in order to celebrate this day with the royal family.

Arriving at the hospital, the Rolls-Royce made its way through the crowd and stopped near the entrance where the Shah disembarked and entered the hospital through the front entrance. As anticipation mounted for the royal couple and their newborn to leave the hospital, the crowds began to grow larger as many more arrived at the hospital in hope of catching a glimpse of both the present and the future Monarch.

At 2:30pm in the afternoon, the royal couple emerged from the hospital, and made their way to the Phantom IV. The nurses and staff of the hospital had gathered in the courtyard where they were greeted and thanked, by the royal couple, for their service. The royal couple then proceeded to board the Phantom IV and headed back to the Palace in the Phantom V, with a motorcade of security guards in tow.

Throughout the route, crowds gathered alongside, hoping for a glimpse of their future sovereign, and even, as per tradition, placed their personal Persian carpets on the road to be driven over. One of the most outstanding and memorable events to take place was the erection of four temporary gates for the motorcade to pass under, each one of these gates being made up of 1.5 million flowers each, and, after passing the last gate, the Rolls-Royces entered a special path laden with flowers and entered the Palace. It was quite a debut for the Crown Prince on his first "royal outing."

OPPOSITE: **Queen Farah** and the newborn Crown Prince in the Rolls-Royce Phantom IV, chassis number 4CS6, enroute to the Palace. (November 4, 1960) *(Borzou Sepasi)*

THIS PAGE: Heading back to the Palace from the hospital. The Rolls-Royce Phantom IV is in the lead with the royal couple on board followed closely behind by the Rolls-Royce Phantom V, chassis number 5LAS39. Both cars are protected by a motorcade of motorcycles. (November 4, 1960) *(Borzou Sepasi)*

The Rolls-Royce Phantom IV, chassis number 4CS6, passes a gate decorated with over a million and a half flowers, one of four erected along the route from the hospital to the Palace. (November 4, 1960) *(Borzou Sepasi)*

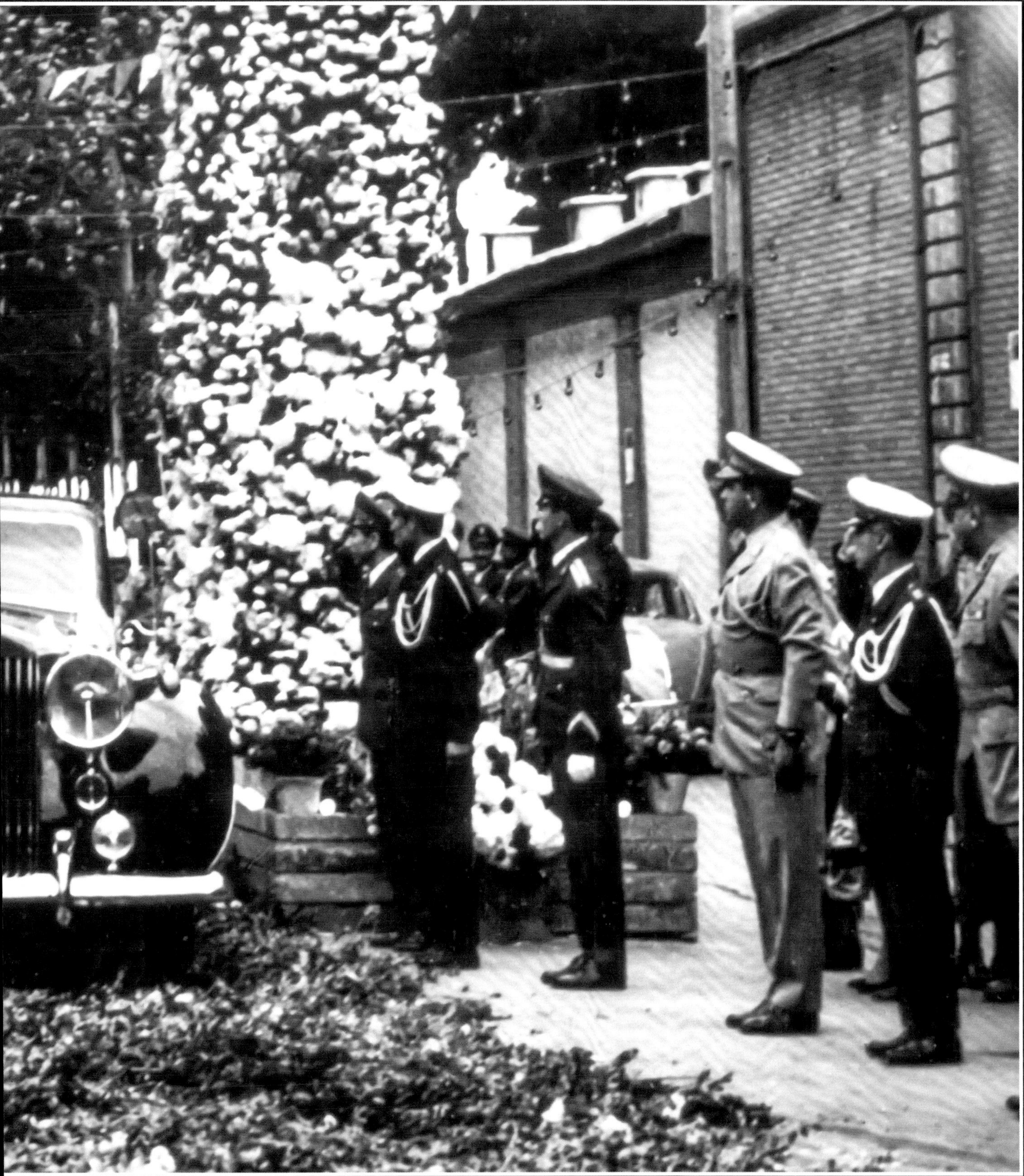

CHAPTER 18

Queen Elizabeth II visits Iran and the Shah visits France

Chapter 18: Queen Elizabeth II visits Iran and the Shah visits France

In reciprocation of the Shah's May 1959 visit to the United Kingdom, from the second to the sixth of March, 1961, Queen Elizabeth II and Prince Philip the Duke of Edinburgh paid an official visit to Iran. The Duke and Queen were met personally at the airport by the Shah and Queen Farah and, after a number of ceremonial formalities at the airport, Queen Elizabeth and the Shah boarded the Shah's Rolls-Royce Phantom IV, chassis number 4CS6, with Queen Farah and Prince Philip following in tow in the Shah's Rolls-Royce Phantom V, chassis number 5LAS39. From the airport the Rolls-Royces whisked the two royal couples towards Tehran's iconic Statue Square (named in honor of the formidable statue of Reza Shah which towered over the square) where the Mayor of Tehran presented Queen Elizabeth a key to the city. A parade route had been arranged lined by cheering crowds which covered the distance from the square to the Golestan Palace, where a new wing had been constructed specially for the stay of Queen Elizabeth. For this portion of the route, Queen Elizabeth and Mohammad Reza Shah Pahlavi switched transportation to a Qajar-era royal carriage built by Carl Marius followed by a second carriage which transported Prince Philip and Queen Farah. The two carriages were escorted by parade horses ridden by specially uniformed honor guards. Later that evening, the Shah feted his fellow royalty in a banquet held in their honor in the famed Mirror Hall of the Palace.

On the second day of the visit, the two royal couples attended a sporting event, held in honor of Queen Elizabeth at the Amjadiyeh Stadium. A little before 3pm, the Shah and Queen Farah arrived at Golestan Palace in the Phantom IV and V and, after picking up

ABOVE & OVERLEAF: The two royal families visit Amjadiyeh Stadium pictured next to the Rolls-Royce Phantom IV, chassis number 4CS6. *(Borzou Sepasi)*

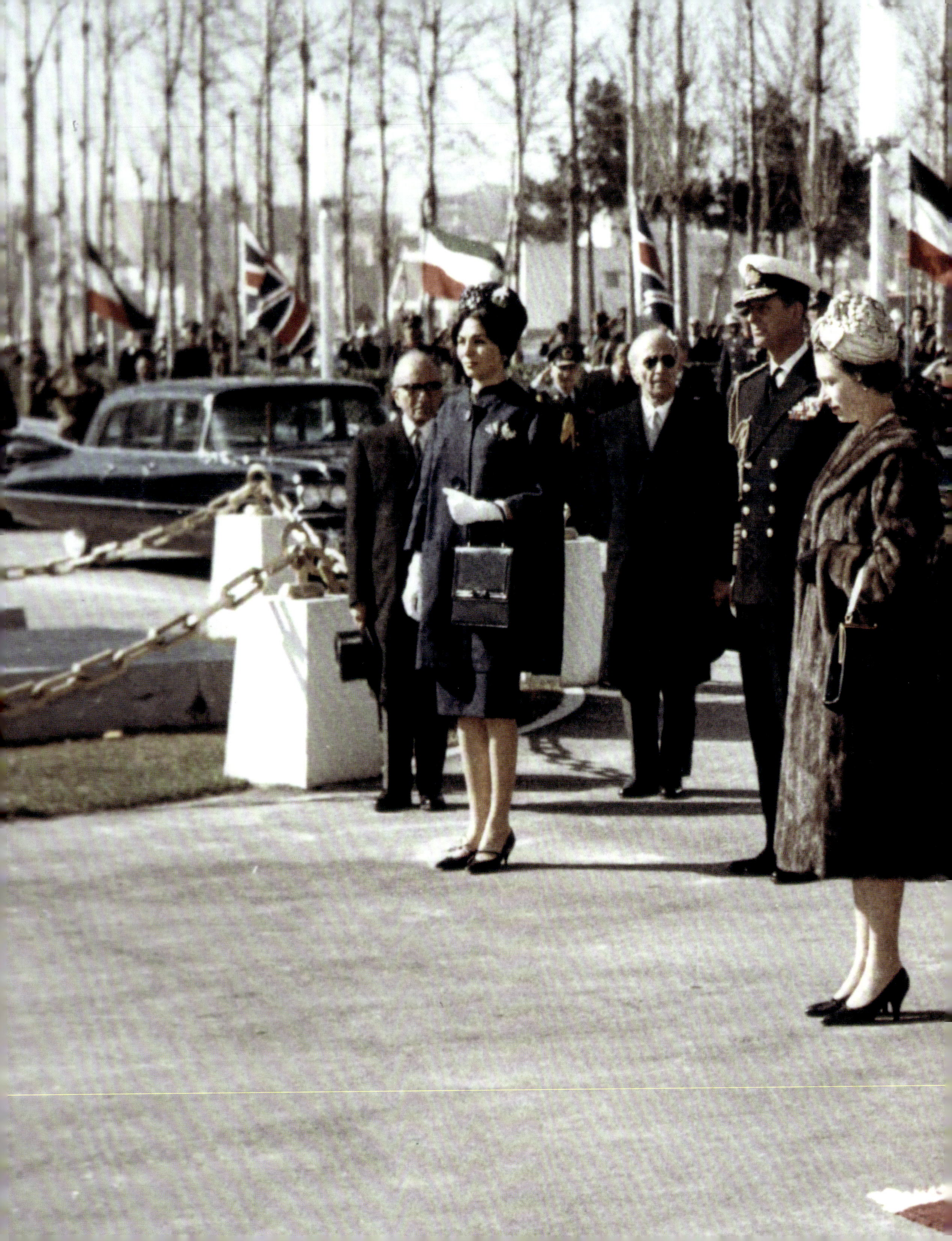

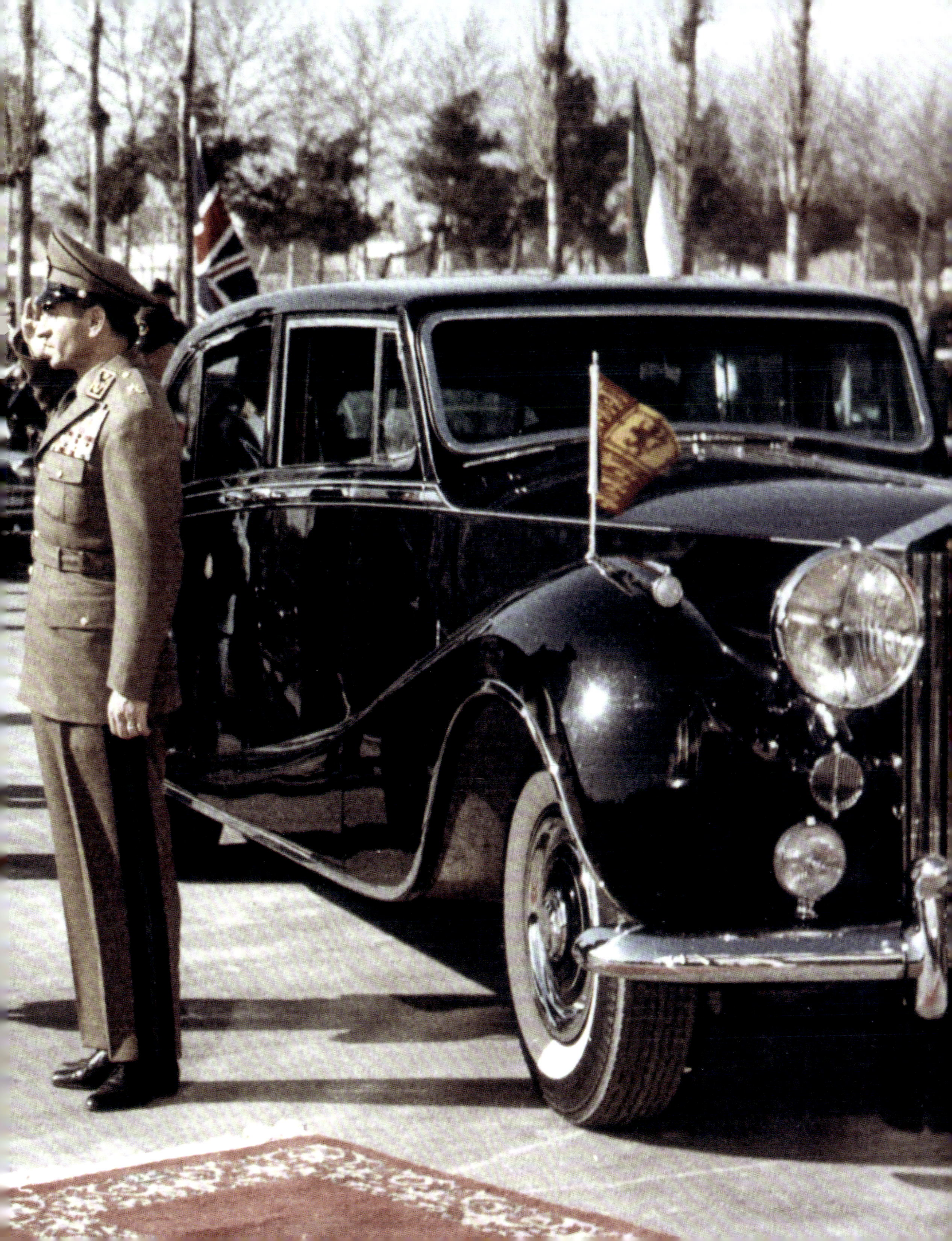

Fit for a King ~ The Royal Garage of the Shah of Iran

their guests, left for the stadium. Upon arrival, a little girl, speaking in English, greeted and welcomed the two royal couples, following which, Queen Elizabeth was then serenaded by a group of young female students followed by other events, finally ending with a performance of the traditional Iranian sport "Pahlevani."

BELOW: **The Rolls-Royce Phantom IV, waiting for Queen Elizabeth and the Shah to board after visiting Amjadiyeh Stadium.** *(Borzou Sepasi)*

LEFT: **Queen Elizabeth and the Shah in the Rolls-Royce Phantom IV.** *(Borzou Sepasi)*

OPPOSITE (BOTH): **Queen Elizabeth in the Iranian Rolls-Royce Phantom IV.** *(Borzou Sepasi)*

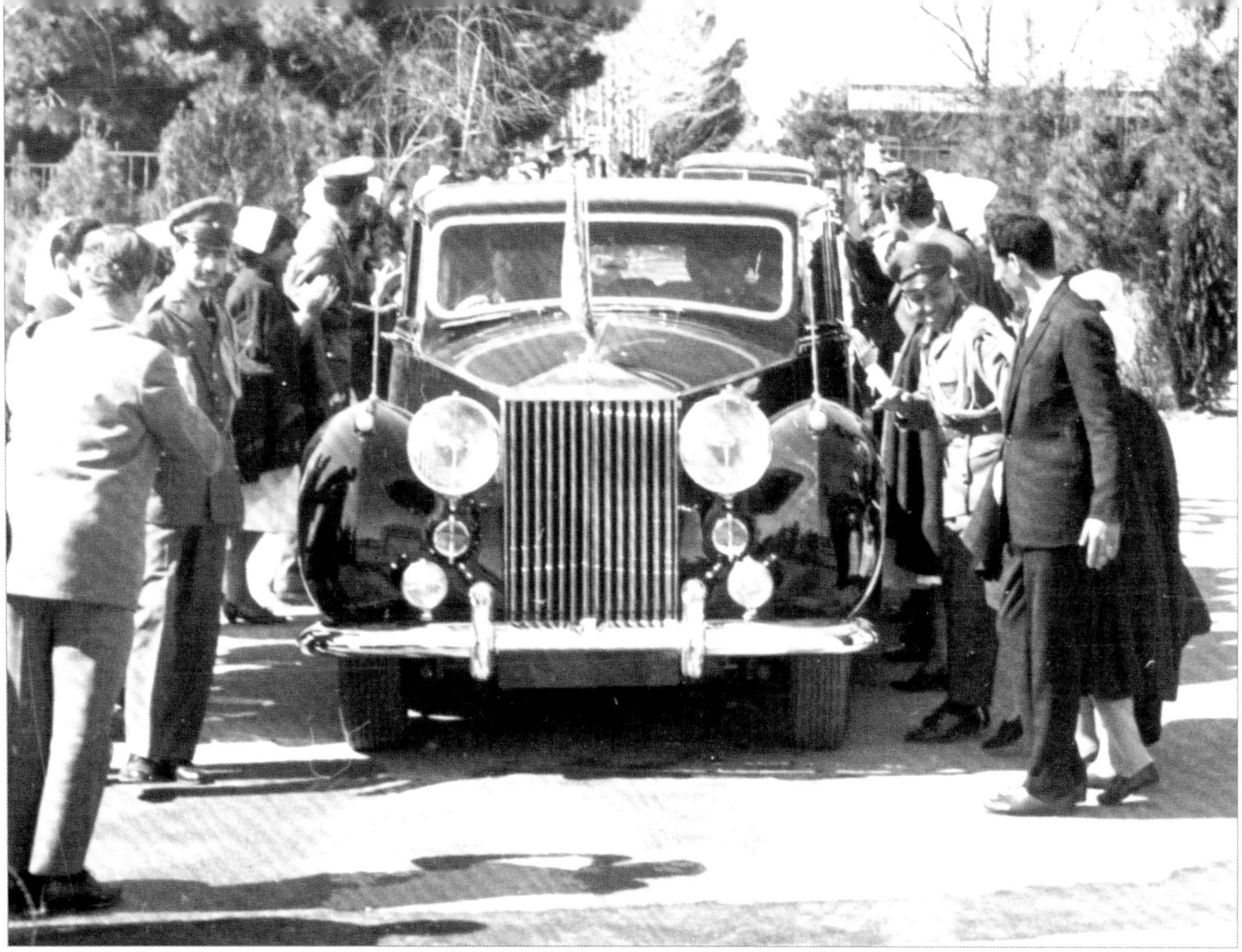

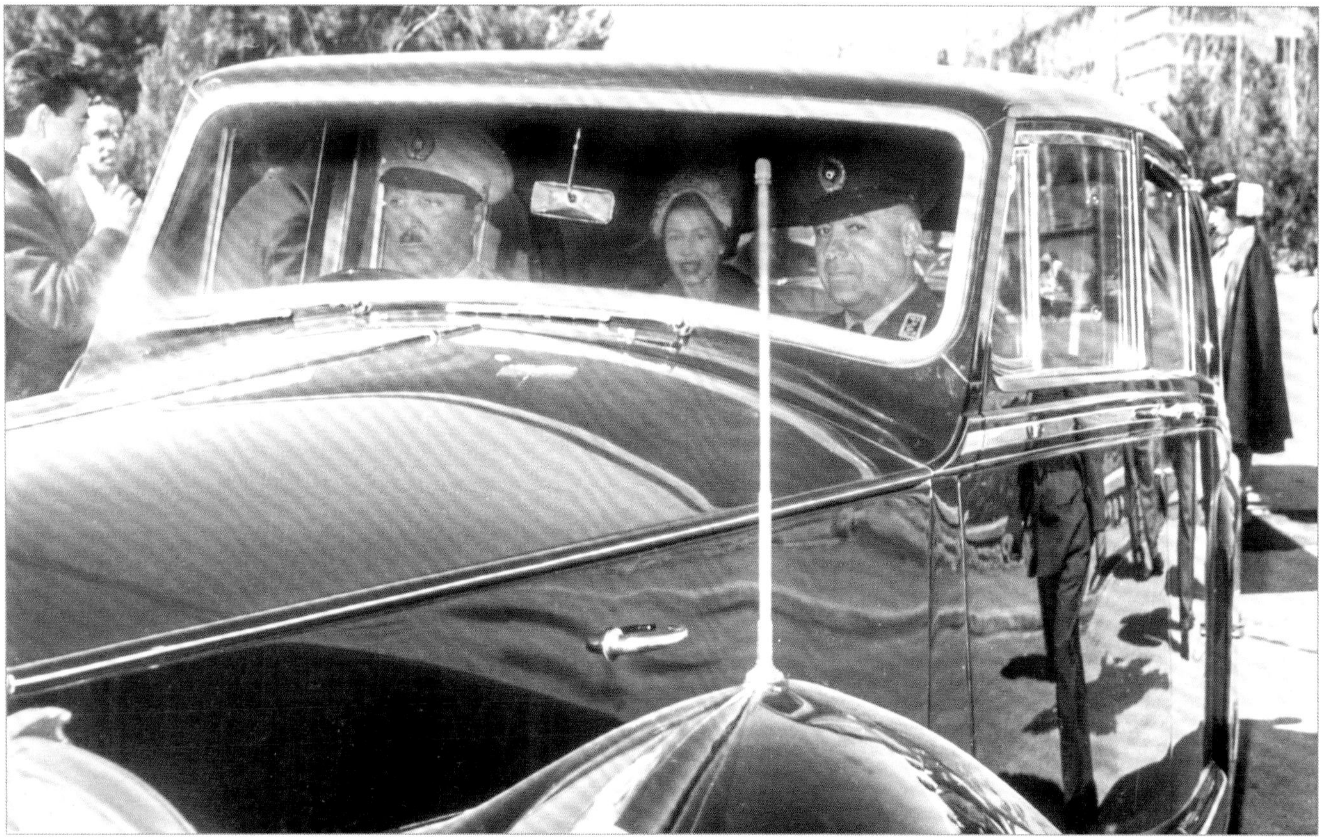

The royal families of Iran and Great Britain in Tehran. *(iichs.ir)*

Chapter 18: Queen Elizabeth II visits Iran and the Shah visits France

From the stadium, the two royal couples ventured on to the Iranian Treasury where the royal jewels were kept in the vaults of the Central Bank of Iran. The collection included several of the world's most famous and historical diamonds, emeralds and rubies, all of which were laid out on display for the Queen of England to appreciate. Yet, none of them could match the amazing pale pink Darya-i-Noor diamond, which, even today, remains one of the largest cut diamonds in the world, a rare stone weighing an estimated 182 carats. This diamond has the same origin and a similar history to that of the famous Koh-I-Noor diamond, which has been a part of the British crown jewels.

The English royal couple were also able to view the Pahlavi crown, the renowned jewel and pearl encrusted coronation crown of the Pahlavi dynasty. After being bedazzled by all the fabulous jewelry, Queen Elizabeth and Prince Philip left the Central Bank together with the Shah and Queen Farah, after signing the Treasury Gold Book.

Later that evening, the Shah and Queen Farah attended a dinner hosted by Queen Elizabeth, at the British Embassy, in Tehran. The flowers for decorating the rooms of the Embassy, as well as the food served that evening, were flown in from London to Tehran.

The next morning, the two royal couples left Tehran for a visit to the historical city of Isfahan. Two Cadillacs were used to transport the royals during their visit. The first Cadillac, used by the Shah and Queen Elizabeth, was a yellow 1955 Series 62 Convertible. The second car, that of Queen Farah and Prince Philip, was a black 1959 Sedan de Ville. All along the road from the airport to Chehel Sotoun, a number of ceremonial gates were erected, all being decorated with the flags and symbols of the two countries. Taking a break from their sightseeing, the royal couples lunched together in the famed Chehel Sotoun, a pavilion built by Shah Abbas II, dating back to the Safavid dynasty (1501-1736), for his receptions and for entertainment. After lunch, the visit continued with visits to a number of historical sites

TOP (BOTH): **The Pahlavi crown (left) and the exquisite Darya-i-Noor diamond (right).**

ABOVE (BOTH): **The Shah and Queen Elizabeth visiting the Safavid Naqsh-e Jahan Square in Isfahan in a Cadillac Series 62 Convertible.** *(Borzou Sepasi)*

including the Safavid Naqsh-e Jahan Square and the beautiful Shah Mosque.

From Isfahan, the two couples, traveled on to Shiraz, and visited the historical monuments of that city, in particular Persepolis.

TOP & ABOVE: The Shah and Queen Elizabeth visit the Shah Mosque in Isfahan. *(Borzou Sepasi)*

RIGHT: The Shah and Queen Elizabeth visit the Naqsh-e Jahan Square in Isfahan. *(Borzou Sepasi)*

Chapter 18: Queen Elizabeth II visits Iran and the Shah visits France

To commemorate her trip, Queen Elizabeth was presented with a gift from the Shah of Iran. This was a special table, decorated with "Khatam", which is an ancient Persian technique of inlaying the surface of wooden articles with delicate pieces of wood, bone and metal, all precisely cut into intricate geometric patterns. The Queen's table though was unique in the fact that it featured non-geometric patterns. In total, eighteen million pieces of Khatam were used in the making of this table. The crafting of the table was completed just a few days before the guests arrived in Iran.

The Shah pays a visit to France

On October 10, 1961, the Shah and Queen Farah made a state visit to France, arriving at Orly Airport, on the outskirts of Paris where they were personally welcomed by General Charles de Gaulle, the French President. In honor of their visit, a number of ceremonies and official visits took place, including a magnificent banquet at the Élysée Palace hosted by President de Gaulle; the laying of a wreath at the tomb of France's Unknown Soldier, as well as a special visit by Queen Farah to an orphanage. The royal couple also attended a number of functions held in their honor, one of which was hosted by the Paris municipality. Additionally, several functions were specially arranged for Queen Farah, who, until two years earlier, was an unknown architecture student in Paris before being plucked from obscurity to become the Queen of Iran. These included an art exhibition where the Queen was personally escorted by André Malraux, the French Minister of Culture, and a fashion show held by the leading couture houses of Paris.

The Shah and Queen Farah also visited the Simca automobile factory, with some pundits surmising that the French government was hoping they could make headway into Iran's nascent automobile industry. Though their state visit officially ended on October 13, the couple stayed on in Paris for a few more days, for a private vacation. During their official visit, the French Presidential car, a Simca Presidence V8 Cabriolet, was put at their disposal. However, pictures taken during

ABOVE & FOLLOWING PAGE: **Arriving in a Simca Presidence V8 Cabriolet Chapron with registration plate 5 PR 75 at the Tomb of the Unknown Soldier at the Arc de Triomphe. (October 10, 1961)** *(Niavaran Palace)*

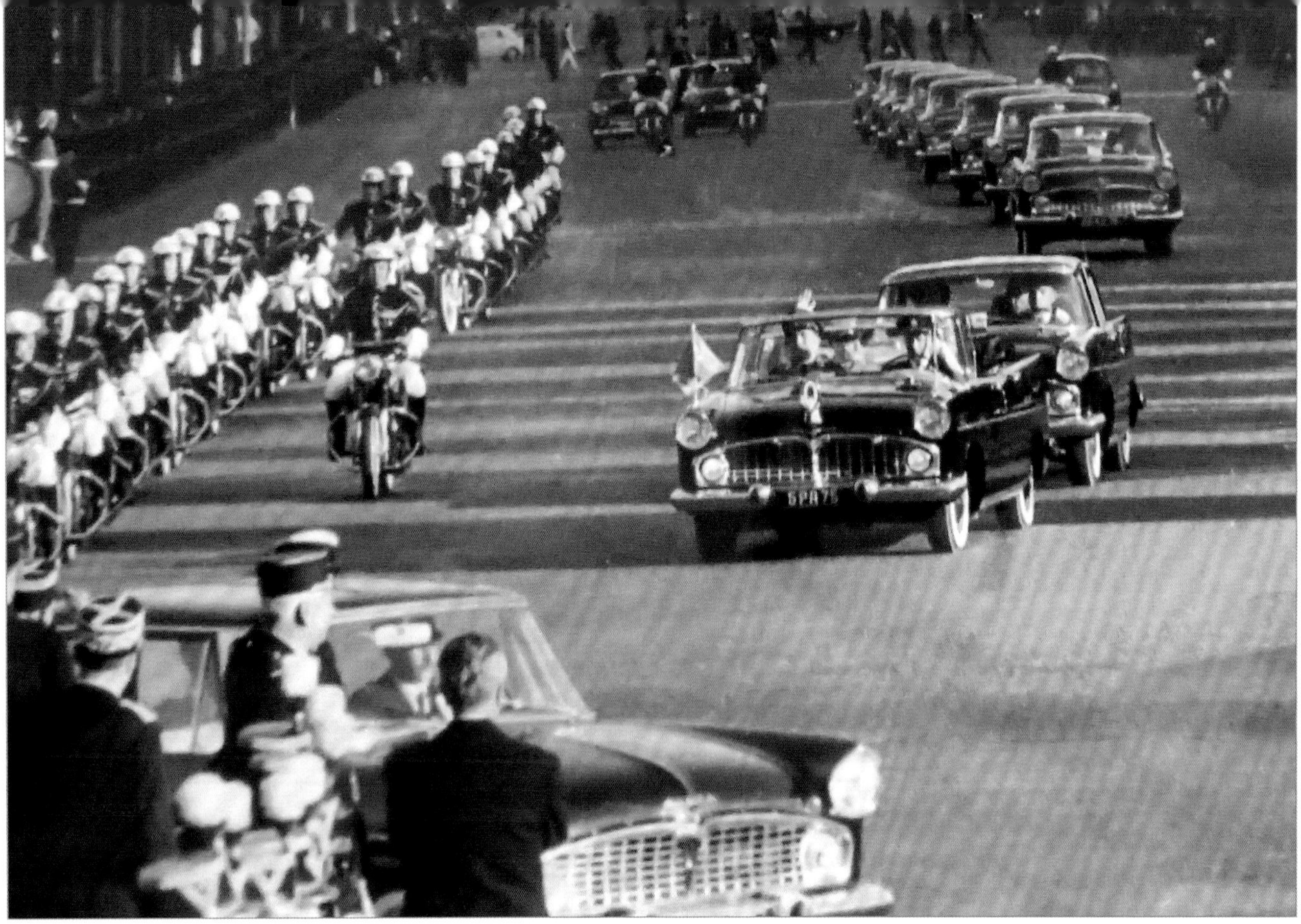

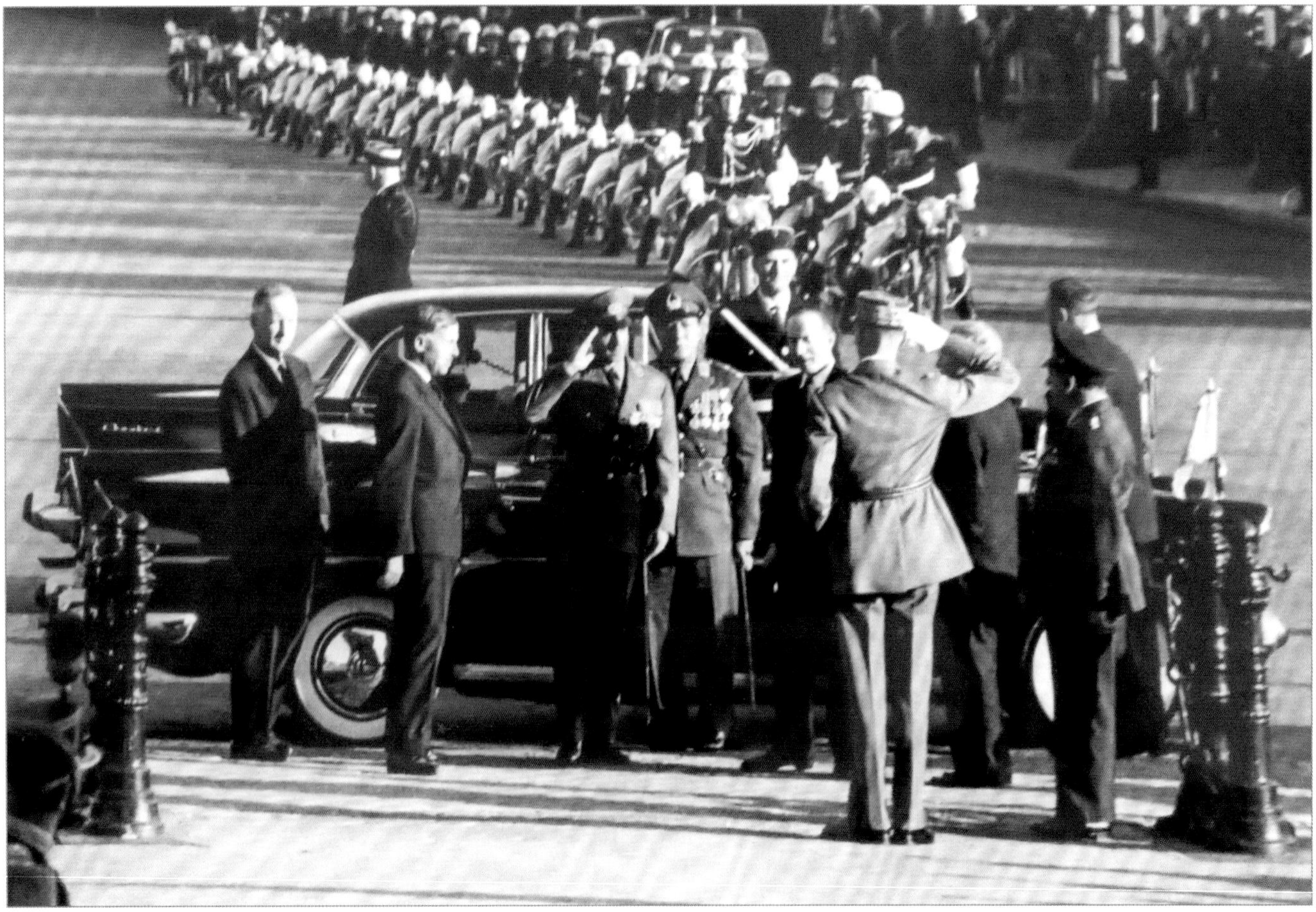

Chapter 18: Queen Elizabeth II visits Iran and the Shah visits France

the private period of their visit show the Shah and Farah driving around Paris in a Facel Vega Facel II. Over the years, it was believed that, as he was wont to do, the Shah would buy the latest exotica of the country he was visiting and that this Facel Vega was no exception. However, as further discussed below, no history of ownership by the Shah of a Facel has ever been discovered, and while some speculate that the Facel II had been put at the disposal of the Shah as a courtesy of the French government, in all likelihood though, it is possible that Facel founder Jean Daninos saw an opportunity in promoting his new car with the Shah of Iran, and so, on his own accord, offered the use of the Facel to the Shah.

The Facel II which the Shah steered through the streets of Paris with the Queen in tow, had not been launched yet into series production and had not even been officially registered, as it had not received its homologation

RIGHT: **Arriving at the Simca factory. (October 12, 1961)** *(Niavaran Palace)*

BELOW (BOTH): **Queen Farah visits the Simca 1000 production line. (October 12, 1961)** *(Niavaran Palace)*

LEFT & BELOW: Facel Vega Facel II, chassis number HK2-A100, lent to the royal couple in the second leg of their visit to France. *(Michel Revoy, "Amicale Facel Vega archives")*

ABOVE & OPPOSITE: During the visit to France, the Shah also used a 1959 Cadillac Series 62 Convertible. *(Internet)*

Chapter 18: Queen Elizabeth II visits Iran and the Shah visits France

certification. The car's temporary registration number then was 3242 W 75 and the Facel II only received its official certification from the French Ministry of Transport and Industry (Service des mines) on December 27, 1961, a little over two months after the Shah's departure from Paris. This dark blue car, which used by the Shah, was, in all likelihood, chassis number HK2-A100, the first car from the production series (and not the prototype car, which was chassis number A099), that was unveiled at the Paris Salon of October 1961. This car was never sold to the Shah of Iran, contrary to what may have been reported or assumed by some enthusiasts. It was a factory car, and was kept by Facel S.A. for another two years, before being sold in December 1963, to a French customer, after it had been registered in June 1963 with the registration number 8759 NW 75.[1]

On October 14, the royal couple celebrated the 24th birthday of Farah Pahlavi in a Paris suburb. Notwithstanding the fact that they were officially on vacation the royal couple participated in the groundbreaking ceremony of the Maison d'Iran (the Iran House), at the university campus of Cité Université, in Paris. The Maison d'Iran was a project for the construction of a center for students who came from Iran to Paris to study. The project was undertaken by Frenchmen Claude Parent and André Bloc, in collaboration with two Iranian architects, Mohsen Foroughi and Heydar Ghiai.

Right at the end of their French sojourn, the Shah met with a number of the Iranian students in Paris, as well as the Iranian Ambassadors stationed in some of the European countries, at the Royal Iranian Embassy in Paris. From there, the Shah and Farah went back to Tehran.

---

[1] *Michel Revoy, "Amicale Facel Vega archives"*

CHAPTER 19

The Start of the 1960s

Chapter 19: The Start of the 1960s

A decade of stability, economic growth, social reform and the birth of the Iranian automotive industry

With the 1953 coup well behind him, and having fully consolidated his power, Mohammad Reza Pahlavi focused his attention on the economic development of Iran. Following in the footsteps of his father, Reza Shah, who towards the promotion and growth of Iranian industry would even organize "Made in Iran" exhibitions, the Shah started to push for the wide scale industrialization of Iran. Capitalizing upon a new generation of technocrats, many of whom had been dispatched to the best western universities during the reign of Reza Shah, Iran experienced record economic growth. At the same time, the population of Iran expanded from approximately 12 million in 1900 to 15 million in 1938 and 19.3 million in 1950. By 1968, the Iranian population would stand at 27.3 million.

During this era, major investments were made not only in industry by the government, but also by the private sector and between the years 1954 to 1969 the economy grew on average by 7 to 8 percent per annum.

The Shah beside his personal Iranian-assembled Jeep Station Wagon, a gift from the Jeep Iran Company. Standing on his left is Mr. Jafar Akhavan, the founder of the Jeep Iran Company.

Given the economy of scale provided by Iran's expanding population combined with the increased prosperity of the era, investment by the private sector grew, even gravitating towards heavy industry, previously the exclusive domain of the government. As a new consumer class with spending power began to emerge, the private sector began to steer investment towards the automobile industry. On October 8, 1959, the first Iranian automobile factory was inaugurated.[1] The company, named the "Jeep Iran Co.", was inaugurated following sixteen months of hard work. The complex, which had a production license from Willys Motors Company was located on the Tehran-Karaj Road, an area which had in recent years been zoned for industrial purposes, in an area covering 16,550 square meters, and employing 180 personnel. The range of products included the Willys Jeep, Willys Jeep Truck, the Willys Jeep Station Wagon, as well as an ambulance derivative.

The Shah arrived at the factory for the opening ceremony at 2pm on October 8. The minister for Industry and Mines, Jafar Sharif Emami, welcomed him and then Jafar Akhavan, the founder and CEO of Jeep Iran Co. introduced the board members followed by a presentation about the company. The Shah was then taken for a visit of the factory and the facilities. At the end of the visit, Jeep Iran Co. bestowed an Iranian-assembled Jeep Station Wagon to the Shah. It was a fully optioned, top-of-the line version, literally custom built for a King.

Following on the heels of the launch of Jeep Iran Co., on May 14, 1961, and to much fanfare, the Shah inaugurated the Saica Co. factory, launched by Fiat's Iranian representative, Hassan Kashanchi and his brother Ali. The factory was located in the "Tehran Now" ('New Tehran') area of the city. Prior to start of the assembly operations in Iran, Kashanchi had been importing cars directly from Fiat. One of the most popular models in the Iranian market was the Fiat 1100, a car which had emerged as the backbone of the Iranian taxi fleet. Given the economy of scale afforded by the sales volume of the 1100 model, Kashanchi established Saica Co. to start the assembly of the Fiat 1100. Saica Co. was a small set-up, with 30 employees, and had a target volume of only 600 cars per year. Gianni Agnelli, the jet-set owner of Fiat, and a personal friend of Mohammad Reza Pahlavi, flew in to Tehran for the launch of the factory. After presenting Fiat's activities in Iran, Agnelli and the Shah made a tour of the factory. At the end of the visit, a pedal car based on the Fiat 1500 Spider, was given to the Crown Prince, Reza Pahlavi, by the Saica company.

---

1   *Technically the first vehicle manufacturing plant in Iran was a TUP Mobile assembly plant set up by General Motors to supply trucks during the Allied occupation of Iran in World War II. With the end of the war, the plant was dismantled.*

BOTTOM LEFT: **Saica production line of the Fiat 1100.** *(Borzou Sepasi)*

ABOVE: **A Fiat 1500 Spider pedal car, a gift from Gianni Agnelli for the Crown Prince.** *(Borzou Sepasi)*

OPPOSITE: **Crown Prince Reza Pahlavi playing with his Fiat pedal car.** *(Borzou Sepasi)*

To oversee the implementation of the White Revolution, the Shah began to personally travel to various provinces. One of the more important cars used for these trips, was the 1958 Cadillac Eldorado Biarritz, the same car used during the visit of President Eisenhower to Tehran. The most important and longest provincial tour of the Shah lasted an unprecedented 18 days – and took place to allow the Shah to personally hand over the deeds of land ownership to the peasants who would now own the land they had labored over for generations as sharecroppers.

OPPOSITE TOP: **The Shah touring Khorasan province in a 1959 Imperial Crown Sedan. (Early 1960s)** *(Niavaran Palace)*

OPPOSITE BOTTOM & THIS PAGE TOP: **The Shah used a 1962 Imperial Crown Convertible during several of his visits to different provinces to check on the progress of the White Revolution. (Early 1960s)** *(Niavaran Palace)*

RIGHT (BOTH): **In most of his visits to the provinces the Shah either personally piloted one of his own planes or that of the IIAF (Imperial Iranian Air Force). These photographs show a de Havilland L-20 Beaver which belonged to the IIAF. In many instances when the Shah had to fly to a destination that had no airfield or runway, he used the L20 as it had STOL (Short Take-off Landing) capability. He is known to have enjoyed flying these planes.** *(Niavaran Palace)*

Fit for a King ~ The Royal Garage of the Shah of Iran

This provincial tour commenced on October 25, 1962, one day before the Shah's 43rd birthday, and started out with a drive to the northern provinces of Iran, notably the provinces outlying the Caspian Sea with dozens of villages visited in the Cadillac.

On April 10, 1962, the Shah and the Queen began an official visit of the United States. The royal couple first arrived in New York city, and after spending the night in the famed Presidential Suite of the Waldorf Astoria Hotel, traveled the next day to Washington D.C., where the Shah and Queen Farah were welcomed by the US President, John F. Kennedy and his wife, First Lady Jacqueline Bouvier Kennedy, at Washington D.C.'s National Airport. Two Presidential Limousines were waiting at the airport, a 1961 Lincoln Continental Presidential Limousine with code number X-100 for the Shah and President Kennedy, and an older Lincoln Cosmopolitan for the Queen and First Lady. Both cars had a glass roof, which made the Iranian guests and their hosts visible for the crowds who had gathered along the streets to see them.

During the first evening, the Shah and Farah Pahlavi were invited to a state dinner held in their honor in the White House. In the following days, the Shah and President Kennedy had several face-to-face meetings and discussions, with the most important topics for these two leaders being the Soviet Union and its Cold War machinations in the region. These discussions were complemented by the Shah's request to receive the latest American military technology to ward off a potential

TOP: **American President, John F. Kennedy welcoming the Shah at Washington Airport.**

BOTTOM LEFT: **A 1961 Lincoln Continental X-100 transported the Shah and President John F. Kennedy from the airport to the White House. (April 11, 1962)** *(Niavaran Palace)*

BOTTOM RIGHT: **A Lincoln Cosmopolitan transported Empress Farah Pahlavi and First Lady Jacqueline Kennedy from the airport to the White House. (April 11, 1962)** *(Niavaran Palace)*

Chapter 19: The Start of the 1960s

Soviet threat against Iran. The visit to Washington D.C. reached its zenith when the Shah was granted the unique honor of addressing a joint session of the United States Senate and Congress, a distinction bestowed only upon the most important visiting dignitaries.

From Washington D.C., accompanied by President Kennedy, the Shah visited the American Space Agency NASA at Cape Canaveral Florida, after which the royal couple bid farewell to President Kennedy and flew on to New York. On April 16, 1962 New Yorkers welcomed the Imperial couple with a ticker tape parade. The car used for this parade was an aptly named 1952 Chrysler Imperial Parade Phaeton, one of three cars used by the New York state government for visiting dignitaries and other state functions. All three were based on the Imperial Crown Limousine chassis, featuring custom bodies with a Virgil Exner design. Each car was a dual-cowl phaeton, with separate front and rear passenger compartments, each with their own windshield. After their first three years of service by the New York State government, the cars were brought back to the factory in 1955 to be updated to the 1956 Imperial design. After the New York visit, as Queen Farah had never visited the United States before, the Shah and Farah decided to take a private vacation to provide her with the opportunity to see the continental United States and their trip to the United States continued unofficially.

As was his habit during his overseas trips, the Shah was continuously on the lookout for the latest auto to catch his eye and take back to Iran. On his visit to the United States, the Shah was shown photographs of a new model to be launched shortly by the Buick Division of General Motors: the Buick Riviera. The Riviera, which was slated for launch on October 1962, immediately caught the attention of the Shah. The Shah was fascinated with

TOP: **At the banquet held in honor of the Shah and Queen Farah at the White House. (April 11, 1962)** *(Niavaran Palace)*

LEFT: **New Yorkers welcoming the Imperial Couple with a ticker tape parade.** *(Borzou Sepasi)*

THIS PAGE: **The royal family with their Buick Riviera.** *(Borzou Sepasi)*

Chapter 19: The Start of the 1960s

the design of the car and promptly proceeded to order one. A few months later, after the Shah and the Queen had returned to Iran, one of the early production Buick Rivieras was sent to Iran and delivered to the Shah.

As the Shah's passion for cars also extended to airplanes and, as a trained pilot, he also proceeded to order a private plane for his own private use. The plane in question, a Lockheed Jetstar, with construction no. 5002, was

BELOW: The Shah flew from Burbank to Palm Springs in a Lockheed Jetstar. The Shah is pictured discussing the plane with Lockheed Vice President, Hibbard (left), and the plane's pilot, Charles Tucker. The Shah piloted the plane for a period during the flight. (April 24, 1962) *(Niavaran Palace)*

BOTTOM LEFT: With Iranian registration EP-VRP, arriving at London Gatwick Airport. (1968) *(Brian Bickers)*

TOP RIGHT & MIDDLE: A scale model of the Jetstar was presented as a gift to the Shah from Lockheed. *(J.N. Alizadeh)*

BOTTOM RIGHT: The Shah and Queen Farah disembarking from the Lockheed Jetstar. (1964) *(Borzou Sepasi)*

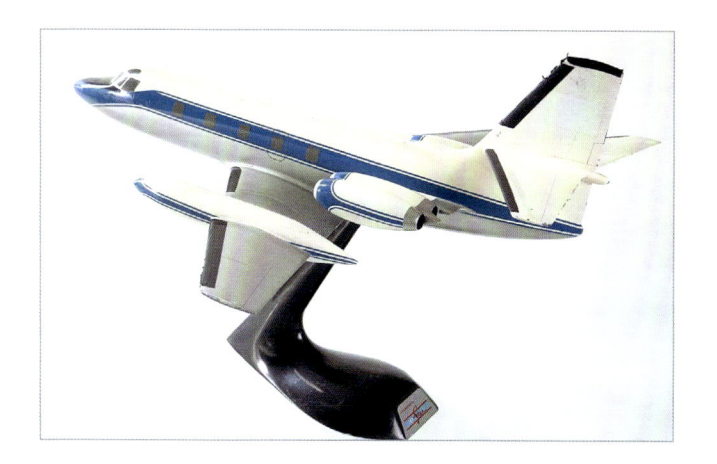

purchased during a visit to the Lockheed works. The plane was subsequently registered under the number EP-VRP.

From the United States, the Shah and the Empress made a short trip to England on their way to Amsterdam to participate in the Silver Wedding Celebrations of Queen Juliana of the Netherlands. During their stopover in the UK, the Shah also had the opportunity to test drive the new Jaguar E-Type convertible, which Jaguar boasted could easily do 150mph. The E-Type he drove was a 1961 model, chassis number 850280, at Chertsey Road, near Richmond, Surrey. In this test drive, two Embassy cars followed, so that no other cars could pass him. After the test drive, the Shah was a bit undecided whether to buy the E-Type and eventually did not go through with the purchase. It is possible that he may have compared the E-Type to his other sports cars, in particular the Maserati 5000GT and the Ferrari 410 Superamerica, and probably found it lacking in power and driving enjoyment. It bears note that when the Jaguar E-Type was launched at the Geneva Show in 1961, it was shown on a Persian hand-woven carpet, but still failed to attract the interest of the Shah.

Some months before their trip to England, the Shah purchased a new royal plane from Britain. The new plane, a Vickers Viscount V.816, construction number 436, was delivered to the Shah on May 1961 when it landed in Tehran's Mehrabad Airport and registered as EP-MRS (Mohammad Reza Shah). With the purchase of the jet-engined Lockheed, the now obsolete turbo-propped Vickers Viscount fell out of favor and, on March 1963, it was leased to the "Iran National Airlines Corporation" as a VIP plane.

The Shah driving a Jaguar E-Type Roadster, chassis number 850280 lent to him by the factory for a test drive. (April 30, 1962)
(Keystone/Hulton Archive/Getty Images)

Chapter 19: The Start of the 1960s

On May 15, 1962, a major flood destroyed the Javadiyeh and Nazee Abad districts located in the poorer southern sectors of the Iranian capital Tehran. The Shah decided to visit the flooded areas and on that day, accompanied by Tehran's mayor, the Chairman of the Joint Chief of Staff of the armed forces, and the Shah's special adjutant the Shah went to visit the flood survivors in a white 1961 Lincoln Continental Convertible, using the open top of the car as a perch to view the damage first hand.

TOP (BOTH): The Shah examines the engine of the E-Type, chassis number 850280. (April 30, 1962) *(Top Foto)*

ABOVE: The royal Vickers Viscount V.816, construction number 436. *(The Samba Collection)*

RIGHT: The Shah in his Lincoln Continental surveying flood-stricken areas in south of Tehran.

Fit for a King ~ The Royal Garage of the Shah of Iran

On July 26, 1962, Mohammad Reza Shah Pahlavi flew to Kabul, the capital of Afghanistan at the official invitation of Afghanistan's King, Mohammad Zahir Shah who personally welcomed him at the airport accompanied by several high-ranking officials. During this visit, the two kings undertook direct negotiations to resolve regional issues between Afghanistan and its neighbor, Pakistan, at the Delgosha Palace. Thereafter, the Shah addressed the members of Parliament at the Afghanistan National Assembly. He also gave a speech in a Kabul stadium, addressed to the people of Afghanistan.

The official car of the Shah of Iran for the Afghanistan sojourn was a Daimler DK-400 All-Weather Tourer, constructed for Mohammad Zahir Shah by coachbuilder Hooper, chassis number 92724. The body number was 10236.

Post Afghanistan, the Shah traveled to Pakistan, to continue with the negotiations, to try resolving the contentious Afghanistan-Pakistan issues.

On March 14, 1963, the Shah made a trip to Khuzestan province for the opening ceremony of the Mohammad Reza Shah Pahlavi dam, now the Dez dam. It was an arched

THESE TWO PAGES: The Shah of Iran and Zahir Shah of Afghanistan riding together in the Daimler DK-400, chassis number 92724, in Kabul. (July 1962) *(Borzou Sepasi)*

Chapter 19: The Start of the 1960s

dam on the Dez River, 23 km northeast of Andimeshk. Constructed between 1959 and 1963, and supervised by an Italian consortium, it was (and still is) owned and managed by the Khuzestan Water & Power Authority. At 203 meters, the dam was one of the highest in the country. At the time of its construction, the Mohammad Reza Shah Pahlavi Dam was Iran's biggest development project. The Shah arrived at the opening ceremony for the dam in his 1959 Cadillac Fleetwood Series 75 Limousine.

On May 3, 1963, King Frederick IX and Queen Ingrid of Denmark arrived in Tehran. The two royal families visited Tehran, Isfahan, Shiraz and Persepolis. Once they returned to Tehran, they headed to the northern beaches of the Caspian Sea, in the Iranian royal train built by Wegmann & Co. Kassel.

In October 1963, Charles de Gaulle, the President of the French Republic, accompanied by the First Lady of France, paid a four-day-long official visit of Iran. De Gaulle visited the Iranian ministry of foreign affairs where he gave a speech to a joint session of both the members of the Iranian Senate and National Consultative Assembly. He also visited the Iran-France Friendship Society while in Tehran. De Gaulle and the First Lady next flew to Shiraz, and then visited Persepolis and Isfahan. At the end of the visit, de Gaulle returned to Tehran, visiting the Pasteur Institute of Iran and the Royal Army College. The official car used for this visit was a white Rolls-Royce Silver Cloud II Drophead Coupe, chassis number LSWC418, with hand-crafted coachwork by H. J. Mulliner. This car was delivered to the royal garage in November 1960. The car was subsequently repainted to Bordeaux red in 1965.

Fit for a King ~ The Royal Garage of the Shah of Iran

Chapter 19: The Start of the 1960s

ABOVE: The Mohammad Reza Shah Pahlavi dam, now the Dez dam.

LEFT: The Shah's Cadillac Fleetwood Series 75 arriving at the ceremony for the commissioning of the Mohammad Reza Shah Pahlavi dam. (March 14, 1963) *(Borzou Sepasi)*

316

Chapter 19: The Start of the 1960s

OPPOSITE TOP: The Shah of Iran and Frederick IX of Denmark on their way to the royal palace from the airport riding together in the Shah's Rolls-Royce Phantom IV, chassis number 4CS6, bodied by Hooper. *(Borzou Sepasi)*

OPPOSITE BOTTOM LEFT: The Shah and Frederick IX riding together in the Iranian Carl Marius royal carriage. *(iichs.ir)*

OPPOSITE BOTTOM RIGHT & THIS PAGE TOP LEFT: The Shah and Queen Farah Pahlavi sightseeing with King Frederick IX and Queen Ingrid in Isfahan. A 1958 Lincoln Continental Convertible was used to ferry the two royal couples around. *(iichs.ir)*

TOP RIGHT, ABOVE & RIGHT: Charles de Gaulle visits the Iranian Senate in a Rolls-Royce Silver Cloud II, chassis number LSWC418, bodied by H. J. Mulliner. (October 1963) *(Borzou Sepasi)*

317

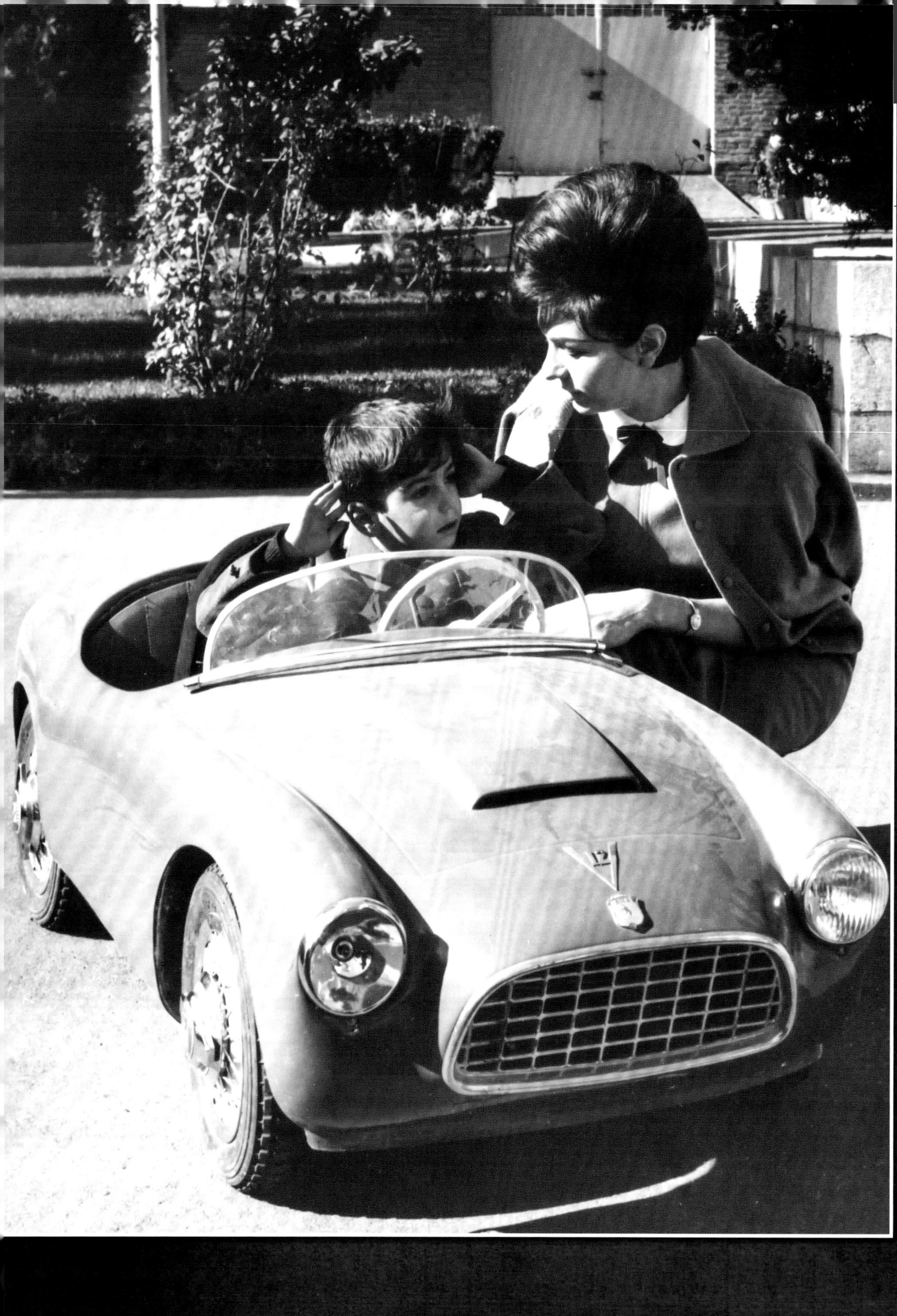

Chapter 19: The Start of the 1960s

As the Crown Prince grew up, the Shah bought him automotive-related toys including a small electric car, the Bimbo Racer V12. This red-colored runabout was a Giovanni Michelotti-design and had been hand-built by S.I.L.A, in Torino, Italy. It was inspired by the Ferrari 375MM Pininfarina Spyder. Powered by a 12-volt electric motor, the little vehicle could travel to a top speed of 7mph. It also featured working headlamps, a three-speed gearbox, brakes on all four wheels, and a horn. When the Crown Prince Reza grew to an age when he could drive it, the Shah ordered the Saad Abad palace garage manager to prepare the runabout for him. As the Crown Prince took a great liking to this toy, the Shah ordered several more of the Bimbo Racers, in shades of white and red.

THESE TWO PAGES: **Crown Prince Reza drives his Bimbo Racer V12. (Early 1960s)** *(Niavaran Palace)*

Fit for a King ~ The Royal Garage of the Shah of Iran

THESE TWO PAGES: The Shah and Farah Pahlavi in front of the Saad Abad "White Palace". The Shah's 1961 Chevrolet Corvette and the Crown Prince's Bimbo Racer V12 are seen adjacent to each other. (Early 1960s) *(Borzou Sepasi)*

Chapter 19: The Start of the 1960s

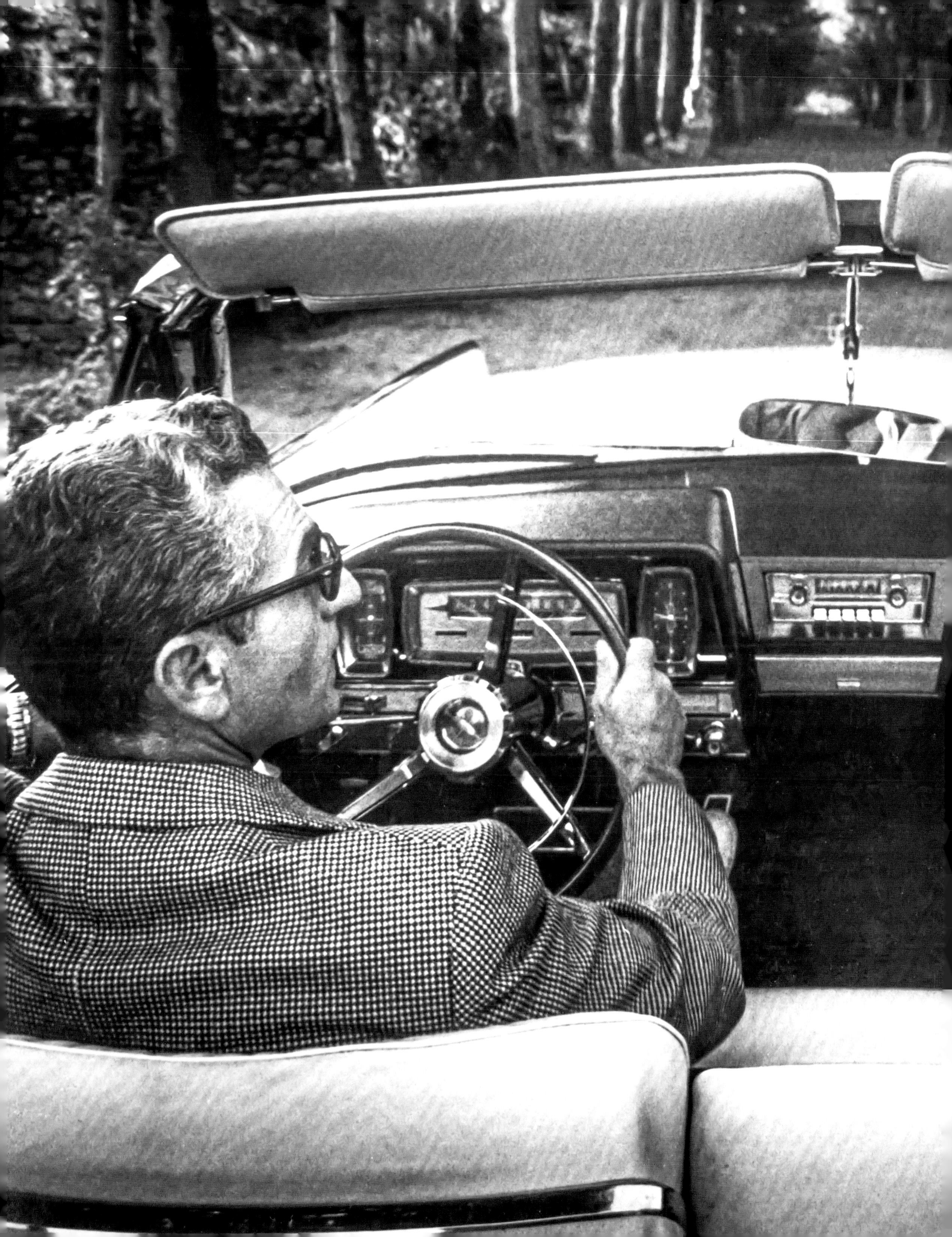

Shah in his 1961 Lincoln Continental in the vicinity of the Babol Palace. *(Borzou Sepasi)*

Fit for a King ~ The Royal Garage of the Shah of Iran

In October 1963, Queen Juliana of the Netherlands accompanied by her children Prince Bernard and Princess Beatrice, arrived in Tehran. In the first part of this visit, both the royal families traveled to the Caspian Sea shores in the Wegmann & Co. Kassel royal train where they stayed at the Babol royal palace. The next day, the Shah and the Dutch royals paid a visit to the Babolsar fishery, in the Shah's 1961 Lincoln Continental Convertible. At a distance, the farmers and the villagers gathered to see them as they drove by in the Lincoln. The Iranian and Dutch royals had lunch in the Babolsar Hotel and in the afternoon, they went to Ramsar, to visit the Farah hospital, a showcase of the Shah's efforts to bring quality medical care to the masses. After spending the night at Ramsar Hotel,

324

Chapter 19: The Start of the 1960s

the next day the Shah and the Dutch royals traveled back to Tehran in the royal train.

Following their return from the Caspian, the two royal families went on to visit Tehran, Isfahan, Shiraz and Persepolis, and the cars used in the various cities were a 1956 Rolls-Royce Phantom IV, chassis number 4CS6, a 1962 Chrysler Imperial Crown Convertible, a 1960 Rolls-Royce Silver Cloud II Drophead Coupe with chassis number LSWC418 and a 1959 Cadillac Fleetwood Series 75 Limousine all belonging to the royal garage.

OPPOSITE (BOTH): The Iranian and Dutch royal families in a Lincoln Continental Convertible in Babolsar. *(Saad Abad Palace)*

TOP LEFT: Visiting Persepolis with two Imperial Crown Convertibles (chassis numbers unknown). *(iichs.ir)*

TOP RIGHT: Visiting the Tehran Royal Jewelry Museum with the Rolls-Royce Phantom IV, chassis number 4CS6, bodied by Hooper. *(iichs.ir)*

MIDDLE (BOTH): The Shah and Queen Juliana in a Rolls-Royce Silver Cloud II Drophead Coupe, chassis number LSWC418. *(iichs.ir)*

ABOVE: Chivu Stoica, Romanian President of the State Council visiting Iran and being transported with a Rolls-Royce Silver Cloud II, chassis number LSWC418, bodied by H. J. Mulliner repainted in Bordeaux. (1967) *(Khandaniha magazine)*

Fit for a King ~ The Royal Garage of the Shah of Iran

Italy visit

In February 1964, the Shah made an official visit to Italy. During this visit, he took delivery of his latest order from the Ferrari factory, a 330GT 2+2, chassis number 5459, the first Ferrari to feature four headlamps. The exterior was in a shade of Oro Chiaro, and inside the

TOP (BOTH): During an official visit with his Rolls-Royce Silver Cloud II, chassis number LSWC418, bodied by H. J. Mulliner. (Early 1970s) *(Borzou Sepasi)*

ABOVE: The Shah at the wheel of his brand-new Ferrari 330GT, chassis number 5459, bodied by Pininfarina.

RIGHT: At Niavaran Palace around 1998, the Shah's former Ferrari 500 Superfast, chassis number 6605SF, bodied by Pininfarina was on display at a classic car exhibition. *(Teymour Richard)*

Chapter 19: The Start of the 1960s

car featured beige upholstery. The car was sent to Iran by plane soon after.

The Shah used this car for a little less than one year, as it seems to have fallen out of favor after receiving his next Ferrari from the factory: a gorgeous 500 Superfast. The Shah took delivery of his Superfast in May 1965, during a second trip to Italy. The car, with chassis number 6605SF (the 20th of 36 made), was sent to Tehran in June 1965, and the Shah was so smitten with it that he started using it as his daily driver. The Shah's 330GT was cast aside, and, as was frequently the case, the Shah simply passed the car on to a relative, in this case, Prince Shahram Pahlavi Nia, the eldest son of the Shah's twin sister, Ashraf Pahlavi. It remained in the possession of the Prince until 1973 though records show that he did not use the car after 1968. According to the documents of the royal garage, it would seem that the car had been suffering from mechanical maladies and had sat abandoned in the royal garage for some years, until it was sold in 1973 to Mr. Parviz Eshghi.

Fit for a King ~ The Royal Garage of the Shah of Iran

Such was the Shah's affinity for the Superfast that in November 1965, the royal court of Iran took delivery of a second Ferrari 500 Superfast, chassis number 7975SF (the 27th car of the 36 produced in total). With a maroon exterior, and with a natural tan shade interior, little is known about this car other than it was subsequently taken out of Iran and since 1976, it has been owned by Hugh Edgley, who displayed the car at the 1996 International Historic Festival, at Silverstone.

On January 7, 1965, Olav V, the King of Norway arrived for a state visit at Mehrabad Airport, Tehran, and was welcomed by the Shah. On that snowy day, the Shah used his 1959 Cadillac Fleetwood Series 75. Olav V stayed for seven days in Iran, and visited several cities, including Tehran, Isfahan and Dezful, and the Khark Island.

BELOW: The Shah and King Olav V at the reception ceremony at Tehran's Mehrabad Airport. The Shah's Cadillac Fleetwood Series 75 can be seen in the background ready to transport the two Monarchs to the royal palace. *(Saad Abad Complex)*

OPPOSITE TOP LEFT: The Shah and King Olav V in the Carl Marius royal carriage. *(iichs.ir)*

OPPOSITE TOP RIGHT: King Baudouin of Belgium paid an official visit to Iran in 1964. The photograph shows the Shah and the Belgian King riding together in the Carl Marius royal carriage. *(Saad Abad Complex)*

OPPOSITE BOTTOM: In 1965, an air show and open house for the general public was held by the USAF at Tehran's Mehrabad Airport and over twenty aircraft ranging from fighter jets to bombers were put on display. In the photo, the tail of a McDonnell F-101 Voodoo fighter and Boeing KB-50 Superfortress bomber are visible. The Shah and Queen Farah paid a visit to the show arriving in the Rolls-Royce Phantom IV, chassis number 4CS6, bodied by Hooper. *(Borzou Sepasi)*

Chapter 19: The Start of the 1960s

329

Fit for a King ~ The Royal Garage of the Shah of Iran

In 1965, the Rolls-Royce Company received a new order from the royal court of Iran. The Shah ordered a Rolls-Royce Silver Cloud III, with Mulliner Park Ward Drophead Coupe coachwork. At the time of receiving order from Iran, the company had only a Bentley S3 Continental, chassis number BC56LXE available, so Rolls-Royce converted the Bentley to a Rolls-Royce Silver Cloud III. This was executed at the factory, and a new chassis number, LCSC83C, was given to the car. The car was finished by Rolls-Royce's coachbuilding arm, Mulliner Park Ward, and displayed at the 1965 Frankfurt Motor Show, and finally delivered to the care of the Imperial Iranian Air Force, who had it transported back to Tehran in a C130 Hercules plane on January 23, 1966.

TOP: The chassis number plate of the Silver Cloud III. *(Borzou Sepasi)*

ABOVE: The royal garage plate "No. 5" fastened to the engine compartment firewall. *(Borzou Sepasi)*

RIGHT: Queen Farah Pahlavi riding in the rear seat of the Rolls-Royce Silver Cloud III, Mulliner Park Ward Drophead Coupe, chassis number LCSC83C. *(Borzou Sepasi)*

330

Chapter 19: The Start of the 1960s

Fit for a King ~ The Royal Garage of the Shah of Iran

Whilst the royal court of Iran had a number of vehicles dedicated for official and ceremonial use, as the Shah's international stature grew, and as the number of visiting dignitaries began to increase, he proceeded to order a very special, new car from Rolls-Royce. At that point of time, the company was producing the Phantom V, and some years earlier, the Shah had bought a "regular" Phantom V, which was first used during the birth of the Crown Prince. In 1963, Rolls-Royce had facelifted the model, using four headlamps, making it even more elegant. Notwithstanding assassination attempts in the past, in light of the political stability Iran had attained in the 1960s, the Shah felt secure enough to order his new Rolls-Royce with a State Landaulette body (convertible top opening at the division windows, as well as a Perspex panel over the driver's compartment body style), notwithstanding the higher security risk that was inherent to such a model. The Phantom V's rolling chassis, chassis number 5LVF29, was sent to Mulliner Park Ward for the body to be fabricated. Although, until then, around 400 standard Phantom V limousines had been produced, only two of them featured the State Landaulette option. The Shah's car was the third one. Painted in a deep Bordeaux red, the car featured a pair of discrete royal coat of arms of Iran on each rear door.

The car was shipped to Iran in August 1966, and after its arrival at the royal garage, a small plate titled "Property of the Imperial Court – Registration Number 12" was affixed to the firewall.

The Shah's State Landaulette Phantom V stands as one of the rarest Rolls-Royce models ever produced with the total number of the State Landaulette Phantom Vs standing at just five cars:

Once pressed into duty in the royal garage the Rolls-Royce Phantom V State Landaulette replaced the older Phantom IV, for most events. The first event that this car had a role to play was for the inauguration ceremony of Aryamehr University, on November 2, 1966.

ABOVE: The Shah and Queen Farah at the opening Ceremony of Aryamehr University pictured talking with the University President, Dr. Mojtahedi. The Rolls-Royce Phantom V State Landaulette, chassis number 5LVF29, bodied by Mulliner Park Ward, can be seen parked near the main entrance of the University. *(Niavaran Palace)*

OPPOSITE TOP: The Shah and King Hassan of Morocco riding together in the Shah's Rolls-Royce Phantom V, chassis number 5LVF29. (March 1968) *(Borzou Sepasi)*

OPPOSITE BOTTOM (BOTH): The Shah making an official visit to Kordestan Province. The Phantom V State Landaulette, chassis number 5LVF29, was transported to the province for this official visit. *(Saad Abad Palace)*

Chassis Number	Production Year	Original Owner
5VD99	1965	Ruler of Tanganyika
5VD83	1965	London Show car/delivered new to the Ruler of Bahrain in August 1966
5LVF29	1966	Shah of Iran
5LVF113	1967	Dr. Earl Heath of the USA (Originally Commissioned by the Romanian government)
5LVF183	1968	L. van Leeuwen in Switzerland

Chapter 19: The Start of the 1960s

The University which was launched with the objective of becoming the leading science and technology University of Iran (and, accordingly was modeled on the Massachusetts Institute of Technology) was dedicated to developing a new generation of locally trained engineers and technocrats who would provide the human resources required for the development of Iran. Given the status afforded to this university, the Shah and Farah Pahlavi personally took part in the inauguration ceremonies of this university and then proceeded to visit the different departments of the University, listening as the University Chancellor, Dr. Mohammad Ali Mojtahedi, one of Iran's leading and most well-known academics, led them on the tour of the university.

In subsequent years, Mohammad Reza Pahlavi would use the Rolls-Royce Phantom V State Landaulette regularly for the welcoming ceremonies of many of his foreign guests as this car became the primary car used for official functions. For instance, when King Hassan of Morocco came to Tehran, in March 1968, the latter was welcomed at the airport by the Shah, and then the two royals drove to royal palace in the Rolls-Royce.

On November 1, 1967, the Shah arrived at Mashhad, the second most populous city in Iran, located in the northeast of the country. The city is named after the shrine of Imam Reza, the eighth Shia Imam who is buried there. The Shah, who was named after this Shiite Saint, first made a pilgrimage to the shrine of this Saint and then proceeded to visit a number of urban development projects including a new student dormitory, and a public park. The car used for this official visit was a 1964 Chrysler Newport Convertible belonging to the Governor of the Province.

Chapter 19: The Start of the 1960s

THESE TWO PAGES: On some of his visits to urban development projects, the Shah preferred to use a Chrysler Newport Convertible (chassis number unknown). *(Saad Abad Complex)*

CHAPTER 20

More Toys for the (Royal) Boy

Chapter 20: More Toys for the (royal) boy

In 1966, Aston Martin made two scale replicas of the James Bond Aston Martin DB5. They were electric DB5 convertible toy cars, with many working gadgets similar to the movie version. Of these two, one of them was given to Prince Andrew, for his sixth birthday, and was presented to Queen Elizabeth during her visit to the Aston Martin Lagonda factory. The second one was a personal gift from Aston Martin owner, Sir David Brown, to the Shah of Iran, for the six-year-old Crown Prince of Iran, Reza.

On December 20, 1966, the second replica was delivered to the Iranian Embassy in London, in the presence of Sir David Brown himself. The seven-year-old son of Aston Martin's Deputy Managing Director, Ian Heggie, test drove the toy Aston Martin DB5, and then it was delivered to Ardeshir Zahedi, the Iranian Ambassador in London.

ABOVE: **Prince Andrew and the first scale model Aston Martin DB5 replica.** *(Shutterstock)*

TOP RIGHT: **Seven-year-old Ian Heggie, the son of Aston Martin's Deputy Managing Director, test drove the scale model Aston Martin DB5 designated for the Crown Prince of Iran at the Iranian Embassy in London. (December 20, 1966)** *(Getty Images)*

RIGHT & FOLLOWING PAGE: **The Crown Prince of Iran with his scale model Aston Martin DB5. (1967)** *(Borzou Sepasi)*

337

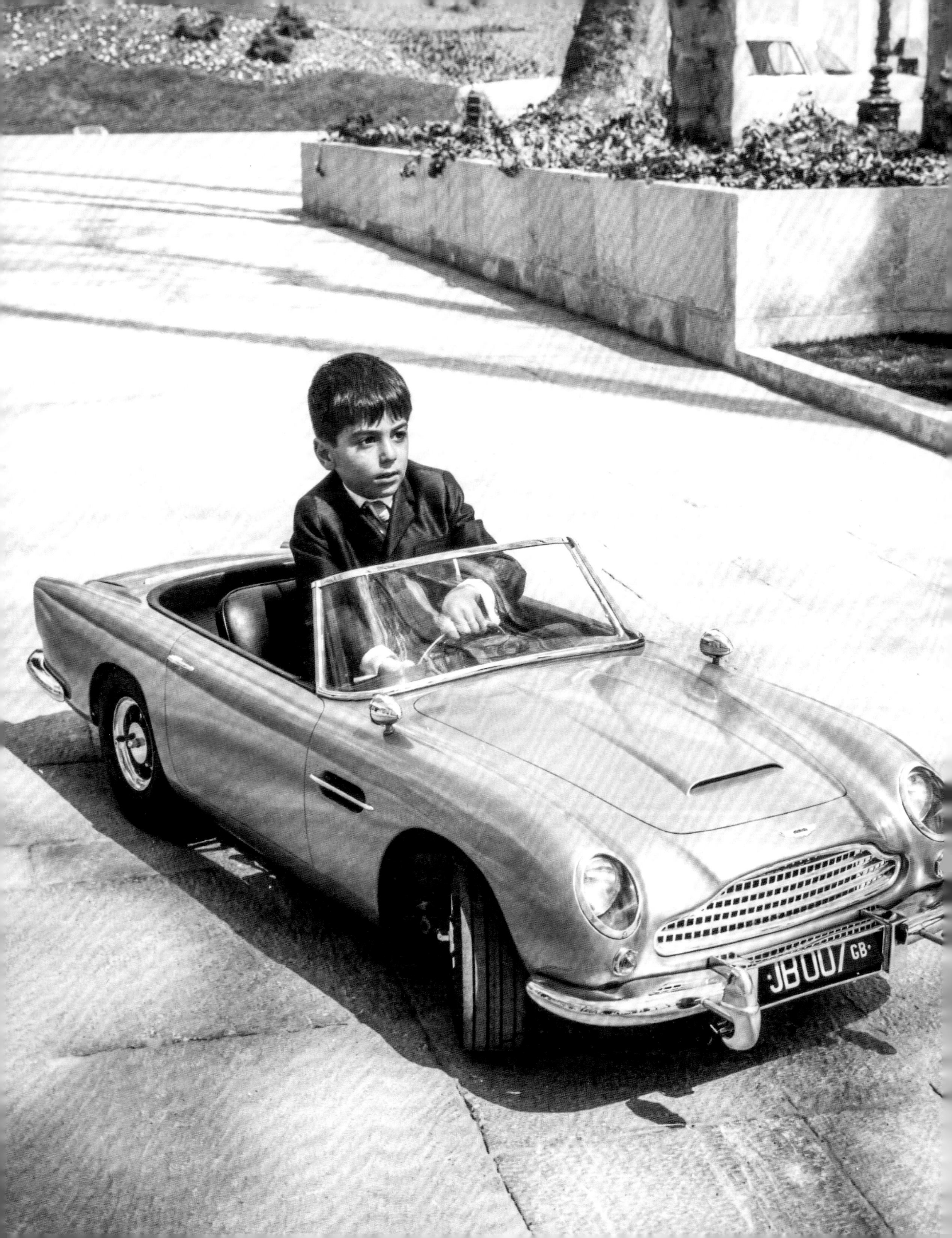
JB007
GB

Chapter 20: More Toys for the (royal) boy

Just like the real James Bond Aston Martin, the Crown Prince's car had revolving number plates, as well as steel plates covering the rear part of the car (which was bullet proof in the real car).

Around the same time, the Shah had commissioned a new Palace which was located in the old grounds of the Sahebgharanieh Palace in the Niavaran district of Tehran. Sahebgharanieh Palace, dated back to the mid-1800s and was a former summer residence of the Qajar Kings. The Shah converted the old Sahebgharanieh Palace to his private office, and in 1967 the royal family moved to the recently constructed Palace which was walking distance to the former Sahebgharanieh Palace that became known as the "Niavaran Palace". Notwithstanding this move, the Shah maintained the Saad Abad Palace for use during the summer and official functions. Designed by the architect Mohsen Foroughi, the Palace drew inspiration from pre- as well as post-Islamic architecture. While Saad Abad was a massive complex where most of the members of the Pahlavi family had their own private Palaces, Niavaran was built exclusively for Mohammad Reza Pahlavi. The Crown Prince now had a big and exclusive yard to play in, with his new Aston Martin and over the years, the royal family bought several scale cars and motorcycle toys for the Crown Prince to ride in the Niavaran Palace grounds. One of the more noteworthy "vehicles" bought for the Prince was a yellow Attex ST/300 6×6, which was used in Niavaran, and also for trips to the Caspian Sea shore.

THIS PAGE: The royal family at the newly built Niavaran Palace. **(1967)** *(Borzou Sepasi)*

339

Fit for a King ~ The Royal Garage of the Shah of Iran

Chapter 20: More Toys for the (royal) boy

ABOVE: Crown Prince Reza Pahlavi is pictured "driving" a "Giordani Ferrari Indianapolis" pedal car. (Early 1960s) *(Saad Abad Complex)*

OPPOSITE LEFT: In November 1963, Leonid Brezhnev, General Secretary of the Central Committee of the Communist Party of the Soviet Union (CPSU) paid an official visit to Iran and presented a Soviet Moskovich pedal car to the Crown Prince Reza Pahlavi. *(irdc.ir)*

RIGHT (ALL): The Crown Prince is pictured driving his Attex ST/300 6×6 in the grounds of the Niavaran Palace. *(Niavaran Palace)*

341

THIS PAGE: **The Shah's children are pictured driving a scale Ferrari 275P alongside their Attex ST/300 6×6 and a Honda ST50 Dax motorcycle in the grounds of the Niavaran Palace.** *(Borzou Sepasi)*

OPPOSITE: **The Crown Prince pictured riding a Honda ST50 Dax.** *(Niavaran Palace)*

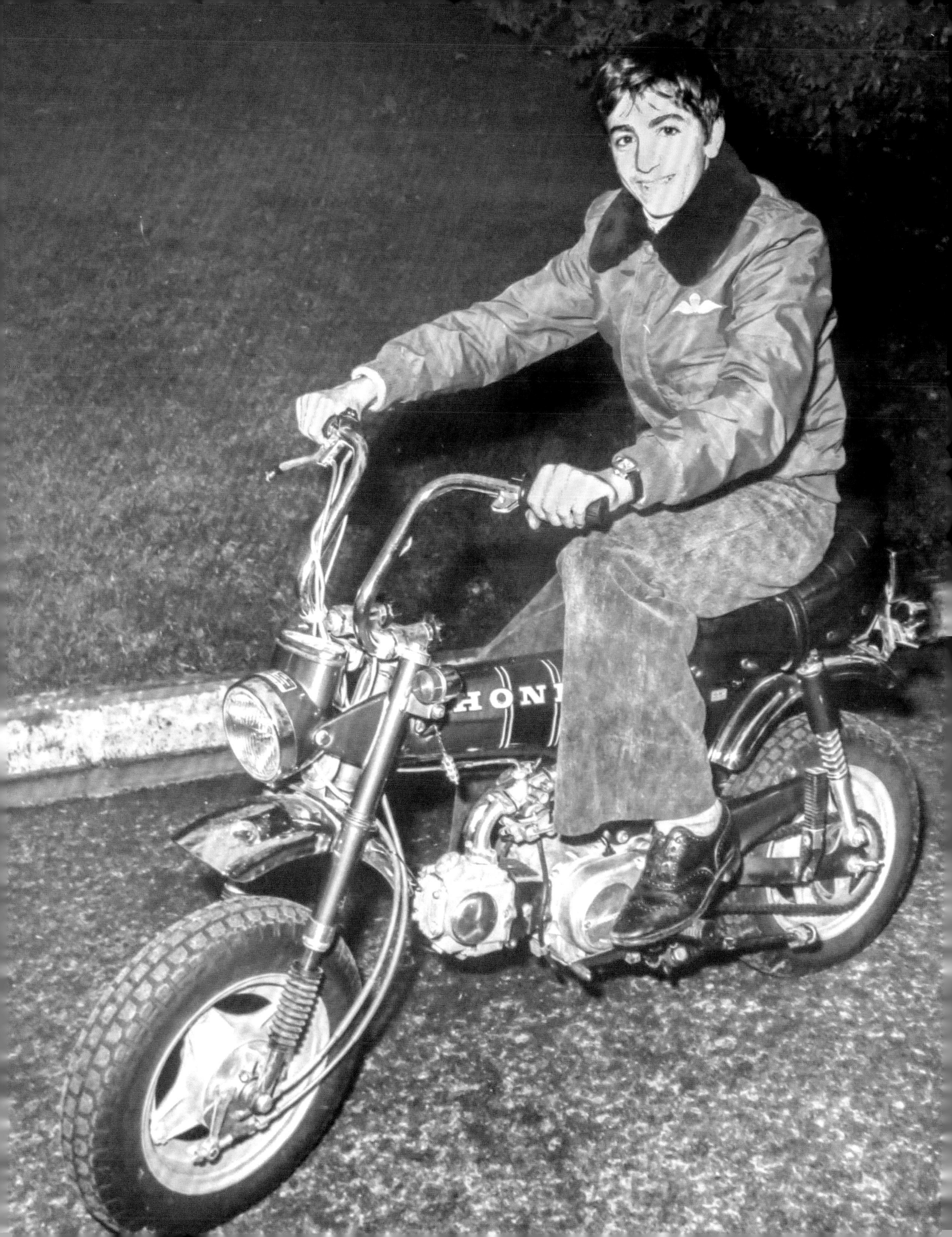

THESE TWO PAGES: Crown Prince
Reza Pahlavi and his Honda ATC-90.
(Niavaran Palace)

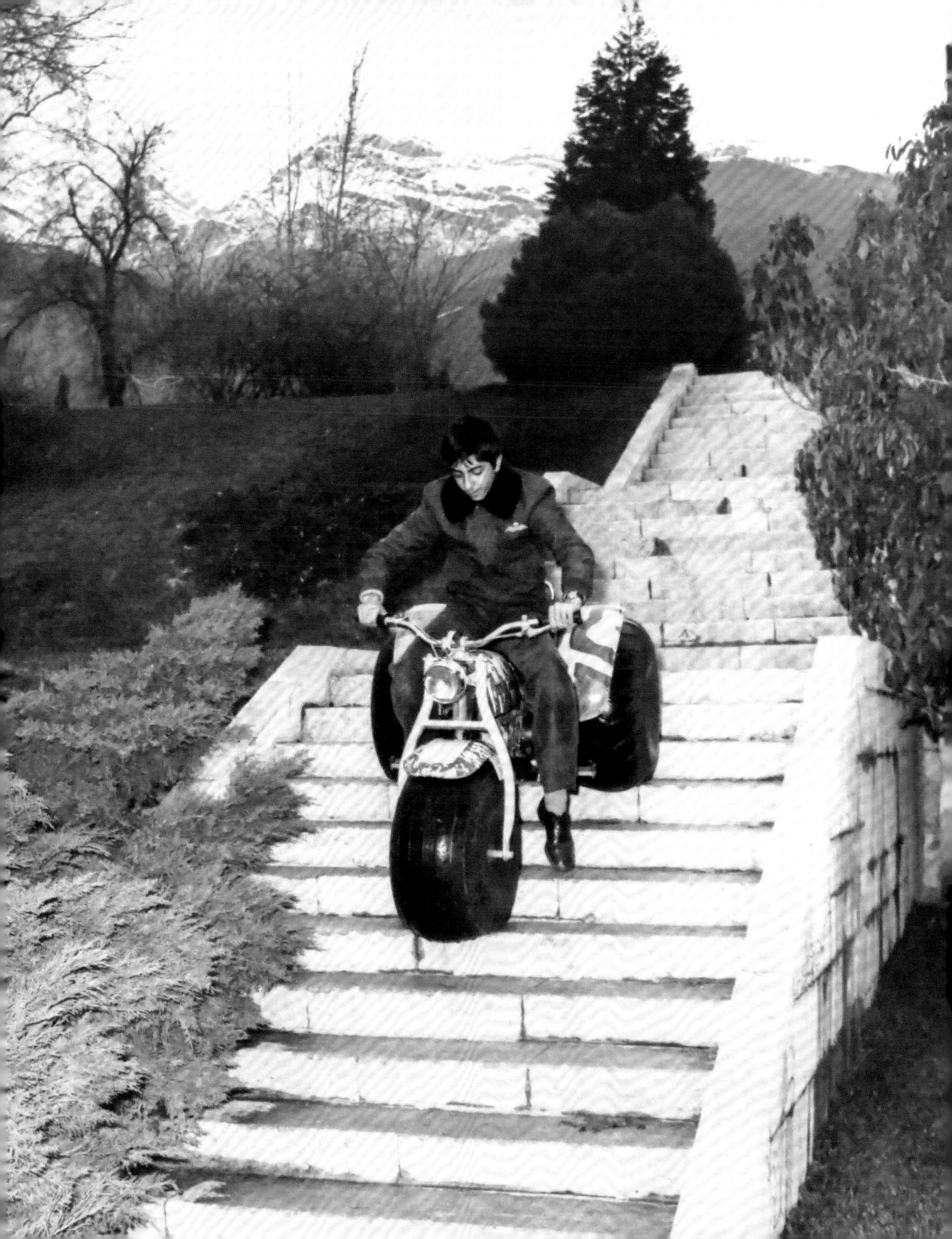

CHAPTER 21

The Mercedes 600 dominates the Royal Fleet

Chapter 21: The Mercedes 600 dominates the Royal Fleet

With the production launch of the 600 (W100) model by Mercedes-Benz in 1963, the Iranian royal court began to order vehicles for use in official ceremonies.

The models procured by the royal court encompassed all four body styles, including SWB (Short Wheelbase), LWB (Long Wheelbase) as well as the two rarest models, namely the Landaulet (with just 59 units produced) and the ultra-rare Presidential Landaulet, of which just ten were produced. The Presidential Landaulet had a unique retractable roof covering the entire rear passenger compartment.

The Landaulet ordered by the royal court was chassis number 100.015.12.001959, while the two Presidential Landaulets used by the royal court were chassis numbers 100.015.12.001207 and 100.015.12.001370. In addition to the royal court, a number of other Iranian governmental organizations used the 600 in their fleets, including the foreign ministry which used 600s in a number of Iranian Embassies. Over the years, a total of 35 Mercedes-Benz 600s were purchased by the Iranian government, making Iran one of the largest customers in the world for this unique car.

With the entry of the Mercedes 600 to the fleet of the royal court, these vehicles began to supplement the Rolls-Royce Phantom V for official ceremonies. By way of example, on November 1970, Nikolai Podgorny, the Chairman of the Presidium of the Supreme Soviet of the USSR, paid an official visit to Iran to participate in the opening ceremony of the Iran-Soviet natural gas pipeline (Hajiqabul-Astara-Abadan Pipeline). This ceremony was held in the city of Astara, in the north of Iran, near the Soviet border. Mohammad Reza Shah and Nikolai Podgorny used the Mercedes-Benz 600 Presidential Landaulet, chassis number 100.015.12.001207 as their transportation during this ceremony.

The 600s were used for not only for different ceremonies and official visits to the provinces, but would also be

A Mercedes-Benz 600 SWB, chassis number 100.012.12.001886, in front of the Shah's villa in Saint Moritz, Switzerland. *(Borzou Sepasi)*

Fit for a King ~ The Royal Garage of the Shah of Iran

transported for use during the Shah's overseas visits. By way of example, the Shah, who owned a villa in the Swiss city of St. Moritz, would frequently travel there on holiday, especially during the winter ski season. It was not uncommon that at least one or two of the Mercedes 600s of the royal court would be flown in for use by the Shah during his visits and then be flown back to the royal garage.

BELOW: Queen Farah and Prince Alireza Pahlavi in front of a 600 SWB with CD (Corps Diplomatique) license plate, in Switzerland. A Rolls-Royce Silver Shadow can be seen parked next to the 600. *(Niavaran Palace)*

BOTTOM LEFT: The Shah and Nikolai Podgorny, Chairman of the Presidium of the Supreme Soviet, riding together in the Mercedes 600 Presidential Landaulet, chassis number 100.015.12.001207, at the Iranian port city of Astara. *(Borzou Sepasi)*

BOTTOM RIGHT: Farah Pahlavi on one of her trips to Europe pictured next to an Iranian Embassy Mercedes 600. *(Niavaran Palace)*

348

TOP: The Crown Prince on the way to a youth soccer tournament in the city of Rezaiyeh in Azerbaijan Province, riding in the Mercedes 600 Presidential Landaulet, chassis number 100.015.12001370 on September 29, 1977. *(Borzou Sepasi)*

ABOVE: Queen Farah Pahlavi visiting the city of Sabzevar riding in a Mercedes 600 SWB, chassis number 100.012.12.002421. *(Borzou Sepasi)*

LEFT: Queen Farah Pahlavi on an official visit to the city of Kerman in the Mercedes 600 Presidential Landaulet, chassis number 100.015.12.001370. *(Niavaran Palace)*

CHAPTER 22

1967 ~ The Year of the Coronation and the global search for a Carriage Maker

Chapter 22: 1967 ~ The Year of the Coronation and the global search for a carriage maker

By 1967, Iran had been witnessing unprecedented economic growth and social development. The Shah had stated that he would not have a coronation and take up the ancient title of Shahanshah (King of Kings) "until he turned Iran into a prosperous and modernized nation".[1]

Now, in the 26th year of his reign, on the date of October 26, 1967, coinciding with the Shah's 48th birthday, the Shah finally held his coronation. The ceremony was held in the Grand Hall of the Golestan Palace in Tehran with the old Palace being extensively refurbished for the occasion.

The ceremony commenced with the opening of the great doors of the Marble Palace, a Palace located adjacent to the Golestan Palace and where the Shah had held

RIGHT: **The royal carriage built by Josef Klicmann following its completion. (1967)** *(Borzou Sepasi)*

BELOW: **The Grand Hall of the Golestan Palace on the day of the coronation.** *(Saad Abad Complex)*

[1] *Shah of Iran's Coronation, www.Royalwatcherblog.com*

Fit for a King ~ The Royal Garage of the Shah of Iran

all three of his weddings. From there, the Shah and Farah proceeded in the royal carriage towards the Golestan Palace with a smaller carriage carrying the Crown Prince following behind them. A battalion of the Imperial Guard and a marching band lead the first carriage, with mounted ceremonial guards on horseback escorting the carriages on both sides. The carriages passed through the Pahlavi, Sepah and Nasser Khosro Streets, and entered the Golestan Palace from the northeast entrance. Upon arrival the Shah made his way towards the Naderi Throne, a gemmed and enameled throne dating back to the time of Fat'h Ali Shah Qajar (1772-1834). The design was unique in that it was also portable, so as to be easily transported when the Qajari Shah made the annual trek to his summer residence.

As the Shah took his seat on the throne, the Queen took her seat next to him on one side and the Crown Prince on the other side. On the right side of the Grand hall, which was the most important wing of the hall, there was a special seat of honor for Karim Agha Khan IV the Imamate of the Nizari Ismaili Muslims and his family, the Begum Aga Khan III and Prince Sadruddin Khan (son of the late Aga Khan III). On the left side, space was dedicated to members of the Iranian political spectrum, as well as foreign guests and their wives. Seated in the third row was the Prime Minister, his cabinet and government officials, and the fourth row was reserved for the presiding boards of the Iranian Senate and Parliament as well as other distinguished guests.

Three minutes after the Empress, it was the Shah who entered the Grand Hall, preceded by three generals, the most senior military officer of each of the three branches of the Armed Forces: The Imperial Navy, the Air Force and the Army. He walked towards the throne, and after a delay of a quarter of a century, and, in an apparent cue from Napoleon, proceeded to crown himself. Minutes later, the, Shah, now officially known as the Shahanshah, lifted the Queen's Crown, a Van Cleef and Arpels Crown made specially for the occasion, and proceeded to crown his Queen and afforded her a new title as "Shahbanu" (wife and Queen of the King of Kings).

ABOVE: **The Shah and his coronation carriage.** *(Saad Abad Palace)*
OPPOSITE: **Shah crowning the Queen.** *(Saad Abad Complex)*

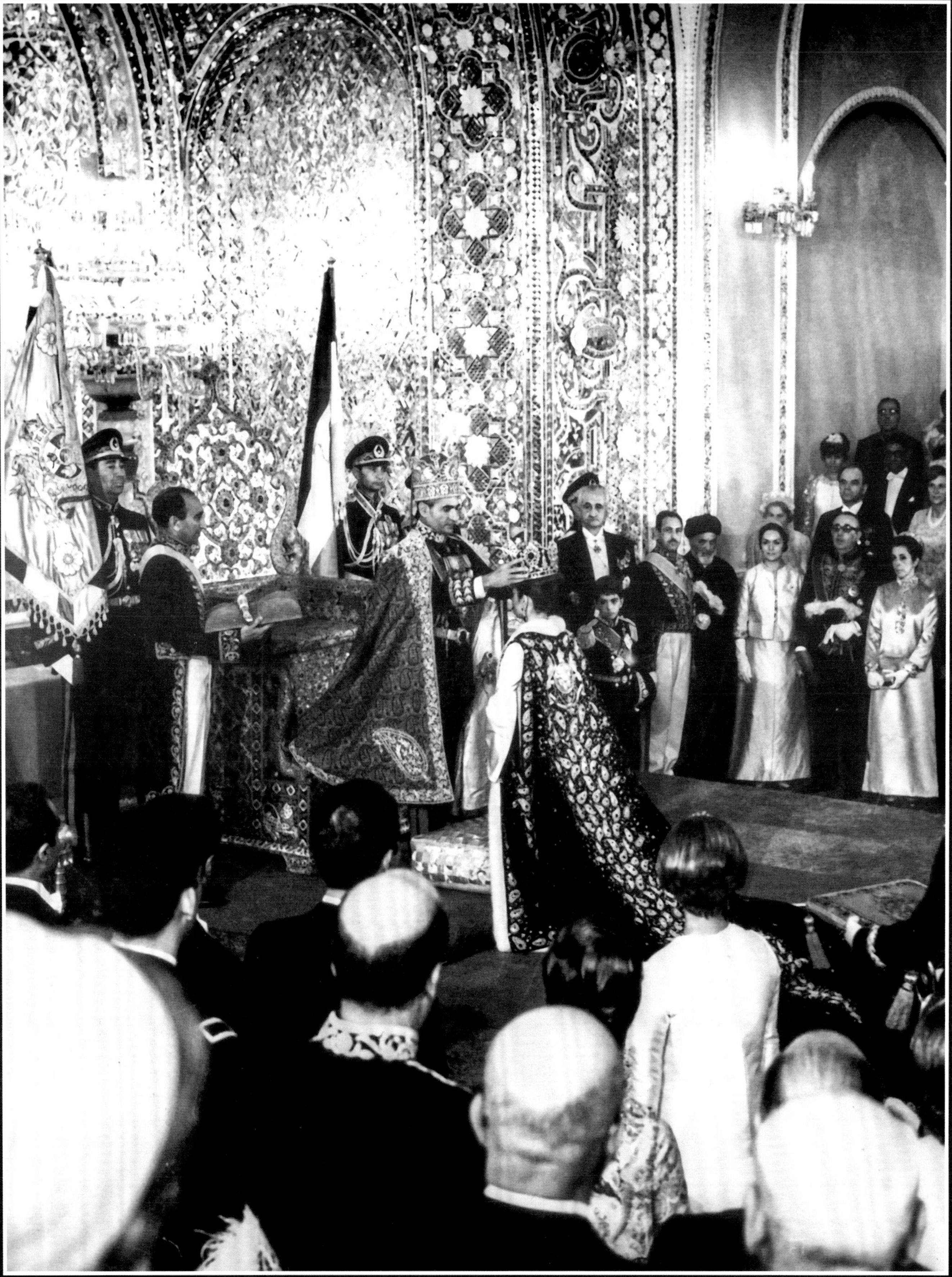

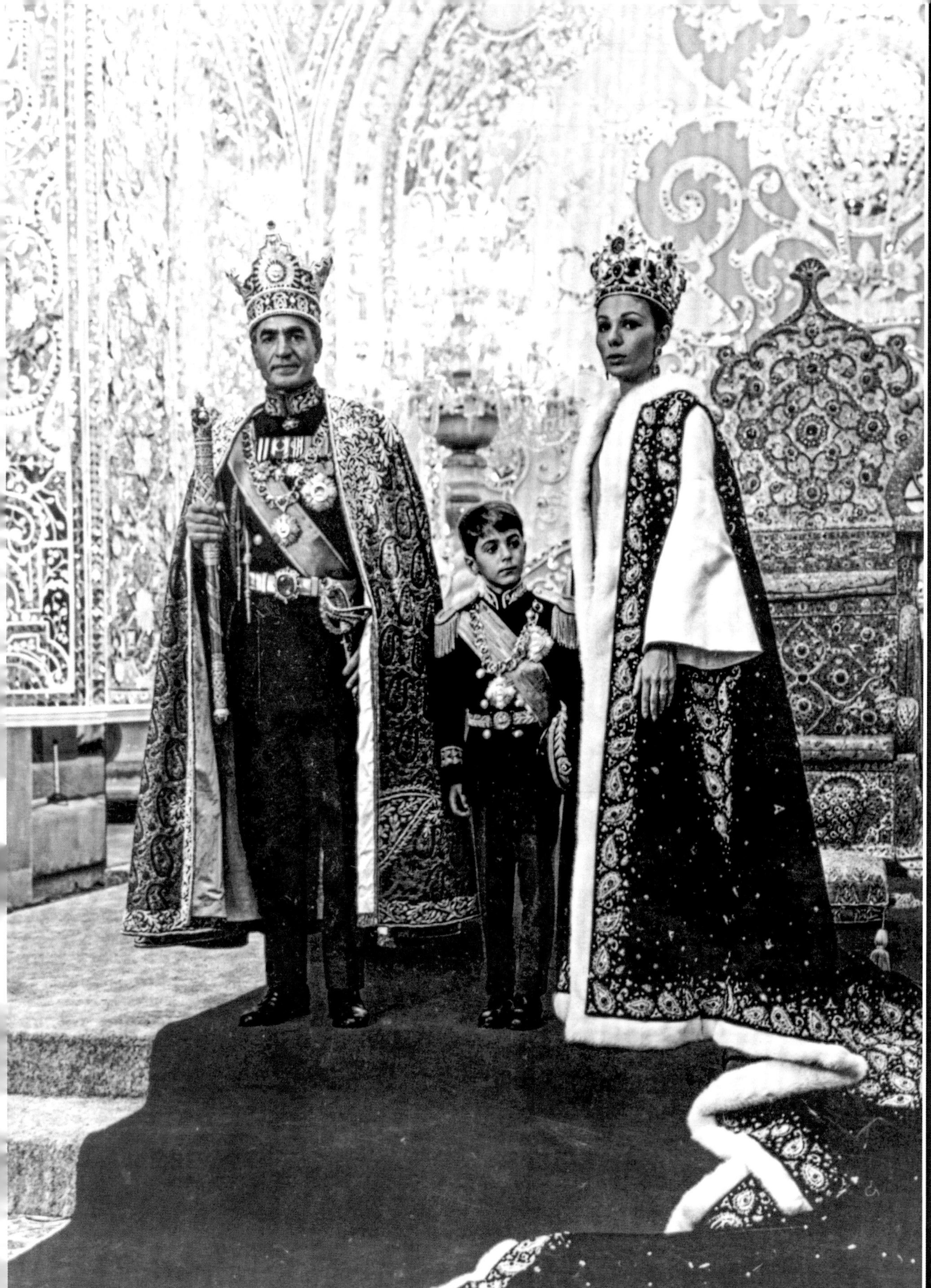

With this ceremony, Queen Farah became the first Empress to be crowned in the 2,500-year history of Persian monarchial rule. Following the crowning ceremony, the Shah addressed the guests and the nation from his throne.

After the ceremony, the Shahanshah, Shahbanu and the Crown Prince proceeded on to the Golestan Palace yard and boarded the royal carriage and, in an extravagant procession through the streets of Tehran, traveled back to the Marble Palace.

LEFT: The Shah, Queen Farah and Crown Prince Reza pictured after the coronation in Golestan Palace. *(Saad Abad Complex)*

TOP, ABOVE LEFT & MIDDLE RIGHT: Shah and Queen Farah departing from the coronation ceremony in the royal carriage. *(Niavaran Palace)*

RIGHT: The royal carriage pictured at Ferdowsi Square after the coronation. *(Niavaran Palace)*

The royal carriage, a replica of a 250-year-old Austrian Imperial carriage used by the Hapsburgs, was drawn by eight white Hungarian horses that had been specially ordered by the Shah for the coronation ceremony from Josef Klicmann's Karosseriebau (carriage maker's shop) in Austria. The Shah settled on Klicmann after an unsuccessful search of a number of countries that still had monarchies such as England, Spain and Holland with the belief that the existence of monarchies would go hand in hand with carriage making. It was during this search that it slowly became apparent that whilst there were still carriage restorers, carriage making was a dying craft and that the manufacture of carriages had virtually ceased. Finally, after unsuccessfully trying to lease a carriage from the Wagneburg Museum in Vienna, the Shah was directed to the only known remaining carriage maker in Europe, Klicmann.[2]

In a span of nine months, Klicmann with a team of 20 artisans built an eight-horse carriage with gilded sides, blue lacquer doors, a silk interior and a golden crown on top. Klicmann traveled to Tehran in July 1967, to assemble the carriage from semi-knocked down parts that had been transported to Iran by plane. The design of the Iranian royal carriage, which was based on a royal carriage from the Habsburg dynasty of Austria, was, and remains, arguably one of the most beautiful carriages in the history of horse-drawn carriages. The carriage weighed some four tons and was made entirely of wood. The body was painted a unique shade of blue, with golden patterns, and the Iranian royal crest with two lions and the Pahlavi crowns were hand painted on the doors. The crown affixed to the roof was a large replica of the Pahlavi crown. Some 4.4 meters long, and with a width of 2 meters and a height of 2.5 meters, the carriage garnered much attention during the ceremony.

There are differing accounts about the ultimate cost of this carriage. However, during these years, the Shah had been coming under growing scrutiny for his perceived lavish personal spending so he wanted to avoid revealing any details about the contract. During his last trip to Austria, some five hundred Iranian students had vociferously protested against him and his profligacy.

---

[2] David A. Andelman, "The Last of Vienna's Great Carriage Makers", *New York Times*, October 29, 1979, p. 9

Chapter 22: 1967 ~ The Year of the Coronation and the global search for a carriage maker

OPPOSITE: The Crown Prince pictured riding in the older Carl Marius carriage of the royal court followed by the new carriage. *(Niavaran Palace)*

RIGHT: The carriage being readied for storage in the royal garage after the coronation. *(iichs.ir)*

BELOW: Until the 1967 coronation, the queens of Persian Monarchs had never been crowned. As a result, it was necessary that a crown be commissioned for Queen Farah. The French jewelers Van Cleef & Arpels were selected for this task. *(Iran Treasury of National Jewels)*

BOTTOM RIGHT: In 1925, Reza Shah ordered a group of Iranian jewelers, under the supervision of the jeweler Haj Serajeddin Javaheri, to create a new crown to symbolize the Pahlavi Dynasty. Inspiration for the design was drawn from paintings and historical references to crowns used during the Sassanid Empire, which had ruled Persia from 224 to 651 AD. The Pahlavi crown was first used for the coronation of Reza Shah in 1926 and then again for the 1967 coronation of Mohammad Reza Pahlavi. *(Iran Treasury of National Jewels)*

CHAPTER 23

The Lamborghini Miura and the Iranian Royal Family

Chapter 23: The Lamborghini Miura and the Iranian Royal Family

Having been sent to complete his secondary education at the renowned Institut Le Rosey boarding school in Rolle, Switzerland, the Shah had a special affinity for Switzerland, an affinity which would continue even after his return to Iran and assumption of the throne. An avid skier, the Shah would plan his annual winter vacation around the ski slopes of Switzerland. During these vacations, in light of the people who made up his entourage, including a multitude of bodyguards, at least ten cars were necessary to ferry this large body of people. For their personal transportation, the Shah and Farah had differing tastes. The Shah generally preferred to use sports cars equipped with snow tires, usually either flown in directly from the royal garage, or, in certain cases, having his latest order delivered to Switzerland for use during his vacation and then subsequently shipped back to Tehran. On the other hand, Queen Farah favored the comfort of one of the Rolls-Royces flown in from the royal garage. During these trips, usually two floors of the famous Dolder Grand Hotel in Zurich were taken over for a week, with the skiing taking place at St. Moritz.

By 1968, in light of the frequency of his visits, the Shah decided to purchase a residence in Switzerland, a process that was exacerbated by the fact that anti-Shah Iranian students tended to gather and protest against his rule in front of the Dolder Hotel. As a result, the Embassy staff in Switzerland were mandated to find a suitable residence and eventually came upon a villa named Suvretta, which was one of the most beautiful villas in the region. The building had large, luxurious halls and was conveniently located near the Suvretta House Hotel, which was suitable for accommodating the Shah's entourage and

ABOVE & FOLLOWING PAGE: **The Shah and his Lamborghini Miura in front of the Suvretta Villa, St.Moritz.** *(Saad Abad Palace)*

Fit for a King ~ The Royal Garage of the Shah of Iran

Chapter 23: The Lamborghini Miura and the Iranian Royal Family

security personnel. The main advantage of this villa was that it was in a secluded location, which made it more secure for the Shah and his family and, no doubt, easier to avoid anti- Shah protestors. Following its purchase in 1968, the Villa Suvretta was extensively refurbished over a two-year period by French and Danish designers and was ready in time to accommodate the Shah and his family for their winter vacation in 1970.

1968 was also the year when the Shah bought his first Lamborghini, a Miura. After years of special commissions for the Shah from the more well-established players like Ferrari and Maserati, the Miura, despite coming from the relative upstart Lamborghini, quickly became the "must have" supercar and the Shah soon emerged as Lamborghini's most important and prestigious customer.[1]

The Shah ordered his Miura P400 directly from the factory in Rosso (dark Orange), with Bianco (white) interior and unique chrome bumpers and painted door slats. The Shah's Miura was chassis number 3303, engine number 1630, with body number 101. Like all first series Miuras it was powered by the 325bhp V12 displacing 3929cc. As with his other acquisitions from Ferrari and Maserati, the Iranian Embassy in Rome handled the details of the purchase.[2]

---

[1] *Simon Kidston, "If Cars Could Talk", Ramp, Edition 38, Summer 2017, p. 118*

[2] *David Lillywhite, "King Miura", Magneto, Issue 2, Summer 2019, p. 100*

The Shah entering his Miura, chassis number 3303, in St. Moritz. *(Borzou Sepasi)*

TOP: The Shah and Queen Farah in their Lamborghini Miura P400, chassis number 3303, in St. Moritz. *(Borzou Sepasi)*

ABOVE (BOTH): Princess Leila Pahlavi beside her father's Miura, chassis number 3303. *(Niavaran Palace)*

Chapter 23: The Lamborghini Miura and the Iranian Royal Family

Completed on February 9, 1968, the Miura was delivered to the Iranian Embassy in Rome on February 18, reaching the royal garage in Tehran on March 15, by plane. The Shah had a particular affinity for this car and would have it shipped to Switzerland from Tehran for his winter vacations. As a result, the car was fitted with studded snow tires and Iranian transit plates "TEH 3988". During these holidays, the Miura would be accompanied by a number of other cars from the royal garage, such as a Porsche 911, and assorted Rolls-Royces, all of which, along with all the luggage and other necessities, would be transported to St. Moritz from Tehran by plane. As the Miura would be shipped in advance, it would be arranged that the Miura would be parked at the steps of the Shah's private aircraft after it had taxied to a stop so that the Shah could drive off to his desired destination, usually with a phalanx of security men trying desperately to keep up.

Such was the affinity of the Shah for his Lamborghini

ABOVE: **Farah Pahlavi and companions in St. Moritz.** *(Saad Abad Palace)*

BELOW: **The Shah in Switzerland beside his Lamborghini Espada, chassis number 7099, behind the Peacock Throne.** *(Minou Reeves)*

363

that when the Espada was announced, the Shah placed one of the first orders. The Shah's Espada, a 1969 S1, was manufactured on January 22, 1969 with chassis number 7099, engine number 2694 and production number 0036. This unique Espada was painted champagne acrillo (champagne) with testa di moro interior (dark brown leather upholstery and carpets) and was kept at the Shah's primary residence, Niavaran Palace rather than the royal garage. It was not uncommon for the Shah to drop off his children to school in the Palace grounds with his Espada.

According to unsealed documents from the royal court, on November 11, 1968, the Shah was involved in an accident when driving his Miura (he did not suffer any injuries) and the extent of the damage to the car is not clear. In light of the fact that the Shah, whose "love of individual cars was famously short-lived"[3] some pundits have taken the view that following the crash, the Miura was then set aside and remained unused in the royal garage until its eventual sale in 1973.

However, given that the Shah only took residence at the Villa Suvretta in 1970, combined with the fact that the Miura has been photographed extensively at the Villa Suvretta during that period, it is thought that the Miura remained in frequent use by the Shah following the accident. It also bears mention that it was rare, if not unheard of, for the Shah to have an auto repaired and put back on the road after an accident, a testament to the fondness that the Shah had for the Miura. It laid the groundwork for his next order from Lamborghini, a unique and more powerful Miura, the legendary SVJ.

The Genesis of the Shah of Iran's Miura SVJ

In late 1969, Lamborghini's Chief Development Engineer the legendary Bob Wallace began work on a one-off Miura incorporating performance upgrades "christened" as the Jota – (pronunciation of the letter "J" in Spanish) as the car was to have qualified for the Appendix "J" racing class of the day.[4] With the project being sanctioned by Ferruccio Lamborghini himself, the Jota became known in the Lamborghini works as "Miura Privata" due to Wallace's "intimate association with it".[5] This high-performance Miura had many modifications including, inter alia, a modified engine and exhaust system, lighter body, dry sump lubrication and external and interior modifications.

The car garnered much attention from the automotive press, and the Jota gripped the imagination of enthusiasts across the world, including the Shah of Iran.

Correspondence discovered in the archives of the royal court points to inquiries made on behalf of the Shah about the "Jota". These inquiries, which were made by the Shah's Chief of Staff, Kambiz Atabai primarily ask about the particular attributes of this version of the Miura. Surprisingly, this correspondence was not addressed to the Embassy but rather to Iran's Ambassador to the United Nations Food and Agricultural Organization (FAO) based in Rome. On March 29, 1971, this gentleman, a man named Hossein Sadegh, responded to Atabai's inquiries, providing detailed feedback on an automobile he names the "Yota". Because this letter sheds insights on how the first Miura SVJ came about, it has been translated as follows:

> "Pursuant to your telegram dated December 18 about the special Lamborghini kindly note as below:
>
> The automobile is named the "Yota" (sic) and as you can see from its specifications it is a fantastic car in all aspects. Fortunately, the automobile under discussion is available and only requires interior work and paint and, in the event that you place the order prior to the end of December of this year, the Lamborghini company can deliver the car prior to the end of January, (19)72.
>
> I respectfully request that you bring this information to the attention of his Highness and if this vehicle meets with his Imperial Majesty the Shahanshah's interest,

---

[3] David Lillywhite, "King Miura", Magneto, Issue 2, Summer 2019, p. 100

[4] Joe Sackey, "The Lamborghini Miura Bible", Veloce Publishing, Dorchester, 2008, p. 58

[5] ibid, p. 54

Chapter 23: The Lamborghini Miura and the Iranian Royal Family

accordingly send a telegraph for the interior and exterior colors which are requested.

The letter from the Lamborghini company providing all the specifications and prices and the only two available pictures are sent for your perusal. The automobile has a radio, tape deck and heater, however the factory advises against the installment of air conditioning.

As can be seen by the invoice issued by the Lamborghini dealer S.E.A. Automobili (based in Rome) on page 367 and the accompanying the letter sent by Ambassador Sadegh on page 366, the sale price for the SVJ was 18 Million Italian Lire, as compared to a standard Miura's ex-factory price of 8 Million Lire.

Less than a week later, Ambassador Sadegh sent a follow-up telegram to Atabai, announcing that the contract for the "special" Lamborghini had been signed and that the car was to be delivered between the 20th and 25th of January, 1972. The telegraph goes on to further state that a down payment of $3,500 had been paid and requests that the amount of $23,000 be sent to him for full payment of the car and "transportation costs and snow tires and other items" prior to January 10, so as to assure timely delivery.

A follow-up letter on the royal court letter head was sent in reply by Atabai inscribed with his own handwriting that the car should be ordered in "candy apple red" and have either a white or black interior.

On the same date, a second letter was sent by Atabai stating that the Shah had expressly requested that the car be delivered to Switzerland no later than January 30, 1972. The letter also goes on to again emphasize that the car be painted metallic candy apple red which is then described as being a "very vivid color" and that "in light of this, the interior should either be black or white". Furthermore, the letter goes on to state that "Mr. Behbahanian" who was the Shah's financial manager was in Switzerland at the time and that he has been instructed to "immediately" wire the money to Ambassador Sadegh. At the end of the letter, Ambassador Sadegh was requested, "if possible, send some more pictures of the car".

Four days later, the head of the royal court, Mr. Assadollah Alam, a former Prime Minister and one of the Shah's closest confidantes, sent a telex to Mr. Behbahanian stating that, "a special Lamborghini for the personal use of the Shah has been ordered by Engineer Sadegh, the Ambassador of his Imperial Highness, and accordingly, this vehicle must be delivered to Switzerland no later than the 30th of January and as a result on an expedited basis the amount of $23,000 must be sent to Mr. Sadegh's account."

A subsequent handwritten note dated December 11, 1970 written by an unidentified officer of the royal court, someone of such standing and seniority that many of the persons involved in the purchase of the Miura are identified on a first name basis, writes to Atabai:

> Dearest Kambiz,
>
> Last night at 12 o'clock, Mr. Alam contacted me stating that a telex had come from the Foreign Ministry stating that the Shah's car had been dispatched and that the junior Mr. Kambiz should be there to personally take delivery of the car at the airport and take it to a garage by truck accompanied by a mechanic. I do not know if you will be coming today and which airplane the (car) will be arriving with. You can check the telexes at the Ministry of Foreign Affairs.

The content and tone of the letter points to the importance that the car has and conveys a direct order by the Shah that the Chief of Staff of the royal court be personally present to take delivery of the car in Switzerland with a mechanic to personally oversee the unloading and to have it taken to a garage in preparation for the Shah's arrival.

While the royal court was scrambling to make sure the car was ready for the Shah's upcoming visit to Switzerland, simultaneously Lamborghini was also taking the final steps for preparing the car for delivery. With the number

شماره ـ ۵۱۴
تاریخ ـ ۵۰/۱۰/۱

PERMANENT MISSION OF IRAN TO FAO
VIA FLAMINIA 362/4
ROMA 00196

جناب آقای کامبیز آتابای

مدیر کل محترم فنی دربار شاهنشاهی

در تعقیب تلگرام مورخ ۱۸ دسامبر راجع به اتومبیل منصوب لامبورگینی محترماً بشرح ذیل اشعار میدارد.

اتومبیل مزبور مدل YOTA نام دارد و همانطور که از مشخصات ملاحظه میفرمائید از هر جهتی اتومبیل فوق العاده جالبی است. خوشبختانه اتومبیل مورد بحث آماده بوده و فقط کارهای داخلی و رنگ آن باقی است و در صورتیکه قبل از سال جدید یعنی تا آخر ماه دسامبر جاری سفارش آن داده شود کمپانی لامبورگینی میتواند آنرا تا آخر ژانویه سال ۷۲ تحویل دهد.

تمنا دارد موضوع را به شرف عرض رسانده و در صورتیکه مورد علاقه اعلیحضرت همایون شاهنشاه قرار گیرد در ضمن تلگرامی راجع به سفارش رنگ داخلی و خارجی آنرا متذکر فرمائید.

نامه شرکت لامبورگینی راجع به کلیه مشخصات و قیمت و تنها دو عدد عکس موجوده جوفاً ارسال میگردد. اتومبیل فوق دارای رادیو و TAPE و بخاری میباشد ولی کمپانی نصب دستگاه AIR-CONDITIONING را در این اتومبیل صلاح نمیدانند.

ارادتمند ـ حسین صادت

OPPOSITE: A copy of the correspondence discovered in the archives of the royal court dated March 29, 1971, from Hossein Sadegh, the Iranian representative to the UN Food and Agricultural Organization, who followed up on the inquiries of the royal court providing detailed feedback on the vehicle he named as the "Yota". *(Saad Abad Palace)*

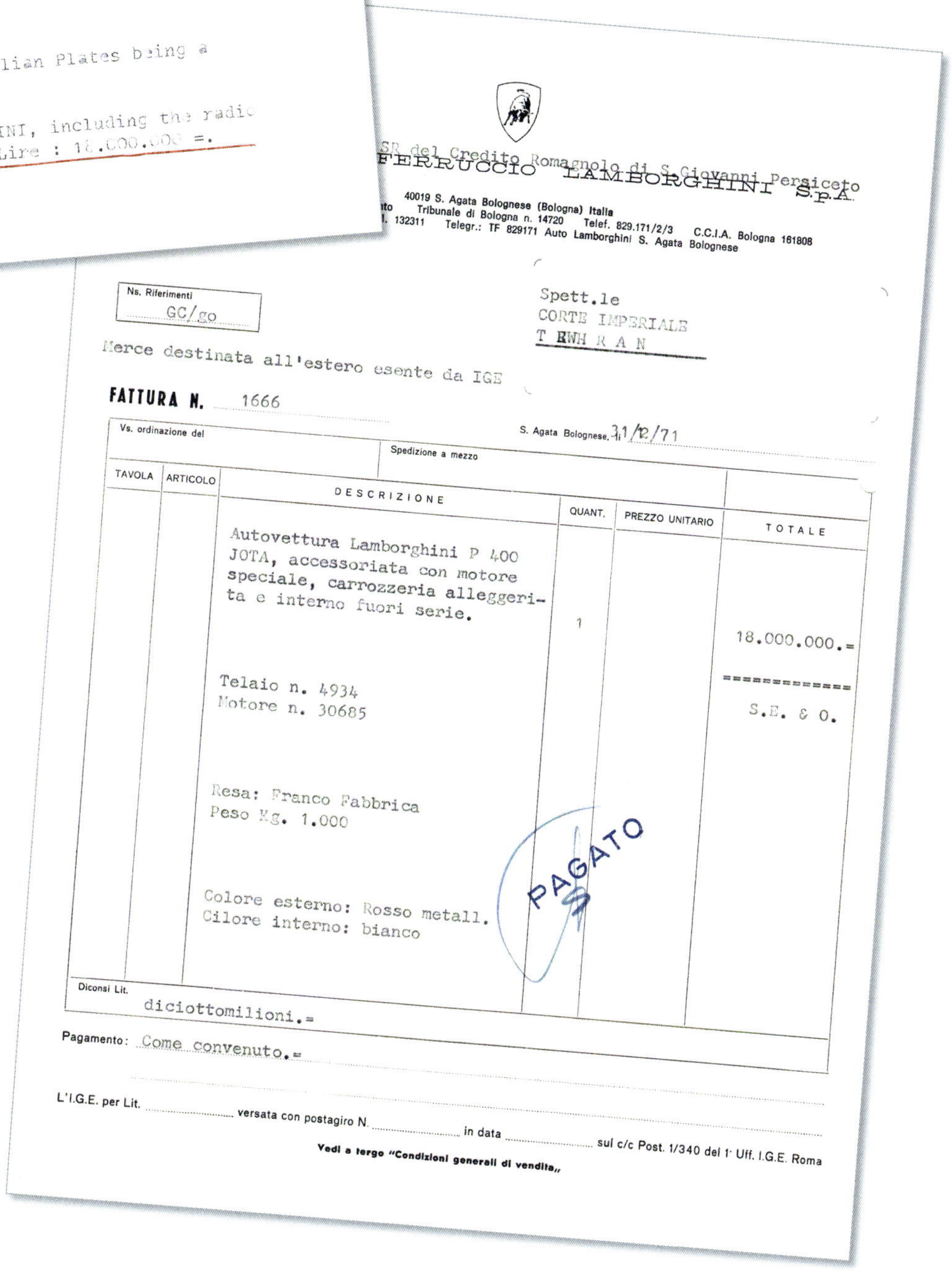

ABOVE: Pre-delivery invoice of the Italian Lamborghini dealer, S.E.A. Automobili, who processed the order for the Miura SVJ, chassis number 4934. Of note is the sentence stating that the SVJ cannot be registered with Italian license plates as it is a competition car. *(Saad Abad Palace)*

RIGHT: Lamborghini factory invoice dated December 31, 1971, for the Miura SVJ, discovered in the archives of the royal court. *(Saad Abad Palace)*

ABOVE: **The SVJ prior to delivery at the Lamborghini works in Sant'Agata, 1971.** *(Brooks Europe sales catalog, March 12, 1997)*

BELOW: **The Shah preparing to drive the SVJ for the first time immediately upon disembarking from his plane after arrival in Switzerland.** *(Keystone)*

of modifications carried over from the original Jota, the completed car was re-named by Lamborghini as the Miura SVJ (Super Veloce Jota) and, while not painted "candy apple red" as originally requested, was instead repainted a metallic burgundy over Bertone's dark blue original. Prior to shipping off the car to Switzerland, the newly christened SVJ underwent some 500-600 km of testing by Bob Wallace personally. The car was finally delivered, complete with specially-commissioned Pirelli studded snow tires, to the Shah in time for his visit to St. Moritz on January 30, 1972.

The car was driven and parked alongside the Shah's private plane after it had finished taxiing, whereupon the Shah promptly sat inside and drove to one of his many haunts in Switzerland. After the visit, the SVJ was subsequently flown to Tehran, and such was the Shah's fondness for this car, that lore has it that it would be flown via Iranian air force air transport for servicing at the factory. As can be seen in the following chapters, the SVJ was one of the few cars that the Shah kept

Chapter 23: The Lamborghini Miura and the Iranian Royal Family

until the end of his reign, most importantly, enjoying an enhanced status among his other cars as it was not kept at the royal garage but rather on hand at his residence in the Niavaran Palace for the occasional, usually late-night, high-speed spin through the streets of Tehran.

The delivery of the SVJ led the Shah to retire his P400 and a year later the car was sold to an intimate of the royal court and renowned car enthusiast, Mr. Firouz Saeid Ansari, on November 21, 1973 for a price of 100,000 Iranian Tomans approximately $14,285. Ansari was known to have driven the car enthusiastically and would even enter the Miura in local automotive races.

The Other Miuras of Iran

There were a number of other Miuras exported to Iran some of which have had their ownership mistakenly attributed to the Shah. These Miuras were:

Chassis number 3153: In April 1969, the royal garage received a second Miura P400, ordered by the Shah's twin sister Princess Ashraf Pahlavi. Painted blue, and having a mustard interior, according to the documents of the royal court it was delivered to Iran by an Italian by the name of Luigi Bosio. After a while, the car was sold to a successful businessman, Eskandar Aryeh, who was the owner of the Irana Tile Company. He changed the color of the Miura to yellow.

A copy of an official letter dated May 18, 1969 regarding the Miura's, chassis number 3153, clearance from customs. *(Saad Abad Palace)*

Fit for a King ~ The Royal Garage of the Shah of Iran

Chassis number 4479: In 1970, Lamborghini received another new order from Iran. It was placed by the Shah's eldest daughter, Shahnaz Pahlavi, the progeny of his marriage to his first wife, the Egyptian princess Fawzia. Shahnaz's Miura was an S version, with a white exterior, and blue interior. This car was delivered to the dealer G. G. Nations on April 7, 1970, and was then shipped to Iran. Apparently having inherited automotive enthusiast genes from her father, Princess Shahnaz was a car buff in her own right and over the years she is known to have owned, amongst others, a Rolls-Royce, Range Rover, Mercedes-Benz 280S, two Paykans, and the Miura. Princess Shahnaz kept her Miura for three years before it was sold in 1973 to Dr. Kaivon Saleh, a well-respected physician who later became a deputy minister of health.

When Dr. Saleh started using the car, he did not remove the royal garage registered license plates, and for many years, he could be spotted driving the car with royal plates. Dr. Saleh's home was located in one of Tehran's most luxurious districts, Fereshteh Street, and subsequently both his home and his Miura were featured in the January 1975 issue of *National Geographic* magazine. This particular Miura received further media

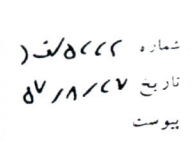

Chapter 23: The Lamborghini Miura and the Iranian Royal Family

coverage when the Iranian mass circulation women's magazine *Ettelaat Banovan* published a story about the car and its incredible price (by Iranian standards) of 800,000 Tomans ($1= 7 Tomans, circa 1976). With the start of the street protests in Iran, which eventually culminated in the 1979 revolution, Dr. Saleh apparently tried to secure the Miura's documentation from the royal garage, in order to be able to receive regular license plates, and hide the car's royal provenance, and its link to the royal court from the revolutionaries. These efforts failed and eventually the new revolutionary government seized his Miura.

اتومبیل ۸۰۰ هزار تومانی

رئیس یکی از بیمارستان های تهران ، علاقه عجیبی بخرید اتومبیل های مختلف دارد . او بتازگی یک اتومبیل ((لامبرکنی)) ((مدل میرا)) را که ۱۲ سیلندر است و ۳۲۰ کیلومتر در ساعت سرعت دارد ، خریداری کرده است . بهای این اتومبیل در ایران ۸۰۰ هزار تومان است . ساخت اتومبیل های لامبرکنی از سال ۱۹۶۸ آغاز شد و تا سال ۱۹۷۲ ، در حدود ۱۵۰ نمونه ، از این اتومبیل ها در دنیا عرضه گردید و بعد ، کار ساخت آن متوقف شد ٠ ، سه اتومبیل آن در ایران است ـ ۷ سال قبل ٠ اسکندر اریه یکی از این اتومبیل ها را خریداری نزده بود .

اطلاعات بانوان

OPPOSITE TOP LEFT: Shahnaz Pahlavi, the owner of the Miura S, chassis number 4479.

OPPOSITE TOP RIGHT: Dr. Kaivon Saleh and his Miura S as published in the January 1975 edition of *National Geographic* magazine. *(National Geographic, Jan. 1975)*

OPPOSITE BOTTOM RIGHT: The official letter of the royal court dated December 18, 1978, just two months prior to the revolution, requesting that the Miura receive license plates in the name of its owner, Dr. Kaivon Saleh. *(Borzou Sepasi)*

LEFT: The article printed in *Ettelaat Banovan* magazine on Dr. Saleh's Miura S titled, "The 800,000 Toman Car". *(Borzou Sepasi)*

371

The Miura S, chassis number 4479, at Dr. Kaivon Saleh's house. The original registration plate 22914/Tehran-D is visible on the car. **(Mid 1970s)** *(Mr. Mehrdad. Vahid)*

Chapter 23: The Lamborghini Miura and the Iranian Royal Family

Chassis number 4870: On July 21, 1971, a new Lamborghini Miura SV was delivered to Iran through the dealer S.E.A. Automobili, in Rome. The SV was an updated version of the Miura, with modifications such as a widened rear, which changed the overall width and stance of the car, to incorporate wider wheels and tires, as well as improved engine and suspension. The customer was Patrick Ali Pahlavi, the son of Alireza Pahlavi, the Shah's deceased younger brother. Prior to the birth of Crown Prince Reza, Patrick Ali, who was of mixed Iranian and French parentage, was heir presumptive to the throne after the Shah. After shipping the car to Tehran, unlike the common practice for other royals, Patrick Ali eschewed royal plates for his car and instead had the car registered with the regular license plates "56917/Tehran-D".

Patrick Ali apparently used this vehicle for only a few months, and in the summer of 1972, it was sold to a local automotive enthusiast and collector, Mr. Farshid Esfandiary, by Professor Yahya Adel, the head of Patrick Ali Pahlavi's office.

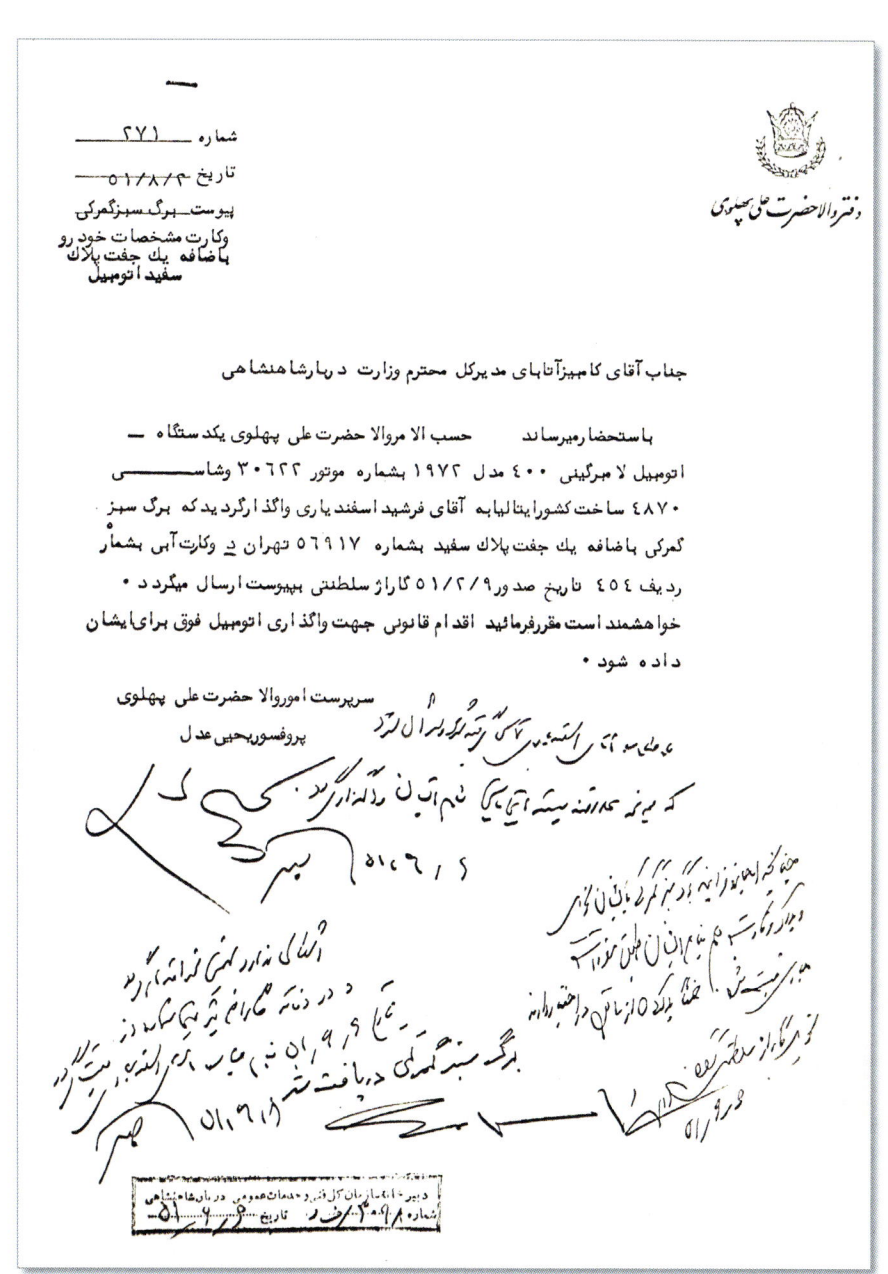

Sales document of Miura, chassis number 4870, from Patrick Ali Pahlavi to Mr. Farshid Esfandiary. *(Borzou Sepasi)*

Fit for a King ~ The Royal Garage of the Shah of Iran

Was the first customer Countach destined for the Shah?

During the course of the research for this book, a number of significant royal garage documents were uncovered. One of the more intriguing ones pertains to file number "26-6 Lamborghini Countach". The file contains a specification sheet for a Lamborghini LP500 GT with the word "Countach" written in hand above the name. In particular, the sheet lists the engine as being a 440bhp V12 with a capacity of 4971cc hence the "500" moniker identifying the vehicle as having a 5-liter engine. A top speed 300 km/h is also specified and a price, hand inscribed, stating "About 20,000,000 Lire".

The specifications would seem to be derived from the first Countach prototype which was also designated as the LP500 and debuted at the 1971 Geneva Motor Show. The proposed vehicle stands in contrast to the production Countach which had a 3929cc (3.9L) engine and was named LP400 accordingly.

TOP RIGHT: The official royal garage folder pertaining to the "Lamborghini Countach". *(Saad Abad Palace)*

ABOVE: The car which is generally recognized as being a Countach, chassis number 1120002, purportedly delivered to Iran. *(joesackey.com)*

OPPOSITE: Inside the folder there is only one sheet of paper that details the specifications of the vehicle named Lamborghini LP500 GT with the name "Countach" added by hand on the top of the page.

At the bottom of the specification sheet, there are handwritten instructions in Farsi, dated June 22, 1973 instructing a Mr. Rostampour to open a file on the car, in all probability as a prelude to purchase. Many pundits believe that the royal court went ahead with a Countach purchase for the Shah, the car being chassis number 1120002, the first production LP400 which made its debut at the 1974 Geneva Motor Show. Ostensibly, given the Shah's affinity for Lamborghini combined with his clear preference to receive the first production model of the cars he bought, lends credence that it could have been owned by the Shah despite there not being any evidence of ownership in the archives of the royal court. This probability could be further buoyed by the fact that the factory was actively courting the Shah as a customer for the soon-to-be unveiled car. At the time of the printing of this book, the author could not verify whether the car was indeed a part of the royal garage.

374

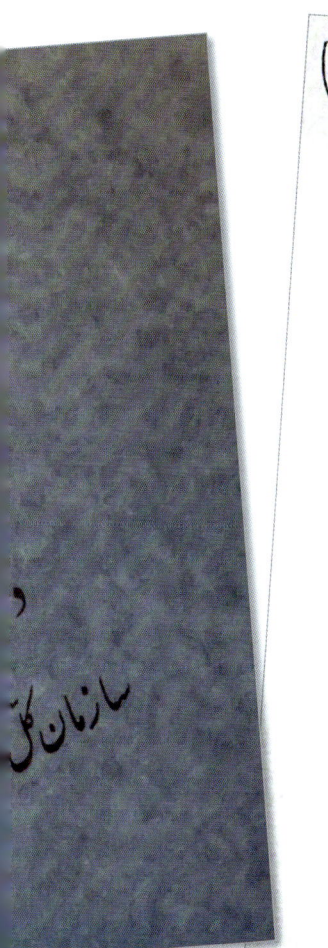

Chapter 23: The Lamborghini Miura and the Iranian Royal Family

"COUNTACH"

LAMBORGHINI LP 500 GT

Bodywork:
2 seater berlinetta (Bertone)
Spare wheel and battery located in front
Rear trunk capacity 175 liter
Retractable alogen headlights
Laminated windscreen - tinted glasses

Engine, transmission:
V-12 (60°) longitudinal middle engine rear located between gearbox and differential (LAMBORGHINI system)
Capacity 4971 cc (85x73 mm)
Compression ratio 10.5:1
Maximum power 440 bhp at 7400 rpm
Light-alloy castings
7 crankshaft bearings
2x2 overhead camshafts (chains)
Single ignition over 1 twin distributor
6 hor. twin carburetters Weber 42 DCOE
Pressurised cooling system over 2 cross-flow radiators and 2x2 electric fans
Lamborghini 5+R speed gearbox all syncromesh
Constant velocity final drive shafts
Electrical equipment 12 V - battery 56 Ah - alternator 770 W.

Chassis:
All-steel body of monocoque construction
Independent suspension front and rear consisting of double transverse wishbones with coil springs, telescopic dampers, and anti-roll bar front and rear.
Ventilated disc braking system with independent circuit to front and rear.
Cast magnesium rims: front 7Lx14", rear 9Lx14"
Low profile radial tires

Dimensions, weight:
Wheelbase 2450 mm
Track front 1500 mm
Track rear 1520 mm
Lenght 4010 mm
Width 1870 mm
Height 1030 mm
Curb weight 1130 kg

Performance:
Top speed 300 km/h

Price - About 20.000.000 Lit.

A Maserati Ghibli among the bevy of Lamborghinis

During the period when the Shah's affinity for Lamborghini was increasing, he still had an interest in Maseratis and, in-between the orders for his Lamborghinis (Miura P400 in 1968, Espada in 1969 and Miura SVJ in 1971), a Ghibli was ordered from Maserati in 1970.

The Ghibli, chassis number AM115.1394, was the Shah's first documented purchase from Maserati since the order for his "Scia di Iran" 5000 GT in 1959. This Ghibli, in addition to its royal provenance, also has an interesting back story, as when one of the Shah's nephews, Prince Kamyar Pahlavi completed his university studies, the Prince volunteered to undergo pilot training as part of compulsory military conscription in Iran. Unlike other royal peers who usually found ways to evade conscription, the fact that this nephew, Kamyar Pahlavi, voluntarily joined such a rigorous program greatly impressed the Shah.

Prince Kamyar, like the Shah, was said to have had an affinity for high-performance cars and, according to local lore, the Shah, in reward for the Prince's sense of duty, offered him a choice of "any car from the royal garage". Apparently, Prince Kamyar chose the Miura SVJ, to which the Shah is reported to have replied "any car but that one".[6] In substitution, Prince Kamyar is said to have settled on the Ghibli. Whether or not the reported exchange between uncle and nephew is fact or fiction, as per the document shown on page 377, on October 7, 1975, the royal court was instructed by the Shah to transfer ownership of the Ghibli to Prince Kamyar Pahlavi.

ABOVE: **The Shah's daughter, Farahnaz, posing beside her father's Maserati Ghibli, chassis number AM115.1394, circa early 1970s.** *(Borzou Sepasi)*

OPPOSITE: **The official letter transferring ownership of the Maserati Ghibli, chassis number AM115.1394, from the Shah to Prince Kamyar Pahlavi.** *(Saad Abad Palace)*

---

[6] *www.miuraregister.com: Chassis 4934, December 27, 2011*

Chapter 23: The Lamborghini Miura and the Iranian Royal Family

شماره ۸٤٧٢

تاریخ ۱۶/۷/۱۳٥٤

پیوست دفتروالاحضرت شاهپور عبدالرضا

خیلی فوری است
=========

جناب آقای کامبیز آتابای مدیر کل محترم دربار شاهنشاهی

خواهشمند است دستور فرمائید یک زوج پلاک برای اتومبیـــــــل مازراتی دو درب مرحمتی اعلیحضرت همایون شاهنشاه آریامهــــر بوالاحضرت کامیار پهلوی بدفتر والاحضرت تحویل نمایند.

رئیس دفتر والاحضرت ــ جمشید خبیر

377

CHAPTER 24

The Shah of Iran and
the Birth of the G-Class Mercedes

Chapter 24: The Shah of Iran and the Birth of the G-Class Mercedes

More than any other of his predecessors, the Shah lavished attention on his armed forces. The Shah was said to have had a Gaullist view of Iranian 'gloire' and independence. In other words, Iran's armed forces were to be a reflection of the Iran's standing in the world.[1]

As a result, issues of defense and the armed forces occupied the largest portion of the Shah's time, and the Shah was known to closely manage the Iranian Army, even "down to monitoring the appointment of middle ranking officers".[2]

By the late 1960s, the Shah had come to the belief that the Iranian Army needed a new multi-purpose vehicle, and, as such, it was no surprise that the Shah would take a direct role in the selection of the next generation of utility vehicle for the Iranian Armed forces.

Up until this point, the primary backbone of Iranian military utility vehicles were Jeeps, Land Rovers and some Russian and Romanian units. The Shah decided that something new was needed for the next generation. The Shah who was a fan of Mercedes-Benz products, believed that the combination of reliability and durability of both its passenger and commercial vehicles made this company the ideal candidate to supply the Army. The main impediment was simply that the German vehicle maker did not have any product in its portfolio to answer their needs. The Shah shared his idea with the Daimler-Benz management and the story of Mercedes-Benz G-Class began.

---

[1] *Robert Graham, "Iran: the Illusion of Power" St. Martin's Press, New York, 1979, p. 168*

[2] *ibid, p. 168*

ABOVE & FOLLOWING PAGE: **The Shah riding in the passenger seat of a Steyr-Puch Haflinger. (January 1969)** *(Borzou Sepasi)*

In January 1969, the Shah paid an official visit to Austria, where he visited the Steyr-Daimler-Puch works, which later signed an agreement with Daimler-Benz to cooperate in bringing the Shah's idea of a utility vehicle to fruition. During this visit, the Shah personally tested the Haflinger vehicle in the Mayr-Melnhof forests. The Haflinger was a small, lightweight, four-wheel-drive vehicle, powered by a 643cc horizontally-opposed flat twin, with the air-cooled engine mounted at the rear. This vehicle fell into the category of a light utility vehicle.

In 1971, the two companies commenced their collaboration, and, by 1972, they agreed on the design and performance targets required to fulfill the Shah's ideal of a utility vehicle. Mercedes-Benz engineers in Stuttgart were in charge of the design and testing, while the team in Graz at Steyr-Daimler-Puch developed the production plans. The first wooden model was presented to the Daimler-Benz management in 1973, with the first drivable prototype test in 1974 using a multitude of driving environments including German coalfields, the Sahara Desert, and the Arctic Circle. In 1975, construction commenced on a production facility in Graz, where the new cross-country vehicle would be initially assembled, almost entirely by hand.

In 1975, a delegation of top Iranian Army officers, including General Hassan Toufanian, the head of procurement for the Iranian armed forces, visited the Daimler-Benz factory to check upon the development of the Shah's pet project. On that visit, one of the first prototypes was shown to them, and, after testing the vehicle's capabilities, the Iranian team signed off on the new vehicle. It has been rumored that after this visit the Shah put in a pre-production order for 20,000 of the new G-Wagen for the Iranian armed forces.

Unfortunately, mass production of the G-Wagen (Gelandewagen) in Graz did not start until late 1979. The first batch of the G-Wagen were delivered to Tehran just before the collapse of the Shah's regime, and this batch was also the last, as with the advent of the revolution, one of the first acts of the revolutionary government was to cancel all of the Pahlavi regime military contracts.

Chapter 24: The Shah of Iran and the Birth of the G-Class Mercedes

ABOVE: Haflinger parade in front of the Shah. (January 1969) *(Borzou Sepasi)*

RIGHT & FOLLOWING PAGE TOP: A delegation of senior officers from the Imperial Iranian Army observing the capabilities of a long wheelbase G-Class prototype. (1975) *(Borzou Sepasi)*

Fit for a King ~ The Royal Garage of the Shah of Iran

Chapter 24: The Shah of Iran and the Birth of the G-Class Mercedes

OPPOSITE BOTTOM: The Iranian delegation also visited the Mercedes-Benz Museum. (1975) *(Borzou Sepasi)*

RIGHT: General Hassan Toufanian, Chief of Procurement of the Imperial Iranian Armed Forces sitting in a Mercedes-Benz C111 Concept. (1975) *(Borzou Sepasi)*

BELOW: Mercedes-Benz G-Model production started in 1979 but too late for the Shah to realize his dream. *(Borzou Sepasi)*

383

CHAPTER 25

The Shah's "Utilitarian" Tastes and the Cars of Summer

Chapter 25: The Shah's "Utilitarian" Tastes and the Cars of Summer

While the Shah and his family were known to own a broad gamut of ultra-luxury cars ranging from Miura supercars to a number of Rolls-Royces, they also owned simpler, more (relatively) mass-market forms of transportation.

By way of example, the royal court ordered several golf carts, for use in travel around the grounds of the Shah's primary summer and winter Palaces in the capital Tehran, namely the Saad Abad and Niavaran Palaces, as well as a number of retreats outside of Tehran such as Kish Island in the Persian Gulf and Nowshahr near the Caspian Sea where the Shah also kept Palaces.

Of the carts, one stands out, a Westinghouse-Marketeer 436. Ordered in 1968 and delivered to the Niavaran Palace the same year, it would seem that there was a particular affinity for this cart as the royal family used this vehicle not only at their primary residential Palaces in Tehran, but also when traveling to other Palaces across Iran and would be photographed extensively in it.

The fact that the Shah of Iran was a bona fide automotive enthusiast was not lost on many of the world's automotive manufacturers, whether large or small. It soon became common practice for many of these companies to send pictures and documentation of their latest models and special editions to their Iranian Embassies with the hope that they would be passed on to the Shah and catch his eye. One of the proposals that was submitted to an Embassy and resulted in an order was for a Fiat Shellette. The Shellette was designed by Michelotti, on a Fiat 850 chassis, essentially for beach use. The Shah's car, a 1968 model with chassis number 100GB 1226009 was ordered with a pink exterior and wicker seats and dashboard. The Shellette was produced in extremely low volume, with just 80 being produced.

One of the Shah's favored retreats was his Palace at Nowshahr, located on the shores of the Caspian Sea in northern Iran. The Shah and his family would visit this Palace every summer and when enjoying the beach, they would primarily use a wooden beach house which was located on the edge of the seashore. This small building had one bedroom, a sitting room where the Shah met his guests, a kitchen and a covered balcony. During the day, the royal family and their guests prepared for swims and water skiing jaunting back to the cabana for a change of clothes and lunch and, at night, watched movies at this building. Next to the cabana were accommodations for

A widely-circulated photograph of the Shah and his family in their Westinghouse-Marketeer 436 golf cart. (Early 1970s) *(Saad Abad Palace)*

386

security guards and a storage area for swimming gear. While it was far from the opulence of the nearby Palace, the Shah and his family are believed to have greatly enjoyed their stays there. During their visits, the Shah's children would receive water skiing and other aquatic sport lessons from General Mohammad Amir Khatami, the Commander of the Imperial Iranian Air Force. General Khatami was also related to the Shah by virtue of his marriage to Princess Fatemeh Pahlavi, the half-sister of the Shah.

It was during these carefree summer holidays that the Shah would be seen driving the Fiat 850 Shellette along the coast on an almost daily basis, only in later years switching to a more sporting dune buggy, a Volkswagen-powered EMPI Imp.

THESE TWO PAGES: **The Pahlavi royal family in Nowshahr with their Fiat 850 Shellette, chassis number 100GB 1226009, bodied by Michelotti. (Early 1970s)** *(Niavaran Palace)*

Fit for a King ~ The Royal Garage of the Shah of Iran

LEFT: Queen Farah in the wet grounds of the Nowshahr Palace near the Fiat 850 Shellette. (Early 1970s)
(Borzou Sepasi)

BELOW: Members of the royal family taking a ride in the grounds of the Niavaran Palace with a Westinghouse-Marketeer 436 and Cushman golf cart. (1970s)
(Niavaran Palace)

OPPOSITE TOP & BOTTOM LEFT: The Shah, Queen Farah and their children at the Nowshahr Palace riding side by side with their Westinghouse-Marketeer 436 golf cart and a Volkswagen EMPI Imp dune buggy. (Early 1970s)
(Niavaran Palace)

OPPOSITE BOTTOM RIGHT: The Crown Prince at the wheel of the Westinghouse-Marketeer 436 in the grounds of the Nowshahr Palace. (Early 1970s) *(Saad Abad Palace)*

Chapter 25: The Shah's "Utilitarian" Tastes and the Cars of Summer

CHAPTER 26

An Aston Martin for Summer Fun

Chapter 26: An Aston Martin for Summer Fun

In light of the Shah's proclivity for high-performance automotive exotica, it is not surprising that the Shah's carefree summer days at his Palace at the Caspian Sea were not just limited to the Fiat Shellette and Dune Buggies. The Shah also kept on hand at the Nowshahr Palace an Aston Martin V8, which the former staff of the royal garage refer to as the Shah's "summer car".[1]

The Shah's Aston Martin V8 was delivered to the royal garage on June 18, 1973, and subsequently transported to the Nowshahr Palace. This particular model was not just any model, but the first model built for export, in line with the Shah's preference of receiving the first in series of most of the new cars that he would order. It was in Tudor green and was complemented by cream Connolly hide upholstery and matching Wilton carpets.[2] The Shah's Aston Martin V8 was the third to be built, having chassis number V8/11004/LCA. The V8's predecessors the first and second versions on chassis numbers 11002 and 11003 had been development mules that were not delivered to the public.

Prior to taking delivery of this V8, a year earlier in 1972, the Shah had purchased an Aston Martin DBS, chassis number DBS/5503/LC. However, the six-cylinder engine was not to the Shah's liking and he requested

---

[1] *Brooks Europe Auction Catalog (March 12, 1997)*

[2] *ibid*

Queen Farah with the former King of Greece, Constantine II and his wife Anne-Marie at Nowshahr Airport. Pictured is the Shah's Lockheed Jetstar 8, construction number 5137 and registered EP-VRP. (1973) *(Niavaran Palace)*

Fit for a King ~ The Royal Garage of the Shah of Iran

Chapter 26: An Aston Martin for Summer Fun

that the officers of the royal court replace the car with an Aston Martin V8. Accordingly, on July 12, 1972, the DBS was returned to the factory via an Imperial Iranian Air Force Lockheed C-130 Hercules. For this journey, it was affixed with the transit registration plates TEH-6440. The plane landed at Lyneham Airport and the car was sent to the Iranian Embassy in London where it was then sold back to the Aston Martin factory. As the DBS was now considered a used car, albeit one with very low mileage, the factory purchased the car back at a price of £2650 but only after deducting £850 for having to return the left-hand drive car back to right-hand drive and a further deduction of £300 for taxes. Ultimately, the Aston Martin factory issued a credit note for £1500 to the royal court against the purchase price of the new Aston Martin V8, which, was ultimately sold to the Shah for a final price of £6781.

The Shah socialized with a number of his peers, including former King Constantine II of Greece, King Hussein of Jordan and Juan Carlos of Spain. Usually accompanied by their families, all three gentlemen traveled to Iran a number of times and would meet with the Shah and his family. King Hussein in particular shared a mutual affinity with the Shah for high-powered supercars and in 1974 gifted the Shah two Ferraris, both in rare Verde Pino Metallizzato. The first Ferrari was a Gran Turismo 365 GT4 2+2, chassis number 18263, and the second was a mid-mounted 365 GT4/BB, chassis number 18181. Both cars were originally delivered to King Hussein in Amman, Jordan before being transferred by plane for delivery to the Shah in Tehran.

OPPOSITE TOP: **The Shah and the former King of Greece, Constantine II in a Riva 2000. (1973)** *(Niavaran Palace)*

OPPOSITE BOTTOM: **In Nowshahr, the Shah at the wheel of his 1970 Rolls-Royce Corniche, chassis number DRX9983, along with Queen Farah and their guests, Constantine II the former King of Greece and his wife, Anne-Marie of Denmark. (1973)** *(Niavaran Palace)*

BELOW (BOTH): **A fellow car buff, King Hussein of Jordan and the Shah were known to exchange the latest supercars. Pictured are the Ferrari 365 GT4/BB, chassis number 18181, (left) and Ferrari 365 GT4 2+2, chassis number 18263 (right), both given by King Hussein to the Shah.** *(Borzou Sepasi and Brooks Europe)*

CHAPTER 27

The Shah's affinity for the Range Rover

Chapter 27: The Shah's affinity for the Range Rover

At that time, the import duty into Iran on new vehicles was 350 percent, which made imports economically impractical. However, the Shah was impressed by the Range Rover that he decided he wanted fifty for his Pahlavi Foundation. He thus reduced, for a period of six months only, the import duty to fifty percent, specifically for off-road vehicles.
  Anthony Rosen
  An UnOrdinary Life, 2007

When the British Leyland Company launched its Range Rover in 1970, it quickly gained favor with the Iranian royal family and over ten were initially ordered directly by the royal court. These vehicles were subsequently used by the Queen, the Crown Prince and even the Shah's eldest daughter from his first marriage, Princess Shahnaz. The Shah and Princess Shahnaz were frequently at odds over her lifestyle choices and, in particular, his pique at her second marriage to a gentleman the Shah viewed as being a "hippy". According to the diaries of Asadollah Alam, the Minister of the royal court and one of Shah's closest confidantes, "…Just as I was about to take my leave, HIM (His Imperial Majesty) asked who owned the magnificent Range Rover he'd seen parked in front of the Palace. I replied that it belonged to Princess Shahnaz who was there to go skiing with HMQ (Her Majesty the Queen). 'Astounding', he said in an angry tone. 'That husband of hers doesn't stint on all the luxuries, for all his hippy pretensions. A Rolls and a Lamborghini to swan about town in, and now a Range Rover to go skiing'…[1]

---

[1] Asadollah Alam, "The Shah and I", I.B. Tauris and Co. Ltd., 2008, p. 347

ABOVE & FOLLOWING PAGE, TOP: **The above photographs show the Shah and his Arctic White Range Rover during a "tree planting day" ceremony. (1976)** *(Borzou Sepasi)*

The Shah who preferred that his cars stand out from others, was known to have ordered a number of Range Rovers for his personal use, usually fully optioned by London-based coachbuilders, Wood & Pickett Ltd, choosing most of the options available from their catalog. His preferred option was air conditioning and bucket seats. In most of the official letters between the royal court and the Leyland Company, probably in reference to the relatively anemic 130 hp of the Range Rover's V8, this sentence was repeated: "please provide the most powerful engine available".

OPPOSITE: The Shah is driving one of his Range Rovers in St. Moritz Switzerland. (Early 1970s) *(Borzou Sepasi)*

OVERLEAF, LEFT: Crown Prince Reza Pahlavi in front of his own separate Palace in the Niavaran Palace Complex. His Range Rover and Innocenti Mini are pictured behind him. (Mid 1970s) *(Niavaran Palace)*

OVERLEAF, RIGHT: Queen Farah posing next to her Range Rover. (Mid 1970s) *(Niavaran Palace)*

Chapter 27: The Shah's affinity for the Range Rover

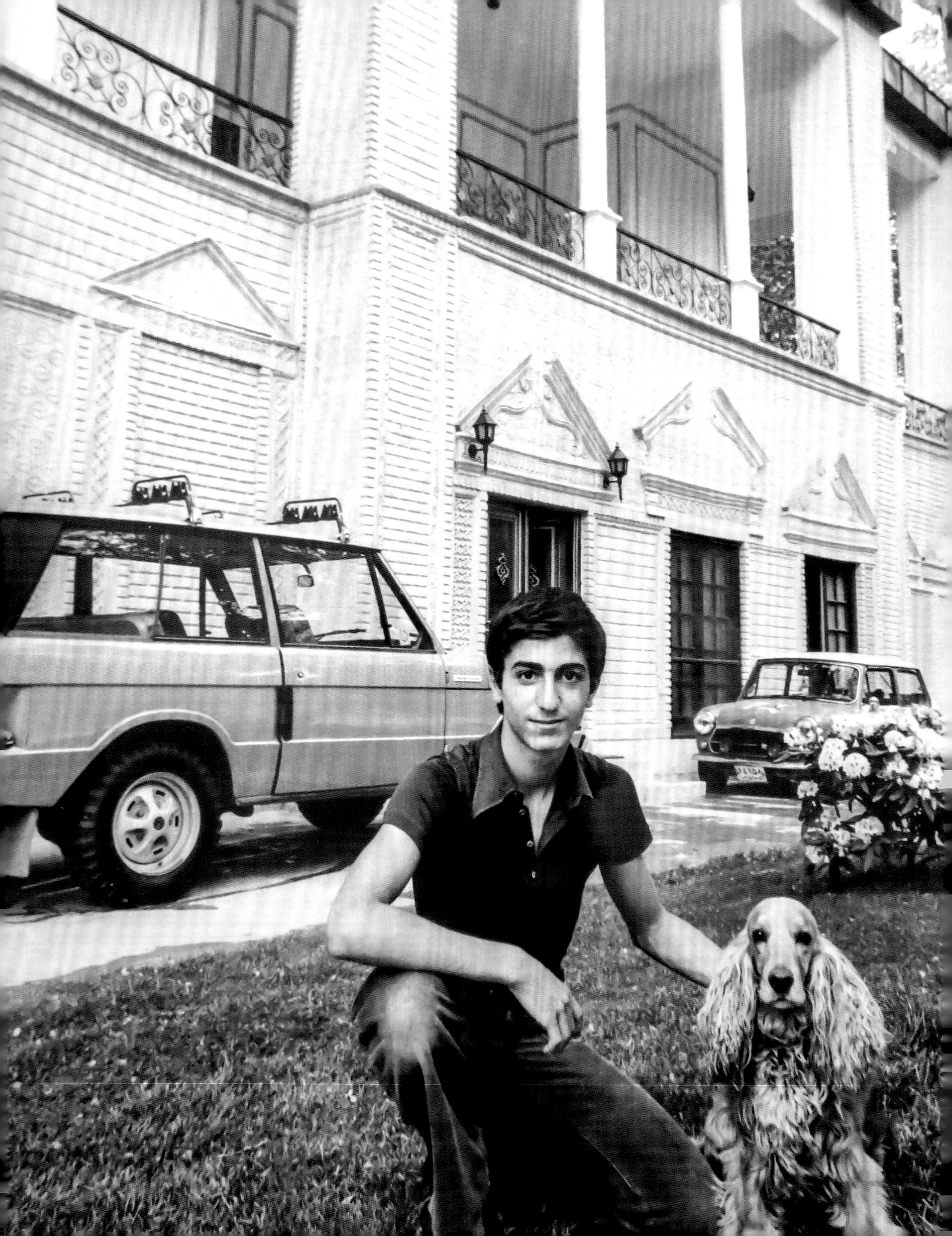

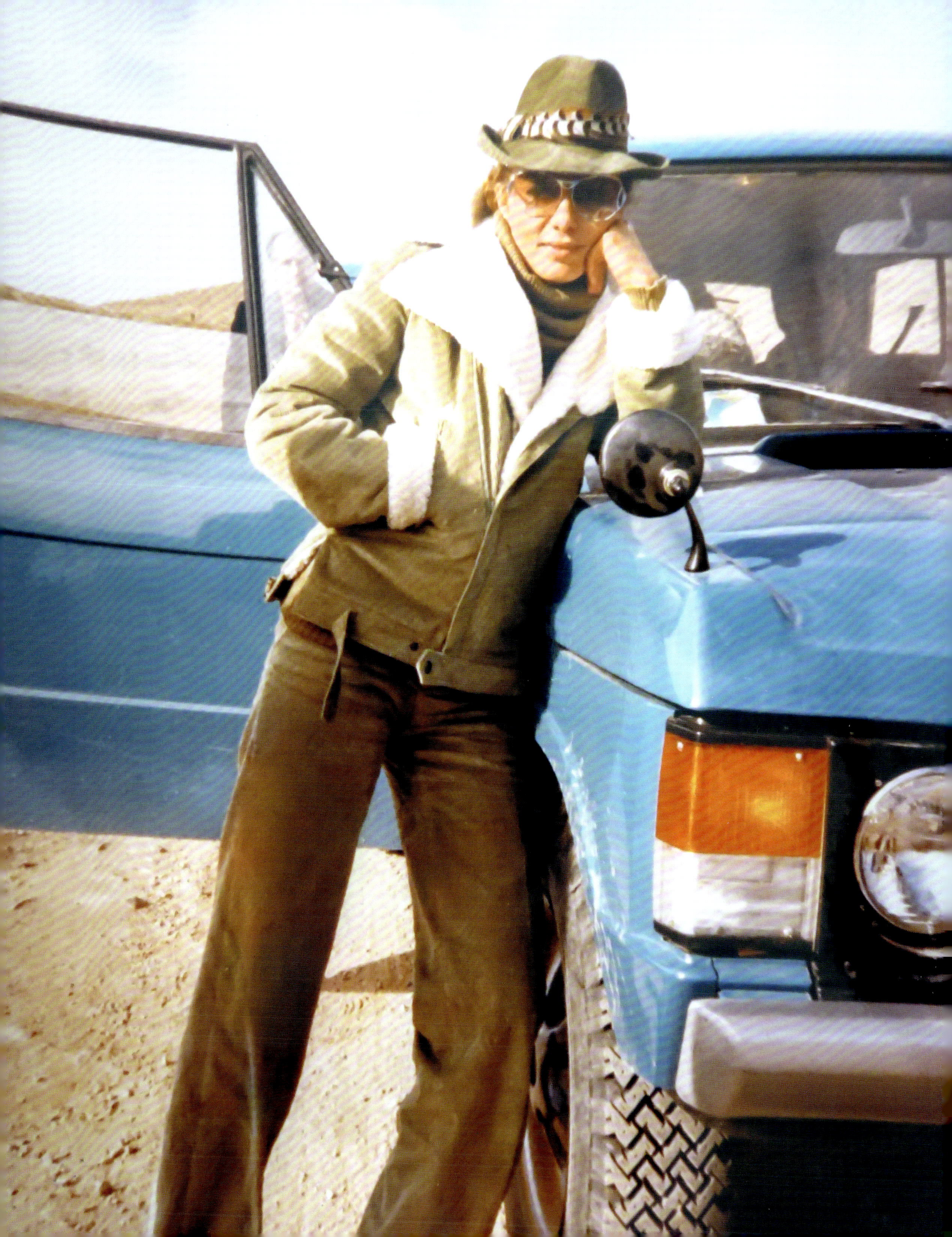

CHAPTER 28

Celebrating 2,500 Years of the Persian Empire

Chapter 28: Celebrating 2,500 Years of the Persian Empire

Traditionally an agrarian society, by the end of the 1960s Iran had experienced momentous industrialization and economic modernization. In order to draw the world's attention to this transformation, the Shah decided to hold a commemoration to not only celebrate the 2,500th year of the founding of the Persian Empire but also the founding of the Imperial State of Iran by Cyrus the Great. The objective of the event was to not only demonstrate Iran's ancient civilization and history, but to also showcase the country's contemporary advances.

For this celebration, the Shah chose the ancient ruins of Persepolis, the ceremonial capital of the Achaemenid Empire, also known as the First Persian Empire, founded by Cyrus the Great.

Amir Asadollah Alam, one of the closest confidantes of the Shah, a former Prime Minister and the Minister

THIS PAGE: Ceremony at the Tomb of Cyrus the Great.

401

of the royal court, known as the Shah's "go-to man" was assigned the monumental task of organizing the ceremony. Alam's ministry, which carried out all of the affairs of the royal court, whether it be the supervision of the ordering and timely delivery of the Lamborghini Miura SVJ to overseeing the day to day affairs of the Palaces, prepared to organize an event on a scale unheard of in the 20th century.

BELOW LEFT: **Parade at Persepolis.** *(Saad Abad Palace)*

BELOW RIGHT: **The President of the Soviet Union and Madame Podgorny welcomed by the Shah and Queen Farah next to the Shah's Rolls-Royce Phantom IV, chassis number 4CS6.** *("Celebration at Persepolis" book)*

BOTTOM: **The Shah in his new Rolls-Royce Phantom V State Landaulette, chassis number 5LVF29, parked in front of the Tent City.** *("Celebration at Persepolis" book)*

Chapter 28: Celebrating 2,500 Years of the Persian Empire

To ensure the success of the celebration, all of the activities ultimately came under the direct supervision of Queen Farah Pahlavi who had final say on all matters.

The challenge faced by the organization committee was monumental. The nearest city, Shiraz, had no airport which was capable of handling large commercial aircraft resulting in the expenditure of tens of millions of US dollars to upgrade the airport.[1] Furthermore, Shiraz only had one luxury hotel which was woefully inadequate for the hundreds of world leaders and dignitaries who were to converge for the celebrations. As a result, a city of tents was erected near the ruins of Persepolis with the project outsourced to Jansen AG, the world's most expensive tent maker. The tents that Jansen designed were not only fireproof and air-conditioned but could also withstand winds of up to 100kph.[2] Each tent had its own unique interior; a living room, two bedrooms and two bathrooms.

Waiters were brought in from Europe, some of them unsurprisingly from the hotel of the Shah's winter retreat of St. Moritz with food flown in from Maxim's of Paris. Guests included twenty kings, five queens, twenty-one princes, sixteen Presidents and sixty-nine Prime Ministers. The diversity of guests varied from the Chairman of the Presidium of the Soviet Union, the Vice President of the United States to the Emperor of Ethiopia.

All in all, the British Embassy in Iran described the event as "a sumptuous celebration… of daring enterprise" a "good idea but marred by the element of excess".[3] In 1980, Guinness World Records chose the ceremony as the most extravagant party on record.

While the celebration had both its detractors and proponents, what stood out was the eclectic mix of cars used during the ceremonies. While some pundits have stated that over "two hundred and fifty Mercedes-Benz bulletproof limousines were bought to ferry the heads of state"[4] the only evidence of cars imported specifically for the ceremony point to some sixty Mercedes-Benz 300SELs, without armor or bullet proofing, all painted

The Shah's Rolls-Royce Silver Cloud III Mulliner Park Ward Drophead Coupe, chassis number LCSC83C, at the Persepolis celebrations. *("Celebration at Persepolis" book)*

---

[1] *Abbas Milani, "The Shah," Palgrave Macmillan, New York, 2011, p. 122*

[2] *ibid, p. 323*

[3] *ibid, p. 325*

[4] *ibid, p. 323*

403

in the colors of the cars of the royal court, Bordeaux. Their primary use was for the transfer of the guests from Shiraz Airport to the venue.

The Shah himself would travel during the ceremonies in his Rolls-Royce Phantom V State Landaulette, chassis number 5LVF29, usually followed by a Chrysler Convertible with bodyguards in tow. It was not the only Rolls-Royce at the ceremony – several other Rolls-Royces of the royal garage were also pressed into service including the Shah's cherished Phantom IV, chassis number 4CS6, a Silver Cloud II Convertible, chassis number LSWC418, the Shah's other Phantom V, chassis number 5LAS39, and the Silver Cloud III with Mulliner Park Ward Drophead Coupe bodywork, chassis number LCSC83C. Almost all of the cars used for the ceremony were in the royal court shade of Bordeaux, and even the Shah's Silver Cloud II Convertible, chassis number LSWC418, was repainted from white to Bordeaux for use in the ceremony. Accompanying the sixty 300SELs imported specifically for the ceremonies, were also a number of Mercedes-Benz 600s of the royal garage which were used to ferry the more important guests to the ceremonies. Among these were the two rare Mercedes-Benz 600 Presidential Landaulets, chassis numbers 100.015.12.001207 and 100.015.12.001370, of the royal court.

The grand finale of the ceremony was marked by the transfer of the guests to Tehran by chartered Iran Air planes. Upon arrival to Tehran, the guests were accommodated at the Tehran Royal Hilton Hotel. In Tehran they partook in the opening ceremony of the Shahyad (Memorial of the Shah) monument. This monument had been designed by a young budding Iranian architect, Mr. Hussein Amanat who was chosen after a nationwide contest. It was a unique combination of Islamic and pre-Islamic era architecture and quickly emerged as a national symbol of Iran.

Mercedes-Benz 600 Pullman pictured in front of the Persepolis tent city. *(Borzou Sepasi)*

Chapter 28: Celebrating 2,500 Years of the Persian Empire

The Shah of Iran shaking hands with Abdul Halim of Malaysia in front of the Shah's Mercedes-Benz 600 Presidential Landaulet, chassis number 100.015.12.001207. *(Borzou Sepasi)*

As the ceremony was to showcase not only Iran's ancient civilization and history but to also highlight Iran's contemporary advances, especially as a rapidly industrializing country, a microcosm of these advances can be witnessed in the pictures of the Rolls-Royces and Mercedes-Benzes used in the ceremony. If one looks closely, in the background of all of these pictures, shadowing the ultra-luxurious vehicles pressed into service for the ceremony, one particular make of car stands out, the AMC Rambler. With Iran's nascent automotive industry growing, in 1967, Iran Jeep Company signed a contract with the American Motors Company to assemble the AMC Rambler American under a CKD (Complete Knock Down) license agreement, a significant technological leap from its initial assembly activity of producing Jeeps under the license of Willys. The progression from the assembly of Jeeps to passenger cars reflected the growing industrial maturity of the Iranian automotive industry. The Iranian version of the Rambler was offered in two separate trim levels, the Aria, which was a full option version, including an automatic transmission and the Shahin which, with a manual transmission was the base model. Both cars were equipped with a 232 cu. in (3.8-liter) in-line six-cylinder engine and, unique for the Iranian market, both were available with air conditioning.

The launch, and subsequent success of the Rambler in Iran reflected the fact that the target market, the upper and middle classes of Iran had grown prosperous during this period of the Shah's reign.[5] As Iran's economic prosperity continued to increase, in 1972, Jeep Iran formed a joint venture with General Motors and, in 1974, with the formation of General Motors Iran, 46% owned by General Motors, the Rambler was phased out first, in favor of the Opel Rekord (named locally as the Chevrolet Iran) which was then subsequently replaced by the production launch of the Chevrolet Nova, Buick Skylark and, most notably, the Cadillac Seville.

---

[5] *Jim Mann, "Beijing Jeep", Touchstone Books, New York, 1989, p. 37*

Chapter 28: Celebrating 2,500 Years of the Persian Empire

The opening ceremony of the Shahyad Monument in Tehran. *(irdc.ir)*

CHAPTER 29

The Shah tries a
1971 Mercedes-Benz 300SEL 6.3

On May 10, 1971 the Shah ordered what was known in its day as the fastest saloon car in the world, the Mercedes-Benz 300SEL 6.3. Through the local Mercedes dealer Merrikh Co., the Mercedes-Benz passenger car agent and distributor in Tehran, the Shah ordered a fully-optioned car with sunroof and sand beige metallic paint, color code number 467. Upon its completion, the car, chassis number 109.018.12.005924,

بسوی مدرسه ــ شاهنشاه، والاحضرت ولیعهد و والاحضرت فرحناز را برای رفتن به مدرسه همراهی میفرمایند.

LEFT: The October 30, 1974 edition of the mass circulation daily newspaper *Kayhan* published an article about the royal family. In the picture, the Shah is about to drive his children, Crown Prince Reza and Princess Farahnaz, to school with his Mercedes-Benz 300SEL 6.3, chassis number 109.018.12.005924.

ABOVE (ALL): Some outtakes from a television documentary made by the French "Actuel 2" television channel. In the documentary the Shah and Queen are seen getting in the 300SEL 6.3, in front of the steps of the Saad Abad Palace. (1974)

was shipped to Iran by Baumann & Co and delivered to Merrikh's warehouse in Tehran's business district, Saadi Street. From there, the car was taken to the royal garage and registered, but never had its registration plate affixed as the Shah disliked his cars having license plates. For a number of years, the car was driven personally by the Shah and three years after its delivery, the car was featured prominently in a 1974 television documentary made by the French "Actuel 2" channel focusing on the daily life of the Shah, his wife and their children. In one scene, the royal couple are shown to be descending the stairs at the Saad Abad Palace and entering the 300SEL 6.3 with the Shah behind the wheel and Queen Farah alongside. They are then filmed driving the Mercedes in the heavy morning traffic of Tehran, to the Niavaran Palace.

Queen Farah posing next to the Shah's 300SEL 6.3 in Nowshahr. (Early 1970s) *(Borzou Sepasi)*

The Royal 450SLC

It is rare to see the Shah pictured driving his cars. However, as with the 6.3, another car which has shown up in pictures more frequently than others is the Mercedes-Benz 450SLC pictured on the following page. As can be seen from the frozen frame of a promotional film clip featuring the daily routine of the Shah, it is this "daily driver" 450SLC which is parked by the entrance of the Niavaran Palace, ready to be driven by the Shah for his short trek to the office located on the Palace grounds. Other photographs are also available with the Shah behind the wheel of this very car. Unfortunately, as of the date of publication, the particulars of this car have not been found in the documents of the royal court.

Chapter 29: The Shah tries a 1971 Mercedes-Benz 300SEL 6.3

ABOVE: The Shah at the wheel of his Mercedes-Benz 450SLC. *(Borzou Sepasi)*

RIGHT: In 1978, a documentary was made about the daily routine of the Shah and the Queen. In one sequence, the Shah is filmed coming out of the Niavaran Palace to go to his office. He then signals that he wishes to walk to his office instead of taking the 450SLC and a staff member then drives the car presumably back to the Palace garage. (1978)

A new royal plane for the Shah

In 1974, the Shah took delivery of a Boeing 727 to be used for his trips around the world. It was first delivered by Boeing to ANA (All Nippon Airways) in 1967 with serial number 19577, registered JA8321. It was later transferred to the Ford Motor Company in August 1972 and re-registered as N329K, before finally being bought in June, 1974 by the Imperial Iranian Air Force (IIAF) and being retrofitted as a luxury transport for the Shah.

Following delivery to the IIAF, the plane once again received a new registration number "EP-MRP", signifying the use by Mohammad Reza Pahlavi and was named Shahbaz.

The Shah's Boeing 727 named Shahbaz, registered EP-MRP. (January 1977) *(Ron Monroe)*

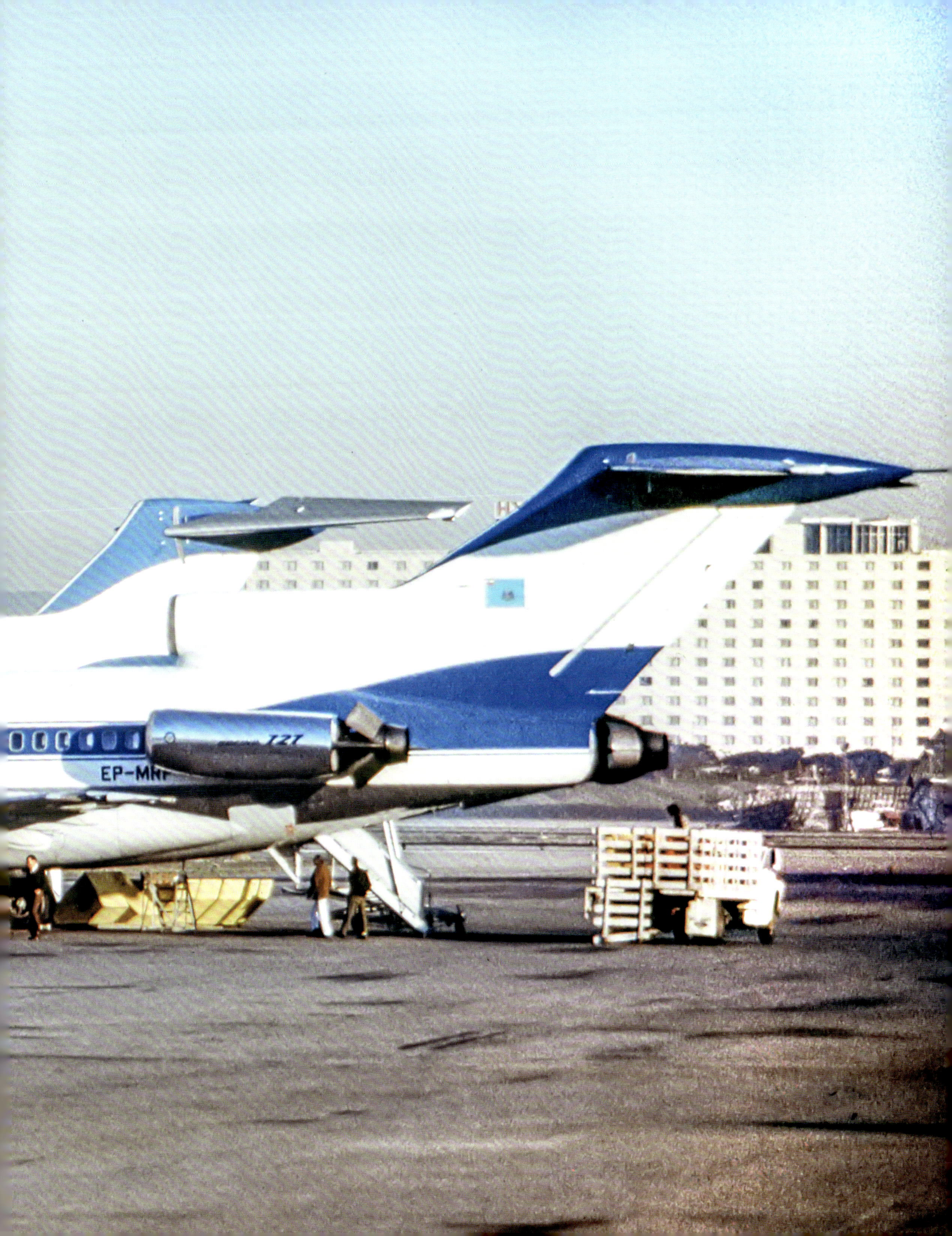
727
EP-MRF

CHAPTER 30

The Crown Prince receives a Mini Benz

Chapter 30: The Crown Prince receives a Mini Benz

Reminiscent of the 1930s with the world on the brink of World War II, when Germany made a major effort to curry favor with the Crown Prince Mohammad Reza with the gift of a Mercedes-Benz 500K Autobahnkurier, in 1971, with the world again on the brink of economic upheaval from rapidly increasing oil prices, the German government once again attempted to curry favor with the Pahlavi dynasty and an emergent Iran by bequeathing Crown Prince Reza with a specially-made German "hot rod".

As a prelude, on October 17, 1971, the Crown Prince received a scale model of a car protected by a Plexiglas display case, from an emissary of the German government, accompanied by an official letter from German Chancellor, Willy Brandt. This gift was a scale model of a hand-built car which was under assembly as a joint project between Mercedes-Benz, Porsche and Volkswagen, and was to be presented as a special birthday gift from the German government to the Crown Prince. No doubt taking a cue from the Shah's penchant for unique and high-performance vehicles, it is assumed that as the twelve-year-old Crown Prince began to mature into a young man, the German government banked on the prospect that the Shah's automotive interests would pass on to the Crown Prince as well.

During this period, as a means to prepare him for his future duties, the Crown Prince lived separately from his parents in his own Palace in the grounds of the Niavaran Palace, close by to his parent's residence. It was a relatively small Palace, which was in the past used by Ahmad Shah Qajar as a summer residence. Reza displayed the new model car prominently in his library on the second floor of his Palace and awaited excitedly for the real car to arrive.

The young Crown Prince's anticipation should have been of no surprise. The car in question, a single seat, open cockpit, mid-engine car was designed to look like the original C-111 Mercedes, with an orange body and having the three emblems of Mercedes-Benz, Porsche and VW

ABOVE & FOLLOWING PAGE: Scale model of the Mercedes-Porsche-VW car delivered to the Crown Prince in October 1971. *(Borzou Sepasi)*

415

affixed on the left pillar. The car was unique in other ways as well. According to the unpublished memoirs of Wolfgang Berger, former Project Engineer at Porsche, who carried out the bulk of the work on the project, the car was to have two separate keys, one in gold, obviously with the speed-loving Shah of Iran in mind, which allowed rapid acceleration and a top speed of 180 km/h and the other, in silver, no doubt for the safety of the twelve-year-old Crown Prince, which effectively served as a speed limiter to approximately 40 km/h. With the second key, the position of the pedals would automatically adjust for driving by the young Crown Prince.[1]

Despite carrying Mercedes and Volkswagen insignia as well, Porsche was the project manager and offered Berger the job as the lead engineer. According to Berger, after accepting the project (after some hesitation), he proceeded, on what he states to have been a tight budget causing him to have to "do a lot of things myself, at times I even had to spend out of my own pocket".[2]

As a first step, Berger proceeded to purchase a Formula V vehicle, without a motor, from Rutesheimer

---

[1] *Wolfgang Berger, "Personal Memories of Wolfgang Berger – Former Project Engineer of Porsche, Unpublished Memoirs"*

[2] *ibid*

Chapter 30: The Crown Prince receives a Mini Benz

Rennwagenbauer Fuchs. A 1679cc, 80bhp Volkswagen four-cylinder, air-cooled engine was mounted and the final package, weighing in at barely 560kg served to showcase the strengths and engineering prowess of the three manufacturers.[3]

Particular emphasis was placed on safety. In this regard, according to Berger, the front of the body was reinforced with a deformable impact absorber for front crash protection, and according to the technical literature accompanying the car, it had a "rigid structure protecting the driver from exterior forces of impact".[4] The car also had side and roll-over protection.

According to Berger, "we undertook extensive testing to make sure that the car functioned correctly" and that the hodgepodge of parts fused together from the parts bin of the three companies all functioned smoothly together on the Formula V chassis. Once the project was done, Mercedes had a mechanic trained to service the vehicle once it entered into the royal garage.[5]

With Berger's job done, on August 29, 1972, the German Ambassador in Tehran arrived at the Saad Abad Palace to personally hand over the keys to this very special gift. Crown Prince Reza and some members of the royal court were on hand to receive and welcome the Ambassador.

The Ambassador proceeded to personally hand over the two keys of the car, and a technician, presumably the same technician from Mercedes trained to service the car, demonstrated the workings of the car to the Crown Prince. It would seem that the German government's gamble to appeal to two generations of the crown paid off, as, with his interest piqued, the Shah himself emerged from the Palace, took a detailed look at the car, and then proceeded to drive it himself for a short distance.

After receiving the car, the Crown Prince began using it in the grounds of both the Saad Abad and Niavaran Palaces. After some months, the Shah requested the mechanics of the royal garage to add two indicator lights to the car, as he believed that it would be useful for the Crown Prince to better his driving skills. As a result, VW turn indicators were subsequently installed on the front fenders of the car.

The fact that three leading German auto makers would cooperate together on such a joint project should come as no surprise. By the mid-1970s, a rapidly developing Iran had emerged as one of their fastest growing markets as exemplified by the fact that the first export of a complete knock down truck assembly by Mercedes had been to Iran in 1966, whilst Volkswagen had been doing a brisk business having aligned itself with one of Iran's most successful businessmen Habibollah Sabet Pasal. Even Porsche had found a relatively small, but growing market with Iran's elite including the Shah. By the late 1970s Iran had emerged as one of BMW's largest, if not the largest export market.

---

[3] *1972 Mercedes-Porsche-VW User Manual*

[4] *Wolfgang Berger, "Personal Memories of Wolfgang Berger – Former Project Engineer of Porsche, Unpublished Memoirs"*

[5] *ibid*

ABOVE: **The Mercedes-Porsche-VW being tested by its Project Manager Wolfgang Berger prior to delivery to Iran.** *(Wolfgang Berger)*

OVERLEAF: **The Shah test drives the Crown Prince's new car.** *(Borzou Sepasi)*

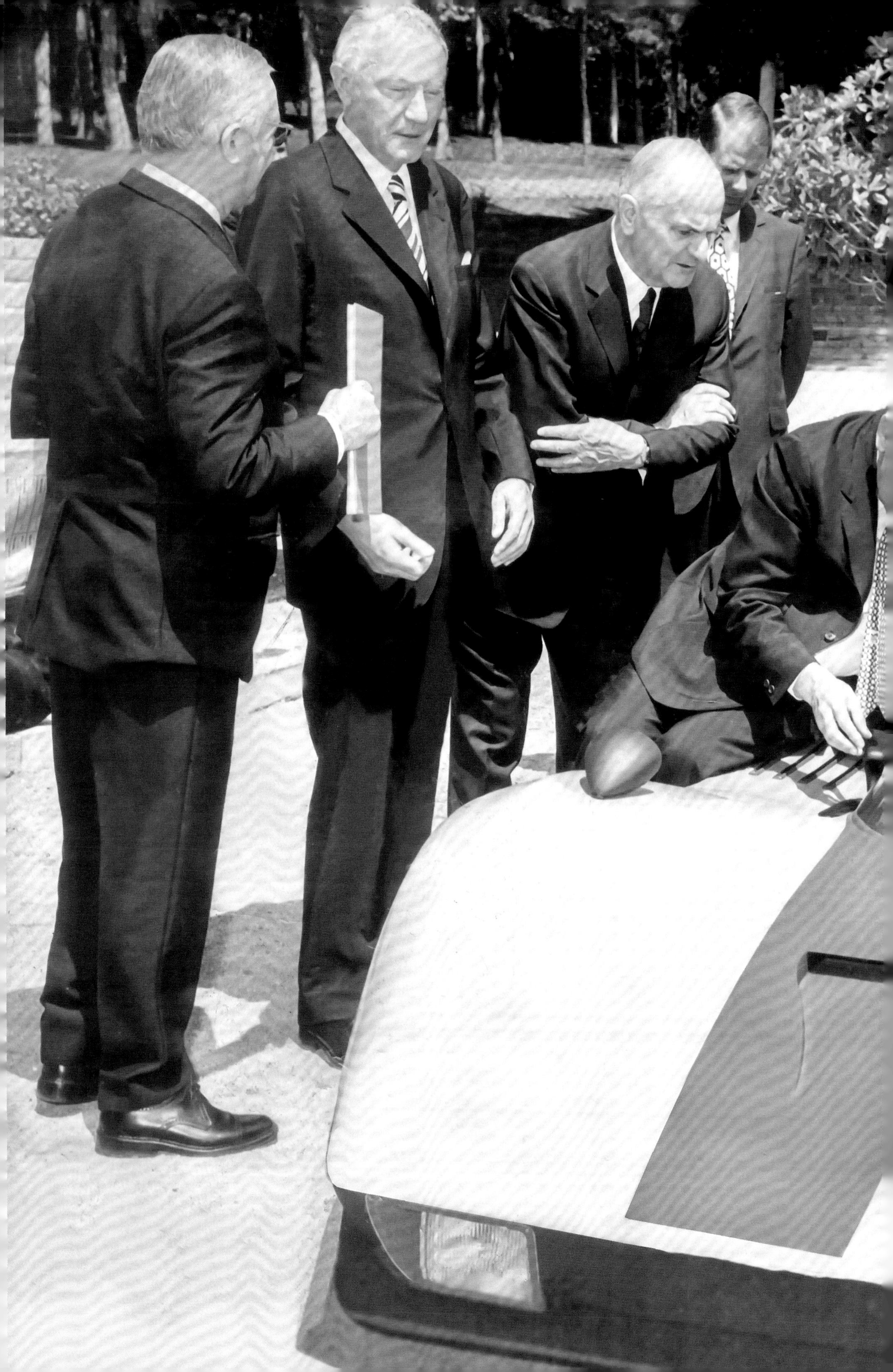

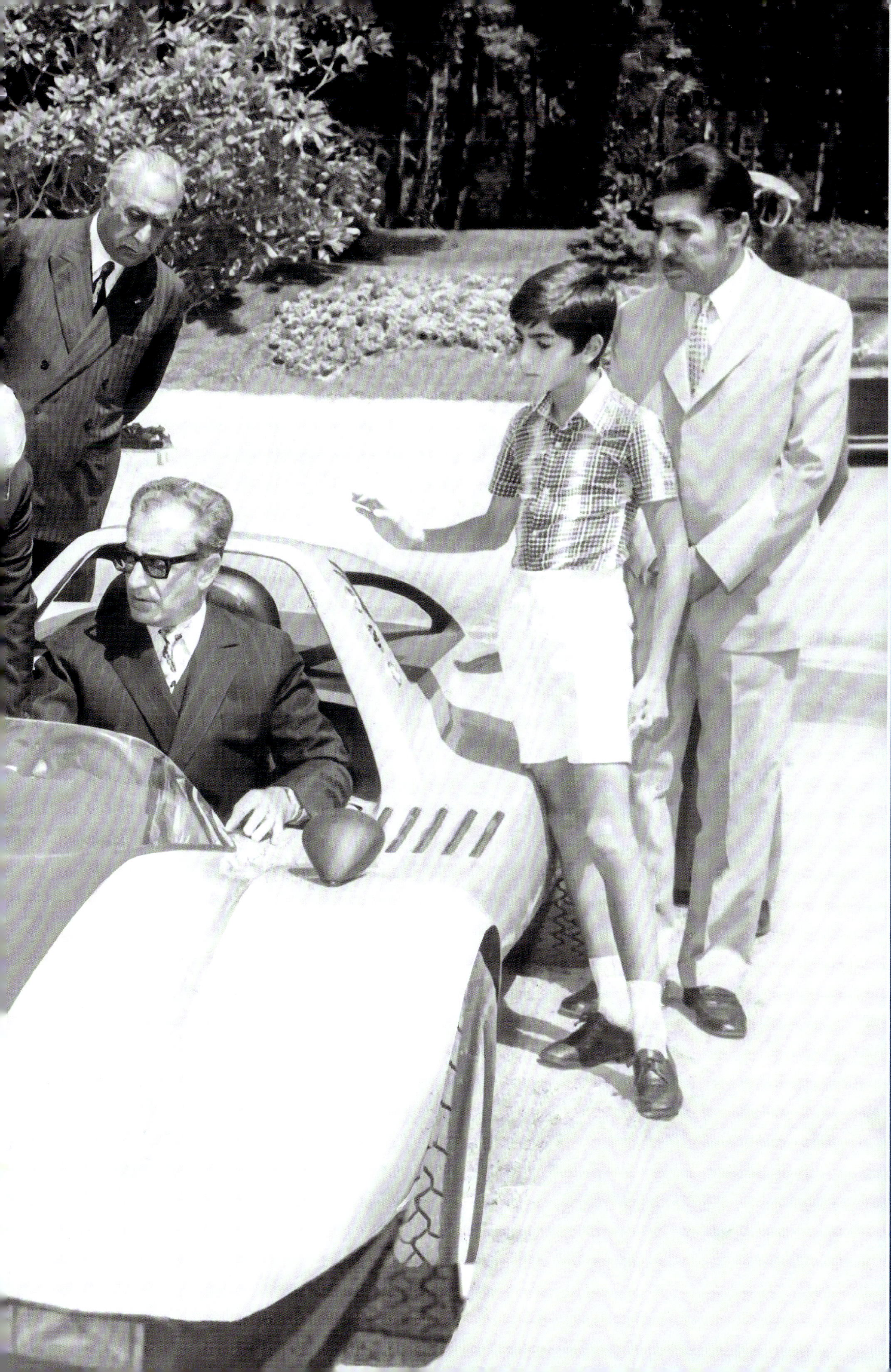

CHAPTER 31

Visiting with an American President

Chapter 31: Visiting with an American President

On May 31, 1972, American President Richard Nixon and first lady Patricia Nixon arrived in Tehran for an official visit. The visit, the first for an American President since the half-day stopover of Dwight Eisenhower in 1959, reflected Iran's growing stature in the region. President Nixon, who enjoyed a close relationship with the Shah had already visited Iran in 1953 in his capacity of Vice President during the Truman Administration. Eschewing protocol, and ostensibly for security reasons, the Shah and Richard Nixon rode together from Mehrabad Airport to Saad Abad Palace, not in one of the limousines of the royal garage, but in the US Presidential limousine, a 1969 Lincoln Continental. During Nixon's earlier visit back in 1953, the official car was a Cadillac Fleetwood Series 75 from the royal garage.

Vice President Richard Nixon being greeted by the Iranian Prime Minister Fazlollah Zahedi next to the royal Cadillac Fleetwood Limousine at Mehrabad Airport. (1953) *(Borzou Sepasi)*

The Shah and President Nixon waving to the crowds in Tehran in the Presidential Lincoln Continental limousine. *(Borzou Sepasi)*

The Shah repays Nixon's visit

In reciprocation of President Nixon's visit, from 24-26, July 1973, the Shah paid an official visit to the United States – his ninth since taking the throne in 1940. This four-day trip had two critical matters on the agenda.

The first, pertained to Iran's decision on the selection of its next generation fighter jet. The Shah, who was not only a trained pilot but also Commander of the Iranian armed forces had the final say on the matter. The decision came down to the selection between the McDonnell Douglas F-15 and the Grumman F-14, a decision that would have a critical impact on American naval strategy as well.

The fighter plane selection process was fraught with numerous, behind the scene maneuverings, on two counts. The first being that the Grumman Corporation, the developer of the F-14, was teetering on the edge of bankruptcy and a sale to the Iranian Air Force would have extended a critical lifeline. The second arose from the fact that the United States Navy had a vested interest in the sale of the F-14 to Iran as it had already selected the F-14 as its next generation carrier-based aircraft and, without the sale to the Iranian air force, the collapse of Grumman would also be sending the US Navy back to the drawing board for a new fighter jet.

An F-14 for a Chevy and a major victory against the oil giants

Following the Shah's visit, in December 1973, the Iranian air force officially announced that Iran had selected the F-14 "Tomcat" and a contract for thirty F-14s was signed followed by a second order for another fifty units. At the same time, the Melli Bank of Iran provided a 75 million dollar loan to the Grumman Company, not only saving Grumman from imminent collapse, but also the United States Navy from having to select a next generation fighter jet from scratch.

In 1975, the United States returned the favor. Due to a dispute with the Iranian government over a worker share participation scheme, General Motors began to seriously contemplate either withdrawing from the Iranian market or removing its name from the joint venture. According to Lew Wilkins, the general manager of GM Iran, it was only after a number of high level consultations with the White House that in September 1975 General Motors agreed to remain in Iran, paving the way for the subsequent launch of a new generation of vehicles in Iran, including the Cadillac Seville (see page 425).

Such was the importance that the Shah had attached to the investment of GM in Iran that he had threatened to cancel the F-14 contract if General Motors withdrew or scaled down its investment in Iran.[1] The second key matter on the Shah's agenda during his visit to the United States was the "Oil Consortium Contract" under which America and Britain controlled Iranian Oil production. In a ground-breaking agreement, the Consortium handed over its operations to the National Iranian Oil Company (NIOC) and Iran was able to gain

Chapter 31: Visiting with an American President

OPPOSITE: The Shah preparing to take a test flight in a two-seat version of a Northrop F5 Tiger during his visit to the United States.

THIS PAGE: The Shah greeting the crowds in Tehran, following his triumphant return from the United States, in his Rolls-Royce Phantom V State Landaulette, chassis number 5LVF29. *(Borzou Sepasi)*

BELOW: The royal Rolls-Royce Phantom V State Landaulette, pictured on the front page of the mass circulation daily newspaper, *Kayhan*. (July 29, 1973)

full sovereignty over its oil resources.[2] This was ratified during the Shah's 1973 visit to the United States. It was during this same visit of the Shah, that Iran, now virtually free from foreign control over its oil resources, announced a joint venture agreement with the American company Ashland Oil, to market Iranian oil products in the United States, the first such deal between a Middle East oil producing country and an American company.

On the return home, upon entering Iranian airspace, a triumphant Shah was met by an escort of eight Iranian air force F-4 Phantom fighter jets. The Iranian media lauded the end of the Consortium as a turning point in the centuries-old struggle to have full sovereignty over its national resources and thousands of people lined the streets to hail the Shah as he was driven from the airport to the Saad Abad Palace.

No doubt that for such a major occasion a very special car had to be used. Unsurprisingly, the Shah requested that the Rolls-Royce Phantom V State Landaulette, chassis number 5LVF29, be brought to the airport as the landaulet top would enable him to stand during his triumphant return and waive to the crowds as he was driven to the Palace.

The drive back to the Palace, and the massive crowds that gathered to cheer the Shah received widespread coverage in the Iranian media, with the mass circulation *Kayhan* newspaper publishing a large headline "Welcomed by one million Tehranis" accompanied by a large photograph of the Shah waving to the crowds in the Rolls-Royce on the route back the Palace.

GM Stays in Iran

"I was met by an official of the Palace who told me that the Shah had gone to another, even smaller Palace along the coast, having an even smaller airfield.

It seemed he was test driving his new Cadillac Seville."

      William H. Sullivan
      Mission to Iran: The Last US Ambassador

---

[1]   Robert Graham, "Iran: the Illusion of Power" St. Martin's Press, New York, 1979, p. 95

[2]   *ibid, p. 36*

With GM's commitment to stay in Iran re-affirmed and the threat to cancel the F-14 contract abated, the presence of GM in Iran reflects one of the little-known anomalies about the Iranian auto industry. While Willys is generally recognized as being the first company to set up assembly operations, it was General Motors that can in fact lay claim to such an assertion, but with objectives vastly different from Willys. In 1942, with Iran being under Allied occupation, the Allies set up a supply route through Iran into Soviet Azerbaijan by which British supplies and American Lend Lease aid was provided to Russia as it fought off the Nazi invasion. This massive supply operation became known as the "Persian Corridor". Supplies to Russia were carried out either by railroad or in long truck convoys. Of the 17.5 million tons of American Lend Lease Aid provided to Russia throughout World War II, 7.9 million tons (45%) was sent via Iran.[3]

To back this major operation, a large contingent of US military technicians were dispatched to Iran where they demonstrated their prowess for industrial organization "on a colossal scale".[4] At its peak, in mid-1944, approximately 7,500 tons per day were being transported by road[5] and it became apparent that it would be easier to send the trucks required for such a massive operation in KD (Knock Down) form for subsequent assembly at a GM facility established in Iran for such purpose under the wartime TUP mobile assembly plant program.[6]

The success of the US contingent was not just limited to truck assembly as evidenced by the fact that their activities ranged from the micro (bakeries, laundries, ice cream

---

[3]   *Steven R. Ward, "Immortal: A Military History of Iran and its Armed Forces", Georgetown University Press, Washington D.C., 2014, p. 176*

[4]   *James Buchan "Days of God", Simon & Schuster, New York, 2012, p. 57*

[5]   *ibid, p. 58*

[6]   *Louis F. Fourie, "On A Global mission: The Automobiles of General Motors", Friesen Press, Altona, 2016*

Chapter 31: Visiting with an American President

plants) to the macro (replacing of graded washboard roads with modern highways, replacement of the light rails which had buckled under the war time tonnages and the like). Such was the success of this operation that even an assembly plant for Curtiss P-40 fighter planes destined for Russian was established. All in all, by the end of the second World War, the US is believed to have left behind in Iran assets worth over $100 million.[7]

Some three decades later, GM again returned directly to Iran to undertake manufacturing operations, but under much different circumstances. In 1972, via a joint venture pursuant to which GM acquired 46% of the shares of the Iranian automaker Iran Jeep, the partner of AMC and Willys in Iran. With the share purchase, the company was restructured with a new name, "General Motors Iran" and, in 1974, the company launched a local version of the Opel Commodore B which was re-named and re-branded as the "Chevrolet Iran". By 1976, Opel assembly was phased out in favor of the Chevrolet Nova and Buick Skylark followed in 1977 by the Cadillac Seville.

The local production of the Cadillac Seville was a milestone for the Iranian automotive industry and reflected the growing maturity and economy of scale provided by an economically and industrially developing Iran. By 1978, GM Iran held 7% of the Iranian passenger car market. With the February 1979 revolution in Iran, General Motors abandoned the plant following its expropriation by the revolutionary government and the company subsequently reverted to the name of Pars Khodro. Notwithstanding this turn of events, the production of GM vehicles continued intermittingly until 1987 by running down remaining stocks and receiving knock down kits which GM subsequently delivered after receiving compensation for the expropriation of its assets from the Iranian government. In the end, a total of 2653 Cadillac Sevilles were manufactured in Iran during a ten-year span between 1977 to 1987.[8]

With the exception of the involvement of Pininfarina in the 1959 and 1960 versions of the Cadillac Eldorado Broughams and the 1987 to 1993 Allante, the launch of the assembly of the Cadillac Seville in Iran made it the only post-World War II country to assemble Cadillacs outside the United States. It was not until 1997 when the Cadillac Catera was built in Germany by Opel that Cadillac once again carried out assembly operations overseas.

---

[7] *James Buchan "Days of God", Simon & Schuster, New York, 2012, p. 58*

[8] *Louis F. Fourie, "On A Global mission: The Automobiles of General Motors", Friesen Press, Altona, 2016*

Start of production of GM Iran with the "Chevrolet Iran" (Opel Commodore). (1974)

CHAPTER 32

Six Daimlers join the Royal Garage

Chapter 32: Six Daimlers join the Royal Garage

1973 also marked the year that the royal garage took delivery of six Daimler DS420s. Shipped from England to the port of Khorramshahr in southern Iran, all were in black and were left-hand drive. Unlike the Mercedes-Benz 600s of the royal garage which were backed by comprehensive after sales services through the local agent "Merrikh Co.", the Daimlers were soon faced with the problem that there were no service facilities for these vehicles. As a result, the royal garage was obliged to ask the Daimler company to send technicians to Iran on a periodic basis. This was not uncommon practice as companies that had limited sales, primarily to the royal garage and the Iranian elite, including Rolls-Royce, Lamborghini and Maserati, had the same practice as the small volume of exported cars would not justify a full-fledged service center.

The Daimlers were primarily pressed into service for use during the provincial visits of the Shah and Queen Farah. These trips had taken on a newfound frequency as by the 1970s both the Shah and Queen Farah had increased their visits to the Iran provinces to check first-hand on projects under execution. Queen Farah especially took an interest in the provinces as she had under her patronage numerous cultural projects.

It is interesting to note that notwithstanding the use of the six Daimlers for provincial visits, it was not uncommon for the Shah and Queen Farah to also use an eclectic mix of other vehicles ranging from a 1972 Chevrolet Impala Convertible to an Iranian Army GAZ-69.

During one of the Queen's provincial visits a young girl jumped in front of the Queen's Daimler DS420, chassis number 1M 20088, to hand her a message. A bodyguard is seen getting out of a Mercedes-Benz S class escort to protect the Queen. (Early 1970s) *(Borzou Sepasi)*

427

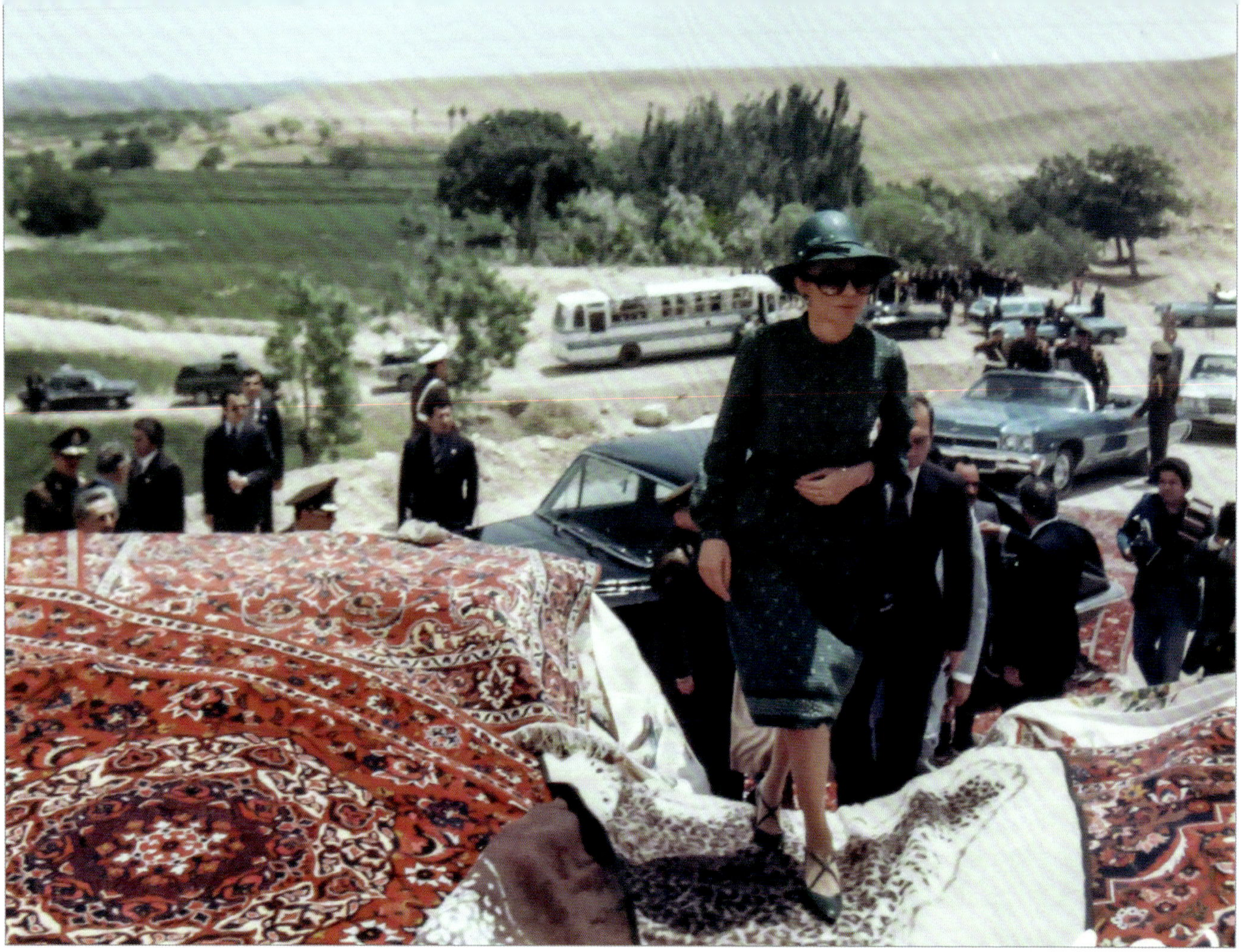

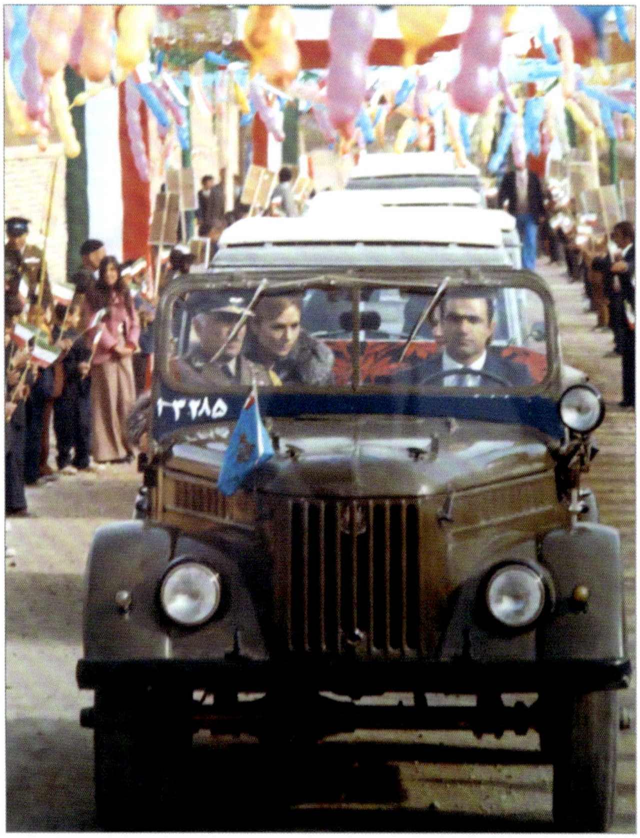
۲۳۲۸۵

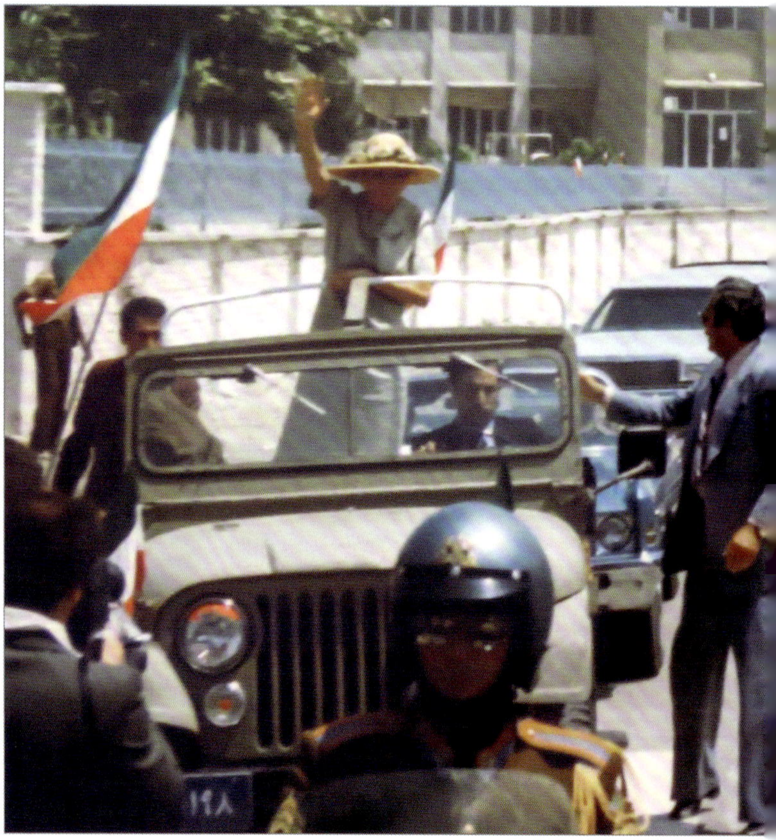
۱۲۸

Chapter 32: Six Daimlers join the Royal Garage

THESE TWO PAGES: In the mid-1970s, Queen Farah made visits to the provinces to follow the projects which she had under her patronage.
The images pertain to her visits to the provinces of Gilan, Mazandaran and Lorestan with a wide range of transportation as evidenced by the pictured 1972 Impala Convertible and Gaz-69 of the Iranian Army. *(Niavaran Palace)*

CHAPTER 33

A Camargue for the Shah and... one for Queen Farah?

Chapter 33: A Camargue for the Shah and... one for Queen Farah?

By 1975, the Shah had over the years amassed a broad collection of Rolls-Royces which virtually included an example of every model produced by the company, including, inter alia, a Phantom I, III, IV, V and VI and a Corniche ultimately culminating in 1975 with the first left-hand drive Camargue.[1]

The Pininfarina-designed Camargue, the first post war Rolls-Royce not designed in-house, became the flagship of Rolls-Royce and the most expensive production car in the world. The combination of price and the fact that it would take six months to assemble each Camargue made it one of the most exclusive vehicles in the world. This unique combination would no doubt garner the interest of the Shah and it is of no surprise that almost immediately after its launch in Italy in January 1975, Roger Cra'ster a Rolls-Royce delivery driver and company factotum drove a Camargue from Italy to Switzerland to present it to the Shah, who at the time was on one of his perennial winter vacations at St. Moritz.

By the time Cra'ster reached his destination, it was early evening, yet he was surprised to learn that one of the Shah's aides was anxiously waiting for his arrival stating, "good you've arrived. The Shah heard you had crossed the border and wants to see the car".[2] The Shah's emissary was undeterred by Cra'ster's protestations that the car was dirty and that it was dark. The emissary was adamant that the Shah was coming to see the car now and there. When the Shah arrived, while he was dissuaded from driving the car in the dark, obviously smitten, he agreed to postpone the test drive and in place sat in the car and tried out the controls, a process that lasted over twenty minutes.

The Shah who was known for his punctuality, arrived at 9:00 am sharp the following morning, taking the wheel of the Camargue with Roger Cra'ster beside him and Amir Houshang Davlloo, a Qajar Prince and the Shah's right-hand man in Europe, in the back.

Escorted by a Swiss police car in front and with two limousines in tow, ostensibly with body guards, the Shah drove to the airport where his private plane was waiting to return to Iran. Before boarding, the Rolls-Royce factory color charts were reviewed by the Shah (the Camargue having its own exclusive range) with the Shah settling on gold. On being told that this factory color was named "Crown", the Shah remarked that it was no doubt an "appropriate" selection. Cra'ster proceeded to contact the factory in order to convey the Shah's order only to be rebuffed and, instead, was entrusted with the delicate task of informing this very important customer that he could not have the color he wanted. The reason was the Rolls-Royce factory had been so confident that the Shah would place an order for a Camargue that they had already proceeded to build one for him even before he had set eyes on the car. As his preceding order from Rolls-Royce had been a cobalt blue 1970 Drophead Coupe, chassis number DRX9983, the factory had apparently taken it for granted that his next order would be for the same color as well and had already built one in this color accordingly.

Faced with such a dilemma, Cra'ster came up with a solution. He suggested to the Shah that he should order a second Camargue which would be painted gold.

The Queen preparing to sit in her Rolls-Royce Camargue, chassis number JRX23260. *(Youtube.com)*

---

[1] Bob Montgomery, Irish Times, "The car connoisseur's collection of choice", www.irishtimes.com/life-and-style/motors/the-car-connoisseur-s-collection-of-choice-1.1234237

[2] Peter Pugh, "The Magic of a Name: The Rolls-Royce Story, Part 2: The Power Behind the Jets", Icon Books Ltd, London, 2012

"What a good idea. I will give it to my wife as a birthday present",[3] replied the Shah and that was how Roger Cra'ster was the first and perhaps only person to take two orders for a Camargue in one day.

It was with such a background that Rolls-Royce Camargue, chassis number JRX19741, painted cobalt blue, became the first export car to go to a customer and the first production example to be fitted with a Solex carburetor. The car was air freighted to Tehran and, on September 25, 1975, David Plastow (Chairman of Rolls-Royce) and Roger Cra'ster arranged for it be positioned at the foot of the Palace steps. As Rolls-Royce was at the time also negotiating the sale of tank engines to the Iranian Army, they timed the delivery of the car to coincide with their negotiations with the Shah. If they had hoped that timing the delivery of the Camargue concomitant with their negotiations would have provided them with a negotiating edge, they had clearly miscalculated as the Shah was so engrossed with his new car that he lost all interest in negotiating the tank engines.

The second Camargue, chassis number JRX23260 and finished in Crown, was originally put in as a production order as a right-hand drive car for London dealer H.R. Owen but modified to left-hand drive and delivered to the Shah in St. Moritz Switzerland in the spring of 1976. While it is not known whether or not Queen Farah was delighted with her "birthday present", subsequent photographs and film attest to the fact that the car was subsequently sent to the Niavaran Palace where the Queen can be seen driving it to her office.

[3] Bernard L. King, "Rolls-Royce Camargue: Crewe Saviour", Complete Classics, Weedon, England, 2019, p. 203-204

The 1975 Camargue price list discovered in Saad Abad Palace. The Farsi handwriting says, "to be filed in the Rolls-Royce folder, 18th of Esfand, 1353". (March 9, 1975) *(Saad Abad Palace)*

Chapter 33: A Camargue for the Shah and... one for Queen Farah?

CHAPTER 34

The Crown Prince graduates to an Italian Supercar

Chapter 34: The Crown Prince graduates to an Italian Supercar

In 1977, in celebration of his 17th birthday, the Crown Prince received a very special gift from his aunt, Ashraf Pahlavi, the twin sister of the Shah and somewhat of a car aficionado herself. It was a Lamborghini Countach Periscopio, chassis number 1120190, in Rosso Granada color. It was bought from Gabriel Cavallari's Monaco Motors, and delivered to the Hotel de Paris, in Monte Carlo, to Princess Ashraf.

Immediately after delivery, the Lamborghini was sent to Tehran in a C130 Hercules of the IIAF (Imperial Iranian Air Force) and delivered to the royal garage on October 25, 1977 before being handed over to Crown Prince Reza on October 31, the day of his birthday.

Though the Crown Prince has been photographed with the car and is believed to have driven it on occasion, it is doubtful that it saw much use. The Crown Prince, a trained pilot since the age of 11, was dispatched less than a year later to the United States for fighter jet training in August 1978 as a cadet in the Imperial Iranian Air Force. He was never to return to Iran again.

ABOVE & FOLLOWING PAGE: Lamborghini Countach, chassis number 1120190, pictured in front of Gabriel Cavallari's Monaco Motors before being sold to Princess Ashraf Pahlavi. The registration plate on the car is a Monaco "Transit Temporaire" export plate. *(Andreas Birner)*

Fit for a King ~ The Royal Garage of the Shah of Iran

LEFT: Crown Prince Reza Pahlavi pictured with his Innocenti Mini Cooper 1300. The Crown Prince was known to drive quite spiritedly and had a tendency to break away from his security cordon and to have "sped off in his Mini Cooper, leaving the drivers of his tail car shaking their fists in traffic".[1] *(Niavaran Palace)*

OPPOSITE: Crown Prince Reza Pahlavi with his two sisters Princess Farahnaz and Princess Leila posing beside his Lamborghini Countach. *(Borzou Sepasi)*

---

[1] Andrew Scott Cooper, *"The Fall of Heaven"*, Henry Holt and Company, New York, 2016, p. 186

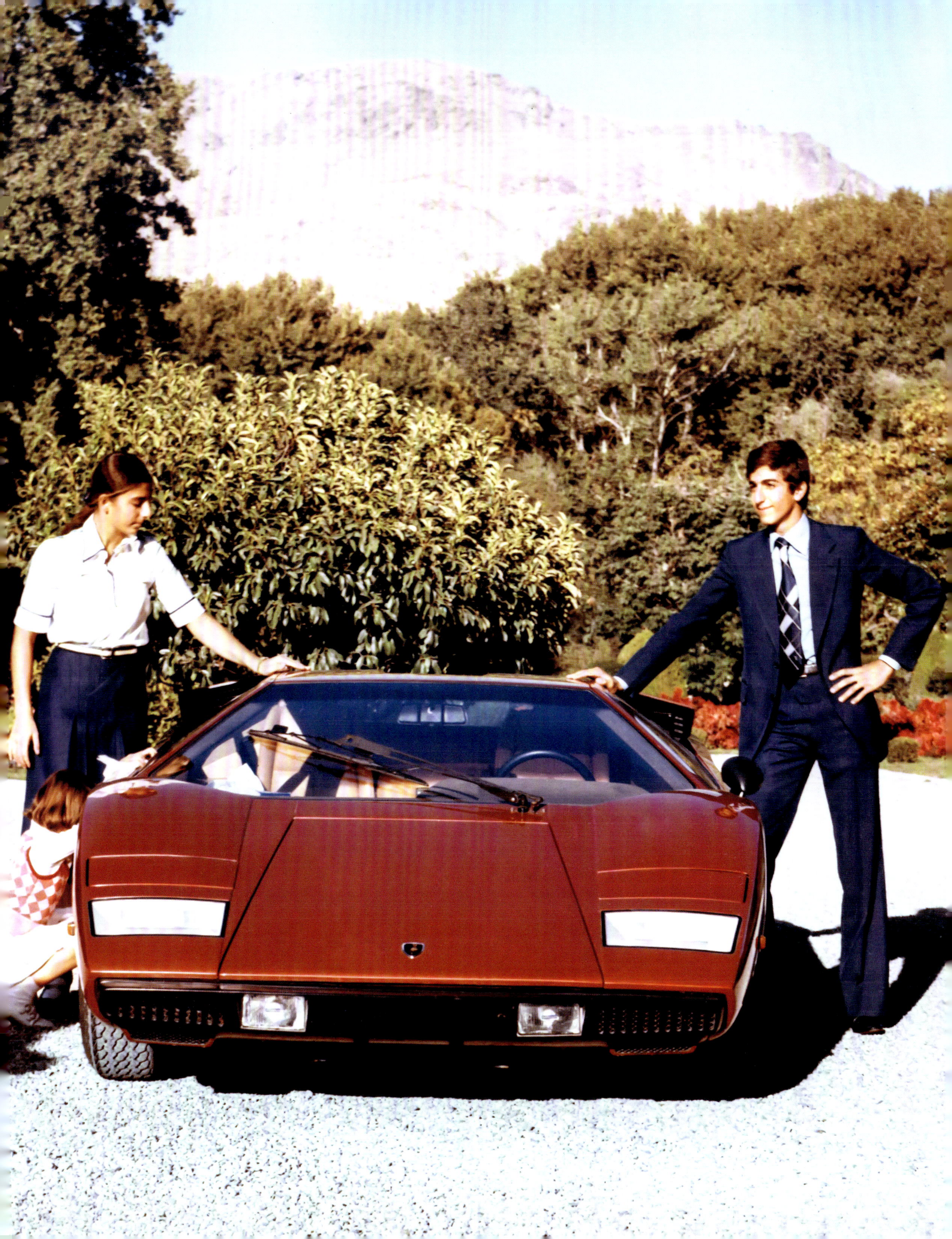

ABOVE: Delivery documents issued by the royal court for Lamborghini Countach, chassis number 1120190, acknowledging its delivery to the royal garage. (November 9, 1977) *(Borzou Sepasi)*

OPPOSITE: IIAF (Imperial Iranian Air Force) cargo manifest for Countach, chassis number 1120190. *(Borzou Sepasi)*

Chapter 34: The Crown Prince graduates to an Italian Supercar

			CARGO MANIFEST
Type of aircraft	Aircraft No	**I.I.A.F.** (Log Air Command)	Manifest No
Type of vehicle	Vehicle's No		Manifest Destination

No.	No. of Page	Nature of Goods	Original	Destination	Weight-in Lb	Consignee	Number of pieces	Remarks
1								
2								
3								
4								
5		HOM S.A.I. ACHRAF PAHLAVI						
6		ADRESSE HOTEL DE PARIS						
7								
8		IDENTIFICATION DU VEHICULE						
9		MARQUE LAMBORGHINI						
10		TYPE COUNTACH LP 400 GENRE V.P						
11		No dan sis SERIE du TYPE 1 20.120						
12		Puissance 23 Cyl 12						
13		S. ENERGIE ES Places 2						
14		carrosserie C.I 2P couleur ROUGE						
15		V.N						
16		1 Mise en circulation 21 JUIN 1976						
17		167 JJ						

TOTAL

All items listed on this manifest have been Received. data
Signature

CHAPTER 35

The Shah and Crown Prince's Last Rides

Chapter 35: The Shah and Crown Prince's Last Rides

One of the smaller niche market players that seemed to have caught the attention of the royal family was Panther Westwinds. Founded by Robert Jankel in 1972, the company was rapidly able to carve out a niche for itself in the luxury segment by producing cars using modern mechanicals and retro-based styling. Jankel would also design unique (if not off beat) vehicles as well.

In 1976, it is believed that Iran's Crown Prince took delivery of two vehicles from the Panther works. The first being the one-off Panther Lazer, a wedge shaped three abreast open roadster perhaps to some in the spirit of a grand tourer while others saw it as a caricature of the "Wacky Racers" cartoon series. This particular vehicle had been originally ordered by Panther's Canadian importer as a present for his wife. Though the design tended to polarize, Jankel's many engineering talents were on

Panther Lazer prior to delivery to Iran. *(Internet)*

display as the car had energy absorbing bodywork with box section crumple zones.

Delivered to its original customer in August 1974, and notwithstanding the labor of love that the car represented, the Lazer was promptly returned to Panther as the car was rejected after "it failed to impress the lady for who

441

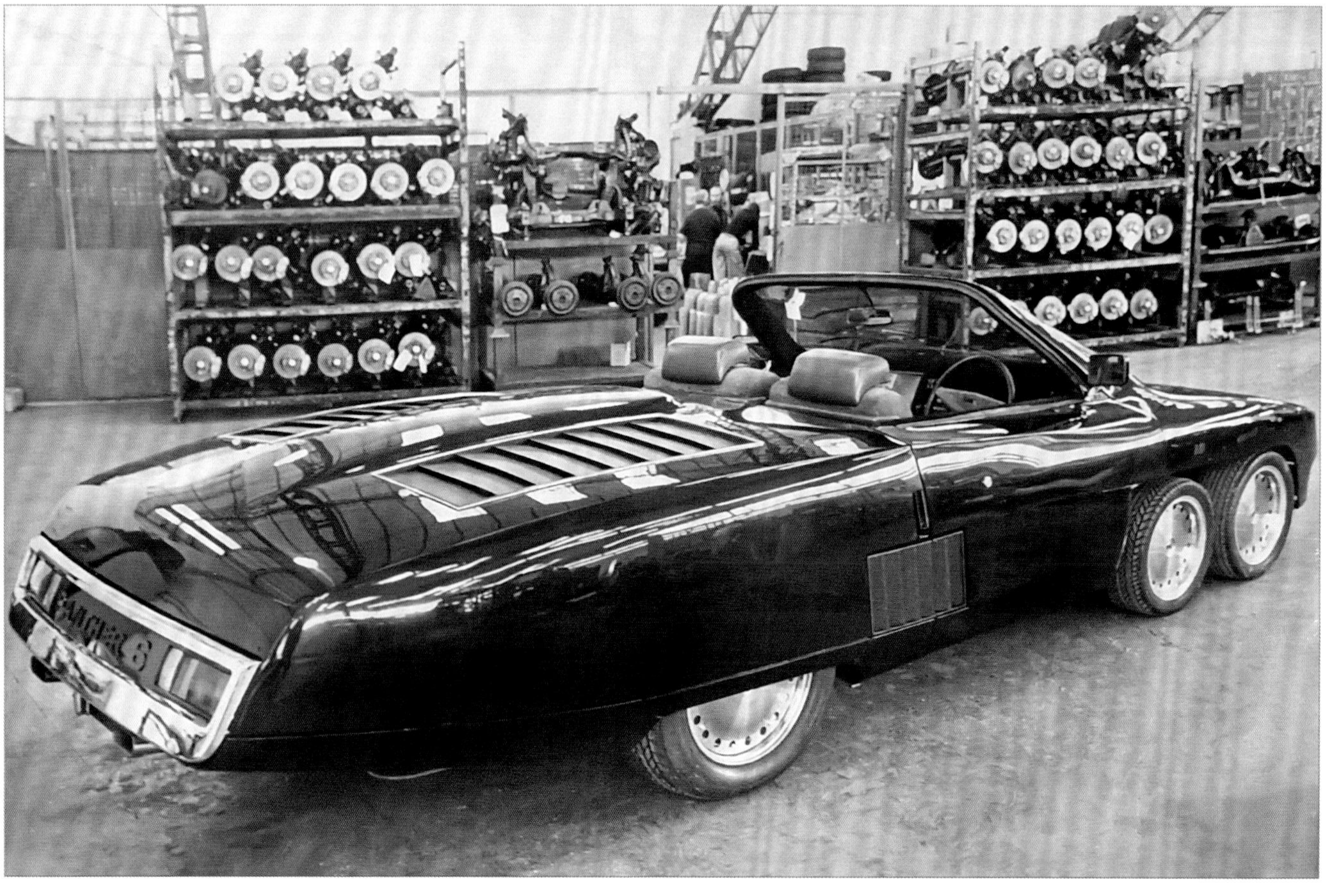

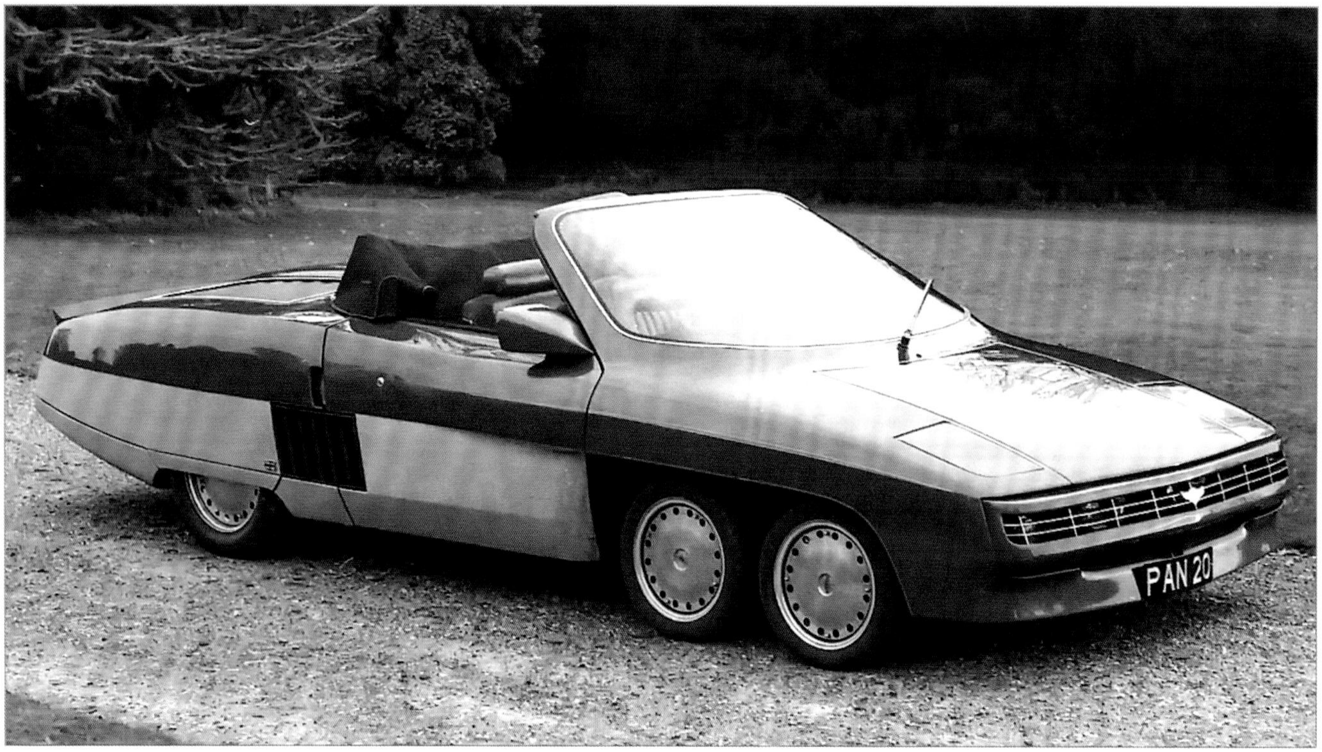
PAN 20

Chapter 35: The Shah and Crown Prince's Last Rides

it had been built".[1] After languishing for more than two years in the Panther works, at some point in 1976, the car caught the eye of the 16-year-old Crown Prince Reza Pahlavi who proceeded to buy the car. It is also believed that the Crown Prince bought a second Panther, a model J.72, chassis number 294L, in September 1976 as well. The J.72 had styling derived from the classic Jaguar SS-100 with modern Jaguar XJ mechanicals, with an asking price twice the amount of contemporary Jaguar models.

In January 1978, less than thirteen months before the Iranian revolution and the fall of the monarchy, the Shah ordered a third Panther, a new Panther 6. Though the Shah was known for his interest in one-off and limited-edition vehicles, the ordering of a six-wheeled convertible, powered by a mid-mounted 8.2-liter Cadillac V8 seemed out of step with the Shah's tastes and some pundits are of the view that the order could have been on behalf of the Crown Prince. At the time of the order, the production car was not ready. As a result, with a price of approximately £38,000, the royal court made a down payment of £20,000. The Shah ordered the car in a dark blue shade and optioned with air conditioning, electric windows, radio/cassette system, electric door mirrors, digital clock, automatic transmission, power-assisted steering, gas plasma instruments, leather upholstery and automatic fire extinguishers. A removable hardtop was also requested, along with a telephone and a television. After all the options were ordered on behalf of the Shah by the royal court, Panther announced that the final price would come to £39,950.

In June 1978, Panther sent an official letter to the Iranian royal court and informed them that in the engine compartment a special area had been designated to engrave the name of the purchaser, and they needed to know who this should be.

During this period, with Iran on the brink of a revolution, the day to day activities of the royal court also began to grind to a standstill and nobody from the court ever responded to Panther's request, nor was the order followed through. Eight months later, in January 1979, the Shah of Iran and his family left Iran for a life of exile and the revolution became victorious less than a month later. The production of the Panther 6 was limited to exactly two cars. The first car was a right-hand drive version, and the second car, with left-hand drive, was the one prepared for the Shah but was never to be delivered.

The last Hurrah – The Shah's 928

On the third of June 1978, an Imperial Iranian Air Force C-130 was dispatched to Munich Airport in Germany to pick up the Shah's latest order, a Porsche 928. On board was a mechanic from the royal garage, Peter Voss, who was told to pick up the 928 and transport it to the royal garage. The 928, chassis number 9288101733, had been ordered via the Iranian Consulate in Munich, and according to correspondence between the Consulate and the Office of the royal court, the car was to be in black with an automatic transmission.

Upon arrival, the 928 was delivered directly to the royal garage, where subsequent correspondence showed that the car suffered from warning lights indicating brake problems, and the Consulate was requested to secure service booklets from Porsche as the local dealer was not able to fix the malady.

---

1. *www.aronline.co.uk, The Converters: Panther Lazer*

PAGE 441 & OPPOSITE TOP: **Photographs of the first Panther 6 sent to Iran as part of a promotional pitch to the Shah. (1977)** *(Saad Abad Palace)*

OPPOSITE BOTTOM: **The Panther 6 after being repainted.**

The last jet of the Shah of Iran

In April 1978, the Shah took delivery of what would be his last private jet. It was a Boeing 707-386C, construction number 21396, and was named the "Shahin" (Eagle). The plane, which was delivered in April 1978, was registered as EP-HIM (His Imperial Majesty).

The plane has the reputation of being one of the most luxurious private aircraft of the era and was fitted with accoutrements including gold-plated fittings, a fully stocked bar intricately carved out of wood and most notably, a hand-made twelve seat conference table carved in the tradition of the Iranian handicraft of "khatam" a form of marquetry, an art form made by inlaying small delicate pieces of wood, bone and metal in precisely cut intricate patterns and which took over 6,000 man-hours to create. The plane also had six toilets, five of which were for use by guests and located in the aft of the plane and one in the fore with gold fittings for exclusive use by the Shah and Queen Farah.

Complementing these luxurious fittings were a state-of-the-art telephone and telex system which would provide the Shah with airborne contact across the globe. The plane was staffed by twenty attendants who could only board after showing a special security pass.

At a time when a regular Boeing 707 passenger jet was priced in the vicinity of $42 million, the final price of the Shahin at the time of delivery was $135 million.

As the winds of revolution loomed closer, on January 16, 1979, the Shah and Queen Farah boarded this plane and left Iran for a life of permanent exile.

LEFT: On January 16, 1979, the Shah and Queen Farah boarded the Shahin for a new life in exile.

OPPOSITE (BOTH): The Shah's last royal plane, a Boeing 707-386C, construction number 21396, and named the "Shahin" (Eagle).

Chapter 35: The Shah and Crown Prince's Last Rides

APPENDIX 1

The Story Continues

An alphabetical guide to the known fates of the vehicles featured in this book after the revolution

Appendix 1: The Story Continues

During the compilation of this book, a recurring question that would consistently arise was the ultimate fate of the vehicles of the royal garage, especially after the 1979 revolution and the overthrow of the monarchy. Iran's revolution was in many cases a backlash against the growing schisms of a society undergoing many changes, including a rejection of the pomp and excesses of the royal court.

One of the most visual and accessible remnants of the monarchy to bear the brunt of the fervor of the revolutionaries were the cars of the Shah and his associates. With the fall of the palaces to the revolutionaries, many cars, motorcycles, utility vehicles and even the toy cars and bicycles of the Shah's children were immediately expropriated, with some being damaged in the heat of revolutionary fervor. Many were either put away in storage for years in various warehouses or languished locked away in palace garages (or even, in some cases, former horse stables) while others were sold at auction, pursuant to which many were then quickly spirited out of Iran. Some remained hidden by associates of the royal family until their discovery or some, perhaps, remain hidden to this day.

One of the most well-known auctions to take place after the revolution was for the sale of a single lot of ten cars which, for the most part, based on their pedigree and history, were closely associated with the Shah himself. Held in 1993, the auction resulted in a sales contract with a bidder from the United Arab Emirates, Mr. Mohammad Ibrahim Al-Sadegh. The auction was held by the Bonyad Shahid (Foundation of the Martyrs),

The sale comprised of the following vehicles:

Year/Model	Chassis Number
1973 Daimler 4.2-liter Limousine	1M 20088
1973 Aston Martin V8	V8/11004/LCA
1969 Lamborghini Espada	7099
1975 Rolls-Royce Camargue	JRX 19741
1975 Rolls-Royce Camargue	JRX 23260
1974 Ferrari 365 GT4 2+2	18263
1969 Rolls-Royce Silver Shadow	SRX 7256
1965 Cadillac Fleetwood Series 75	ST 04A 65-69733 DC 766 KR 2 EA
1970 Rolls-Royce Drophead Coupe	DRX 9983
1971 Lamborghini Miura SVJ	4934

a foundation which was granted control of a portion of the assets of the royal family and others associated with the Pahlavi regime. The Foundation had been established to generate income to support the families of those killed during the revolution and the subsequent eight-year war with Iraq (1980-1988).

The Bonyad Shahid co-existed alongside a second foundation, the Bonyad Mostazafan (formerly the Bonyad Mostazafan va Janbazan – Foundation of the Poor and Self-Sacrificers), which had been established to assist the poor and those who had suffered injury from the revolution and the subsequent war with Iraq, and, in fact, was granted the control of the majority of the assets of the Shah, his family and his associates. It was not uncommon for these two Foundations to sporadically auction off the vehicles in their possession. Fortunately, in the year 2003, with the persistent lobbying of a group of Iranian enthusiasts and sympathetic managers in the Bonyad Mostazafan, the first National Automobile Museum was inaugurated and the cars and other vehicles that still remained in the possession of the Bonyad Mostazafan were transferred to the ownership of the museum and, ultimately, further sales of the vehicles in the possession of entities such as the Bonyads were ended.

This chapter will try to trace, in alphabetical order, the known current status of a number of cars and vehicles having a royal lineage.

1966 Aston Martin DB5 James Bond Electric Toy Car

As touched upon earlier, not only were the cars and other property of the Shah and his family expropriated, but also the playthings of his children. By the mid-1980s the sale and auction of the Shah's assets reached a peak as Iran was embroiled in full scale war with Iraq and in order to raise funds, both the Bonyad Mostazafan and the Bonyad Shahid would hold auctions encompassing everything from land holdings to the Shah's motorcycles.

TOP: The Crown Prince and his sister Princess Farahnaz with his scale toy Aston Martin DB5. (1967) *(Borzou Sepasi)*

ABOVE & OPPOSITE LEFT (ALL): The Crown Prince's Aston Martin DB5 as discovered in the basement of a home by the author. (2003) *(Borzou Sepasi)*

448

Appendix 1: The Story Continues

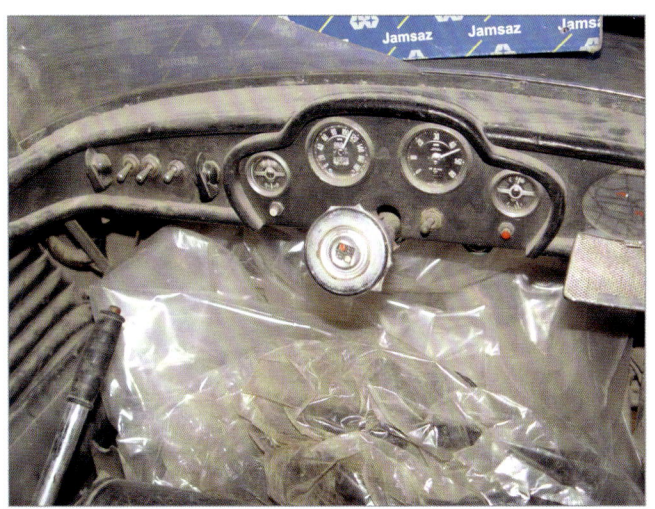

In one such auction, the Crown Prince's scale Aston Martin DB5 was sold off. The purchaser, an Iranian airline pilot bought it for his young son and, over the years as his son grew up, the car was subsequently stored away in his basement among other clutter.

1973 Aston Martin V8
Chassis Number: V8/11004/LCA

Given the fact that the majority of the vehicles that were seized after the revolution were divided primarily between the Bonyad Mostazafan and the Bonyad Shahid, most of the vehicles that were in the Shah's primary winter residence, and where he last resided before leaving Iran, the Niavaran Palace (as opposed to the royal garage) when the revolution took place, ended up in the possession of the Bonyad Shahid. For the most part, these were the cars that the Shah kept near and on hand, including the famed Lamborghini Miura SVJ which the Shah was known to take out on spirited midnight runs and is believed to have been his favorite car.

Grouped among the lot of ten cars in the possession of the Bonyad Shahid, was the Shah's green Aston Martin V8, chassis number V8/11004/LCA. Each summer, this car was transported to the royal palace by the Caspian Sea to be used for the Shah's frequent stays during the summer months. Following the revolution, the Aston Martin was stored away in an unknown warehouse in

The Shah's Aston Martin V8, chassis number V8/11004/LCA as it sat in a warehouse in Iran before its sale. (1980s) *(Mehran Afshar)*

449

Fit for a King ~ The Royal Garage of the Shah of Iran

251

Formerly the Property of His Imperial Highness the late Shah of Iran

1973 ASTON MARTIN V8

Chassis no. V8/11004/LCA   Engine no. V/540/1104

The handsome DBS of 1967 saw Aston Martin back in the limelight but it was not until the new V8 engine arrived two years later that the marque was restored to its rightful place among supercar manufacturers. The V8 was a car with the pace to match its looks, delivering 150mph performance whilst clothed in the coachbuilders equivalent of a Savile Row suit. As a gentleman's supercar the V8 had few real rivals until its demise in the late 1980s, and even today the model is sadly missed by many.

It was almost an Aston Martin tradition that the first export example of any new model should go to the Shah of Iran, and indeed this is the first carburettor-fed V8 built for export, chassis numbers 11002 and 11003 being development hacks which were not sold. The car was made for the Shah in a very appropriate combination of Tudor Green complimented by cream Connolly hide upholstery and cream Wilton carpets, and left England for Iran on 18th June 1973. It was to be the Shah's last Aston Martin.

We understand from former staff in the Imperial Garage that the V8 was primarily the Shah's summer car, and as such was kept at Nowshahr, his summer residence on the Caspian Sea, before being returned to Tehran for his use there. The odometer reading now stands at 10,912km.

Should the car remain in Switzerland local import taxes will be liable. If the car is to be re-exported from Switzerland, this must be arranged through Brooks Europe.

Cette élégante Aston fût commandée par le Shah en vert 'Tudor', intérieur en cuir Connolly et tapis, crème. La voiture restait dans la résidence d'été du Shah sur la mer Caspienne. Elle n'affiche que 10,912 km. Voiture non-dedouanée en Suisse.

Estimate SFR36,000 - 50,000

The page dedicated to Aston Martin V8, chassis number V8/11004/LCA in the auction catalog published by Brooks Europe. The Aston was designated as Lot No. 251. (March 12, 1997) *(Brooks Europe)*

Appendix 1: The Story Continues

Tehran along with the nine other cars until all the cars were sold in one lot to Mr. Mohammad Ibrahim Al-Sadegh, a national of the UAE in 1994. Following its sale, the Aston was shipped to United Arab Emirates and, with the other nine cars, stored in a warehouse near Sharjah for a further three years, out of sight until the new owner decided to sell the whole lot at an international auction to be held by the renowned auction house, Brooks in Geneva, Switzerland.

In order to prepare the cars for auction, the Aston and others were brought out of storage and photographed by professional photographers in preparation for the auction catalog and were then transported to Switzerland. On March 12, 1997, all ten cars, including the Aston, were sold one by one and with that, important parts of Iranian automotive history, including the first "export" Aston Martin V8, was lost to Iran forever.

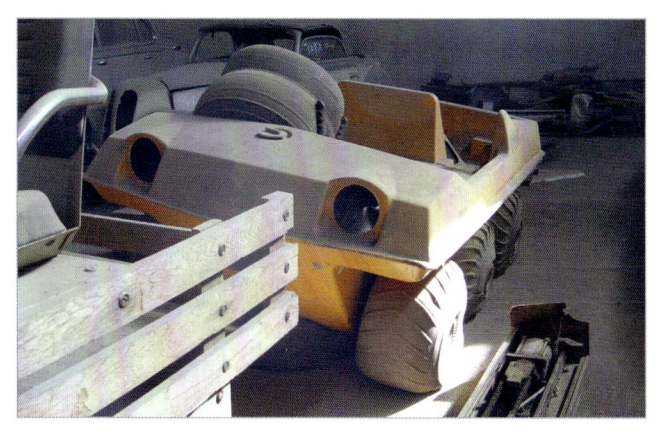

Attex ST/300 6x6

Prior to the onset of the 1979 revolution, Crown Prince Reza Pahlavi had moved to the United States to train as a fighter pilot. For this reason, alongside his other vehicles, his yellow Attex ST/300 6×6 had already been stored away in the royal garage before the revolution. Following the revolution, the Attex was among the vehicles that were handed over to the Bonyad Mostazafan and subsequently stored in a warehouse in Karaj, Iran. As of the printing of this book, the Attex still remains in storage in the same warehouse.

TOP RIGHT: **Crown Prince Reza Pahlavi at the wheel of the Attex ST/300 6×6 while his grandmother Farideh Ghotbi looks on. (Early 1970s)** *(Niavaran Palace)*

TOP LEFT & ABOVE (BOTH): **Crown Prince Reza's Attex ST/300 after the revolution, damaged and dusty parked beside a Ferrari 365 GT, chassis number 11417. (2004)** *(Borzou Sepasi)*

451

1955 Bentley R-Type Continental, bodied by H. J. Mulliner

Chassis Number: BC73D

The Shah's 1955 Bentley R-Type Continental, which had been bought during his official visit to Britain in 1955, eventually found its way to the United States at some point in the 1960s, most probably after being sold during one of the periodic house cleanings of the royal garage. The car was eventually located in the United States and purchased in 2006 by the UK-based Rolls-Royce and Bentley specialists, Frank Dale & Stepsons. At the time of purchase, the car was in poor condition and brought to London for a complete restoration. Following its restoration, including an overhaul and rebuild of the engine, gearbox, suspension, chassis, coachwork and interior, the car was sold to a Dutch owner and was displayed at the Concours d'Elegance Paleis het Loo in 2016.

The royal emblems on the doors, an important element of the history of the car, have been removed and the color of the car has been changed to black.

Appendix 1: The Story Continues

OPPOSITE & BELOW (BOTH): The Shah's Bentley R-Type Continental, chassis number BC73D, bodied by H. J. Mulliner photographed prior to its complete restoration. *(Giles Crickmay, Frank Dale & Stepsons, London)*

RIGHT: The royal emblems still visible on the doors prior to restoration. *(Giles Crickmay, Frank Dale & Stepsons, London)*

BOTTOM: Bentley R-Type Continental, chassis number BC73D, bodied by H. J. Mulliner after the complete restoration by Frank Dale & Stepsons, London. *(Giles Crickmay, Frank Dale & Stepsons, London)*

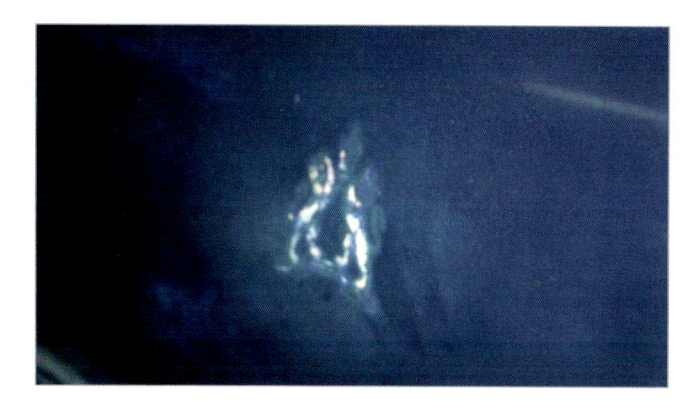

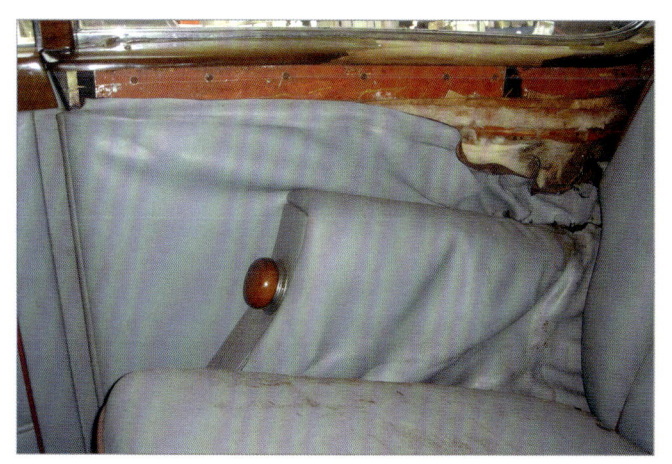

1960 Bentley S2 Continental Drophead Coupe
Chassis Number: BC8AR

This Bentley is believed by some pundits to be the very car that the Shah drove to the hospital to visit his newborn son, the Crown Prince. It is believed that the car was sold by the royal garage in 1968 to a Mr. Khazeni, who would drive the car frequently. Apparently, the Bentley was prone to overheating and correspondence still exists where the new owner contacted the management of the royal garage and requested that he be afforded a time slot during one of the periodic visits of the mechanics of Rolls-Royce and Bentley to the royal garage. After the revolution, the car was stored away in a private garage until 2019 when the owner brought it out in virtually a time capsule state.

ABOVE & OPPOSITE LEFT TOP: The Bentley S2 Continental Drophead Coupe, chassis number BC8AR, seeing sunshine for the first time in almost four decades. *(Teymour Richard)*

OPPOSITE LEFT MIDDLE & BOTTOM: The Bentley S2 Continental Drophead Coupe in time capsule condition being transported. It will be started and driven for the first time in four decades. *(Teymour Richard)*

Appendix 1: The Story Continues

1957 Bimbo Racer V12

The Crown Prince had not one, but four Bimbo Racer V12s, two in red, one in dark red and one in white. As with the other assets and belongings of the royal family, all are believed to have been auctioned off after the revolution and, until the recent discovery of one in 2018, were believed to have been lost forever. The pictured vehicle (bottom), which was discovered in a serious state of neglect outside of Tehran, has now been bought by a sympathetic collector and is currently under restoration.

TOP RIGHT: **The Crown Prince in his Bimbo Racer V12. (Late 1960s)** *(Niavaran Palace)*

ABOVE: **The "barn find" Bimbo Racer as discovered in the outskirts of Tehran. (2018)** *(Ehsan Darougin)*

1939 Bugatti Type 57C Vanvooren
Chassis Number: 57808

As covered in Chapter 15, following a major house cleaning of the royal garage, the Shah's Bugatti Type 57C Vanvooren was sold with a salvage title in 1959 to Mr. Houshang Jaili. Jalili then sold the Bugatti to Mr. Salim Bahary, following which the car was subsequently driven by Bahary under its own power to Holland, and over the years the Bugatti eventually found its way to the United States. The car, which had been driven by the Shah frequently, especially to the Caspian Sea via the Shah's favorite driving road, had been subjected to the wear and tear that continued high-speed driving over crude roads could inflict. As a result, when the car was sold by the royal garage, the car was showing deterioration and even some trim items are believed to have been missing.

For years, perhaps due to the missing trim, the car was believed to have been bodied by Figoni et Falaschi.

LEFT: The royal Bugatti Type 57C bodied by Vanvooren, chassis number 57808, prior to restoration. (1960s) *(Petersen Automotive Museum)*

BOTTOM & ABOVE (BOTH): The Bugatti Type 57C, under restoration by specialist Rod Jolley. *(Rod Jolley)*

OPPOSITE TOP LEFT, MIDDLE & INSET: The only negative point in the restoration of this car was the use of a non-original registration plate. A black plate with white numbers has no historical background in Iran. Under ownership of the Shah, the car had no registration plates but after its auction by the royal garage it received a standard license plate in white with the license plate number 20011 T(Tehran)-38. (1959) *(Sam Noroozi and Jack Braam Ruben)*

OPPOSITE RIGHT TOP: Such is the timeless beauty of the Shah's Bugatti that in the 2017 Rétromobile show a car was debuted to the public which was very similar to the Shah's Bugatti but in a different color. Actually it was a replica made by "Auto Classique Touraine" on a Bugatti Type 57C chassis as a customer order. *(Mahnaz Beedel)*

OPPOSITE BOTTOM: The Bugatti Type 57C, at its current home in the Petersen Automotive Museum. *(Petersen Automotive Museum)*

Appendix 1: The Story Continues

However, when the car was brought to the attention of Claude Figoni, son of the founder of Figoni et Falaschi, it was discovered that Figoni et Falaschi had never had any involvement with this car.

The true origins of the Bugatti were subsequently discovered by renown automotive historian Alain Dollfus, who wrote in the Winter 1985 edition of the French journal, *Automobiles Classiques,* that the Bugatti had been copied from a Delahaye Type 165 which Crown Prince Mohammad Reza Pahlavi had admired at the Paris Salon several months before his wedding and that the French

457

government had commissioned the French coach builder Vanvooren, not Figoni et Falaschi, to build a car similar to the one admired by the future Monarch.

In 1986, the car was acquired by the Blackhawk Classic Automobile Collection. The next owner was Mr. Oscar Davis before it was sold to its current home, the Petersen Automotive Museum.

1953 Cadillac Series 75 Convertible Ghia Special, bodied by Carrozzeria Ghia
Chassis Number: unknown

This car was a special order to Carrozzeria Ghia by King Saud of Saudi Arabia in 1953. This unique limousine was ordered as a convertible and was used during the official visit of the Shah to Saudi Arabia in 1957. After being decommissioned from official use, the car remained in the Saudi royal garage and was then transferred to the King Abdolaziz Historical Center where it is now on display. The car is missing its original hubcaps and requires a cosmetic restoration.

Alongside the 1953 Cadillac Series 75 Convertible Ghia Special, the Saudi government also had in their fleet a number of other specially-bodied Cadillacs. By way of example, in late 1951, King Ibn Saud (Abdolaziz) ordered twenty new Cadillacs with custom-built bodies from Hess & Eisenhardt for a total amount of $250,000, to transport his four wives (and one hundred former wives). These cars each had six doors, electric fans and special windows so the women could see out but no one could see in.

Appendix 1: The Story Continues

1955 Chrysler K-300 Ghia Special
Chassis Number: 3N551511

The Shah was known to have been very fond of this car and had ordered that it be kept as an artifact of the Pahlavi dynasty. Accordingly, at the time of the 1979 revolution, the car was kept at the royal garage in pristine condition. Unfortunately, when the royal garage fell to the revolution, this car, along with others, bore the brunt of revolutionary fervor and suffered damage to both the front end and left rear fender. In the late 1980s, the Bonyad Mostazafan decided to repair some of the damaged cars that it had in its possession and the repair of the Chrysler was turned over to a local expert, Mansour Kamranfar, whom, along with his team, were able to return the Chrysler to close to its original condition. Kamranfar's team only worked on the exterior with the interior still being in need of some repair.

OPPOSITE: March 11, 1957, the Shah of Iran paid a state visit to Saudi Arabia where he is driven in a 1953 Cadillac Series 75 Convertible Ghia Special. In this picture, the Shah is sitting alongside King Saud. *(Borzou Sepasi)*

LEFT TOP & MIDDLE: 1953 Cadillac Series 75 Convertible Ghia Special on display in the King Abdolaziz Historical Center.

ABOVE: One of the twenty Hess & Eisenhardt Cadillacs prior to delivery to Saudi Arabia. (1951) *(www.professionalcarsociety.org)*

RIGHT (BOTH): The official photographs of the Chrysler K-300 Ghia Special, chassis number 3N551511 at the time of the transfer of ownership to the Bonyad Mostazafan. A portion of the damage the car suffered during the revolution can be witnessed by the broken rear light. The car's wooden dashboard with gold-plated instruments and HIGHWAY HI-FI Phonograph and refrigerator remain intact. (1980s) *(Bonyad Mostazafan)*

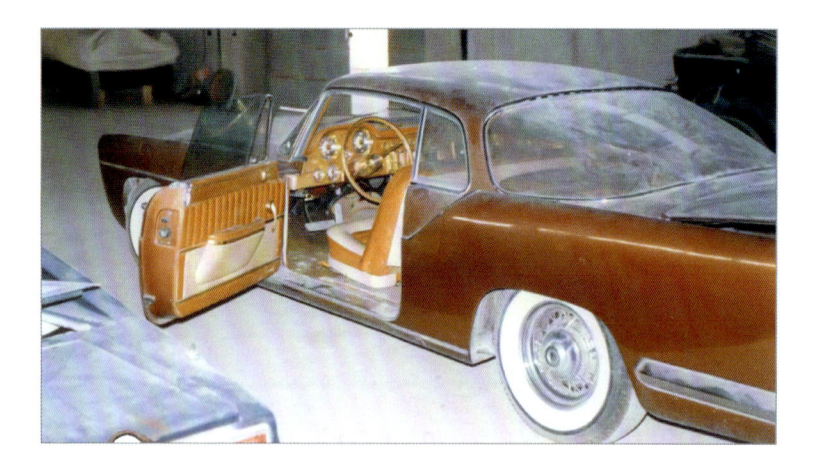

BELOW (BOTH): Mansour Kamranfar led a team to restore the Chrysler K-300 Ghia Special. (Late 1980s) *(Mansour Kamranfar)*

LEFT: The Chrysler K-300 Ghia Special in the Karaj warehouse of the Bonyad Mostazafan. (Late 1980s) *(Mansour Kamranfar)*

Daimler DK-400 All-Weather Tourer, bodied by Hooper (King of Afghanistan)
Chassis Number: 92724

This car was owned by Mohammad Zahir Shah, the former King of Afghanistan. Though not having any direct or indirect ownership by the Shah of Iran, this vehicle was prominently on display during Mohammad Reza Shah's official visit to Kabul in 1962. In the 1990s, with the monarchies in Iran and Afghanistan both overthrown and Afghanistan in political turmoil with the ascension of the Moudjahidin, this vehicle, which was being kept as part of the National Museum collection, was taken out and used for target practice by the Mudjahidin (later Taliban) and eventually scrapped.

ABOVE: Mohammad Zahir Shah, the King of Afghanistan rides in the Daimler DK-400 All-Weather Tourer, chassis number 92724, bodied by Hooper in Kabul. (1968)

BELOW: An Afghan Mujahedin with what remains of the royal Daimler DK-400 All-Weather Tourer. This picture was taken in the yard of the Afghan National Museum in Kabul in the Spring of 1995. In the background (left), the remains of the burned and looted national museum can be seen while on the right, the shell of the destroyed Darussalam Palace. (1995)
(Swen Conrad/ Yume Vision)

Fit for a King ~ The Royal Garage of the Shah of Iran

250

Formerly the Property of His Imperial Highness The Late Shah of Iran

1973 DAIMLER 4.2 LITRE LIMOUSINE
COACHWORK FINISHED BY VANDEN PLAS

Chassis no. 1M 20088   Engine no. 7M 2553

This left-hand drive limousine was built on 4th June 1973 and despatched on 20th July 1973 to the Imperial Court of Iran. In dark blue/black paintwork with blue/grey upholstery and interior trim (in cloth in the rear passenger compartment), the car features flag masts, a central division and occasional seats, and general condition of the paintwork, chrome, carpets and interior is said to be good, and commensurate with the extremely low recorded mileage of just 4,141 kms.

The car is representative of the last coachbuilt Daimlers. It is powered by the 4.2 litre six cylinder overhead camshaft engine, and has automatic transmission, all-independent suspension and disc braking. In store since the 1979 revolution, the car has nonetheless been regularly started. It is offered with a Jaguar Daimler Heritage Certificate confirming its Imperial origins.

Should the car remain in Switzerland local import taxes will be liable. If the car is to be re-exported from Switzerland, this must be arranged through Brooks Europe.

Cette voiture, conduite à gauche, a été livrée à la cour Impériale d'Iran en Juillet 1973. De couleur bleu foncé, intérieur bleu/gris, elle n'a que 4141 km au compteur.
Voiture non-dedouanée en Suisse.

Estimate SFR9,000 - 15,000

1973 Daimler DS420

With the nationalization of the palaces and the dissolution of the royal court, the six Daimler D420s of the royal court were expropriated by the state and of these, one was handed over to the Bonyad Shahid with the remaining five going to the Bonyad Mostazafan. The Daimler that went to the Bonyad Shahid was subsequently sold as part of the ten vehicles that were sold to Mohammad Ibrahim Al-Sadegh and then auctioned off by Brooks Auction House in Switzerland, in March 1997 and the rest remain in the ownership of the Bonyad Mostazafan languishing in a warehouse since the revolution.

1949 Delahaye 135M, bodied by Ghia
Chassis Number: 800514

As detailed earlier in the book, following its sale by the royal garage, the Shah's Delahaye 135 was in Holland for a number of years and, as late as 1965, was still garnering coverage in Dutch automotive magazines. The car subsequently crossed the Atlantic where it became part of the Blackhawk Collection, remaining there until 1989. After undergoing restoration in the early 1990s, the Delahaye became part of the O'Quinn Collection. The Delahaye was auctioned in Monaco in 2010 and was bought by a French collector who is said to have used the car sparingly before re-selling at the 2016 Artcurial auction held at the Rétromobile event in Paris.

OPPOSITE: Daimler DS420, chassis number 1M20088, that was sold at auction by Brooks in Geneva in 1997.

LEFT: One of the five Daimler DS420s still remaining in Iran in storage at the warehouse of the Bonyad Mostazafan in Karaj Iran. (2005) *(Borzou Sepasi)*

BELOW: The Shah's Delahaye 135M, chassis number 800514, bodied by Ghia offered by Artcurial at Rétromobile in 2016. *(Artcurial)*

1964 Ferrari 330GT 2+2
Chassis Number: 5459

The Shah's Ferrari 330GT 2+2, chassis number 5459, is believed to initially have been one of his favorite cars, arranging for it to be transported by air to Iran from the factory. However, with the arrival of the sleeker, more powerful and faster Ferrari 500 Superfast in 1965, the Shah seemed to have lost all interest in this car and, in 1968, passed it on to his nephew, Prince Shahram Pahlavi Nia, son of his twin sister, Princess Ashraf Pahlavi. Prince Shahram apparently never took delivery of the car as it was suffering from a number of mechanical maladies and the car languished unused in the royal garage until Prince Shahram sold it to a Mr. Parviz Eshghi in 1974. Because of its private ownership, the car escaped the clutches of the new revolutionary government and avoided confiscation. The last time that the car was spotted inside Iran was in the early 1990s where it was photographed as it was being transported by trailer along with a yellow Corvette to an unknown destination. In the accompanying pictures it is apparent

Appendix 1: The Story Continues

that the original color "Oro Chiaro" (light gold) was repainted to red. Since its last spotting, the trail of this car in Iran has run cold with some surmising that the Ferrari was subsequently taken out of Iran.

1974 Ferrari 365 GT4 2+2
Chassis Number: 18263

King Hussein of Jordan shared with the Shah not only a deep-rooted friendship, but also a passion for fine automobiles. In 1974, King Hussein gifted two Ferraris to the Shah of Iran, one of which was Ferrari 365 GT4 2+2, chassis number 18263. Following the revolution, this Ferrari ended up in the possession of the Bonyad Shahid.

As covered earlier in this chapter, when the Bonyad Shahid proceeded to sell off ten of the cars in its possession to an Emirati buyer, Mohammad Ibrahim Al-Sadegh, this Ferrari was included in the sale. Al-Sadegh subsequently sold this car alongside all the other cars he bought from the Bonyad Shahid through the Brooks Europe auction held in Geneva in March 1997.

1974 Ferrari 365 GT4/BB
Chassis Number: 18181

The fate of the second Ferrari bequeathed by King Hussein of Jordan to the Shah was much different than the 365 GT4 2+2. This Ferrari, a 365 GT4/BB was separated from the 365 GT4 2+2 and ended up in the hands of the Bonyad Mostazafan, where it remains today under the care of the National Automobile Museum of Iran. It has been put on public display from time to time in a number of classic car shows that have been held over the years.

OPPOSITE & TOP LEFT: The royal Ferrari 330GT 2+2, chassis number 5459, in rough condition repainted in red, spotted near Isfahan. (1990s) *(Borzou Sepasi)*

LEFT: Ferrari 365 GT4 2+2, chassis number 18263, in a local workshop before being shipped out of Iran. (February 1994) *(Abbas Soleymani)*

ABOVE: The Shah's Ferrari 365 GT4/BB, chassis number 18181 on display in the National Automobile Museum of Iran. (2005) *(Borzou Sepasi)*

1957 Ferrari 410 Superamerica Series II, bodied by Pininfarina
Chassis Number: 0717SA

Despite the lore that this Ferrari was given to Queen Soraya in 1958 following her divorce from the Shah, this car was not only purchased after the Shah's divorce from Soraya, but remained in the possession of the Shah for a number of years after the divorce. As covered earlier, the Shah would be frequently photographed whisking about town in this car with his new Queen, Farah Diba. In 1967, the car ended up in the United States and was in the hands of Tom Barrett of Scottsdale, Arizona. In 1971, the Ferrari was traded for a Ford Thunderbird and $3,000 cash. In 1980, it was chosen as "Best in Show" in the Ferrari Club of America Annual Meet held in Hershey, Pennsylvania and in 2001 it underwent a restoration at Gran Turismo Motors in Glendale, California, with the paint and metal work carried out at Beckman's Metalworks of Costa Mesa, California. Since then, the Ferrari has gone on to win a number of awards in shows and events. At the 2015 Pebble Beach show, Gooding & Company successfully auctioned the car for $5,087,500.[1]

---

[1] www.goodingco.com/lot/1957-ferrari-410-superamerica-series-ii-coupe-2

LEFT: The Shah of Iran Ferrari 410 Superamerica, chassis number 0717SA, bodied by Pininfarina being prepped for restoration at Gran Turismo Motors. (2001)

TOP RIGHT & BELOW: The Ferrari 410 Superamerica was sold at auction by Gooding & Company for $5,087,500. (August 2015) *(Sam Noroozi)*

Appendix 1: The Story Continues

1965 Ferrari 500 Superfast
Chassis Number: 6605SF

The Shah's Ferrari 500 Superfast, chassis number 6605SF, is unique in that it has been expropriated by the Iranian government not once, but twice. The first expropriation took place after the car was sold by the royal garage on December 22, 1973 to Mr. Farshid Esfandiary, a relative of the Shah and a noted local car enthusiast. With the onset of the 1979 revolution, due to his ties with the royal family, all of Mr. Esfandiary's assets were subject to expropriation, including this 500 Superfast, the ownership of which was transferred to the Bonyad Mostazafan. As the car was slightly damaged at the time of the transfer, the Bonyad commissioned a light repair of the damages that the Ferrari had sustained, including the replacement of a broken rear taillight with a Land Rover unit.

THIS PAGE & NEXT PAGE TOP LEFT: **The Shah of Iran's Ferrari 500 Superfast, chassis number 6605SF, in Bonyad Mostazafan ownership. Some minor damage is visible on the body and trim. (Early 1980s)** *(Bonyad Mostazafan)*

467

Fit for a King ~ The Royal Garage of the Shah of Iran

The ownership of the car then took a tragic turn when the Superfast was sold to Mr. Fazel Khodadad, a scion of one of Iran's most well-known pre-revolution merchant families. Mr. Khodadad, a car enthusiast who had returned to Iran following the revolution and was seeking the release of his family assets which had been expropriated by the Bonyad Mostazafan and during the course of negotiations, also had apparently succeeded in purchasing a number of cars which were in the possession of the Bonyad, including the Superfast. Subsequently, Mr. Khodadad was caught up in one of the largest economic corruption scandals in Iranian history and, on August 22, 1995, Mr. Khodadad was convicted of "sabotaging the country's economic system" and sentenced to death on November 22, 1995. Before his arrest, Mr. Khodadad had planned to ship the Superfast out of Iran and, with his sentencing, the Ferrari was expropriated for a second time and returned to the warehouses of the Bonyad Mostazafan. In 2003, concomitant with the founding of the National Automobile Museum of Iran, the Superfast went on permanent display where it sits today.

1968 Fiat 850 Shellette, bodied by Michelotti

Chassis Number: 100GB 1226009

The Shah's Fiat 850 Shellette was confiscated by the Bonyad Mostazafan along with the Nowshahr Palace on the shores of the Caspian Sea. The Fiat, which had sat in the palace garage, was removed and transferred to the Karaj warehouse of the Bonyad Mostazafan. When the author came across this vehicle, the dashboard had suffered minor damage and the wicker seats were found to have been replaced by regular vinyl-covered seats when the car was still under the ownership of the Shah. Apparently, the Shah did not find the original wicker seats to be comfortable and had the royal garage change them to regular vinyl.

MIDDLE: The Ferrari 500 Superfast, chassis number 6605SF, on display in the National Automobile Museum of Iran. (2010) *(Mahnaz Beedel)*

ABOVE: The 500 Superfast in the late 1980s after a light refurbishment. The left reverse light is borrowed from a Land Rover! *(Borzou Sepasi)*

The Fiat 850 Shellette in storage at the Karaj Warehouse. The wicker seats had been replaced by regular vinyl-covered seats when still in the possession of the Shah. (2003) *(Borzou Sepasi)*

1931 Hispano-Suiza J12, bodied by Saoutchik
Chassis Number: 13010

As covered earlier, in 1957 when the Shah decided to undertake a house cleaning of the royal garage, several cars were kept on due to the significance they had both in his life and that of his family. It was not surprising that of the cars that were kept, cars such as his father's Pierce-Arrow would be included. However, one of the cars that many were surprised to see that he would let go was the 1931 Hispano-Suiza J12. This car had played a big part in his youth, being the first car to be picked and bought by him, and used on his first day of school at Le Rosey, his return to Iran and his marriage to Queen Fawzia.

In any case, after the sale of the car to Mr. Salim Bahary (who at a later point in time went on to purchase the Bugatti Type 57C Vanvooren, chassis number 57808), from its new owner following its sale from the royal garage, the Hispano-Suiza subsequently ended up first in Israel and then in 1966, the United States in the hands of Mr. Bob Ortenberger of Oklahoma, who had answered an ad placed by Bahary in *Road & Track* magazine. In 1979, having only covered 23,000 km from new, the car was sold to New Zealander Roy Southward. Under Southward's care, due to the Hispano's low mileage, it was only in 2006 that Southward commissioned a complete engine rebuild. Additionally, the body was restored, which included a change of color to white with black fenders.

The car remained in Southward's family until 2011 when it was sold to fellow New Zealanders Mark and Sonia Richter. Since taking ownership, the couple have used the vehicle frequently for journeys across New Zealand and started a Facebook page: "Hispano-Suiza J12 Journeys" where they share photographs of their many trips in the J12.

By 2017, under the ownership of the Richters, the car had traveled over 35,000 km. Notwithstanding this extensive use, the car was successfully entered into the 2017 Pebble Beach Concours d'Elegance where it not only won best in Class (European Classic Early) but also the Alec Ulmann Trophy, an award bestowed upon the car that best embodies the combination of excellence in performance and elegance in design. The award of such a prize to the Hispano-Suiza, some eighty-six years after a twelve-year old Mohammad Reza Pahlavi personally chose this car

Appendix 1: The Story Continues

as his first from among the greatest motoring marques of the period, would seem to serve as an early prelude of things to come in the unique automotive tastes of Pahlavi, a taste which would only further manifest itself through the years.

OPPOSITE TOP: **The Hispano-Suiza J12, chassis number 13010, prior to being added to the Roy Southward Collection. (1979)** *(Lawrence Southward)*

OPPOSITE RIGHT (BOTH): **The rolling chassis and body of the Hispano-Suiza under restoration.** *(Lawrence Southward)*

TOP LEFT: **The Facebook page "Hispano-Suiza J12 Journeys" which is dedicated to the trips by the Shah's Hispano around New Zealand.**

TOP RIGHT & MIDDLE: **During one of its many journeys across New Zealand.** *(Mark and Sonia Richter)*

RIGHT: **The royal Hispano-Suiza J12 at the 2017 Pebble Beach Concours d'Elegance.** *(Sam Noroozi)*

Fit for a King ~ The Royal Garage of the Shah of Iran

1976 Lamborghini Countach LP400

Chassis Number: 1120190

When the revolution occurred in 1979, Crown Prince Reza's Lamborghini Countach was being kept in the royal garage at the Firouzeh Palace in east Tehran and had only 2,215 km on the odometer. The revolutionaries subsequently transferred the Countach to the main Karaj warehouse of the Bonyad Mostazafan in the early 1980s where it remained in storage, being brought out only on certain sporadic occasions such as car shows (where the organizers would receive permission from the authorities to put it on display). In 2004, the Countach was put on permanent display at the National Automobile Museum of Iran where it sits today.

ABOVE (BOTH): Honda ATC-90s in Niavaran and Saad Abad Palace garages. (2004) *(Borzou Sepasi)*

BELOW: The royal garage in July 1979, six months after the revolution. The odometer of the Crown Prince's Lamborghini Countach LP400, chassis number 1120190, showed only 2,215 km. (July 1979) *(Keyvan Banihashemi)*

OPPOSITE TOP LEFT: The Countach when it sat in the Bonyad Mostazafan's Karaj warehouse. (2003) *(Borzou Sepasi)*

OPPOSITE TOP RIGHT: The Countach is just barely seen beside the Mercedes-Benz 500K Autobahnkurier, chassis number 130898, at a classic car show in Saad Abad Palace. A problematic front door is not closed correctly. (2004) *(Borzou Sepasi)*

OPPOSITE BOTTOM: In the National Automobile Museum in Tehran on jack stands, ostensibly to protect the original tires. There is a MC (Monte Carlo) sticker affixed in place of a license plate. (2010) *(Ghazal Jami)*

Honda ATC-90 tricycle

The Niavaran and Saad Abad Palaces had a number of Honda ATC-90s for use by the Shah's children on the palace grounds. As can be imagined, with the onset of the revolution and the fall of the palaces, these vehicles, along with bicycles and other children's playthings were left abandoned in the two palaces until 2010 when, with the initiative of the curator of the garage of the Niavaran Palace, Mrs. Shahnaz Pakniyat, the Niavaran Palace Auto Museum was founded and two of the ATC-90s were refurbished and put on permanent display.

Appendix 1: The Story Continues

Fit for a King ~ The Royal Garage of the Shah of Iran

252

Formerly the Property of His Imperial Highness the late Shah of Iran

1969 LAMBORGHINI ESPADA
COACHWORK BY BERTONE

Chassis no. 7099   Engine no. 2694

The Espada was one of Lamborghini's greatest achievements, a car which finally fulfilled Ferruccio's ambition to create a four seater luxury supercar. Stylistically inspired by the futuristic Marzal show car of 1967, the Espada was unveiled at the 1968 Geneva *Salon* and, following the trend started by the Miura, its name was taken from bullfighting folklore. The Espada used the four cam 3,929cc V12 engine fitted to the Miura, whilst its luxurious passenger cabin was intended to offer levels of comfort and refinement not previously seen in a car of such high performance. Innovative details abounded, marking the Espada as the choice of the VIP with taste.

This early Espada, boasting numerous attractive features which were to disappear on later cars, was delivered to HIH The Shah of Iran in January 1969, joining a growing collection of the Sant' Agata marque in the Imperial garage. Its paintwork was finished in Champagne with brown leather upholstery and carpets, all of which show little wear. The odometer reading stands at just 6,975km and the car, whilst being regularly started, has not been driven since the 1979 revolution.

This is surely the lowest mileage Espada in existence, and it is hard to imagine one with a more fascinating provenance.

Should the car remain in Switzerland local import taxes will be liable. If the car is to be re-exported from Switzerland, this must be arranged through Brooks Europe.

Cette Espada, une des premières, fût livrée au Shah d'Iran en Janvier 1969. Elle fût livrée Champagne, cuir marron et n'affiche que 6975 km. Voiture non-dedouanée en Suisse.

Estimate SFR35,000 - 45,000

ABOVE: The Lamborghini Espada featured in the Brooks Europe Auction catalog, March 1997.

OPPOSITE: 1969 Lamborghini Espada, chassis number 7099, as it sat abandoned in the Niavaran palace garage in the early 1980s. *(Ali Gorji, the author extends his appreciation to Mrs. Shahnaz Pakniyat for securing the permission to use this photo.)*

474

1969 Lamborghini Espada S1
Chassis Number: 7099

With the fall of the Niavaran Palace, accompanying the Miura SVJ was the Shah's Espada S1. Despite the fact this car was a decade old at the time of the revolution, it still enjoyed a coveted spot in the Niavaran Palace garage rather than the royal garage, a reflection of the affinity that the Shah had for this car, especially as he was known to drive his children to school in it. As with the Miura SVJ, after the revolution the Espada lay virtually abandoned in the palace garage until it, along with the Lamborghini Miura SVJ, chassis number 4934, were subsequently transferred to an unknown warehouse under the control of the Bonyad Shahid. The two Lamborghinis were then sold together along with eight other cars in auction to UAE citizen Mohammad Ibrahim Al-Sadegh. Al-Sadegh subsequently put the Espada alongside the SVJ up for auction at the Brooks Europe Auction on March 12, 1997 where it fetched $23,000. After years of coexisting side by side in the Niavaran palace garage and then under the control of the Bonyad Shahid, the two cars were finally separated at the Brooks Auction. The buyer was a Turkish collector by the name of Cengiz Artam who shipped the car to Turkey and owns it to this day.

1968 Lamborghini Miura
Chassis Number: 3303

1976 Porsche 934 RSR
Chassis Number: 9306700168

The histories of this Lamborghini and Porsche are uniquely intertwined. In 1973, the Shah's first Lamborghini Miura, chassis number 3303, was sold by the royal court to Mr. Firouz Saeid Ansari, one of Iran's best known car collectors of the period and the son of the Chief of Staff of the Shah's older sister, Princess Shams. Ansari effectively used the car as a daily driver and would race it on weekends at the makeshift Aryamehr Stadium circuit. In 1977, Ansari upped the ante against his fellow competitors when he purchased and imported a former Max Moritz-prepared Porsche 934 RSR, chassis number 9306700168, which had international wins under its belt prior to being imported to Iran.

It is believed that sometime around the purchase of the 934 RSR in 1977, Ansari sold the Shah's Miura to

Firouz Saeid Ansari preparing for a race in his Porsche 934 RSR, chassis number 9306700168, at the Aryamehr circuit. (1978)
(Hamid Kooshanfar)

renowned Iranian architect, Nezam Amery. Amery stands out in Iranian history for two reasons, namely he was the only Iranian architect to have studied directly under the tutelage of Frank Lloyd Wright (and then went on to become the Middle East representative of Taliesin

ABOVE (ALL): **Firouz Saeid Ansari's Porsche 934 RSR, chassis number 9306700168, as it sits in storage at the Bonyad Mostazafan's Karaj warehouse. (Early 2000s)** *(Borzou Sepasi)*

Associated Architects, an architectural firm founded by Wright to carry on his architectural vision after his death) and he was the son of Sheikh Khazal, the Arab separatist and nemesis of the Shah's father, Reza Shah whom, as covered extensively in Chapter 2, he crushed in 1924 during his rise to power. It is believed that Reza Shah subsequently ordered the assassination of Sheikh Khazal in 1936 when Amery was ten years old.

It is speculated that the connection between Amery and Ansari dates back to the design and construction of the Morvarid (Pearl) Palace, the primary palace of Princess Shams. Located in Mehrshahr, outside of Tehran (due to the Princess' asthma), the Princess, whose eccentric tastes were well known to Iranian society, ordered a Palace that was to come in the shape of a pearl. This unique project, which Firouz Ansari's father (as Chief of Staff of the Princess) no doubt played a key role, was contracted to Taliesin Associated Architects and Nezam Amery. With construction having started in or around 1966, the Palace was completed in 1972 at an estimated cost of $3.5 million. The truly unique palace was built on roughly 420 acres of land and was surrounded by an artificial lake. Though this architectural marvel is currently suffering from years of neglect, nonetheless in 2003 it was finally registered as an Iranian national heritage site and today is awaiting a long overdue restoration.

With the onset of the revolution, due to their close ties to the royal court, all of the properties of both Ansari and Amery were confiscated by the state, including their cars. The ownership of the both Ansari's Porsche and Amery's Lamborghini ended up in the possession of the Bonyad Mostazafan and were subsequently sent into storage in one of their many warehouses used to store expropriated property and belongings. Throughout the 1980s, several auctions were held by the Bonyad Mostazafan in which a number of cars in their possession were sold. In 1987, the Miura was put up for auction at the Dafineh building. The Dafineh was one of the most famous buildings in Iran and an architectural landmark located in northern Tehran. Designed by none other than Nezam Amery, this renown building was also confiscated from its owner and transferred to the ownership of the Bonyad Mostazafan.

Appendix 1: The Story Continues

TOP: Pictured is Miura, chassis number 3303, with its Lamborghini insignia removed in preparation for being rebadged as a Fiat. *(Classic_cars_oldpic Instagram page)*

ABOVE: The Shah's Miura, chassis number 3303, prior to restoration. *(Simon Kidston)*

At the auction, the Miura was offered for sale alongside the Shah's Porsche 928, which went unsold, and a BMW 7 series (original owner unknown). The irony of the sale of Nezam Amery's Miura in a building which was one of his crowning achievements was not lost on many. In June 2020, the restoration of this magnificent building was awarded the World Architecture Community Award.

What took place during the auction is subject to two separate accounts from a single source, as classic car dealer Simon Kidston, who has been intimately associated with Miura 3303, renders two separate accounts.

In one account, Kidston is quoted as stating that the bidder for the Miura was none other than the Shah's second son, Prince Ali Reza Pahlavi. With "cunning sleight of hand, the car was bought by the Shah's younger son Alireza, Prince Alireza Pahlavi, with his best friend Alireza Itthadieh acting as intermediary".[2]

The Miura was subsequently shipped out of Iran and, by 1988, the car was in the hands of Prince Alireza in London, having been shipped out of Iran as a Fiat, "with badges removed for good measure".[3] In the early 1990s, with less than 10,000 km showing on the odometer, the Prince commissioned an overhaul with the car being repainted in orange. The Miura subsequently made its debut in 1993 at the London Huntingham Club where it went on display at the Louis Vuitton Concours d'Elegance.

In a separate account, Kidston states that the Miura was offered at auction by the Bonyad Mostazafan at a starting price of 9,000,000 Rials (equivalent to just under $7,500 at the time) setting off a bidding war between two Iranian brothers, Manuchehr and Mehrdad Satvat with Manuchehr Satvat winning the bidding war at a final price of 30,000,000 Rials ($25,000).[4]

According to Kidston, Manuchehr Satvat then proceeded to register the car in his wife's name and the car received the license plate 41825 Tehran 21, with the Tehran-21 prefix representing that the car had been sold at auction.[5] At some point later, the car was then sold to Manuchehr Satvat's brother Mehrdad for a price equivalent to nearly $100,000.

Based on the information published by Kidston, in the early 1990s the Miura was exported to Switzerland using an Iranian transit plate TEH-86761 and then found its way to the United Kingdom where it was bought by the Shah's younger son Prince Ali Reza via an intermediary.[6]

---

[2] *David Lillywhite, "King Miura", Magneto, Issue 2, Summer 2019, p. 104*

[3] *ibid*

[4] *Simon Kidston, "The Lamborghini Miura Book", Kidston SA, 2020*

[5] *ibid*

[6] *ibid*

Sometime in the early years of the decade 2000, Kidston made direct acquaintance with Prince Alireza who confided in him that he really did not know what to do with the Miura, "he'd used it once or twice but every time he went out he found the clutch too heavy and the car too hot, too noisy and uncomfortable. He really did not have the patience to deal with it"[7]. In 2010, the Prince sold the car to an Iranian friend by the name of Dariush Fouladi, with the odometer showing just 10,545 km. A year later, the Prince, suffering a battle with depression, ended his own life.

In 2015, the new owner offered to sell the car to Simon Kidston. At the time, Kidston was in the process of forming on behalf of a client "the world's ultimate Miura collection" and, having already secured the Shah of Iran Miura SVJ for the collection, the SVJ's former stablemate, the Shah's P400 was deemed a necessary addition to the collection. According to Kidston, "we ended up paying quite a high price for the car" and after purchasing the car, the new owner decided "to go all-out and do the absolute ultimate Miura restoration"[8]. However, before the car went to restoration, the new owner allowed Kidston to make a film in homage to the Shah and the Miura. Titled *A Winter's Tale*, in the film, the Miura is shown being driven by a Shah look alike through the Shah's old haunts in St. Moritz, at speed, and on snow-covered icy roads, as the Shah was known to do during his annual visits.

Having had the benefit of a world class restoration, the Miura was first put on display at Simon Kidston's stand at the 2019 Rétromobile show before being shown at the 2019 Pebble Beach Concours d'Elegance. Today, the Shah's P400 is in the hands of renown collector and former Microsoft executive, Jon Shirley.

On a side note, Firouz Ansari's Porsche 934 RSR was never sold and remained in the possession of the Bonyad Mostazafan at its Karaj warehouse for decades until it was finally put on display at the National Automobile Museum of Iran in 2004. In 2021, it was subjected to an amateur restoration by the museum, where any trace of Ansari's ownership of the car was erased. In the same year, Firouz Ansari was found murdered in his office in Italy in what apparently was a business deal gone bad.

---

[7] *David Lillywhite, "King Miura", Magneto, Issue 2, Summer 2019, p. 104*

[8] *ibid*

Appendix 1: The Story Continues

OPPOSITE TOP: The Shah's Miura, chassis number 3303, while being filmed in St. Moritz for the film, *A Winter's Tale*, an homage to the Shah's ownership of the Miura. *(Simon Kidston)*

TOP (BOTH): On display at Simon Kidston's stand at the 2019 Rétromobile classic car show in Paris. Note the reproduction of the original Iranian transit plates. *(Mahnaz Beedel)*

ABOVE: On display at the 2019 Pebble Beach Concours d'Elegance. *(Sam Noroozi)*

The inter-connection between the Shah's first Miura, Firouz Ansari, Nezam Amery and the Pahlavi family is a microcosm of the complexities of the Pahlavi era aristocracy where the son of an assassinated tribal leader would rise to prominence serving the progeny of the very same person who ordered the death of his father. In the end, the one issue other than the shared history of the ownership of Miura that united the three families, was the wave of the revolution that changed their lives forever.

1970 Lamborghini Miura P400S
Chassis Number: 4479

While at times this car has been mistakenly attributed to the ownership of the Shah and, at times, to his twin sister Princess Ashraf, in reality Lamborghini Miura S, chassis number 4479, was first owned by the Shah's firstborn, Princess Shahnaz from his first wife, Queen Fawzia. The Shah had complained about the paradox between the Princess' hippie pretensions and her predilection for luxury cars but, in any case, the Princess inherited from her father an appreciation for fine automobiles, and this Miura was among a number of the unique cars she owned.

In 1973, the Miura was sold to Dr. Kaivon Saleh, a well-respected physician and noted car aficionado. Following its purchase by Dr. Saleh, during the ensuing winter season of that year, the entire engine was rebuilt in makeshift quarters at his home over a period of four months under the auspices of Reza Dardashti, one of Iran's most respected mechanics who years earlier successfully repaired the Shah's Chrysler Ghia K-300.

Following the revolution, Dr. Saleh's possessions were confiscated due to his purported ties with the Pahlavi regime. However, the Miura was all but missing for over a decade until it was found hidden in the greenhouse of a villa confiscated by the revolutionaries. Apparently, when the car was put into hiding, the wheels and tires were removed for good measure and put away in an unknown location where, until today, they have not been found. The Miura, sans wheels, was discovered balanced on a number of logs. When the car was confiscated by the Bonyad Mostazafan, the technicians of the Bonyad had to search for suitable replacement wheels and tires that could be fitted to the Miura. After checking a number of cars in their possession, the technicians

Appendix 1: The Story Continues

OPPOSITE: Lamborghini Miura, chassis number 4479, still being balanced on logs after being fitted with Ferrari rims and tires. (2003) *(Borzou Sepasi)*

BELOW: Dr. Kaivon Saleh's (ex-Princess Shahnaz Pahlavi) Lamborghini Miura S as it sits in storage in the Bonyad Mostazafan warehouse. (2003) *(Borzou Sepasi)*

BOTTOM: The cracks in the paint of Princess Shahnaz's former Miura after years of being hidden away in a greenhouse. *(Borzou Sepasi)*

RIGHT: Ferrari 365 GT, chassis number 11417, with registration plate 99945 Tehran-T, sitting on jacks which to this day serves as the donor car for the rims and tires of Princess Shahnaz's former Miura. *(Borzou Sepasi)*

MIDDLE & BOTTOM RIGHT: With the opening of the National Automobile Museum of Iran in 2004, the ex-Princess Shahnaz Lamborghini Miura S, chassis number 4479, was one of the first cars selected for display, using Ferrari wheels and tires from the donor car. *(Mahnaz Beedel)*

decided to make use of the wheels and tires of Ferrari 365 GT, chassis number 11417. As of the publication of this book, the Miura is on display at the National Automobile Museum of Iran with the Ferrari wheels and tires still fitted on it. The car has been recently subjected to a general refurbishment by the museum. The Ferrari remains in storage on jacks.

1971 Lamborghini Miura P400 SV
Chassis Number: 4870

A second Miura that has been extensively represented as having been formerly owned by the Shah is Miura P400 SV, chassis number 4870. In fact, the car was originally owned by Patrick Ali Pahlavi. Prior to the birth of Crown Prince Reza, Patrick Ali stood second in line to the throne to succeed the Shah (as he was next in line to the throne following the death of his father – the Shah's second full brother, Prince Ali Reza – in a plane crash). As with his uncle the Shah, Patrick Ali had an affinity for sports cars, and was known to drive around the United States in a Shelby GT500. In 1972, the Prince sold the Miura to Mr. Farshid Esfandiary, who had also successfully purchased the Shah's Ferrari 500 Superfast, chassis number 6605SF. After the revolution, Mr. Esfandiary lost the ownership of his Ferrari 500 Superfast by way of expropriation by the state but was able to successfully keep his Lamborghini Miura SV hidden away from the authorities at his villa. It may have helped that, unlike the Ferrari, the ownership of the Miura could not be traced back directly to the Shah. Unlike many of those who had lost property following the revolution due to their ties to the Pahlavi regime (real or perceived), Mr. Esfandiary and his wife chose to stay on in Iran (though they frequently traveled to the United States). With the Miura, Mr. Esfandiary faced a dichotomy, on the one hand he had successfully held on to his Lamborghini and escaped having it expropriated but, on the other hand, he was hesitant to drive the car for

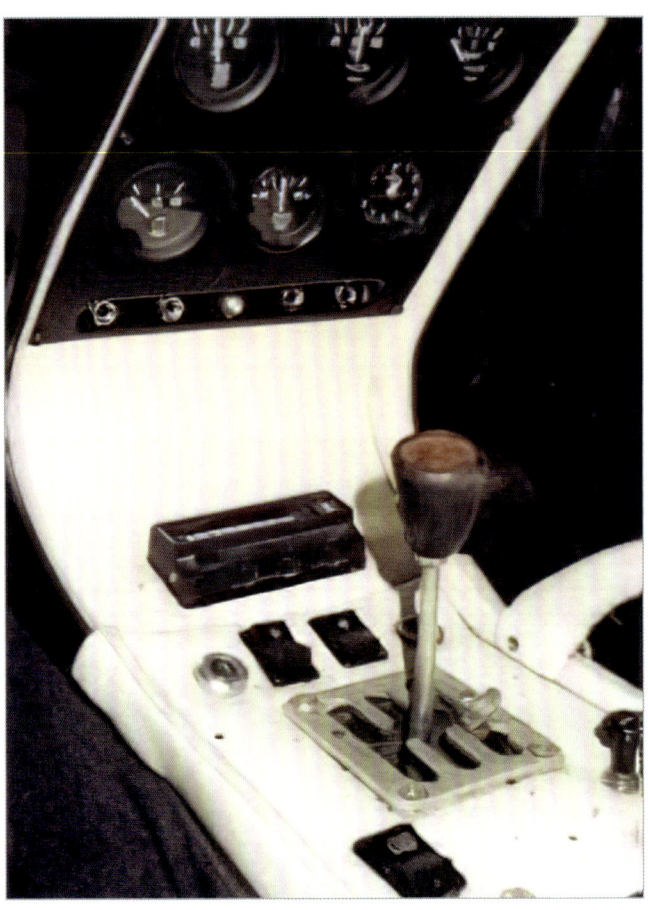

Appendix 1: The Story Continues

1971 Lamborghini Miura SVJ
Chassis Number: 4934

The Shah's Lamborghini Miura SVJ, chassis number 4934, was to emerge as one of the Shah's favorite cars and Tehran was rife with sightings of high-speed midnight runs in the SVJ, primarily in the vicinity of northern Tehran near his two main palaces. It was of no surprise then that with the onset of the 1979 revolution, and the fall of the Niavaran Palace in February 1979, the SVJ, despite being nearly eight years old at the time, was discovered not in the royal garage in the Firouzeh Palace located in east Tehran, but rather in the Shah's primary residence at the Niavaran Palace garage where the Shah wanted it kept close by and on hand for a late-night run.

After the revolution, the SVJ languished in the Niavaran Palace garage, kept company by the Shah's Lamborghini Espada Series I, chassis number 7099, and his two primary ceremonial vehicles, namely the Rolls-Royce Phantom V State Landaulette, chassis number 5LVF29, and Phantom VI, chassis number PRX4861. In the early 1980s, for reasons unknown, the SVJ and the Espada were removed from the garage and their

fear of attracting the undue attention of the authorities and having the car seized as had happened already with his Ferrari.

At some point during the Miura's history, the front end had suffered damage and, in a makeshift repair carried out by Iranian master mechanic Reza Dardashti, Jaguar headlights were used to replace the damaged pop-up units.

Eventually the car ended up in Italy in the 1980s where it was bought by BMW dealer Manfredi Sinistrario and restored locally. From there the car was exported to the United States and bought by Miura collector Joe Sackey, who again had the car refurbished by noted Miura expert Gary Bobileff. During this period, the car was said to have belonged to the Shah of Iran, with the transit plates used to transport the car out of Iran being represented as "royal plates". Since then, the car has passed hands several times, apparently still being represented as having been personally owned by the Shah.

OPPOSITE (ALL) & ABOVE: Miura, chassis number 4870, with fixed lamps borrowed from a Jaguar. The license plates on the car have been wrongly stated to have been the Shah's personal license plates. In reality they are international license plates issued by the FIA under the auspices of the local touring and auto organization. As this car was to be sent to Italy from Iran, it was issued these plates by the Touring and Automobile Club of Iran with the understanding that the car would be returned to Iran. *(Internet)*

The fall of the Niavaran Palace to the revolutionaries in February 1979. The photographs of the Shah and Queen Farah are still hanging on the wall. (February 1979)

483

Fit for a King ~ The Royal Garage of the Shah of Iran

Appendix 1: The Story Continues

OPPOSITE TOP LEFT: The main gate of the Niavaran Palace on the day of its surrender. One of the tanks used to guard the palace is bearing a white flag of surrender and the royal coat of arms on top of the palace gate has been covered by a picture of Ayatollah Khomeini.

OPPOSITE TOP RIGHT: The Lamborghini Miura SVJ as it sits covered in dust at the Niavaran palace garage in the early 1980s. *(Ali Gorji, the author extends his appreciation to Mrs. Shahnaz Pakniyat for securing the permission to use this photo.)*

OPPOSITE BOTTOM: A rare photograph of the garage of the Niavaran Palace shortly after its fall in February 1979. Pictured are the Lamborghini Miura SVJ, Rolls-Royce Phantom V State Landaulette, chassis number 5LVF29, and barely seen in the back is the Phantom VI, chassis number PRX4861. (February 19, 1979) *(Hossein Partovi/ Borzou Sepasi)*

TOP: A torn snippet which is the only surviving photograph of the Miura SVJ, 4934, when it was transferred from the Palace to an unknown warehouse owned by the Bonyad Shahid before being taken out of Iran. *(Mehran Afshar)*

RIGHT (ALL): The photographs show the SVJ at the Tehran Pars workshop with by-standers, including local children, freely sitting and leaning against the car and taking photographs as mementos. The Shah's 1975 Rolls-Royce Camargue, chassis number JRX19741, is also visible. (February 1994) *(Abbas Soleymani)*

485

ownership transferred to the Bonyad Shahid, who, in turn proceeded to sell the two Lamborghinis as part of the ten-car package sold to Emirati Mohammad Ibrahim Al-Sadegh.

In 1993, an Iranian classic car collector residing in France (preferring to remain anonymous) received word that a number of the cars in the possession of the Bonyad Shahid would be put up for sale. He immediately flew to Tehran in order to gather more information. It was then that he became aware that a package of ten cars, including the Shah's famed Miura SVJ (which had not been seen in public for over a decade) would be offered for sale. After submitting his bid, he discovered that when the tender documents were opened in February 1994, he had been outbid by Emirati Mohammad Ibrahim Al-Sadegh.

In a last ditch attempt to purchase the SVJ, the collector

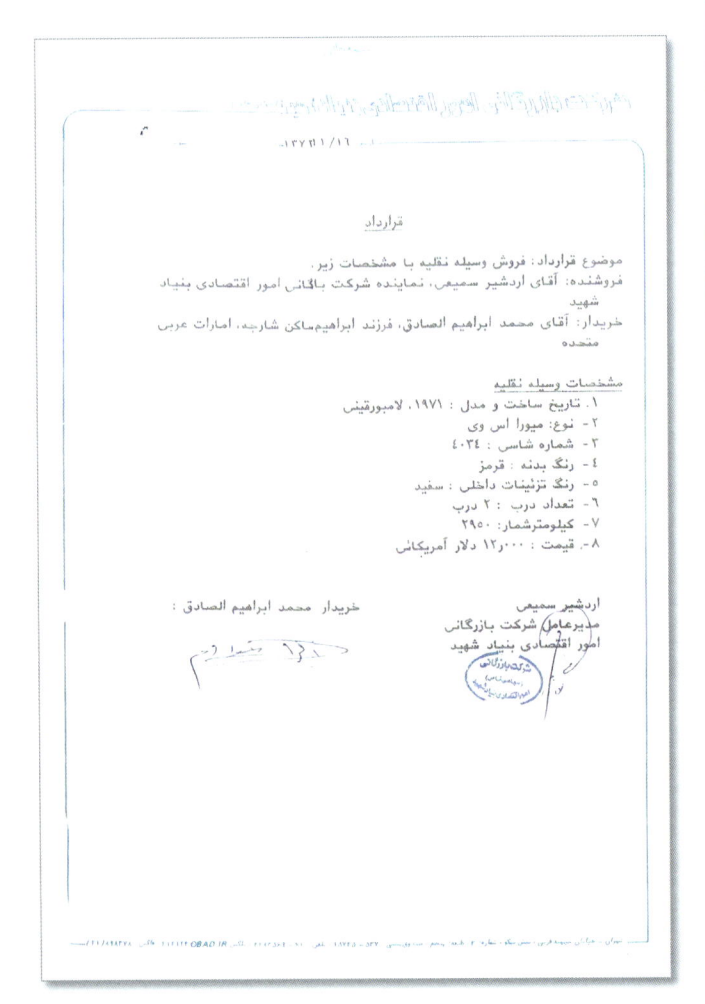

Appendix 1: The Story Continues

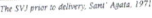

OPPOSITE FAR LEFT: The sales contract for the Lamborghini Miura SVJ, chassis number 4934. Some very important details can be seen in this document, namely (i) the odometer showed just 2950 km at the time of sale and (ii) the sales price was only $12,000. Also notable are some mistakes in the text such as the spelling of the name of the car and that the model is stated to be an "SV". *(Simon Kidston)*

OPPOSITE TOP: The Miura SVJ, chassis number 4934, and a number of the other royal cars purchased by Al-Sadegh photographed after their arrival to the UAE and put in storage at a plastic products warehouse near Sharjah. *(Simon Kidston)*

OPPOSITE SECOND: Mr. Mohammad Ibrahim Al-Sadegh (pictured right), the new owner of the Miura SVJ with Brooks Europe expert, Piet Pulford, and the owner's mechanic checking the Miura SVJ before shipping it and the other cars to auction in Switzerland. The Shah's Lamborghini Espada S1, chassis number 7099 and King Hussein's gift to the Shah, Ferrari 365 GT4 2+2, chassis number 18263, are also visible alongside the Miura. *(Simon Kidston)*

OPPOSITE THIRD & BOTTOM: The Miura SVJ being readied to be photographed for inclusion in the 1997 Brooks Europe Sales catalog. *(Simon Kidston)*

THIS PAGE: The Brooks Europe catalog featuring the Miura SVJ on the cover page. The car was sold as lot number 259 to the actor Nicolas Cage. (March 12, 1997) *(Brooks Europe)*

487

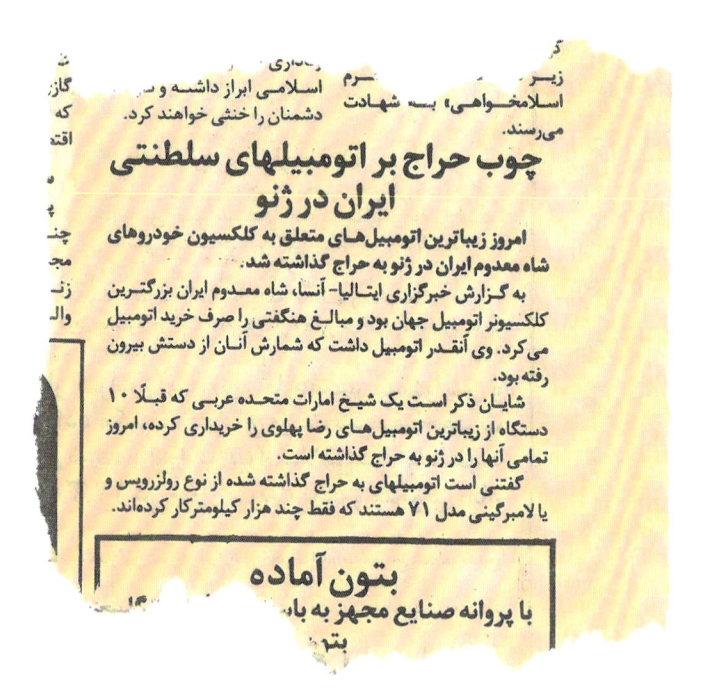

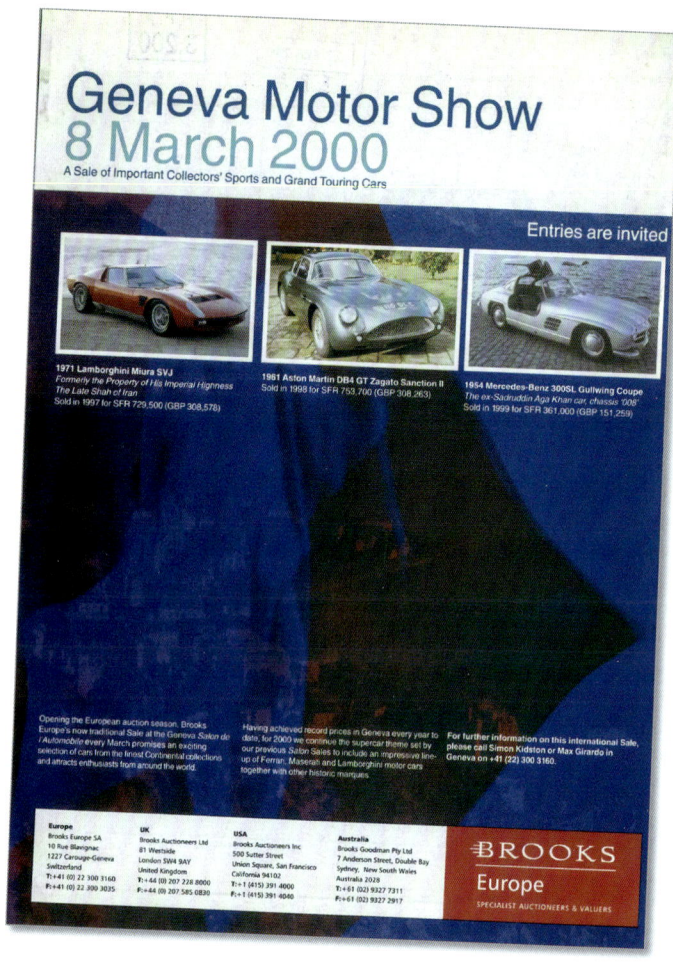

Fit for a King ~ The Royal Garage of the Shah of Iran

TOP LEFT: The auction of the cars in Geneva made it to the local Iranian newspapers. This article was published in the mass circulation Kayhan daily newspaper regarding the Brooks Auction. Unfortunately, while the article touches upon the rarity and the beauty of the cars sold, no mention is made that these national treasures were lost to Iran forever. (*Kayhan* newspaper, March 13, 1997) *(Borzou Sepasi)*

LEFT: *Thoroughbred & Classic Cars* magazine did a feature on the Lamborghini Miura which included the Shah's SVJ, chassis number 4934. (July 2000)

ABOVE: In the year 2000, Brooks Europe pointed out the record breaking price achieved for the Miura SVJ as part of their successful track record. (March 2000) *(Brooks Europe)*

OPPOSITE TOP: The Miura SVJ leading other Miuras in the 40th Anniversary Miura tour. (2006) *(Simon Kidston)*

OPPOSITE BOTTOM: The Lamorghini Miura SVJ reunited with its former stablemate in the royal garage, Miura, chassis number 3303, directly behind it at the stand of noted classic car dealer, Simon Kidston, during the 2019 Rétromobile Show in Paris. *(Borzou Sepasi)*

Appendix 1: The Story Continues

sought out Mr. Al-Sadegh and found him staying at the Esteghlal (Independence) Hotel, formerly known as the Royal Tehran Hilton, prior to the revolution.

Negotiations subsequently fell through and Mr. Al-Sadegh had the cars he had purchased, including the SVJ, transferred to a local workshop in the Tehran Pars district of Tehran (eastern Tehran) for servicing and then had them shipped to the UAE.

When the Shah's Miura SVJ went up for auction in Geneva on March 12, 1997, Brooks Europe succeeded in selling the car at a price exceeding all expectations. The winning bidder was none other than acclaimed American actor Nicolas Cage, whose bid was just shy of half a million dollars, was three times the estimate and the most expensive car sold at auction in 1997. Several years later, after facing a litany of financial issues, Cage sold the car to Iranian film producer, big game hunter, watch designer and all-round bon vivant, Reza Rashidian. Rashidian, whose family history with the Pahlavis is a story unto itself, entered the car in a number of events, including the Miura 40th Anniversary Tour organized by classic car dealer Simon Kidston in June 2006. In 2008, Rashidian sold the car to Danish racing driver and scion of an ancient Syrian-Kurdish noble family, Juan Barazi, who is also known for his extensive classic car collection. In 2009, Barazi sold the car, with only 10,000 km on the odometer, to a collector who was putting together the "world's ultimate Miura collection" where, at one point, the SVJ sat among a collection of twelve other notable Miuras. As of the date of the publication of this book, the collection of Miuras have all been sold and the SVJ is currently in Monaco under new ownership.

Fit for a King ~ The Royal Garage of the Shah of Iran

Appendix 1: The Story Continues

Marmon-Herrington Truck

TOP: As detailed in Chapter 10, this Marmon-Herrington truck was used on May 7, 1950 to tow the cannon and carry the coffin of Reza Shah during the funeral procession held when his body was returned from South Africa to be reinterred in Iran. Following the revolution, the truck was abandoned in an army garrison until the 1990s when it was transferred to the War Museum of the Saad Abad Palace and parked outside using logs in place of jacks. Currently there is no shelter to cover the truck from the elements. *(Borzou Sepasi)*

ABOVE: The Bofors cannon which was used to carry Reza Shah's coffin during the funeral procession. The cannon is currently on display at the Afif Abad museum located in the city of Shiraz. *(Borzou Sepasi)*

LEFT: The Shah's Miura SVJ, chassis number 4934, returned to St. Moritz in 2019 and was driven in the snow at the St. Moritz International Concours of Elegance. *(Fredi Vollenweider/ Mehrdad Mani)*

1959 Maserati 5000GT
Chassis Number: AM103.002

As shown on page 236, based on documentation discovered in the archives of the royal court, the Shah's Maserati 5000GT remained in Iran until either late May or early June of 1966 when it was sent to Europe for repairs by way of an Iranian Air Force transport plane. Though it would follow that the car would be serviced by the Maserati works, there are no records of such a service in the Maserati archives. What is now known, is that the car was believed to have been kept in either Italy or Switzerland until 1971 where it was then subsequently "imported" by Nicholas Hahn and registered with Zurich license plates ZH 174258 on August 27, 1971. As of today, the car still bears Swiss registration. Some pundits surmise that given the delicate nature of the 5000GT's gear-driven Maserati 450S racing engine, and the huge appetite of the engine for spark plugs and numerous other spares, perhaps the Shah decided to keep the car in Europe where it could be more easily serviced before selling it to Nicholas Hahn in 1971.[9] In 1972, the 5000GT was sold via Swiss journalist and broker Rob de la Rive Box to the English dealer, Colin Crabbe.

On May 28, 1974 the car was purchased and exported to the United States by Richard P. Rechter of Bloomington,

---

[9] *Email correspondence with prominent Maserati historian, Adolfo Orsi with the author, June 2, 2021*

Appendix 1: The Story Continues

Indiana. At some point in time, the car was then exported to Europe where it was featured in 1989 in an article by the French enthusiasts periodical, *Auto Passion* magazine, following which the car was auctioned by Claude Boisgirard on December 10, 1989 in the Grand Hall of Hippodrome de Vincennes of Paris where it was purchased by one of the scions of the Peugeot family. Today the car is still in France and remains in separate hands where it is being lovingly cared for.

OPPOSITE (ALL): The Shah's Maserati 5000GT, chassis number 103.002, bodied by Carrozzeria Touring Superleggera in Europe after being flown out of Iran by the royal court ostensibly for repairs but then subsequently sold off and registered in Switzerland. The car is pictured after its sale with Swiss plates (Zurich registration). (1970s) *(McGrath Maserati Facebook page)*

BELOW: An article about the Shah's Maserati 5000GT in the French enthusiasts' magazine, *Auto Passion*, dated December 1989. *(Teymour Richard)*

RIGHT: The Shah's Maserati 5000GT was sold at auction on December 10, 1989 by Claude Boisgirard.

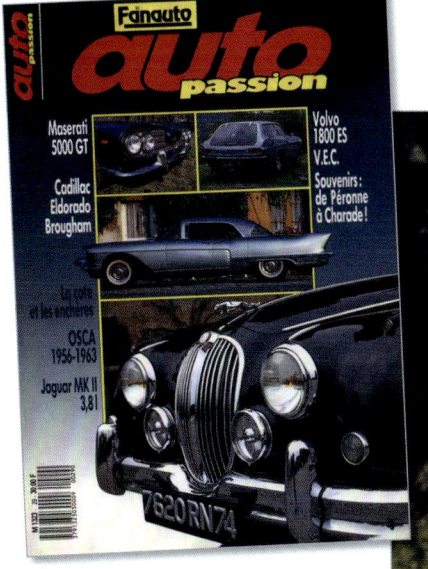

493

1970 Maserati Ghibli Coupe
Chassis Number: AM115.1394

One of the cars owned by the Shah is this 1970 Maserati Ghibli. Originally imported by and for the Shah, this car was subsequently bequeathed to his nephew Prince Kamyar Pahlavi. Prince Kamyar stood out among his peers in the royal family as he not only successfully completed his studies at Harvard, but returned to Iran afterwards to carry out his military training which was compulsory for each Iranian male. Prince Kamyar volunteered to become a pilot and was accepted for pilot training, so impressing the Shah that (as already covered in Chapter 23), according to local lore, he offered Prince Kamyar his choice of "any car from the royal garage". Apparently, when Prince Kamyar requested the Miura SVJ, the Shah is reported to have replied "except that one". The Ghibli was kept in the royal garage, as the young Prince found little time to drive the car as he completed his military training. With the onset of the revolution, and with less than 900 km on

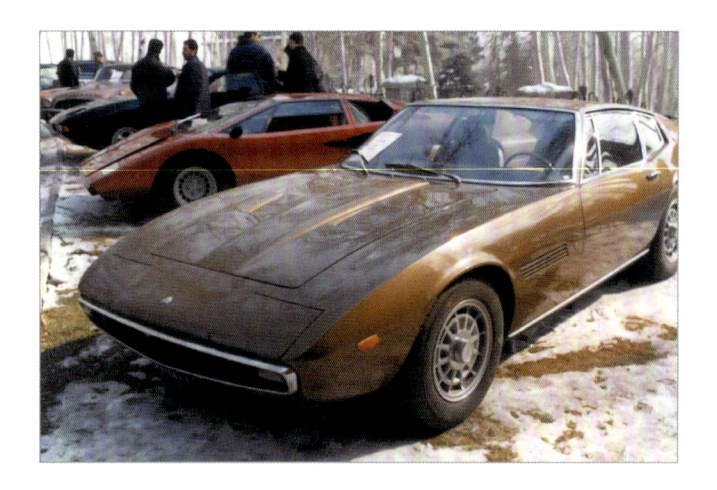

ABOVE: The Shah's Maserati Ghibli Coupe, chassis number AM115.1394, in the Tehran Classic Car show in Saad Abad Palace. (1999) *(Alireza Pourakbari)*

BELOW: The Ghibli Coupe on display at the National Automobile Museum of Iran with jacks fitted under the car, ostensibly for preservation of the original tires. (2008) *(Mahnaz Beedel)*

OPPOSITE TOP (BOTH): The Ghibli Coupe in Bonyad Mostazafan Karaj warehouse. (Early 1990s) *(Borzou Sepasi)*

Appendix 1: The Story Continues

the odometer, the ownership of the car was transferred to the Bonyad Mostazafan and registered as vehicle number 1625. Over the years the car was displayed at a number of car shows before becoming part of the collection of the National Automobile Museum of Iran in 2004.

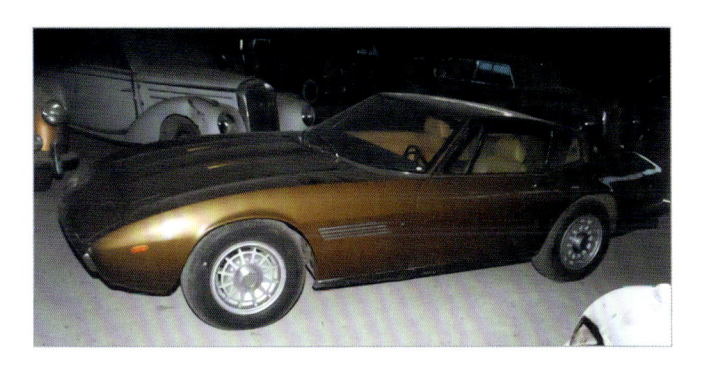

During the research of this book, the author found this advertisement for a 1968 Ghibli which came with unique vertical side vents. It is claimed that this car was formerly owned by the Shah of Iran. It was offered by API Autoputer, Inc. in an advertisement published in the May 1988 issue of *Autocar* magazine. According to correspondence with Adolfo Orsi of the Maserati factory, only one Ghibli with vertical side vents was produced by Maserati. That car was produced by the factory for a customer by the name of Mr. Wax, residing in Genoa, a long-standing customer of Maserati who liked to have his cars customized by the factory. The present situation of the car in unknown.

(Borzou Sepasi)

The Automotive Legacy of the Shah: The G-Class

As discussed in Chapter 24, the Shah's decision to equip his army with a versatile all-round utility vehicle led to the creation of the Mercedes-Benz 'G' Class by Daimler. Having placed an initial order for twenty thousand such vehicles, the mass production launch of the vehicle coincided with the Iranian revolution, leading to the cancellation of the order by the new revolutionary government, under the guise that the order was a symbol of the Shah's excesses. Despite the cancellation, a number of the early production cars were delivered whilst others were put in storage in Austria at the Steyr Plant by Daimler until they were gradually sold.

As a result of the cancellation, with the invasion of Iran by Iraq in September 1980, the Iranian Army found itself without a versatile multi-purpose vehicle which could negotiate the tough terrain of the battlefield, especially as the existing fleet of Iranian Army Romanian Aros and British Land Rovers proved to be woefully inadequate and unreliable. Accordingly, having canceled the order for the G-Class, the Iranian army turned to the import of thousands of Toyota Land Cruisers as a replacement.

The subsequent success of the G-Class is a testament to the vision and foresight that went towards the design and engineering of this timeless vehicle. One of the first hand-built G-Class delivered for the Shah is still in service today and is used by Iranian Supreme Leader Ayatollah Khamenei during annual troop review ceremonies.

LEFT: Mercedes-Benz 240 GD of the 460 model series, open-top vehicle with short wheelbase. Press photograph for the world premiere of the G-Class. (1979) *(Media.Daimler.com)*

TOP & MIDDLE: With the invasion of Iran by Iraq in September 1980, the Toyota Land Cruiser replaced the G-Class after the post-revolutionary government canceled the order in 1979. *(Borzou Sepasi)*

ABOVE: Iranian Supreme Leader Ayatollah Khamenei was still using one of the first G-Classes ever made by hand for the Shah and delivered to Iran before the revolution. The vehicle was primarily used for troop reviews. The Mercedes-Benz star has been removed from the grille. *(Borzou Sepasi)*

Appendix 1: The Story Continues

1971 Mercedes-Benz 300SEL 6.3
Chassis Number: 109.018.12.005924

As per Chapter 29, in the early 1970s the Shah would frequently drive a sand beige metallic Mercedes-Benz 300SEL 6.3, chassis number 109.018.12.005924. The Shah was a great fan of Mercedes-Benz and usually kept one or two of the latest models on hand. Following the revolution, as with the Miura SVJ and Espada, this car did not end up in the hands of the Bonyad Mostazafan, but rather the Bonyad Shahid took ownership. Apparently, at some point in its life it was put back into organizational service by the Bonyad Shahid, before being auctioned off in the 1990s as a regular Mercedes, its royal lineage being lost in the ensuing years.

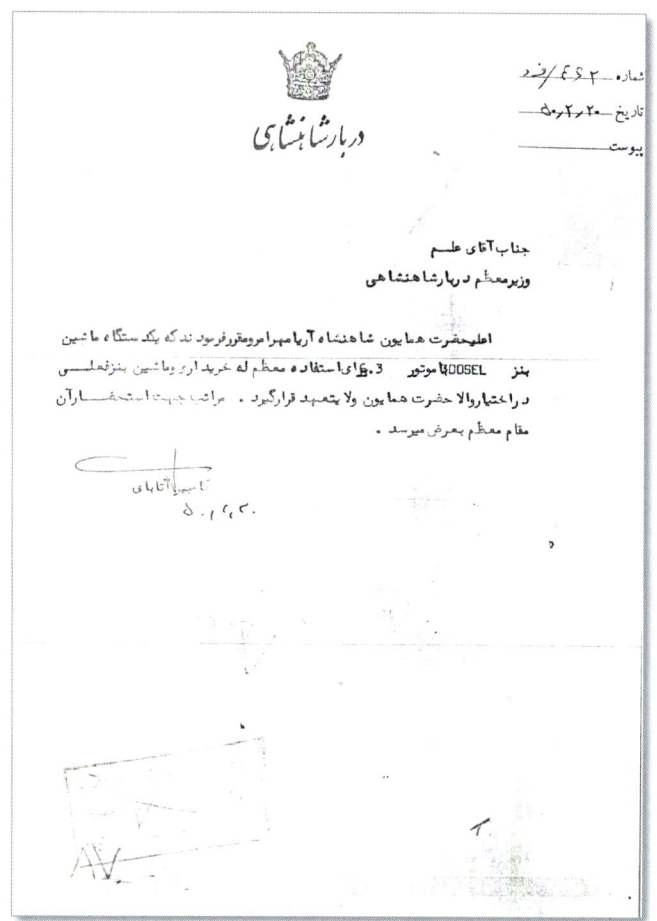

LEFT TOP: The ex-Shah of Iran Mercedes-Benz 300SEL 6.3, chassis number 109.018.12.005924, parked on the side of a street with a 'For Sale' sign on the back window. Note the original alloy wheels in the front have been replaced. The license plate has a Tehran-21 registration plate which indicates that the car was sold at auction by a governmental organization. (Early 2000s) *(Borzou Sepasi)*

LEFT: The Mercedes-Benz 300SEL 6.3 sitting in a workshop outside of Tehran where it was discovered by the author. The new registration plate is visible on it and shows that the car was registered in Karaj (Alborz Province) at the time. (2019) *(Borzou Sepasi)*

ABOVE: One of the documents discovered in the archives of the royal garage was this official letter dated May 10, 1971 regarding the Shah's order for a Mercedes-Benz 300SEL 6.3. *(Borzou Sepasi)*

Following its original sale, the car changed hands four times, being used mostly as a daily driver, and as of 2015 the car was in Isfahan for a number of years before appearing in the city of Karaj. At one point in time, one of the owners was so fed up with its thirst for fuel that he parked it on the side of the street with a big for sale sign. Apparently, he contemplated removing the M100 engine and replacing it with a more fuel efficient one.

Over the years, the car lost its alloy wheels and showed all the dents and bruises of a daily driver. It was only in 2019, during the research for this book, that the royal lineage of this Mercedes was discovered among the documents of the royal garage. Accordingly, the car was rescued by a new owner who is now preparing the car for a ground-up restoration. In 2018, FIVA (Federation International Vehicles Anciens) recognized the history and provenance of this car.

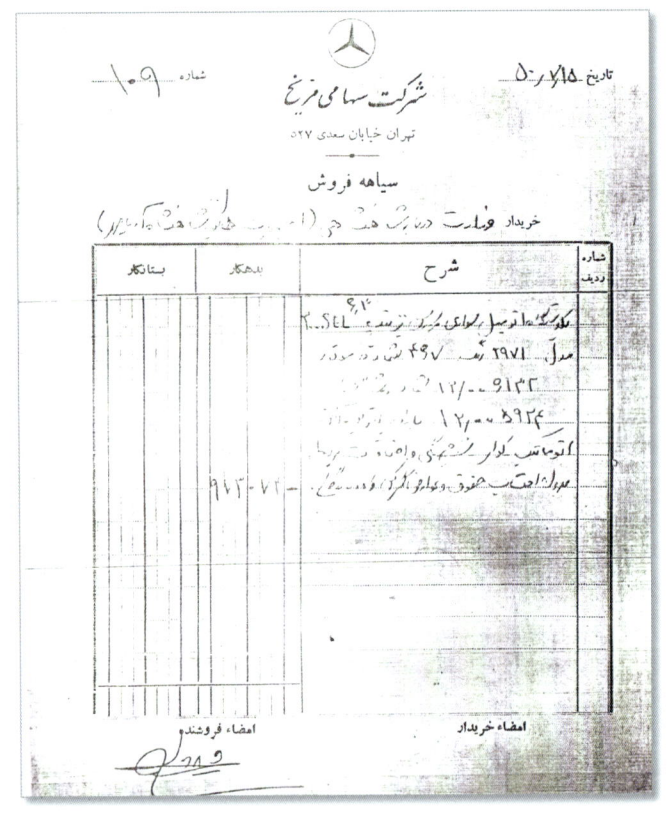

LEFT: **The official invoice dated October 7, 1971 issued by Merrikh Co.** *(the official agent and distributor in Iran of Mercedes-Benz at the time)* **for their very special customer, the Shah of Iran. The invoice states: Passenger car – Mercedes-Benz 300SEL 6.3; model year 1971; color code 467; engine number 12.006132; chassis number 12.005924 with radio stereo; automatic antenna; air conditioning; tinted glass and all available options (exempt from customs duties for a total price of 973074 Rials).** *(Borzou Sepasi)*

BOTTOM: **The ex-Shah 300SEL 6.3 today as it awaits a ground-up restoration. (2020)** *(Khashayar Rabbanian)*

Appendix 1: The Story Continues

The official auction catalog photograph of the Shah's 300SL Gullwing, chassis number 198.040.55.00111, at the Bonhams and Goodman sale in 2006.

1955 Mercedes-Benz 300SL Gullwing
Chassis Number: 198.040.55.00111

Based on available documentation, the Shah's Mercedes-Benz 300SL Gullwing was kept in Iran as late as 1961. At some point in time before this date, the ownership of the car had been transferred to the Shah's English doctor. In or around 1961, the car was taken out of Iran by this gentleman. By the year 2006, it had passed through four owners and, having ended up in Australia, was sold by Bonhams and Goodman at auction for 777,240 AUD at the Collectors' Cars and Number Plates sale in Sydney on October 22, 2006. As of the publication of this book, the car is believed to be in the Middle East and its color has been changed to red.

1936 Mercedes-Benz 500K Autobahnkurier
Chassis Number: 130898

The Shah of Iran's fabled Mercedes-Benz 500K Autobahnkurier, chassis number 130898, was discovered by the revolutionaries in the house of Mr. Fuad Majzub, when they came to seize his property due to apparent ties to the Pahlavi regime. Majzub was perhaps Iran's best known car collector and can be credited with saving many of Iran's automotive treasures. Despite missing its original engine (utilizing a Cadillac engine in place) Majzub had strived to preserve the car's originality. The car was transported from Majzub's home to the Bonyad Mostazafan's Karaj warehouse where it joined many of its former stablemates of the royal garage. In the early

499

1980s the Mercedes was put on temporary display at the Khorram Amusement Park (re-named Eram Amusement Park as the complex had also been expropriated from its former owner Rahim Ali Khorram) before being stashed away in storage for over a decade until being put on display at Iran's first post-revolution car show held at the Esteghlal Hotel (formerly known as the Royal Tehran Hilton, prior to the revolution) in 1993. The car was put on display at a classic car show held at the Niavaran Palace in 1997 and again in 2006 at a classic car show held at the Saad Abad Palace where it was parked in front of the same palace stairs where once upon a time it would wait for its original owner.

Today, the car is on display at the National Automobile Museum of Iran where it is in need of a professional restoration. However, no doubt due to the efforts of the late Fuad Majzub, the car, sans engine, is surprisingly original.

LEFT: The Mercedes-Benz 500K Autobahnkurier, chassis number 13089, on display at the Esteghlal Hotel car show in Tehran. (1992) *(Teymour Richard)*

BELOW: The official photograph of the Shah of Iran's Mercedes-Benz 500K Autobahnkurier. (1980s) *(Bonyad Mostazafan)*

OPPOSITE TOP LEFT: The Autobahnkurier and the Saad Abad Palace reunited once again at the Classic Car exhibition that took place there. (May 2006) *(Borzou Sepasi)*

OPPOSITE TOP RIGHT: Mercedes-Benz 500K Autobahnkurier on display at the National Automobile Museum of Iran. *(Mahnaz Beedel)*

OPPOSITE MIDDLE RIGHT: Mercedes-Benz 500K Autobahnkurier in storage at the Karaj warehouse of the Bonyad Mostazafan during the decade of the 1990s. The original turn signal lights have been replaced with one sourced from a VW Beetle! (1990s) *(Borzou Sepasi)*

Appendix 1: The Story Continues

Mercedes-Benz 600 (numerous)

During the Pahlavi era, Iran accumulated the largest collection of Mercedes-Benz 600s in the world as the car was selected to be the backbone of the fleet for governmental organizations, including the royal court, different ministries, a number of Iranian Embassies in different countries and several quasi-governmental organizations. A number of 600s had been imported by private owners. After the revolution, the majority of 600s, including the two rare (of a total of ten manufactured) Presidential Landaulets, chassis numbers 100.015.12.001207 and 100.015.12.001370, were transferred to the ownership of the Bonyad Mostazafan where today, many still remain in storage.

The Mercedes-Benz 600 most closely associated with the Shah is the Presidential Landaulet, chassis number

Many Mercedes-Benz 600s in Bonyad Mostazafan Karaj warehouse. *(Borzou Sepasi)*

501

Fit for a King ~ The Royal Garage of the Shah of Iran

00.015.12.001207. In one film, the Shah is seen driving this vehicle himself and using it as a virtual school bus as he transports all of his children to their first day of school at the Niavaran Palace. Other films show this car in use for transporting guests to the office of the Shah on the grounds of the Palace, including the American Ambassador. The current situation of this ultra-rare car is, for lack of better words, painful. The original hub caps are missing, the convertible top shows damage and, apparently as the car has never been started since the revolution, the windows have remained open for the last forty-three years and the inside is covered in dust and grime.

As of the time of publication of this book, the National Automobile Museum in Tehran has refurbished and put on display a number of Mercedes 600s, including the second Presidential Landaulet, chassis number 100.015.12.001370, and Saad Abad Palace museums have a number of 600s which are on display at a makeshift museum in the Palace.

There is also one 600 which was auctioned off by a governmental organization which is now undergoing a sympathetic restoration by a private owner.

ABOVE: A 1980's photograph of the Mercedes-Benz 600 Presidential Landaulet, chassis number 100.015.12.001370. *(Bonyad Mostazafan)*

TOP & MIDDLE: The ultra-rare Mercedes-Benz 600 Presidential Landaulet, chassis number 100.015.12.001207, seen in an early 1970's film in which the Shah was driving his children to the Niavaran Palace school in front of a group of journalists, and then as it sits in the Karaj warehouse of the Bonyad Mostazafa. *(Borzou Sepasi)*

ABOVE & OPPOSITE TOP (BOTH): The Queen Mother's 600 LWB, chassis number 100.014.12.002475. The original documents were discovered by the author after four decades in the archives of the Saad Abad Palace. *(Borzou Sepasi)*

OPPOSITE BOTTOM (BOTH): Following the revolution, a number of 600s were put into use by the new revolutionary government like this SWB 600, chassis number 100.012.12.001205, which was used by Ayatollah Khamenei during his Presidency. Though the car now lays in storage, it still dons its plastic registration plate sporting the emblem of the Islamic Republic. *(Borzou Sepasi)*

Appendix 1: The Story Continues

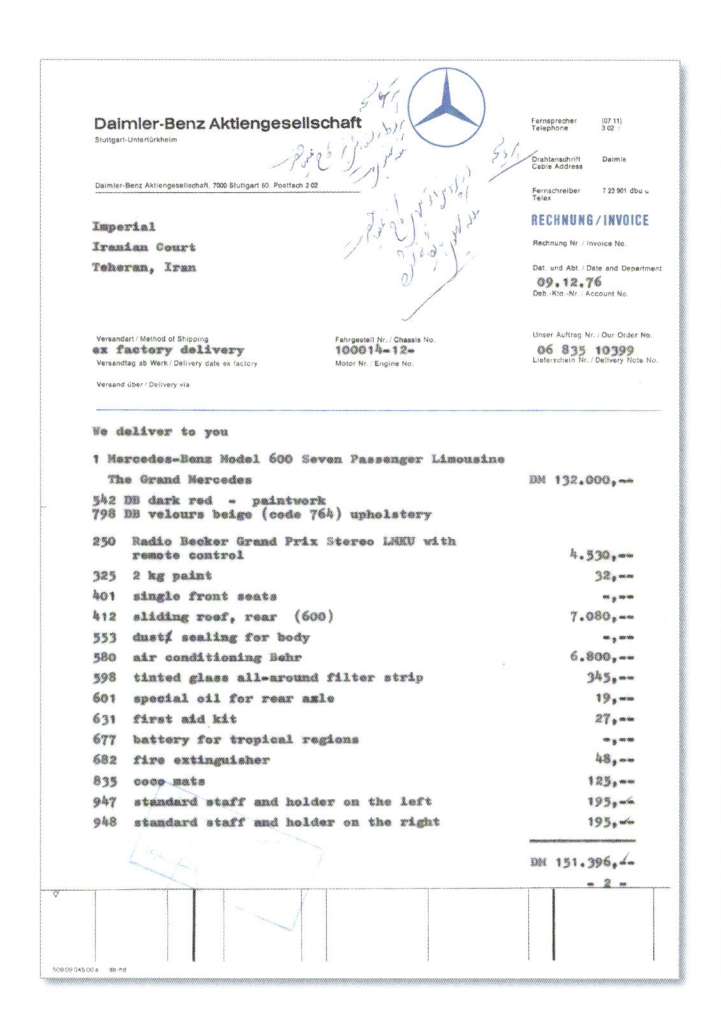

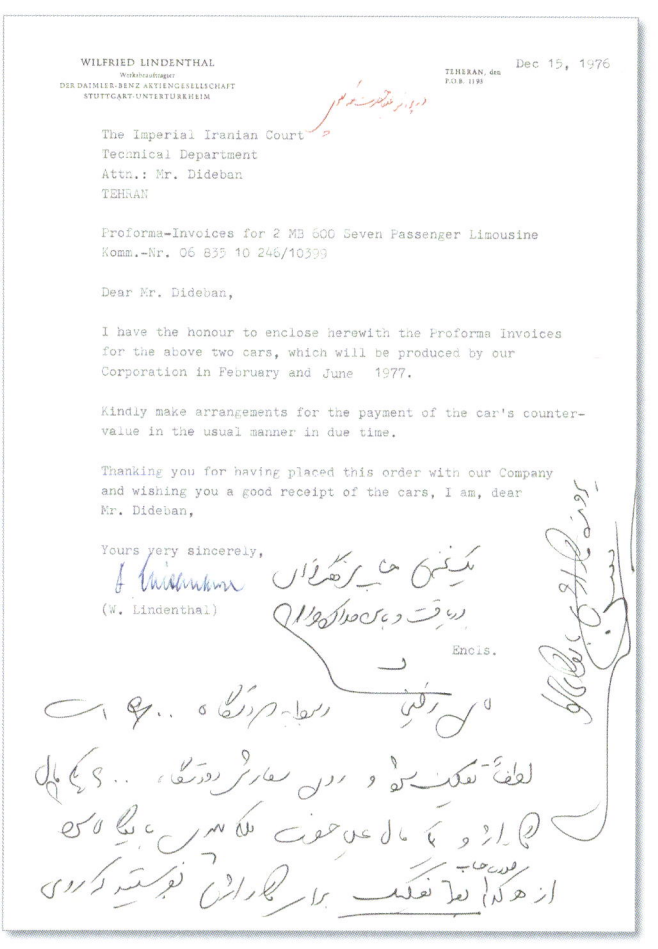

503

Fit for a King ~ The Royal Garage of the Shah of Iran

LEFT (ALL) & TOP: In 2006, five Mercedes-Benz 600s, two Cadillacs and one Lincoln Limousine were transferred to Saad Abad Palace from the warehouse of the Foreign Ministry of Iran. The above photographs show them on the date of their arrival at the Palace. Because of problems with their pneumatic suspension all the cars were balanced on logs in lieu of jacks. *(Borzou Sepasi)*

MIDDLE RIGHT & ABOVE: One of the Foreign Ministry 600s transferred to the Saad Abad Palace museum was this LWB, chassis number 100.014.12.002375, which was repaired and ready for a test drive and photography by the author. The related article was published in the Iranian automotive periodical *Machine Magazine* in the same year. The post-revolution registration plate which says "Protocol" is still affixed to the car. The above photograph is taken in front of the Shah's White Palace at the Saad Abad Complex. (2007) *(Borzou Sepasi)*

Appendix 1: The Story Continues

1972 Mercedes-Porsche-VW

The history of this one-off car given by the German government to Crown Prince Reza Pahlavi is covered extensively in Chapter 30. By the onset of the revolution in 1979, the odometer only read 118 km and the only modification on the car was the installation of two VW Beetle turn signals on the front fenders in order to better assist the teenage Crown Prince to practice his driving skills. As with almost all the other cars of the royal garage, this car was also subsequently transferred to one of the warehouses of the Bonyad Mostazafan. After years of neglect and storage in the warehouse (the leather seats and dashboard showed signs of cracking), the car was finally transferred to the National Automobile Museum of Iran where it sits today under much better conditions.

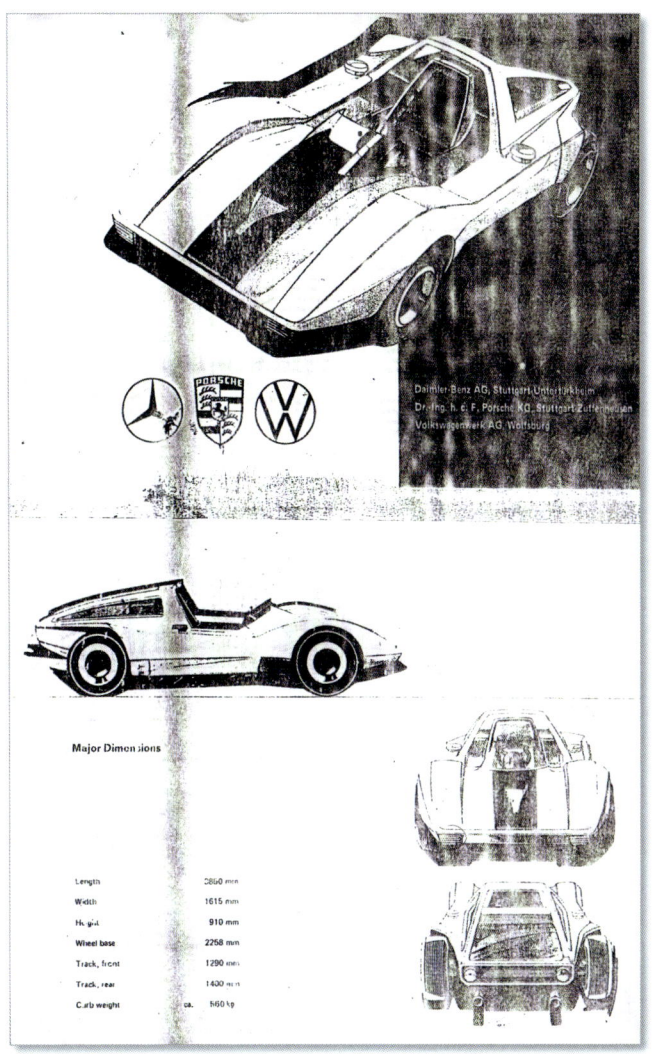

LEFT: The Mercedes-Porsche-VW as it sat in the royal garage some seven months after the revolution. (July 1979) *(Keyvan Banihashemi)*

BOTTOM LEFT: The Mercedes-Porsche-VW pictured in storage in the Bonyad Mostazafan warehouse with open engine cover. (2008) *(Borzou Sepasi)*

ABOVE: A copy of the user manual found in Karaj warehouse. The original copy is lost. *(Borzou Sepasi)*

505

Fit for a King ~ The Royal Garage of the Shah of Iran

The Crown Prince's Mercedes-Porsche-VW as it sits today in the National Automobile Museum of Iran. *(Borzou Sepasi)*

1974 Panther Lazer
Chassis Number: N/A

This car was in the royal garage when the revolution took place. As with the majority of the other cars kept in the royal garage, its ownership was transferred to the Bonyad Mostazafan where it then sat for years in one of their warehouses. In 2004, it went on permanent display with the opening of the National Automobile Museum of Iran.

The Panther Lazer on display in the National Automobile Museum of Iran. (2004) *(Mahnaz Beedel)*

Appendix 1: The Story Continues

1930 Pierce-Arrow Model A
Chassis Number: 3025354

With the end of World War II and the post-war launch of a multitude of new and more advanced cars by the world's manufacturers, the Shah began to let go of many of the cars he had accumulated during the pre-war years, replacing them with the latest models from a number of manufacturers. As a result, by 1959 a number of his best known pre-war cars such as the Bugatti Type 57C and his Hispano-Suiza had been sold and replaced by more modern vehicles such as his Mercedes-Benz 300SL Gullwing. During this same period, having inherited his father's Pierce-Arrow Model A Town Car, chassis number 3025354, the Shah decided to keep this unique automobile as a tribute to his father, Reza Shah, founder of the Pahlavi dynasty.

LEFT TOP: The Pierce-Arrow Model A Town Car, chassis number 3025354, bodied by Brunn & Company, on exhibit in Tehran in 1975. *(Mansour Kamranfar)*

LEFT: The last photograph of the Pierce-Arrow Model A on the eve of the revolution in 1978 showing the car in perfect condition in the royal garage. One year later the car was damaged by the revolutionary crowds who attacked and took over the royal garage. (1978) *(Borzou Sepasi)*

TOP: The Author (wearing a dark blue shirt, far left) assisting the authorities of the Bonyad Mostazafan in identifying the Pierce-Arrow and its rich history. (2003) *(Masih Kaviani)*

ABOVE: The Pierce-Arrow Model A during its storage in the Karaj Road warehouse of the Bonyad Mostazafan. (2003) *(Masih Kaviani)*

The Pierce-Arrow Model A, chassis number 3025354, bodied by Brunn & Company on display at the National Automobile Museum in Tehran. (2010) *(Ghazal Jami)*

In 1960, the royal garage put the Pierce-Arrow on jacks in order to protect the original tires and by the mid-1970s, under the patronage of Queen Farah, the initial steps towards the establishment of Iran's first automobile museum had been commenced. Accordingly, the first car selected to be put on display was Reza Shah's Pierce-Arrow Model A. Following this decision, after years of being stored in the royal garage, the car was brought out and displayed at an exhibition held in Tehran in 1975. In 1978, one year before the revolution, whilst the car was being cared for in the royal garage, the last pre-revolution photograph of it was taken showing the car to be in original and pristine condition.

Unfortunately, during the revolution, the car was damaged by the marauding crowds that poured into the Pahlavi palaces following their fall or abandonment, including the Firouzeh Palace where the royal garage was based. Unfortunately, not only was the Pierce-Arrow's upholstery (in the rear seat) damaged, but also a number of the gold tinted windows were broken and one of the two jewels embedded in the Pahlavi crests on the rear doors was stolen.

As with many of the other cars of the royal garage, following the expropriation of the Pahlavi family's assets, the Pierce-Arrow was transferred to the Karaj warehouse of the Bonyad Mostazafan, its storied past lost to the revolution, until, with the assistance of the author, the rich history of the car was uncovered and brought to the attention of the authorities. In 2004, the Pierce-Arrow, with a delay of just under a quarter of a century, finally achieved its status as being one of the first cars to be put on permanent museum display in Iran.

1978 Porsche 928
Chassis Number: 9288101733

The Shah's Porsche 928 suffered two strokes of bad luck, the first being that it was delivered to the royal garage on the eve of the revolution and, second, following its arrival, it was apparently plagued by electrical gremlins, offering the Shah little or no time to enjoy the car. Accordingly, this car, despite being put up for auction several times following the revolution, remained unsold and after years of storage in the warehouse of the

ABOVE: The Shah of Iran's Porsche 928, chassis number 9288101733, with Iranian registration plate number 72832 Tehran-24 as it sat in the royal garage five months after the revolution. (July 1979) *(Keyvan Banihashemi)*

OPPOSITE TOP LEFT: The Porsche 928, on display in the National Automobile Museum of Iran. (2015) *(Mahnaz Beedel)*

Appendix 1: The Story Continues

Bonyad Mostazafan was put on display in the National Automobile Museum of Iran in 2004, with only 25 km on the odometer, making it one of the lowest, if not the lowest mileage Porsche 928 in the world.

1975/1976 Rolls-Royce Camargues, bodied by Pininfarina

Chassis Numbers: JRX 19741/JRX 23260

As covered extensively in Chapter 34, the Shah bought two "his" and "hers" Camargues, cobalt blue for himself, chassis number JRX 19741, and the second, in crown gold, chassis number JRX 23260, provided to Queen Farah as a birthday present. Both cars were in Niavaran Palace when the revolution took place. Shortly thereafter, along with their Italian stablemates at the palace garage, the Lamborghini Miura SVJ and Espada, the two Camargues were removed from the Niavaran Palace to an unknown warehouse ostensibly belonging to the Bonyad Shahid. The Bonyad Shahid eventually sold both "his" and "hers" Camargues as part of a ten-car package in February 1994 to a buyer from the UAE by the name of Mohammad Ibrahim Al-Sadegh. Al-Sadegh went on to sell both Camargues, as well as the eight other royal cars on March 12, 1997 through the auction house, Brooks Europe, in Geneva, Switzerland.

RIGHT (BOTH): The Brooks Europe Auction catalog had two pages dedicated to the royal Camargues of Iran, chassis numbers JRX 19741 and JRX 23260. (March 12, 1997)

509

1970 Rolls-Royce Drophead Coupe, bodied by Mulliner Park Ward
Chassis Number: DRX9983

The Shah's 1970 Rolls-Royce Drophead Coupe, chassis number DRX9983, was believed to have been one of his most favored cars and he would arrange to have it transported with him on his annual trips to Switzerland. At the time of the revolution, the car was being kept at the royal garage, yet, surprisingly, this car was not transferred to the Bonyad Mostazafan and, instead was separated from the other cars and sent to an unknown warehouse believed to have been under the control of the Bonyad Shahid. Shortly, thereafter, nine other cars, most of which were directly owned by the Shah such as the Miura SVJ joined the Rolls-Royce. All ten cars were subsequently sold off in one lot in February 1994 to Mohammad Ibrahim Al-Sadegh who then proceeded to sell them all, including the Shah's Drophead Coupe, in March 1997 through auction by Brooks Europe in Geneva.

Appendix 1: The Story Continues

In this auction, the Drophead Coupe was mistakenly advertised as having been owned by the Shah's former son-in-law (and one time Foreign Minister), Ardeshir Zahedi. According to the research of the author and photographic evidence, it is believed that this car belonged to the Shah himself. Such a mistake may have no doubt occurred due to the wrong information provided by the original seller in Iran.

1926 Rolls-Royce Phantom I, bodied by Hooper
Chassis Number: 72DC

Rolls-Royce Phantom I, chassis number 72DC, was extensively used by Reza Shah during his reign. Following his exile, it was tucked away in the Saad Abad Palace garage where it apparently lay virtually abandoned for nearly three decades until it was turned over to the royal garage in 1971.

Pursuant to Queen Farah's efforts to launch a motor museum in the mid-1970s, the royal court arranged that the car, having only 2,819 km on the odometer, in or around 1977, be sent to the Rolls-Royce works for restoration. With its restoration complete, the car was returned to Iran at some point prior to the revolution. After the revolution, the car was transferred to the Bonyad Mostazafan's Karaj Road warehouse. This car is one of the few that has not been seen in public since 1941 and it has not even been put on display in the National Automobile Museum of Iran.

On a side note, alongside Reza Shah's Phantom I there exists a second Rolls-Royce Phantom I, chassis number

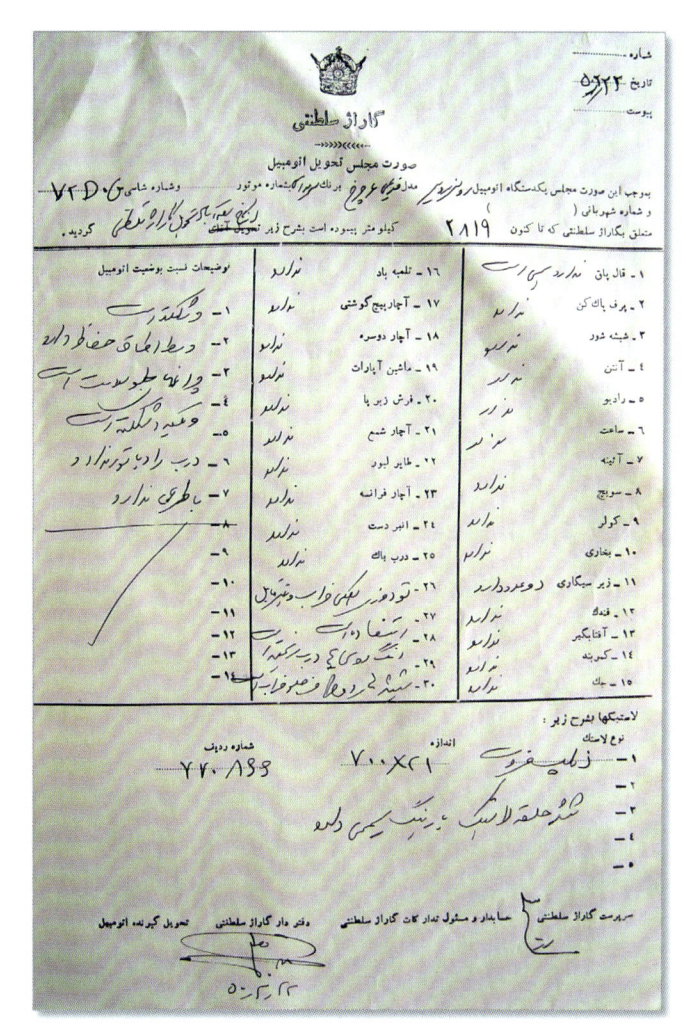

OPPOSITE TOP: **The Rolls-Royce Drophead Coupe as published in the Brooks Europe catalog. (March 12, 1997)**
(Brooks Europe)

OPPOSITE BOTTOM: **The Shah driving his 1970 Rolls-Royce Drophead Coupe in Switzerland in heavy snow. (Early 1970s)**
(Borzou Sepasi)

TOP: **The Rolls-Royce Phantom I, chassis number 72DC, in perfect condition after being returned to the royal garage following its restoration by the Rolls-Royce works. This picture was taken less than one year before the revolution. (1978)**
(Borzou Sepasi)

RIGHT: **Checklist of the Rolls-Royce Phantom I, chassis number 72DC, bodied by Hooper, dated May 12, 1971 which was prepared by the Saad Abad Palace in preparation for hand over to the royal garage. This document proves that the car was in the Saad Abad old garage for several decades until being handed over to the royal garage.** *(Saad Abad Palace)*

Reza Shah's Rolls-Royce Phantom I, chassis number 72DC, bodied by Hooper, gathering dust in the Bonyad Mostazafan Karaj Road Warehouse. (2004) *(Borzou Sepasi)*

64DC, in the Bonyad warehouse which, as evidenced by the fact that it has a private license plate, 4961 Tehran-20, issued in 1941, most probably has no royal lineage.

While the public has not been able to see Reza Shah's Phantom I since 1941, Phantom I 64DC played a starring role in a critically acclaimed historical Iranian television drama called *Hezar Dastan* ('One Thousand Hands'), produced and directed by internationally-renowned Iranian director Ali Hatami. The production of the show lasted nearly eight years, commencing in 1979 (following the revolution) and ending in 1987. For the purpose of historical accuracy, Hatami constructed a large set to represent Tehran both during the Qajar dynasty and Pahlavi era (up through World War II), effectively leading

Phantom I, chassis number 64DC, bodied by Park Ward in one of the scenes of "Hezar Dastan".

Appendix 1: The Story Continues

to the establishment of Iran's first professional movie studio and backlot, named Ghazali Cinema Town. As he was in need of classic cars to accurately reflect the eras depicted in the film, he contacted the Bonyad Mostazafan and they agreed to lend him a number of cars in storage from their Karaj Road warehouse. Among the cars lent to Hatami was Phantom I, chassis number 64DC. Since the wrapping up of the set of *Hezar Dastan*, 64DC has joined 72DC and remains in storage hidden away from the public.

1939 Rolls-Royce Phantom III, bodied by Park Ward
Chassis Number: 3DL138

As covered in Chapter 7, Rolls-Royce Phantom III, chassis number 3DL138, was a wedding gift from Great Britain to the Crown Prince Mohammad Reza Pahlavi on the occasion of his first marriage to the Egyptian Princess Fawzia Fuad. It was one of the cars that the Shah kept through the years in the royal garage and the car even survived the revolution unscathed.

In 1983, an exhibition of classic cars was held by the Bonyad Mostazafan at the Eram Amusement Park where Rolls-Royce Phantom III, chassis number 3DL138, was put on display. The amusement park was formerly called "Khoram Park" (the last name of its original owner) before its expropriation and transfer to the Bonyad Mostazafan and, with the opening of the exhibit of the cars whose ownership had been transferred to the Bonyad, the term "corporate synergies" took on a whole new meaning. It is interesting to note that at the time the Bonyad did not have any automotive experts who could correctly identify and classify the cars. As a result, the display stands in front of each car only stated the name of the manufacturer, without providing any information on the year or model of the car.

TOP: The Shah's Rolls-Royce Phantom III, chassis number 3DL138 and bodied by Park Ward, on display adjacent to a Corniche Coupe and beyond it, the ex-Shah Mercedes-Benz 500K Autobahnkurier, chassis number 130898. (1983) *(Borzou Sepasi)*

MIDDLE & ABOVE: In 2006, the Rolls-Royce Phantom III was reunited with its original home at Saad Abad Palace, albeit temporarily. The car was used for the filming of a historical drama about the Shah called "The Enigma of the Shah". *(Borzou Sepasi)*

1951 Rolls-Royce Phantom IV Drophead Coupe, bodied by H. J. Mulliner
Chassis Number: 4AF6

In 1959, the Shah carried out a house cleaning of the royal garage, selling off many of his pre-war cars such as the Bugatti Type 57C Vanvooren and Mercedes-Benz 500K Autobahnkurier. Among these cars, despite being a relatively new post-war car, the Shah also ordered his Rolls-Royce Phantom IV Drophead Coupe, chassis number 4AF6, not be sold off, but rather be returned to the factory for scrapping. This decision, even today, leaves many automotive historians and pundits alike scratching their heads.

One of the prevailing theories is that the large Phantom IV chassis was unsuited for use as a two-door convertible and that the chassis may have suffered from excessive flex making the car virtually undrivable, prompting the Shah to return the car to the factory. This theory is challenged by a number of experts, as they question how a super strong frame built to carry out the heaviest of limousines could be too flexible when fitted with a drophead body. This argument is buoyed by the fact that other Phantom IVs with drophead bodies, namely 4AF14 and 4AF22, never suffered any similar problems. Furthermore, it would seem doubtful that Rolls-Royce would institute a policy to scrap a chassis.[10]

Others are of the view that while it is doubtful that the chassis flex of 4AF6 was so serious that it may have been

Appendix 1: The Story Continues

rendered undrivable, they give credence to the theory that as the Shah greatly enjoyed driving, he may have been unsettled by the possible scuttle or cowl shake endemic to older open-top cars that 4AF6 may have suffered, causing the bulkhead in front of the passenger compartment to move and vibrate, especially on rough roads.[11] Hence, the Shah may have been prompted to return the car to the factory.

A third theory which the author believes may have

---

[10] *Email correspondence with Rolls-Royce historian, André Blaize with the author, August 24, 2021*

[11] *ibid*

[12] *Email correspondence with Rolls-Royce historian, Steve Stuckey with the author, August 25, 2021*

[13] *ibid*

OPPOSITE: The elegant H. J. Mulliner convertible body on the non-matching Phantom III chassis can be recognized from the 1930s style wire wheels. This image was taken in the 1990s when in the ownership of Tom Barrett of the Barrett-Jackson Auction Company. *(Steve Stuckey)*

ABOVE: The interior of the Rolls-Royce Phantom IV Drophead Coupe, chassis number 4AF6, bodied by H. J. Mulliner. *(Steve Stuckey)*

credence, is that as this car had sentimental value for the Shah, especially during his marriage to his second queen, Soraya and, as it was in effect a "one-off" built for him, he may have ordered it scrapped so as to prevent a car so closely associated with him to be sold to a third party.

Whatever may have been the reason for the decision, based on conversations held with Roger Cr'aster, former Rolls-Royce Export Manager (who, as covered in Chapter 34 personally sold "his" and "hers" Camargues to the Shah) Rolls-Royce indeed scrapped the chassis of 4AF6 in June 1959.[12]

It was at some time during the period where 4AF6 had been returned to the Rolls-Royce factory, that Rolls-Royce also had a Phantom III with a Windovers Limousine de Ville body that had blown its engine. Rolls-Royce kept the chassis, replaced the engine, and sold the Windover's body. The factory then proceeded to place 4AF6's body on the Phantom III chassis. It was subsequently sold by Simmons of Mayfair in July 1961 as a Phantom III with chassis number 3BT15.[13]

As of 2008, the proverbially "reincarnated" 4AF6 is in a Hong Kong collection where, though it is now in effect a Phantom III, on the firewall, which has been carried over with the body, there still exists the original chassis plate stating "4AF6".

515

1922 Rolls-Royce Silver Ghost & 1956 Rolls-Royce Phantom IV, bodied by Hooper

Chassis Numbers: 38PG & 4CS6

The joining together of two Rolls-Royces from two separate eras in this section of the book, while seemingly out of place, is due to a later connection tying the fates of each car together.

As covered earlier in the section pertaining to the post-revolutionary history of the Pierce-Arrow, in the mid-1970s Queen Farah had decided to establish an automobile museum under her patronage. As had been done earlier with Reza Shah's Rolls-Royce Phantom I, chassis number 72DC (covered earlier in this Appendix), accordingly, on May 22, 1977 the chief of the royal court, Asadollah Alam, sent an official letter to the Commander of the Imperial Iranian Air Force requesting the transport by plane of two Rolls-Royces to the Rolls-Royce factory for restoration (see left).

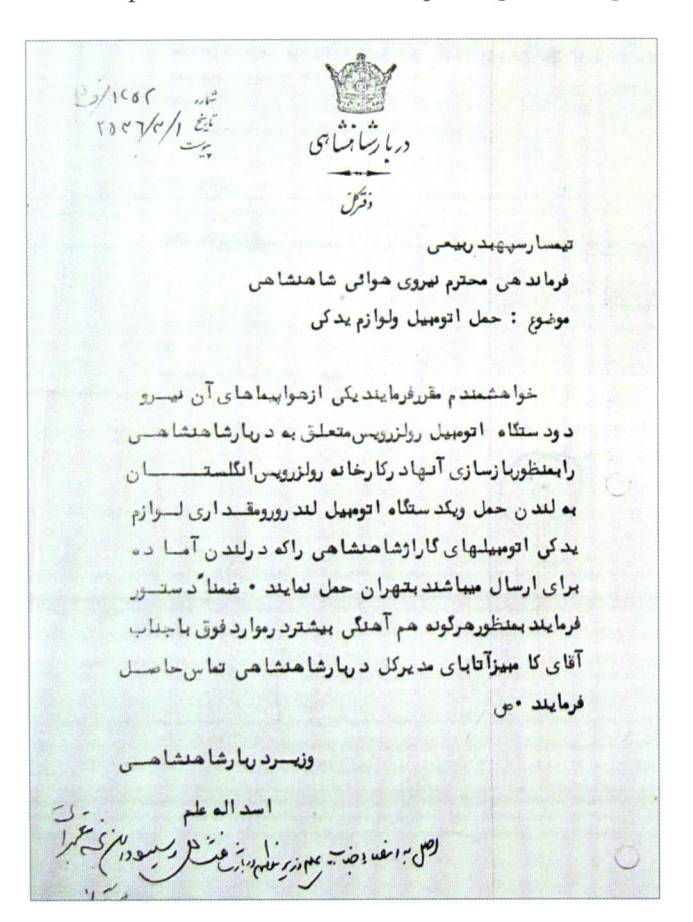

The first car designated for dispatch was Reza Shah's 1922 Silver Ghost, chassis number 38PG, which was covered in Chapter 2, best known as the car used for the proverbial "unveiling" ceremony where Reza Shah, in a public ceremony, proceeded to ban the veil in Iran. Having accumulated 12,600 km from new, after fifty-five years in the royal garage, the car was ripe for restoration in preparation for display at the museum.

The second car singled out for restoration by the Rolls-Royce factory can be considered as one of the most unique and rare Rolls-Royces of the reign of Mohammad Reza Pahlavi: the Phantom IV, chassis number 4CS6, one of eighteen built and, after years of extensive use, apparently in need of a complete overhaul.

Appendix 1: The Story Continues

The restoration of the Phantom IV was not carried out with the objective of display at the museum, but rather for continued service in the royal court. This is evidenced by the fact that the court had requested that the color be changed from black to Bordeaux, the primary color of the cars used by the royal court.

OPPOSITE BOTTOM LEFT: On May 22, 1977, Asadollah Alam, the Minister of the royal court, sent this official letter to the Commander of the Imperial Iranian Air Force requesting the transport by air force cargo plane of two Rolls-Royces, namely the Silver Ghost, chassis number 38PG and Phantom IV, chassis number 4CS6, to England for restoration at the Rolls-Royce factory. *(Saad Abad Palace)*

OPPOSITE TOP RIGHT: The Kashf-e Hijab ("Unveiling") car, Rolls-Royce Silver Ghost, 38PG, after being returned to Iran from the Rolls-Royce factory. The picture was taken outside of the Bonyad Mostazafan's Karaj Warehouse. (Early 1990s) *(Borzou Sepasi)*

OPPOSITE BOTTOM RIGHT: Rolls-Royce Silver Ghost, 38PG, on display in the Contemporary History Museum of Iran located in Tehran. (Early 1990s) *(Hossein Manoochehr Parsa)*

RIGHT: The Rolls-Royce Phantom IV, chassis number 4CS6, bodied by Hooper, on display to the public at the 1993 Tehran Trade Exhibition. This was the first public appearance of the car after its return to Iran. (1993) *(Arash Behzadi, Machine Magazine)*

BELOW: The Rolls-Royce Phantom IV is pictured in the Karaj warehouse of the Bonyad Mostazafan after its return to Iran Tehran. Alongside the car two Silver Shadows are also visible. (Early 1990s) *(Borzou Sepasi)*

With the onset of the revolution, both cars were still in the Rolls-Royce works undergoing restoration. As a result, in the mid-1980s a court case arose in Britain pitting the new Islamic government against the Pahlavi family as both laid claim to the ownership of the cars. The Pahlavis stated that the cars were their personal property, while the new Iranian government argued that the cars were state-owned property. One of the more interesting points of the court case was the position rendered by the Iranian government that the Silver Ghost was bought by the last Qajar Shah of Iran, Ahmad Shah, and that the car was expropriated by the government when Reza Shah Pahlavi seized power from Ahmad Shah in 1925, an event covered extensively in Chapter 2.

Fit for a King ~ The Royal Garage of the Shah of Iran

After a long-drawn out court battle, the British courts ruled in favor of the Iranian government and, in January 1988, the Iranian government took possession of both cars. After an absence of over a decade, both cars arrived in Iran on August 30, 1989.

Following their arrival, as with almost everything else associated with Shah's regime, the ownership of the cars were transferred to the Bonyad Mostazafan, who in turn, put the Silver Ghost on display at a contemporary history museum located in Vali-Asr Street (formerly Pahlavi) in northern Tehran. The Phantom IV joined the remaining cars of the royal garage in storage, only once being put on public display at the 1993 Tehran Trade Exhibition. In 2004, with the founding of the National Automobile Museum of Iran, both cars went on permanent display.

Appendix 1: The Story Continues

OPPOSITE TOP & MIDDLE: The Rolls-Royce Phantom IV sitting and gathering dust while in storage. As evidenced by the paw prints, a cat has taken a liking to the car. (Early 2000s) *(Borzou Sepasi)*

OPPOSITE BOTTOM: The Rolls-Royce Phantom IV on display among the collection of cars of the National Automobile Museum of Iran. (2004) *(Borzou Sepasi)*

BELOW: The last public photographs prior to the revolution of the royal Rolls-Royce Phantom V, chassis number 5LAS39, bodied by Park Ward. (Late 1970s) *(Borzou Sepasi)*

1959 Rolls-Royce Phantom V, bodied by Park Ward
Chassis Number: 5LAS39

The Shah's 1959 Rolls-Royce Phantom V, chassis number 5LAS39, is viewed as being the second most important Rolls-Royce in Mohammad Reza Shah's reign. The car can be seen transporting the Shah in a number of high-profile ceremonies and events, being used by the Shah and the pregnant Queen Farah for transport from the Saad Abad Palace to the hospital for the birth of Crown Prince Reza.

Unfortunately, at some point in time, during or after the 1979 revolution, the trunk of the car was damaged, which, based on a visual inspection by the author, most probably came about in a haphazard attempt to push the car. As with almost all of the cars of the royal garage, this car was transferred to the ownership of the Bonyad Mostazafan where it remains in storage in their Karaj warehouse to this day.

1966 Rolls-Royce Phantom V State Landaulette, bodied by Mulliner Park Ward
Chassis Number: 5LVF29

During the course of the research for this book, in October 2003, the author became the first private citizen to gain access to the garage of the Niavaran Palace, the Shah's primary place of abode. The garage, which had been under lock and key since the fall of the palace to the revolutionaries, was a virtual time capsule, and while the Miura SVJ, Espada and the "his" and "hers" Camargues were long gone, there remained not only the children's bicycles, golf carts and other recreational vehicles, but also the two primary ceremonial cars used by the Shah in the late 1970s, namely the Rolls-Royce Phantom V State Landaulette, chassis number 5LVF29, and Phantom VI, chassis number PRX4861.

TOP: Rolls-Royce Phantom V, chassis number 5LAS39, bodied by Park Ward (right) and Phantom VI, chassis number PRX4860, bodied by Mulliner Park Ward (left) in the royal garage five months after the revolution. Soon thereafter, the ownership of the cars was divided between a number of "revolutionary" foundations, with the majority going to the Bonyad Mostazafan, as were these two cars. (July 1979) *(Keyvan Banihashemi)*

ABOVE: The Rolls-Royce Phantom V as it sits in the Bonyad Mostazafan Karaj warehouse. *(Borzou Sepasi)*

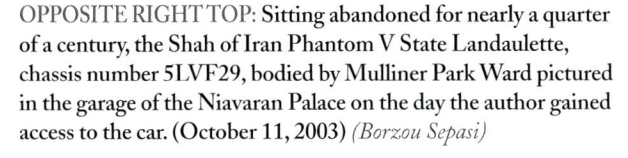

Appendix 1: The Story Continues

OPPOSITE RIGHT TOP: Sitting abandoned for nearly a quarter of a century, the Shah of Iran Phantom V State Landaulette, chassis number 5LVF29, bodied by Mulliner Park Ward pictured in the garage of the Niavaran Palace on the day the author gained access to the car. (October 11, 2003) *(Borzou Sepasi)*

OPPOSITE RIGHT BOTTOM: The royal crest on the rear door covered by dust. (October, 11 2003) *(Borzou Sepasi)*

TOP LEFT: The two royal Rolls-Royces. The Rolls-Royce Phantom V State Landaulette and Phantom VI, chassis number PRX4861 as pictured from the rear. (October, 11 2003) *(Borzou Sepasi)*

ABOVE: The Niavaran palace garage still has a closed warehouse that includes items that have been boxed and stored away. The interesting point is that on its door is written "Sealed by the Imam Khomeini Committee" which means that this section of the garage was sealed in 1979. *(Borzou Sepasi)*

TOP & MIDDLE RIGHT: The Phantom V State Landaulette, 5LVF29, interior virtually untouched for nearly a quarter century. (October 11, 2003) *(Borzou Sepasi)*

RIGHT: The Phantom V, chassis number 5LVF29, handbook supplement is still in the glove box. *(Borzou Sepasi)*

TOP: In an effort by a group of Iranian historical vehicle enthusiasts in 2009, the Landaulet was cleaned, waxed and polished and saw light of day after nearly a quarter century. The public was able to see this car for the first time since the revolution in a classic car show held at the Niavaran Palace in 2009 (where the Landaulet was parked in front of the Palace door seemingly awaiting its former passengers). (2009) *(Mahnaz Beedel)*

ABOVE: In 2012, the garage of the Niavaran Palace was converted into a motor museum. This was due to the tireless efforts of the employees of the Niavaran Palace who have made the palace into a virtual time capsule, and, in particular Mrs. Shahnaz Pakniyat, formerly the curator of the motor museum. Both Rolls-Royce Phantom V, chassis number 5LVF29, and Phantom VI, chassis number PRX4861, are on display as well as a number of motorcycles and other recreational vehicles which were left behind at the Palace following the revolution. (2018) *(Niavaran Palace)*

1960 Rolls-Royce Silver Cloud II Drophead Coupe, bodied by H. J. Mulliner
Chassis Number: LSWC418

The Shah was known to primarily have used this car for protocol and official purposes such as when he welcomed Queen Juliana of Holland to Iran in 1963. Accordingly, it was for this reason that in later years the color of the car was changed from white to Bordeaux, the color of the royal court, in preparation for the Persepolis celebrations of 1971. After the revolution, the car was transferred to the Bonyad Mostazafan Karaj warehouse where, except for sporadic outings such as being put on display at classic car shows, it was kept in storage until being put on permanent display with the launch of the National Automobile Museum of Iran in 2004.

Appendix 1: The Story Continues

ABOVE: The official photograph of the Rolls-Royce Silver Cloud II Drophead Coupe, chassis number LSWC418, taken for the records of the Bonyad Mostazafan. (1980s) *(Bonyad Mostazafan)*

TOP RIGHT: The Rolls-Royce Silver Cloud II Drophead Coupe in storage at the Bonyad Mostazafan's Karaj warehouse. (1990s) *(Borzou Sepasi)*

RIGHT: The Shah's Rolls-Royce Silver Cloud II Drophead Coupe parked next to Princess Ashraf Pahlavi's Rolls-Royce Phantom VI, chassis number PRX4832, bodied by Mulliner Park Ward, at the 2006 Tehran Classic Car Show held in Saad Abad Palace. (May 2006) *(Borzou Sepasi)*

BELOW: The Rolls-Royce Silver Cloud II Drophead Coupe on display (with jacks placed underneath it) at the National Automobile Museum of Iran. (2008) *(Borzou Sepasi)*

1965 Rolls-Royce Silver Cloud III Drophead Coupe, bodied by Mulliner Park Ward

Chassis Number: LCSC83C

As with the Shah's former Ferrari Superfast, his Rolls-Royce Silver Cloud III Drophead Coupe, chassis number LCSC83C (bodied by Mulliner Park Ward), also has the dubious distinction of being expropriated not once, but twice. Having been damaged at some point during or after the revolution, in particular in the front end, the ownership of the car was transferred to the Bonyad Mostazafan from the royal garage. It apparently was subsequently sold off in "as-is" condition to businessman Fazel Khodadad who, in turn, sent the car to famed Iranian mechanic, Reza Dardashti, whose exploits have been covered elsewhere in this book, for repair and restoration. Mr. Khodadad received the car back in pristine condition, but was then caught up in one of the largest banking scandals in Iranian history and was executed for "economic crimes" and all his assets, including the Rolls-Royce, were transferred to Setad Ejraee, another quasi-governmental organization, and stored in their warehouse in western Tehran. Unlike the other organizations having expropriated cars at their disposal, the Setad has looked after the cars in their possession much more professionally and sympathetically. The Setad has four other cars in its custody: Bentley Corniche Convertible, Cadillac Sixty Special (1958), Austin Princess and a Graham-Paige. As with the garage of the Niavaran Palace, the author was the first private citizen to be granted access to the warehouse of the Setad in 2003 and assisted in arranging that these cars be shown to the public for the first time at the 2009 Tehran Classic Car show held in Niavaran Palace.

TOP: The Rolls-Royce Silver Cloud III Drophead Coupe, chassis number LCSC83C, bodied by Mulliner Park Ward pictured prior to the repair of the damage it suffered during the revolution. *(Bonyad Mostazafan)*

LEFT & ABOVE: The Rolls-Royce Silver Cloud III Drophead Coupe after being restored by Iranian master mechanic Reza Dardashti. Before immigrating to Canada in the 1990s, Reza Dardashti was known as one of the most talented mechanics in Iran who had worked on many of the cars of the royal garage prior to the revolution. Following the revolution, he continued to service the royal cars that were sold off to private parties. (Late 1980s) *(Mehrdad Dardashti)*

TOP & MIDDLE LEFT: The Rolls-Royce Silver Cloud III Drophead Coupe, chassis number LCSC83C, bodied by Mulliner Park Ward after being confiscated by the state for the second time and being handed over to the Setade Ejraee. It is pictured alongside a Bentley Corniche Convertible, chassis number DBX24572, also in the possession of the Setade Ejraee. (2003) *(Borzou Sepasi)*

LEFT: Austin Princess and 1958 Cadillac Sixty Special keeping the ex-Shah Rolls-Royce Silver Cloud III Drophead Coupe company in the Setade Ejraee warehouse. Unlike other organizations which had the cars of the royal garage put in their care, the Setade Ejraee maintains the cars in their possession very well. (2003) *(Borzou Sepasi)*

TOP RIGHT: The Rolls-Royce Silver Cloud III Drophead Coupe on display at the 2009 Niavaran Palace Classic Car Show. *(Borzou Sepasi)*

ABOVE: The stablemate of the ex-Shah Rolls-Royce Silver Cloud III Drophead Coupe in the Setade Ejraee warehouse is this Bentley Corniche Convertible, chassis number DBX24572, believed to have a royal lineage. The Bentley is pictured here on display at the 2009 Niavaran Palace Classic Car Show next to one of the sculptures of the famous Iranian sculptor, painter, scholar and art collector, Parviz Tanavoli. *(Borzou Sepasi)*

1920 Rolls-Royce Silver Ghost, bodied by Cunard Motor and Carriage Company

As detailed in Chapter 2, in 1920, the chief officer of the Imperial Bank of Persia, J. McMurray, took delivery of a Silver Ghost bodied by the Cunard Motor and Carriage Company. Following delivery, the car disappeared from sight only to appear again in 1976 when it was displayed in an exhibition commemorating the Pahlavi dynasty. The car was wrongly presented as one of Reza Shah's personal cars. At the time, the vehicle was the property of the Imperial Iranian Army.

Up to the 1979 revolution this car had remained fully intact but, after the revolution, it was left abandoned and exposed to the elements at the Abbas Abad garrison of the Iranian Army for over two decades, and, accordingly, the combination of the elements and neglect took a toll on the car. Finally, steps were taken to save the car and it was transferred to the Saad Abad Palace War Museum where it was put on display in a glass case in "as-is" condition.

Appendix 1: The Story Continues

1970 Volkswagen EMPI Imp

This car disappeared from the Shah's Now Shahr Palace located by the Caspian Sea when the revolution took place, only to show up for sale in 2018. What took place during the ensuing thirty-nine years is unclear, with some pundits taking the view that the car was most probably expropriated by one of the post-revolutionary organizations that took over the Pahlavi family assets or, as had happened from time to time, could have been simply driven off from the Palace grounds by one of the marauding crowds who spilled into each palace following their fall. In any case, when the car was offered for sale, it had no documentation available. When observed closely, the car offered for sale would seem to be the same as the one pictured with the Shah and his family except for the addition of a hand-crafted metal bumper.

OPPOSITE TOP LEFT: **The 1920 Rolls-Royce Silver Ghost, bodied by Cunard Motor and Carriage Company in perfect condition on display at a Pahlavi Era exhibition in Tehran in 1976.** *(Borzou Sepasi)*

OPPOSITE TOP RIGHT: **The McMurray Rolls-Royce Silver Ghost, being viewed in 1975 by General Dean, Commander of the US Army Logistics, at the Abbas Abad garrison.** *(irdc.ir)*

OPPOSITE MIDDLE & BOTTOM RIGHT: **The Imperial Bank of Persia's chief officer, J. McMurray's Rolls-Royce Silver Ghost on display (and placed on what are apparently stools) in a glass case at the Saad Abad Palace Historical Complex. It is still being misrepresented as having been owned by Reza Shah.** *(Borzou Sepasi)*

TOP: **The Shah driving his Volkswagen EMPI Imp with family in tow.** *(Borzou Sepasi)*

BOTTOM: **Most probably the same car after 39 years. It was advertised in an Iranian on-line classic car sales site on Instagram.**

APPENDIX 2

Honorable Mentions

Vehicles not covered in this book but deserving coverage

1949 Alfa Romeo 6C 2500 Super Sport Pininfarina
Chassis Number: 915.773

During the course of research for this book, one of the cars that was discovered languishing in the warehouses of the Bonyad Mostazafan was this 1949 Alfa Romeo 6C 2500 Super Sport Pininfarina. Based on the available documentation, the Alfa was last owned by the renown Iranian classic car collector, Fuad Majzub. As Mr. Majzub had been accused of having ties with the Pahlavi regime, his entire collection of cars, including the Shah's former Mercedes-Benz 500K Autobahnkurier, chassis number 130898, had been expropriated and their ownership transferred to the Bonyad Mostazafan. Following inspection by the author, the Alfa was found to be missing its original chassis number plate, initially making it difficult to piece together the history of this vehicle.

After further research and reviewing the documentation of the car which had been issued when the car was expropriated, a chassis number, albeit having one digit more than other Alfa 6C chassis numbers, was discovered among the documentation. It is speculated that the vehicle may have had a chassis number at the time of its expropriation which could have subsequently been removed or lost over time.

Accordingly, based on the aforesaid documentation combined with the specifications of the vehicle, it is believed that this vehicle is Alfa chassis number 915.773, a Super Sport Pininfarina manufactured on October 27, 1949 and sold in 1950 to a Pia Di Meo of Catania, Italia.

This vehicle was then matched to an old photograph of the Shah at the wheel of an Alfa Romeo 6C. Up to this date, no documents have been discovered that would conclusively link this 6C to the Shah, but some pundits are of the belief that the car may have not been sold new to the Shah, and, rather may have been purchased during his short exile in 1953 when he and Queen Soraya took refuge in Italy following his temporary overthrow.[1]

TOP: The Shah pictured behind the wheel of what is believed to be this very Alfa. (Early 1950s)

MIDDLE: The Alfa Romeo 6C 2500 Super Sport Pininfarina believed to be chassis number 915.773 in the Bonyad Mostazafan Karaj warehouse. (Early 2000s) *(Ramin Salehkhou)*

ABOVE: The official photograph of the Alfa Romeo 6C 2500 at the time of expropriation discovered among the documents of the Bonyad Mostazafan. (1980s)

---

[1] *Stefano Salvetti from 6C2500.org*

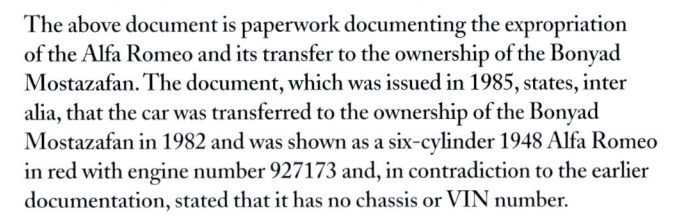

Fit for a King ~ The Royal Garage of the Shah of Iran

The above document is paperwork documenting the expropriation of the Alfa Romeo and its transfer to the ownership of the Bonyad Mostazafan. The document, which was issued in 1985, states, inter alia, that the car was transferred to the ownership of the Bonyad Mostazafan in 1982 and was shown as a six-cylinder 1948 Alfa Romeo in red with engine number 927173 and, in contradiction to the earlier documentation, stated that it has no chassis or VIN number.

1965 Bizzarrini 5300 GT Strada
Chassis Number: IA3.0250

Many are not aware that the Shah possibly also owned a Bizzarrini. This information only came to light after the revolution, where, among the many expropriated cars of the Shah, the royal family and their associates, this Bizzarrini was discovered. Apparently, at some point after the revolution, this car was put up for auction, but found no takers and was stored away in one of the warehouses of the Bonyad Mostazafan. The author, after gaining permission to inspect this car, discovered a plate from the royal garage riveted to the firewall identifying it as vehicle number 119 of the royal garage. This plate is conclusive proof that the

530

car at some point in its history, belonged to either the Shah or a close relation. After languishing in storage for years, the vehicle was refurbished and detailed by a group of enthusiasts who volunteered their services around 2010 and subsequently put it on permanent display in the National Automobile Museum of Iran. At some point, the plexiglass light covers were removed and stowed away in the trunk and the car also shows some damage, believed to have been inflicted during the days of the revolution.

1965 Cadillac Fleetwood Series 75 Limousine

Chassis Number:
ST 04A 65-69733 DC 766 KR 2 EA

Among the lot of ten cars sold by the Bonyad Shahid to Emirati buyer, Mohammad Ibrahim Al-Sadegh (and subsequently auctioned off by Brooks Auctions in Geneva in 1997) was a 1965 Cadillac Fleetwood Limousine. Though not owned personally by the Shah, the car was part of the fleet of the royal court and was used extensively by the Shah and his immediate family for official sojourns. Surprisingly, the very fact that this Cadillac Fleetwood Series 75 Limousine, with chassis number ST 04A 65-69733 DC 766 KR 2 EA, was still in use by the royal family at the onset of the revolution, some fourteen years after its production, reflects the fact that it was one of the mainstays of the royal fleet. A second 1965 Cadillac limousine with an armored body (chassis number unknown) was also in use, however the subsequent fate of that vehicle is unknown.

OPPOSITE TOP RIGHT: **The Bizzarrini 5300 GT Strada, chassis number IA3.0250, during the years in storage before being refurbished and put on display in the museum. (2004)** *(Borzou Sepasi)*

OPPOSITE SECOND: **Royal garage, plate No. 119.** *(Borzou Sepasi)*

OPPOSITE THIRD: **Interior shot of the Bizzarrini.** *(Borzou Sepasi)*

OPPOSITE BOTTOM: **The Bizzarrini after being refurbished and readied for display in the National Automobile Museum. (2010)** *(Borzou Sepasi)*

RIGHT (ALL): **Queen Farah being transported in the Cadillac.**

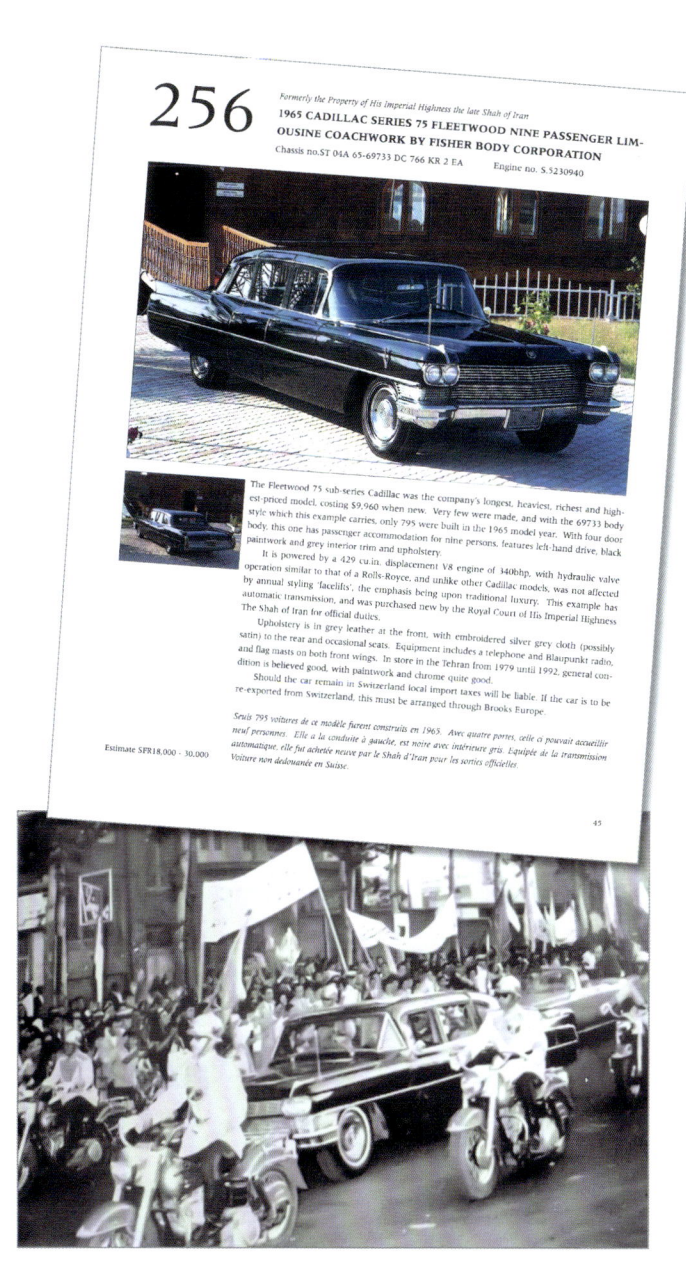

531

1951 Cadillac High top Limousine, bodied by Franay

Complementing the other Cadillacs operated by the Saudi royal court covered elsewhere in this book, was a 1951 High top limousine made by the French coachbuilder Carrosserie Franay. Built for the personal use of King Abdolaziz (Ibn Saud) it utilized a 1951 Cadillac platform. The car still remains in the Saudi royal garage and is in need of a light restoration.

1968 Maserati Ghibli Coupe
Chassis Number: AM115.414

Another car which has been represented as having been owned by the Shah, but, in fact, was formerly owned by Prince Patrick Ali Pahlavi, whom at one time was second in line to the throne, is this white Maserati Ghibli Coupe, chassis number AM115.414, with rare knock-off Borrani wire wheels. When the car was offered for sale in 2017, it was represented as being one of the personal cars owned by the Shah despite having been delivered new to Prince Patrick Ali in 1968. When originally delivered, the Maserati was red and had a black interior. In 1986, it was restored in the United States and subsequently exported to Finland in 1989.

1975 Maserati Indy 4900
Chassis Number: AM116/49*2192

A second Maserati, discovered to have been in the royal garage, but mistakenly attributed to the ownership of the Shah, was a 1975 Maserati Indy 4900, chassis number AM116/49*2192. Adding to the misunderstanding was the fact that this Maserati was consistently pictured parked next to the Shah's former 1970 Maserati Ghibli Coupe, causing many to believe that both cars were owned by the Shah. However, according to the Maserati archives, the Indy had been ordered and owned by the Shah's half-brother, Prince Abdol Reza Pahlavi and not the Shah. It was not uncommon for certain siblings of the Shah to have their cars stored and maintained at the royal garage.

Appendix 2: Honorable Mentions

It bears mention that at the time of the revolution, the Ghibli had already been bequeathed by the Shah to Prince Kamyar Pahlavi, the son of Prince Abdol Reza. In effect, and ironically, the two Maseratis that were being offered for sale side by side were "father and son" Maseratis, namely Prince Kamyar's Ghibli and his father, Prince Abdol Reza's Indy. The Indy, unlike the Ghibli which remained unsold, was sold at auction in the late 1980s and remains in Iran today as part of a private collection.

OPPOSITE TOP & MIDDLE LEFT: The 1951 Cadillac High top Limousine built by Carrosserie Franay.

OPPOSITE BOTTOM LEFT: Maserati Ghibli Coupe, chassis number AM115.414. *(Makela Auto Tuning)*

OPPOSITE TOP RIGHT: *Kayhan* daily newspaper had a report of the royal garage auction. In a series of auctions in 1980s several cars were sold including a 1975 Maserati Indy, chassis number AM116/49*2192, which was the property of one of the royal family. Pictured alongside the Indy, the Maserati Ghibli, chassis number AM115.1394, was not sold. (1980)

TOP LEFT & ABOVE: Prince Abdol Reza Pahlavi at the Maserati factory taking delivery of his Maserati Indy, AM116/49*2192. *(Adolfo Orsi)*

TOP RIGHT: The Maserati Indy 4900, chassis number AAM116/49*2192, before auction. (1980s) *(Bonyad Mostazafan)*

MIDDLE & BOTTOM RIGHT: The sold Maserati Indy in a race in Azadi circuit of Tehran at the hands of its new private owner. **(October 1990)** *(Teymour Richard)*

2018 Maserati Touring Superleggera Scia di Persia

In 2018, the coachbuilder Touring Superleggera launched a new product: the 'Scia di Persia' (The Shah of Persia) in homage to the Maserati 5000GT of the Shah of Iran. Utilizing a Maserati Gran Turismo rolling chassis and a fully hand-made aluminum body, the company subsequently followed up this model with a convertible version.

1948 Oldsmobile 98C "Concept"

Among the cars held in storage by the Bonyad Mostazafan, there sits an Oldsmobile 98C that has been rebodied and would seem to have been a concept car. The front of the car has been totally re-designed with hidden headlights and the modifications extend all the way to the rear of the car. According to the archives of the Bonyad Mostazafan, at the time of the revolution the car had been in the possession of Mr. Fuad Majzub, a car collector par excellence from before the revolution who also had in his collection the ex-Shah Mercedes-Benz 500K Autobahnkurier, as well as a number of other cars believed to have once been owned by the Shah.

Upon more detailed research, the production date of the Oldsmobile coincides with the Shah's first visit to the United States in 1949. Given the Shah's propensity for buying the latest and most interesting cars during his overseas trips, some pundits speculate that at some point the car may have caught the Shah's eye and was bought by him, while others are of the belief that it could have been a gift from either the United States government or General Motors, or both. The author welcomes any available information on this car.

OPPOSITE (ALL): **Touring Superleggera Scia di Persia (The Shah of Persia)** was produced in homage to the Shah of Iran's Maserati 5000GT Touring Superleggera. The Scia Di Persia logo was designed specifically for this car. *(Touring Superleggera)*

TOP: **The mysterious 1949 Oldsmobile 98C (concept?)** sitting in the warehouse of the Bonyad Mostazafan. *(Borzou Sepasi)*

ABOVE: **The Shah of Iran arriving in the United States on board United States Air Force One VC-118 Independence** on his first visit to the United States in 1949 and welcomed by US President Harry S. Truman. (1949)

TOP RIGHT: **The wooden buck of the XNR** used for shaping the sheet metal body parts. *(The Henry Ford Collection)*

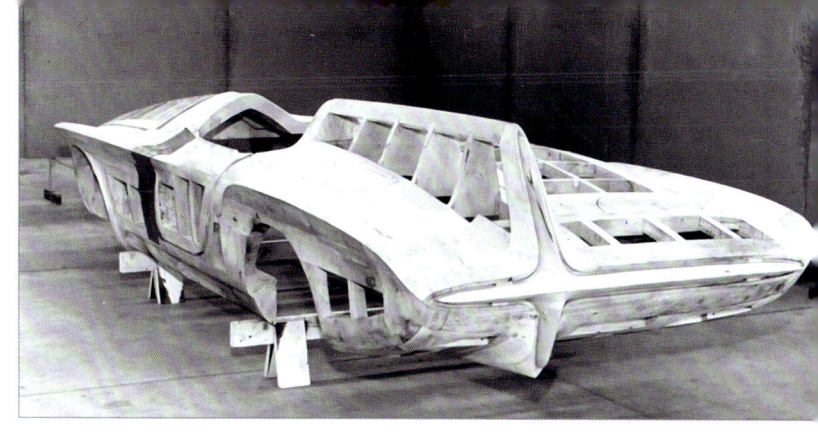

1960 Plymouth XNR Concept
Chassis Number: 9999997

The XNR was created by Chrysler's design chief Virgil Exner and hand crafted by Carrozzeria Ghia in Italy utilizing a Plymouth Valiant chassis. Designed with the objective of adding more pizzazz to the Plymouth brand, the car's in-line six-cylinder engine had been modified to reach a power output of two hundred and fifty horsepower and the car was considered so personal to Exner that he named it after himself.[2]

After being shown on the show circuit, Exner attempted to buy the car, but because of American customs regulations the XNR was sent back to Italy, where, it was sold to an unknown Swiss buyer who apparently then proceeded to sell the XNR to the Shah of Iran. It was subsequently sold to a Lebanese buyer by the name of Anwar al Mulla who resided in Kuwait who, in turn, sold it to another Lebanese citizen and the car was sent to Lebanon. With the outbreak of the Lebanese civil war in the mid-1970s the XNR was stored away in an underground garage until being discovered by Lebanese car collector, Karim Edde. Recognizing its value, Edde made sure the car was kept safe from the local carnage by constantly changing its location. In 2008, it was sent by Mr. Edde to RM Restorations for a comprehensive restoration and was completed in time for the 2011 Amelia Island Concours d'Elegance where the XNR won best in class. Edde put the car up for auction in 2012 where it was bought by New York Investment Banker, Paul Gould, on August 18, 2012 for $935,000 and it joined another Exner/Ghia concept car in Gould's collection, the Dart Diablo.

---

[2] *www.truthaboutcars.com*, "A Car so Personal Virgil Exner named it after Himself, the Plymouth XNR" by Ronnie Schreiber, December 15, 2014

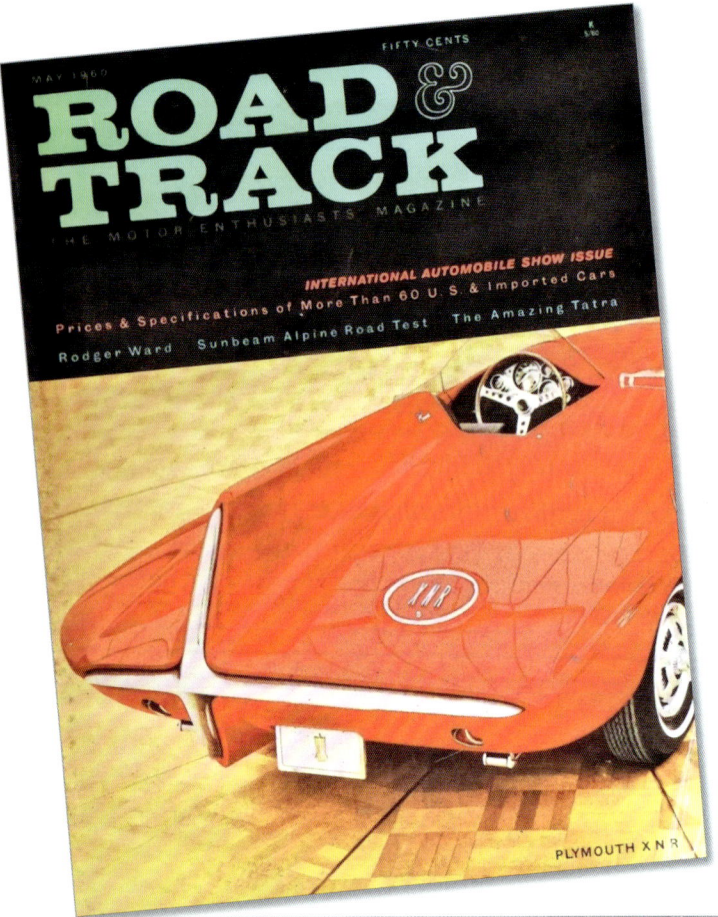

1952 Rolls-Royce Phantom IV four-door Cabriolet, bodied by Franay
Chassis Number: 4AF22

One of the most elegant Rolls-Royces of King Abdolaziz (Ibn Saud) was also built by Franay. Built on a Phantom IV foundation, chassis number 4AF22, and having a four-door cabriolet body, the car was originally painted in a combination of cream and green with a green interior. The color of the car was then later changed to black. The car is currently on display at the National Museum of Saudi Arabia.

Appendix 2: Honorable Mentions

1975 Rolls-Royce Phantom VI, bodied by Mulliner Park Ward
Chassis Number PRX4832

Princess Ashraf Pahlavi's Phantom VI, chassis number PRX4832, bodied by Mulliner Park Ward was discovered by the author in 2002 in storage at the former stables of Saad Abad Palace. The stables had been converted into a makeshift storage area and garage following the revolution and had been under lock and key for over two decades.

As one of the few private citizen to be granted entry following the revolution, the author came across a broad amalgamation of historic items from the palaces, as well as a number of royal cars that included a Mercedes-Benz 300SL Roadster, Rolls-Royce Corniche Coupe, Rolls-Royce Silver Shadow, Mercedes-Benz 600 SWB, VW

OPPOSITE TOP LEFT: **Plymouth XNR, chassis number 9999997, bodied by Carrozzeria Ghia on the cover of** *Road & Track.* **(May 1960)**

OPPOSITE MIDDLE: **Virgil Exner, Chrysler design chief and his masterpiece, the XNR.**

OPPOSITE BOTTOM LEFT: **The ex-Shah Plymouth XNR concept car.** *(Carrozzeria Ghia)*

OPPOSITE RIGHT: **1952 Rolls-Royce Phantom IV Franay Cabriolet, chassis number 4AF22. (Coachbuild.com)**

TOP: **The Rolls-Royce Phantom IV on display at the National Museum of Saudi Arabia.** *(Abd ul-Rahman)*

TOP RIGHT & MIDDLE: **Princess Ashraf's Rolls-Royce Phantom VI, chassis number PRX4832, bodied by Mulliner Park Ward, in the former stables of the Saad Abad Palace. (2002)** *(Borzou Sepasi)*

Meyers Manx, Cadillac Fleetwood Limousine, and also several motorcycles, children's playthings, snowmobiles, and the like. The Saad Abad Complex not only included the Shah's main palace, but also a number of smaller palaces that belonged to the Queen Mother, Princess Ashraf and a number of the brothers and sisters of the Shah. Not all of the items and cars stored belonged to the Shah.

In 1973, another Phantom VI with chassis number PRX4742 was shipped to Iran and delivered to the royal garage. The car was subsequently exported from Iran to the United States in 1978, apparently by Princess Ashraf, most probably anticipating the turmoil that was brewing.

Fit for a King ~ The Royal Garage of the Shah of Iran

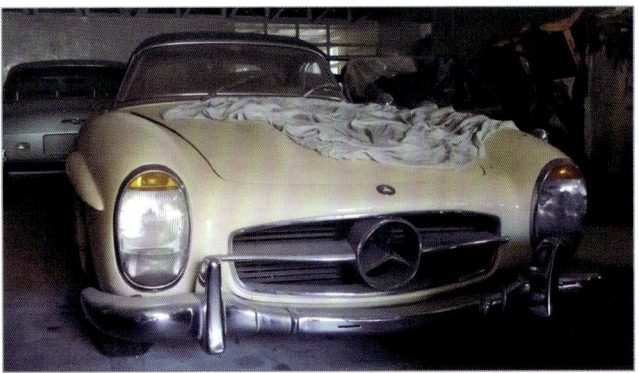

1977 Rolls-Royce Phantom VI, bodied by Mulliner Park Ward
Chassis Numbers: PRX4860 and PRX4861 (The "Twins")

In 1977, the royal court simultaneously ordered two Phantom VI's from Rolls-Royce. Both cars were in the color of the royal court, Bordeaux, and each had royal crests on their rear doors. Neither car was armor-plated but each had a television installed in the rear compartment. The royal court received a 33% discount on the price and instead of the listed price of £86,811.44, paid £68,551.44

LEFT: The busts of the Shah, Queen Farah and the Crown Prince in storage in the former stables of the Saad Abad Palace. (2002) *(Borzou Sepasi)*

MIDDLE: A 1960 Mercedes-Benz 300SL Roadster, chassis number 198.042.10.002444, in the former stables of the Saad Abad Palace. The car is now on display at the Saad Abad Palace Auto Museum. It is believed, but not certain, that the car belonged to Princess Shahnaz Pahlavi. (2003) *(Borzou Sepasi)*

BELOW (BOTH): The former stables of the Saad Abad Palace which were subsequently converted into a makeshift garage and storage area. A number of cars left behind in the Saad Abad Palace following the revolution were hidden away in storage there for over two decades. Seen next to Rolls-Royce Phantom VI, chassis number PRX4832, are: Mercedes-Benz 300SL Roadster, chassis number 198.042.10.002444, Rolls-Royce Corniche, Rolls-Royce Silver Shadow, Mercedes-Benz 600 SWB, VW Meyers Manx and a Cadillac Fleetwood Limousine. Today most of the cars are now on permanent display at the Saad Abad Palace Auto Museum. (2003) *(Borzou Sepasi)*

Appendix 2: Honorable Mentions

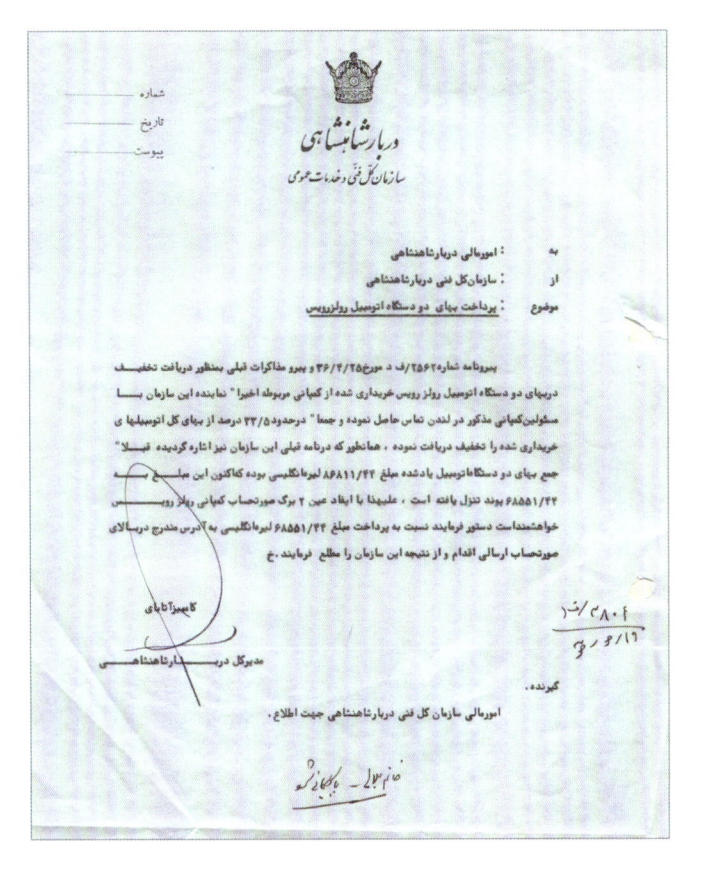

for both cars. They were shipped to Iran in the same year and chassis number PRX4861 was sent to the Niavaran Palace for the personal use of the Shah and chassis number PRX4860 was sent to the royal garage.

Given the fact that the two cars were ordered together and are virtually identical to each other, the author has nicknamed the two Rolls-Royces as the "twins".

LEFT: The official letter dated September 10, 1977 regarding the payment for the two "twin" Phantom VIs, PRX4860 and PRX4861. (Saad Abad Palace)

MIDDLE & BOTTOM: The Rolls-Royce Phantom VI, chassis number PRX4860, and also shown alongside Rolls-Royce Phantom V State Landaulette, chassis number 5LVF29, in the Niavaran palace garage as discovered by the author in 2003 in the Niavaran palace garage. *(Borzou Sepasi)*

BELOW (BOTH): Two pictures from two eras. The passenger compartment of Rolls-Royce Phantom VI, chassis number PRX4861, bodied by Mulliner Park Ward in 1979, eight days after the revolution (top) and the same view of the same car in 2003 (bottom). *(Hossein Partovi/Borzou Sepasi)*

Twenty-three years after the "twins" were separated, the author uncovered the location of each one. Following the revolution, PRX4860 had been transferred from the royal garage to the Bonyad Mostazafan's Karaj warehouse and PRX4861 was found to be still sitting in the Niavaran Palace garage next to Phantom V State Landaulette, chassis number 5LVF29. At the time, both cars had been

LEFT (BOTH): The Phantom VI, chassis number PRX4861, original handbook is still in the glove box. *(Borzou Sepasi)*

ABOVE: The cleaning and detailing of this Rolls-Royce Phantom VI by a group of Iranian enthusiasts in preparation for its debut at a car show held in Niavaran Palace in 2009. (2009) *(Mahnaz Beedel)*

OPPOSITE: The Rolls-Royce Phantom VI on display at a classic car show held in the Niavaran Palace in 2009. The car is parked adjacent to the front door of the Shah's Palace in Niavaran while Rolls-Royce Phantom V State Landaulette, chassis number 5LVF29, is parked directly at the front door. (2009) *(Mahnaz Beedel)*

stored away for nearly a quarter of a century and lay under thick layers of dust.

Phantom VI PRX4861, after having been cleaned, waxed and polished by Iranian enthusiasts, was debuted to the public in 2009 at a classic car show held in the Niavaran Palace alongside Phantom V State Landaulette, chassis number 5LVF29 and a number of other cars having a royal pedigree. It was subsequently put on permanent display at a motor museum established in the former garage of the palace. Its "twin", PRX4860 has not been so lucky and is still languishing under layers of dust in the Karaj warehouse of the Bonyad Mostazafan. In 2020, the National Automobile Museum of Iran began a major overhaul of its facilities and the cars at its disposal. It is hoped that the fate of PRX4860 will change in the near future.

1968 Rolls-Royce Phantom VI, bodied by Mulliner Park Ward
Chassis Number: PRX4182

Rolls-Royce Phantom VI, chassis number PRX4182, was ordered by the royal garage in 1968 in Bordeaux, the color of the royal court. It was armor-plated and had 16-inch wheels as well as upgraded springs to handle its 3.9 ton heft.

Fit for a King ~ The Royal Garage of the Shah of Iran

After the revolution, the car was transferred from the royal garage to the warehouse of the Bonyad Mostazafan. In the early years after the revolution, the car was lent to the Iranian Foreign Ministry for protocol use. Accordingly, the car received a license plate with the registration code Tehran-21, which was the post-revolutionary practice for the identification of confiscated cars that had been subsequently sold off and had been issued with new titles and license plates. During the period it was in use at the Foreign Ministry, the Pahlavi crests on the rear doors had been covered over with plastic and tape.

As the use of a Rolls-Royce limousine was deemed to be too ostentatious and contradicted the "values" of the revolution, the Iranian Foreign Ministry soon returned the car back to the Bonyad Mostazafan whom, in turn, stored the car in their warehouse where it remains until this day. Though the plastic and tape covering of the royal crests have been removed from the rear doors, the outline of where the tape had been applied and pattern of the covering still remain on the car to this day.

1973 Stutz Blackhawk
Chassis Number: 2K57Y3A245367

"I always loved going to the garage. I am not a car nut but His Majesty always had some of the most beautiful cars I have ever seen… there were Lamborghinis, Mercedes-Benz of every description and many other types of sports cars and limousines. At that time there was also parked in the garage a car that had caused much controversy. A Stutz."

– Gail Rose Thompson
All the Shah's Men

According to the memoirs of Gail Rose Thompson, the personal horse trainer of the Shah of Iran, the Stutz Blackhawk was first introduced to Iran when Jim

TOP: The armored Rolls-Royce Phantom VI, chassis number PRX4182, in Karaj warehouse. The post-revolution "Tehran-21" license plates are still in the trunk. (2003) *(Borzou Sepasi)*

SECOND-FOURTH: The chassis number plate and body number plate of Rolls-Royce Phantom VI, chassis number PRX4182, covered under a thick layer of dust. (2003) *(Borzou Sepasi)*

Appendix 2: Honorable Mentions

1973 Stutz Blackhawk, chassis number 2K57Y3A245367, on display at the National Automobile Museum of Iran. (2015) *(Mahnaz Beedel)*

O'Donnell, the New York Banker who had revived the Stutz Motor Company in 1968, put the car on display at the 1975 Tehran International Trade Fair. O'Donnell, having joined forces with the then-retired legendary Chrysler designer Virgil Exner, had targeted the Blackhawk towards a clientele comprising of the most affluent and elite customers across the world. O'Donnell had traveled to Iran with the car in tow in the hope of attracting the interest of the Iranian elite, in particular the Shah and his closest relatives.

According to Thompson, eventually the car was brought to the attention of Kambiz Atabai, Director General of the Imperial Court who, in turn, had the car brought to the royal garage and looked over by its mechanics. Later on, the car was transported to the Imperial Stables at Farahabad where the Shah went to see the car first-hand while there for a riding session. According to Ms. Thompson, the Shah is said to have commented that "he wasn't overly impressed… if Mr. O'Donnell wanted to give it as a gift, he would greatly appreciate it. He would personally pay the import tax on the car".[3] Eventually, the car was impounded for not having proper import duty stickers, and somehow the Stutz ended up back in the Imperial Garage. According to Ms. Thompson, O'Donnell returned to Iran and had the car shipped back to the United States. However, as the pictured car is the only Stutz Blackhawk known to have existed in Iran, and still wears the plates of the exclusive distributor of Stutz, Jules Meyers, many pundits are of the belief that this car is the same car brought by O'Donnell to Iran and that it was never re-exported back to the United States. While the actual facts may never be known, as no documentation on this car has been discovered, according to O'Donnell himself, the Shah did indeed own a Stutz Blackhawk.[4] The Blackhawk would represent the third and last Exner-designed car owned by the Shah following his ownership of the Chrysler K-300 and Plymouth XNR.

1951 Talbot-Lago T26 Record Long, bodied by Saoutchik
Chassis Number: unknown

Saudi King Ibn Saud (King Abdolaziz) received his Talbot-Lago T26 Record Long in 1951. This car was made by the French coachbuilder, Saoutchik, and had a high-roof. The current status of the car in unknown.

The 1951 Talbot-Lago T26 Record Long of the Saudi royal court while in service. *(Borzou Sepasi)*

---

[3] *Gail Rose Thompson, "Iran from Crown to Turbans", Xlibris Corporation, Indiana, 2018*

[4] *James D. O'Donnell, "The Story of Stutz Rebirth of a Classic Car", www.madle.org*

APPENDIX 3

Planes, Rail Carriages and More

Appendix 3: Planes, Rail Carriages and More

During the course of the research for this book, the author came across many royal modes of transport, from planes to carriages to family golf carts, in all of which the royal family was extensively photographed. This section is an overview of their current status.

LEFT (BOTH): A small Formula car was a gift from the Czechoslovakian government to the Crown Prince of Iran. After the revolution it was found in the Niavaran palace garage with only 63 km from new. (2003) *(Borzou Sepasi)*

BELOW (BOTH): The Czech Formula car after being cleaned up for display at the Niavaran Palace Auto Museum. (2004) *(Borzou Sepasi)*

Fit for a King ~ The Royal Garage of the Shah of Iran

ABOVE (BOTH): The Westinghouse-Marketeer 436 as found in the Niavaran Palace garage. The royal family was photographed extensively riding this vehicle. (2003) *(Borzou Sepasi)*

RIGHT (BOTH): The royal family's Cushman golf cart pictured when the author came across it in the Niavaran Palace garage next to the bicycles of the Shah's children. The upper picture was taken when the kart was brought outside to be photographed by the author. (2003) *(Borzou Sepasi)*

546

Appendix 3: Planes, Rail Carriages and More

Carl Marius Royal Carriage

This royal carriage was ordered by Shah Naser Al-Din Qajar in the 1880s. This carriage came into greater prominence following Reza Shah Pahlavi's ascension to the throne, as it was used as his coronation carriage in April 1926. The use of the carriage continued by both Reza Shah and Mohammad Reza Shah. Mohammad Reza Shah used this carriage extensively for welcoming international dignitaries. Following the 1979 revolution the carriage was transferred to a warehouse in Karaj Iran until being put on permanent display at the National Automobile Museum in 2004.

Carl Marius Royal Carriage

The royal court of Iran had at its disposal a second Carl Marius carriage which was also a vestige from the Qajar dynasty. This specific carriage was primarily put to use by both Pahlavi dynasties to greet visiting dignitaries including the Dutch royal family in 1963. At the onset of the revolution, this carriage was being kept at the royal garage in the Firouzeh Palace located in the south of Tehran. After the revolution, unlike the other vehicles stored there, this carriage remained there.

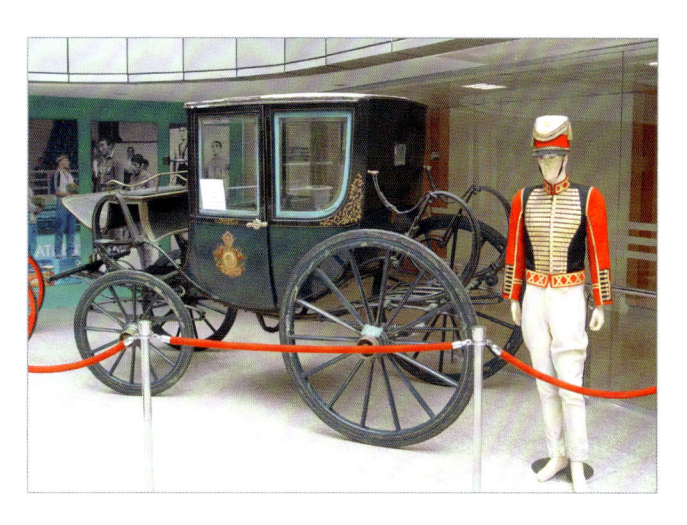

TOP: The Shah and King Baudouin of Belgium in the Carl Marius royal carriage. (1964) *(Saad Abad Palace)*

ABOVE: The Carl Marius royal carriage in the Karaj warehouse. (Early 1990s) *(Borzou Sepasi)*

ABOVE RIGHT: Queen Farah and Prince Bernhard of Netherlands in the second Carl Marius royal carriage. (1963) *(Borzou Sepasi)*

RIGHT: The second Carl Marius royal carriage remained in the former quarters of the royal garage until 2019 before being transferred to Iran's Olympic Museum in Tehran alongside some other carriages. *(Mahnaz Beedel)*

Fit for a King ~ The Royal Garage of the Shah of Iran

As the Firouzeh Palace was subsequently converted to a military base, access to the public was cut off and the carriage remained out of sight for decades. Eventually, in a unique agreement between Iran's National Olympic Committee and the Iranian military in 2019, the carriage was handed over to the Olympic Committee and put on permanent display at the Iran's Olympic Museum where it can be viewed today.

1967 Josef Klicmann Royal Carriage

As covered extensively in Chapter 22, one of the center pieces of Mohammad Reza Shah's 1967 coronation was the blue royal carriage built specially for this event by the Austrian firm Josef Klicmann. After the revolution, alongside the royal family's other vehicles, it too was transferred to the Bonyad Mostazafan's Karaj warehouse and then subsequently put on display in the National Automobile Museum in 2004. The condition is good except for the suspension problem which reduced its height.

BELOW: **The Josef Klicmann carriage pictured while in storage. (2003)** *(Borzou Sepasi)*

BOTTOM: **A number of other royal carriages remain abandoned in the Bonyad Mostazafan Karaj warehouse.** *(Borzou Sepasi)*

548

Appendix 3: Planes, Rail Carriages and More

The Royal Iranian Rail Carriages

Following the 1979 revolution, the royal rail carriages were put in storage in a warehouse located in south Tehran. Though the rail carriages are not accessible to the public, in 2012, the author was granted access and permission to photograph and review their documentation. Fortunately, unlike many of the vehicles which still remain, the carriages have been well-looked after and, as pictured, are in a virtual time capsule state.

1936 Linke-Hofmann-Werke Royal Carriages

THIS PAGE: Reza Shah's private living room in the Linke-Hofmann-Werke royal carriage. The top photograph was taken in the early 1970s and the middle image was taken by the author in 2012. Dishes with the Pahlavi crest engraved on them packed in boxes as they still sit on the kitchen. The Pahlavi crest made of ivory in Reza Shah's private room and the ceiling fan is powered by the wind from the roof. (2012) *(Borzou Sepasi)*

1959 Wegmann & Co. Kassel Royal Carriages

BELOW: The 1959 Wegmann & Co. Kassel and 1936 Linke-Hofmann-Werke royal carriages side by side in storage. (2012) *(Borzou Sepasi)*

BOTTOM: The royal crest of the Pahlavi's from the carriage (production number of 5179) has been removed from the outer body of the carriage and placed in a dog kennel that is located inside the carriage. (2012) *(Borzou Sepasi)*

RIGHT (ALL) & OPPOSITE LEFT (ALL): The royal carriage is located in southern Tehran in one of the warehouses of the Iranian railways. Author is pictured on the lower right. (2012) *(Borzou Sepasi)*

Appendix 3: Planes, Rail Carriages and More

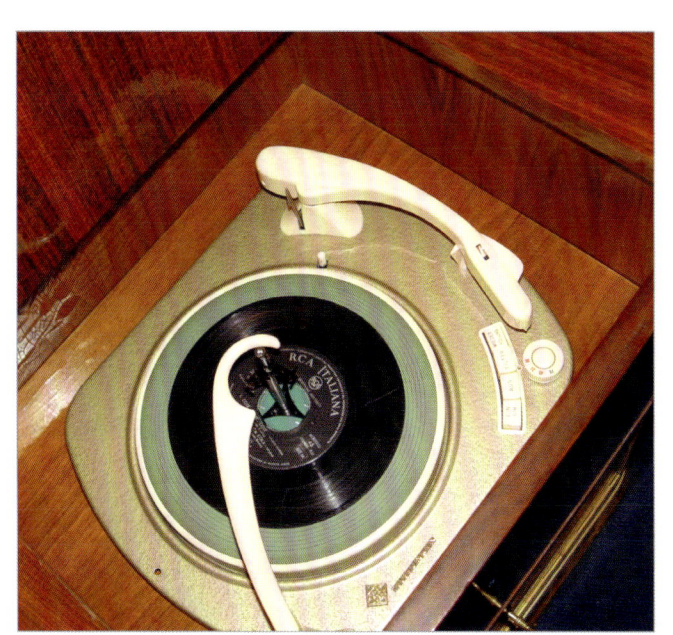

Beechcraft C-45H
Construction Number: A525
Registered: EP-HIH

On August 15, 1953, the American and British intelligence services launched a coup against the popularly-elected Prime Minister of Iran, Dr. Mohammad Mossadegh. The coup, which was carried out with the blessings of the Shah, failed on its first attempt and the Shah, who, along with his then-Queen Soraya were "vacationing" in the Caspian Sea, fled to Baghdad accompanied by their chief of court, Aboul Fath Atabay. The plane used for this flight was a Beechcraft C-45H.[1]

In 1957, the plane was retired from royal service and its ownership transferred to the Iranian Air Force for VIP use. In May 1963, the plane suffered some damage following a crash landing during which time it was being used by the Iranian Plan and Budget Organization. The plane was repaired and used by a private company named Air Taxi until the revolution. After the revolution it was left abandoned in storage. It currently is on display at the Qazvin Azadi Agricultural Airport.

---

[1]   *Iranian Aviation Review, No. 15*

The royal Beechcraft C-45H, construction number A525, installed on a display stand at the entrance of Qazvin's Azadi Agricultural Airport. *(Babak Taghvaee, www.airliners.net)*

551

Ilyushin IL-14
Construction Number: 147001241
Registered: EP-HMI

The Shah's Ilyushin IL-14 covered in Chapter 14 was retired in 1969 from the royal fleet and, at the direct orders of the Shah, handed over to the Air Force. The plane subsequently became the personal transportation of the Commander of the Iranian Air Force, General Mohammad Khatami. The four stars painted on the fuselage and which are still visible, reflect his rank as a four-star general. In March 1971 the plane was retired from active service and subsequently put on display at the Air Force Museum in Dowshan Tappeh Air Force base located in east Tehran. As of the printing of this book, the plane is still on display, but having been exposed to the elements for over five decades shows extensive deterioration. [2]

---

[2]   *Iranian Aviation Review, No. 15*

ABOVE: The royal Ilyushin IL-14, construction number 147001241, on display at the Dowshan Tappeh Air Force Base Museum. (2012) *(Babak Taghvaee, www.airliners.net)*

RIGHT TOP: The Shah's Jetstar, construction number 5002, after being scrapped in Minnesota. *(Vaughn Hangartner, airport-data.com)*

RIGHT: The Shah's Jetstar, former construction number 5137, registration code 5-9001 (EP-VRP) on display during a military exhibition. (2015) *(Erfan Arabzadeh, Jetphotos.net)*

1961 Lockheed L-1329 Jetstar 6
Construction Number: 5002
Registered: EP-VRP

As detailed in Chapter 19, the Shah purchased this plane on his state visit to the United States in 1962. Due to a number of technical maladies, the plane was sent back to Lockheed in 1969 but was not returned to the Shah. Instead, Lockheed replaced the plane with another one and the new plane received the registration of the preceding plane EP-VRP, construction number 5002.

Lockheed then proceeded to re-sell the Shah's L-1329, and in the 1980s, the plane was bought by Padosa Entertainment Corp. and became the official plane of Menudo, the Puerto Rican boy band. In 1987, the plane was decommissioned and scrapped.

The Shah's replacement, construction number 5137 (EP-VRP), was delivered to the Iranian Air Force after the revolution and is still in service. The Shah ordered a third in 1976 (construction number 5203) with registration number EP-VLP. It crashed near Isfahan in 1995.

1967 Boeing 727-81 (Shahbaz)
Construction Number: 19557
Registered: EP-MRP (Mohammad Reza Pahlavi)

As detailed in Chapter 29, the Shah's personal Boeing 727 was used for both domestic and international trips, including official state visits. Following the 1979 revolution, the ownership of the plane was transferred to the Iranian Air Force. In 1982, it was once again transferred to Iran's national airline, Iran Air, and received the registration number EP-GDS with the name changed from Shahbaz to Quds. Despite its transfer to Iran Air, the plane was primarily used to transport government officials. In April 1991, the plane was sent to Germany where it was overhauled by the German airline Lufthansa, and then returned to service for the transport of government officials. In 1998, the plane was decommissioned from service and is now on display at the Air Museum on Karaj Road where it is exposed to the elements and in poor condition.

Boeing 707-386C (Shahin)
Construction Number: 21396
Registered: EP-HIM (His Imperial Majesty)

On January 16, 1979, the Shah boarded the royal Boeing 707 named "Shahin" (falcon) and with Queen Farah flew off to a life of exile. A few days later Captain Behzad Moezzi, the Shah's trusted pilot, flew the plane back to Iran. After arrival, it was parked in a hangar at Mehrabad Airport and subsequently stripped of its luxury accoutrements which were then placed in storage, with their current whereabouts unknown.

As the plane was owned by the Iranian Air Force and in light of the sophisticated avionics that the plane was equipped with, there are some rumors that the plane was used in air operations during the Iran-Iraq War. In 1986, the plane was transferred to the ownership of Iran's state airline, Iran Air, the registration code was changed to EP-NHY and the paint scheme was also changed. In 1999, Iran Air retired its fleet of 707 planes and the Shahin was transferred back to the Iranian Air Force. At the time of the publication of this book, the plane is still in service and primarily used for governmental VIP flights utilizing the registration code of EP-AJE.

LEFT TOP: The Shah's Boeing 727 "Shahbaz" (Shah's Eagle) was initially registered as EP-MRP (Mohammad Reza Pahlavi). Following the revolution, the plane was re-registered as EP-GDS (Ghods=Qods =Jerusalem) and was kept in service for the transport of government officials. *(Perry hoppe, www.airliners.net)*

LEFT (BOTH): The royal Boeing 727 registered as EP-GDS following its decommissioning at the Air Museum on Karaj Road. (2016) *(Borzou Sepasi)*

ABOVE: The royal Boeing 707 with new color and registration code EP-AJE in 2012. *(Alejandro Hernández León, www.Planespotters.net)*

Index

Bibliography

Acknowledgments

Index

MAKE/MODEL	YEAR	CHASSIS/CONSTR.	NOTES	PAGE(S)
Alfa Romeo 6C 2500 Super Sport Pininfarina	1949	915.773	Probably the Shah for a period	529
AMC Rambler American				406
Aston Martin DB5 James Bond Electric Toy Car	1966		Crown Prince toy	448
Aston Martin DBS		DBS/5503/LC	Shah, returned for V8	391, 393
Aston Martin V8	1973	V8/11004/LCA	Shah	391, 393, 447, 449, 450, 451
Attex ST/300 6×6			Crown Prince toy	339, 341, 342, 451
Austin A135 Princess		Not Known	Royal court	256, 264, 524, 525
BA-10 Armored vehicle			Soviet army	133
Bayer-Peacock Garratt			Iran railways locomotive	134
Beechcraft C-45H	1951	A525	Shah plane	186, 551
Bentley R-Type Continental, bodied by H. J. Mulliner	1955	BC73D	Shah	201, 202, 452, 453
Bentley S2 Continental Drophead Coupe	1960	BC8AR	Shah	300, 454
Bimbo Racer V12	1957		Crown Prince toy	319, 320, 455
Bizzarrini 5300 GT Strada	1965	IA3.0250	Royal family	530, 531
Boeing 707 code VC-137			United States VIP transport aircraft	244
Boeing 707 Shahin	1978	21396	Plane	444, 553
Boeing 727 Shahbaz	1967	19577	Shah plane	412, 553
Boeing B-17G Superfortress	1945		Shah plane	164
Bofors Cannon			Iranian Army, for Reza Shah funeral	173
Bugatti Type 57C Vanvooren	1939	57808	Shah	115, 122, 249, 456, 470
Buick collection				183
Buick Limited Series 90	1938		Shah	143
Buick Riviera	1963		Shah	307, 308
Buick Roadmaster Convertible	1952		State	182
Buick Roadmaster Convertible	1937		Royal court	141
Buick Roadmaster Convertible Sedan	1939		King Ghazi of Iraq	111
Buick Series 80 Roadmaster Convertible Phaeton			Royal court	119
Buick Skylark			N/A	406, 425
Buick Super	1946		N/A	143, 147
Büssing trucks			Iranian Army	75
Cadillac 355 Imperial Sedan	1934		Shah	78, 80, 83, 86, 105, 138
Cadillac collection				504
Cadillac Eldorado Convertible	1955		Shah	216, 218
Cadillac Eldorado Biarritz Convertible	1956		Shah, kept in the Iranian Embassy in Switzerland	218
Cadillac Eldorado Biarritz Convertible	1958		Shah	244, 300, 305
Cadillac Fleetwood Series 75	1949		Shah	183, 213, 214, 421
Cadillac Fleetwood Series 75 Limousine	1959		Shah	313, 315, 325, 328
Cadillac Fleetwood Series 75 Limousine	1965	ST 04A 65-69733 DC 766 KR 2 EA	Royal court	183, 213, 214, 314, 315, 325, 328, 421, 447, 531
Cadillac High top Limousine, bodied by Franay	1951	N/A	King Abdolaziz (Ibn Saud)	532, 533
Cadillac Limousine (armored)	1965		Fate unknown	531
Cadillac Saoutchik	1953		King Saud of Saudi Arabia	224, 241, 243
Cadillac Sedan de Ville	1959			289
Cadillac Series 60 Convertible Coupe	1937		Crown Prince Mohammad Reza	78, 80, 144
Cadillac Series 62 Convertible Coupe	1946		Shah	167, 169
Cadillac Series 62 Convertible Coupe			Princess Ashraf	169
Cadillac Series 62 Convertible	1955		Shah	289
Cadillac Series 62 Convertible	1959		Shah, used during French visit	294
Cadillac Series 75 Convertible Ghia Special	1953		King Al Saud of Saudi Arabia	221, 222, 458, 459
Cadillac Series 90 V16 Town Sedan	1938		Shah	137, 139, 141

555

Fit for a King ~ The Royal Garage of the Shah of Iran

MAKE/MODEL	YEAR	CHASSIS/CONSTR.	NOTES	PAGE(S)
Cadillac Seville			Shah	313, 406, 422, 425
Cadillac Sixty Special	1958			524, 525
Cadillac Type 57	1918		Ahmad Shah	29
Carl Marius Royal Carriages	1880s			38, 283, 317, 328, 357, 547
Chevrolet Carryall Suburban			State	83
Chevrolet Corvette	1961		Shah	320
Chevrolet Corvette			Unknown	464
Chevrolet Impala	1972		State	427, 429
Chevrolet Iran			N/A	406, 425
Chevrolet Nova			N/A	406, 425
Chevrolet Styleline DeLuxe			Shah	169
Chrysler 75	1929		Shah	59
Chrysler Airflow	1935		N/A	100, 103
Chrysler C-24 Imperial			Royal court	121
Chrysler Imperial	1951		Shah	182, 193
Chrysler Imperial Crown Sedan	1959		Shah	301
Chrysler Imperial Crown Convertible	1962		State	307, 325
Chrysler Imperial Parade Phaeton	1952		New York state government	307
Chrysler K-300 Ghia Special	1955	3N551511	Shah	197, 199, 200, 459, 460, 480
Chrysler Nardi Boano Corsair II	1955		Prince Moulay Hassan, Prince of Morocco	201
Chrysler New Yorker Convertible	1953		State	179, 191, 269, 270
Chrysler Newport Convertible	1964	Not Known	State	334, 335
Chrysler Special Ghia	1952		Sold to Arab customers	223, 224
Chrysler Windsor Deluxe	1955		Shah	200
Citroën P2 Half-Tracks			Iran Royal Army vehicles	34, 36
Cord 810	1936		N/A	100
Cushman			Royal family golf cart	388, 546
Daimler DK-400 All-Weather Tourer, bodied by Hooper		92724	Mohammad Zahir Shah, King of Afghanistan	312, 461
Daimler DS420	1973	1M 20088	State	427, 447, 463
Daimler DS420 (five cars)				463
DB V-200 001 Prototype locomotive			Locomotive	211
de Havilland Dragon Rapide			Plane	70
de Havilland L-20 Beaver			Iranian Army plane	305
de Havilland Tiger Moth			Iranian Army plane	66, 68, 143, 144
De Soto Adventurer II	1954	14093762	Mohammad V, King of Morocco	201
Delahaye 135M by Ghia	1949	800514	Shah	153, 256, 463
DWL RWD-13	1939	285	Shah plane	123, 128
Facel Vega Facel II	1961	HK2-A100	Facel Vega	293, 284, 295
Fageol			Truck, Crown Prince Mohammad Reza Pahlavi	109
Ferrari 275P Replica			Crown Prince toy	342
Ferrari 330GT 2+2	1964	5459	Shah	326, 464, 465
Ferrari 365 GT4 2+2	1974	18263	Shah	393, 447, 465, 487
Ferrari 365 GT4/BB	1974	18181	Shah	393, 465
Ferrari 410 Superamerica Series II, bodied by Pininfarina	1957	0717SA	Shah	232, 262, 466
Ferrari 500 Superfast	1965	6605SF	Shah	326, 327, 328, 464, 467, 468, 482, 524
Fiat 850 Shellette, bodied by Michelotti	1968	100GB 1226009	Shah	387, 388, 468, 469
Fiat 1100	1961		N/A	298
Fiat 1500 Spider (Pedal Car)	1961		Crown Prince toy	298
Fiat 2800 Torpedo Farina			Italian President Giovanni Gronchi	230, 231

Index

MAKE/MODEL	YEAR	CHASSIS/CONSTR.	NOTES	PAGE(S)
Ford Model T	1919		Reza Shah	31, 33, 37, 38, 65
Ford Truck Hearse			Iranian railways, Reza Shah funeral	170, 171
Frazer-Nash	1947	421/E2	Shah	148, 151, 153, 155, 249, 256
Gardner-Serpollet 10 hp	1900		Mozaffar ad-Din Shah Qajar, the first car in Persia (later Iran)	14, 19, 20, 22
Gardner-Serpollet 50 hp	1903		Mozaffar ad-Din Shah Qajar	23, 25, 27
Gardner-Serpollet 8 hp	1900		Mozaffar ad-Din Shah Qajar	14, 19, 22
Gaz-69			Iranian Army	427, 429
Giordani Ferrari Indianapolis			Crown Prince toy	341
GMC Truck Hearse			Iranian railways, Reza Shah funeral	173
Harley-Davidson RL	1934		Royal court	56
Hawker Aircraft				66, 68, 70, 144, 145
Hawker Hurricane			Iranian Army plane	144, 145
Hispano-Suiza J12, bodied by Saoutchik	1931	13010	Shah	59, 60, 61, 118, 145, 249, 252, 253, 470, 471
Honda ATC-90 tricycle			Crown Prince toy	472
Honda ST50 Dax			Crown Prince toy (motorcycle)	342
Horch 853 Cabriolet by Glaser			N/A	103
Ilyushin IL-14	1956	147001241	Plane	219, 552
Imperial Crown Ghia Special	1956		King Saud of Saudi Arabia	221, 222, 223, 224
Innocenti Mini Cooper			Crown Prince	396, 436
Isotta Fraschini 8B with Touring Dual Cowl Phaeton	1935		King Ghazi of Iraq	106, 111
Isotta Fraschini Tipo 8A			Anushiravan Sepahbody, an Iranian diplomat	103
Jaguar E-Type Roadster	1962	850280	Not Purchased by the Shah	310, 311
Jaguar Mark I		Not Known	Iran embassy in Paris	259, 260, 261
Jeep Station Wagon	1959		Shah	297, 298
Josef Klicmann, the coronation carriage	1967		Royal court	351, 356, 548
Junkers F13			Plane	95
Lamborghini Countach		1120002	Shah? Only probable delivery to Iran	374
Lamborghini Countach LP400	1976	1120190	Crown Prince	374, 435, 436, 437, 438, 472
Lamborghini Espada S1	1969	7099	Shah	363, 364, 376, 447, 474, 475, 483, 487, 497, 509, 520
Lamborghini Miura P400		3303	Shah	361, 369, 376, 475, 477, 478, 479, 482
Lamborghini Miura P400		3153	Princess Ashraf Pahlavi	369
Lamborghini Miura P400S	1970	4479	Shahnaz Pahlavi	370, 371, 372, 480, 481
Lamborghini Miura SV	1971	4870	Patrick Ali Pahlavi	373, 482, 483
Lamborghini Miura SVJ	1971	4934	Shah	364, 365, 367, 368, 369, 376, 402, 447, 449, 475, 478, 483, 485, 486, 487, 488, 489, 491, 494, 497, 509, 510, 520
Land Rover Series I	1948		Iranian Army	156, 160, 163, 213, 379, 496
Lincoln Continental	1969		United States Presidential	421
Lincoln Continental Convertible	1961		Shah	311, 324, 325
Lincoln Continental Convertible	1958		State	317, 323
Lincoln Continental Mark IV	1959		Shah	266, 269, 20
Lincoln Continental X-100			United States Presidential	306
Lincoln Cosmopolitan			Shah	147
Lincoln Cosmopolitan			United States Presidential	306
Lincoln L	1927		Reza Shah	83, 88, 89
Lincoln Zephyr			N/A	100, 134
Linke-Hofmann-Werke Royal Wagons	1936		Reza Shah	87, 89, 91, 92, 115, 269, 549, 550
Lockheed Jetstar 8	1969	5137	Shah plane	391, 552
Lockheed Jetstar	1962	5203	Plane	552

Fit for a King ~ The Royal Garage of the Shah of Iran

MAKE/MODEL	YEAR	CHASSIS/CONSTR.	NOTES	PAGE(S)
Lockheed L-1329 Jetstar 6	1962	5002	Shah plane	309, 552
Mahrouseh (The Egyptian Royal Yacht)			King Farouk of Egypt	111
Marmon-Herrington A7 Scout			Iranian Army	75
Marmon-Herrington Truck		A-30-6-1216	Iranian Army	75, 170, 173, 491
Maserati 5000GT	1959	103-002	Shah	233, 234, 235, 236, 310, 492, 493, 534, 535
Maserati Ghibli Coupe		AM115.414	Patrick Ali Pahlavi	532, 533
Maserati Ghibli Coupe	1970	AM115.1394	Shah	376, 494, 532, 533
Maserati Indy 4900	1975	AM116/49*2192	Prince Abdol Reza Pahlavi	532, 533
Maserati Touring Superleggera Scia di Persia				534
Mercedes-Benz 300S Roadster			Shah	189, 203
Mercedes-Benz 300S Roadster			Princess Ashraf	189, 190, 203
Mercedes-Benz 280S			Princess Shahnaz	370
Mercedes-Benz 300 Cabriolet D			1957 Spain visit	224
Mercedes-Benz 300 Limousine			1955 Germany visit	203
Mercedes-Benz 300c Allungata Convertible Ghia	1956		King Saud of Saudi Arabia	223, 224
Mercedes-Benz 300SEL 6.3	1971	109.018.12.005924	Shah	5, 403, 404, 408, 409, 410, 497, 498
Mercedes-Benz 300SL Gullwing	1955	198.040.55.00111	Shah	203, 207, 208, 230, 256, 499, 507
Mercedes-Benz 300SL Roadster		198.042.7500462	Shah	227, 228, 229, 230
Mercedes-Benz 300SL Roadster	1957	198.042.7500082	Shah	230, 259, 261, 276
Mercedes-Benz 450SLC			Shah	410, 411
Mercedes-Benz 500K Autobahnkurier	1936	130898	Shah	95, 97, 98, 99, 144, 249, 255, 415, 472, 499, 500, 513, 514, 529, 534
Mercedes-Benz 500K Roadster Erdmann and Rossi	1935	123732	King Ghazi of Iraq	106, 109
Mercedes-Benz 540K Cabriolet A	N/A		Reza Shah	134, 138
Mercedes-Benz 600 Landaulet		100.015.12.001959	Royal court	347
Mercedes-Benz 600 Presidential Landaulet		100.015.12.001207	Shah	347, 348, 404, 406, 501, 502
Mercedes-Benz 600 Pullman			Royal court	404
Mercedes-Benz 600 SWB		100.012.12.001886	Royal court	347
Mercedes-Benz 600 SWB		100.012.12.002421	Royal court	349
Mercedes-Benz 600 SWB				348, 537, 538
Mercedes-Benz 770			King Farouk of Egypt	111
Mercedes-Benz 770 Cabriolet B	1940	429319	Present to the Shah from Germany, not delivered	121, 128
Mercedes-Benz 770 Pullman Limousine	1935		Emperor of Japan	237, 239
Mercedes-Benz 770K "Voll & Ruhrbeck" Cabriolet Limousine			King Ghazi of Iraq	106
Mercedes-Benz C111 Concept			Mercedes-Benz	383
Mercedes-Benz G4			Spain royal	85
Mercedes-Benz G-Class			N/A	379, 380, 381, 383, 383
Mercedes-Benz L45 fire engine			N/A	95
Mercedes-Benz O319			N/A	312
Mercedes-Benz W-196			Mercedes-Benz	203, 208
Mercedes-Porsche-VW	1972		Crown Prince	505
Mercury Montclair Cabriolet	1956		Republic of China government visit	237
Morane-Saulnier MS-760 "Fleuret II"	1957	2	Shah plane	230
Moskovich pedal car	1963		Crown Prince toy	341
NOHAB Royal Wagons	1935	1412	Exclusively for use by the Shah and his family	87, 89, 91
Oldsmobile 98C "Concept"	1948	N/A	Probably the Shah	534, 535
Opel Commodore B		N/A		425
Packard 1502 Convertible Sedan	1937		Royal court	115, 117
Packard 250 Convertible	1952		Queen Soraya	179, 182

Index

MAKE/MODEL	YEAR	CHASSIS/CONSTR.	NOTES	PAGE(S)
Packard Custom Super Clipper	1947		Royal court	147, 182, 183, 191
Packard Eight 1405 Limousine	1936		Shah	134, 135, 137
Palang			Warship	70
Panther 6			Not delivered because of the revolution	441, 442
Panther J.72	1976	294L	Crown Prince	441
Panther Lazer	1974		Crown Prince	441, 506
Paykan			N/A	300, 302, 303
Pegaso Z-102 Berlinetta Touring Prototipo	1952	0102.150.0119	Shah	224, 225, 226, 227, 228, 230, 256
Pierce-Arrow 133	1929		Reza Shah	60, 61
Pierce-Arrow Model A Town Car by Brunn	1930	3025354	Reza Shah	51, 52, 53, 54, 56, 173, 175, 183, 249, 507, 508
Plymouth XNR Concept	1960	9999997	Probably the Shah	535, 537
Porsche 356 Speedster	1955		Shah	210, 211
Porsche 928	1978	9288101733	Shah or the Crown Prince	441, 477, 508, 509
Porsche 934 RSR	1976	9306700168		475, 476, 478
Praga E-114	1938	108	Shah plane	123
Range Rover			Shah, Farah, Crown Prince and other royal family members	370, 395, 396, 397, 399
Riva 2000			Shah yacht	393
Rolland-Pilain Type C23 with a Kelsch body	1924		N/A	100
Rolls-Royce Camargue	1975/76	JRX 23260	Farah Pahlavi	431, 432, 447, 509
Rolls-Royce Camargue	1975/76	JRX 19741	Shah	431, 432, 447, 485, 509
Rolls-Royce Drophead Coupe, bodied by Mulliner Park Ward	1970	DRX9983	Shah	393, 431, 447, 510, 511
Rolls-Royce Phantom I		64DC		513
Rolls-Royce Phantom I, bodied by Hooper	1926	72DC	Reza Shah	51, 68, 73, 75, 77, 80, 85, 511, 512, 513, 516
Rolls-Royce Phantom III	1939	3DL138	Shah	121, 122, 124, 513
Rolls-Royce Phantom III with body from Phantom IV, chassis number 4AF6		3BT15	Never in ownership of the Shah, rebodied in 1970s?	254, 515
Rolls-Royce Phantom IV Drophead Coupe, bodied by H. J. Mulliner	1951	4AF6	Shah	177, 178, 187, 194, 195, 196, 254, 514, 515
Rolls-Royce Phantom IV four-door Cabriolet, bodied by Franay	1952	4AF22	Saudi royal car	514, 536, 537
Rolls-Royce Phantom IV Limousine, bodied by H. J. Mulliner		4AF14	Spain royal	224, 225, 514
Rolls-Royce Phantom IV Limousine bodied by H. J. Mulliner		4AF16	Spain royal	224, 225
Rolls-Royce Phantom IV, bodied by Hooper	1956	4CS6	Shah	218, 264, 277, 279, 280, 283, 317, 325, 328, 402, 404, 516, 517
Rolls-Royce Phantom V, bodied by Park Ward	1959	5LAS39	Royal court	273, 274, 279, 283, 404, 519, 520
Rolls-Royce Phantom V State Landaulette	1966	5LVF29	Shah	332, 334, 402, 404, 423, 424, 483, 485, 520, 521, 522, 539, 540, 541
Rolls-Royce Phantom VI, bodied by Mulliner Park Ward	1975	PRX4832	Royal court	523, 537, 538
Rolls-Royce Phantom VI, bodied by Mulliner Park Ward	1977	PRX4860	Royal court	520, 538, 539, 540, 541
Rolls-Royce Phantom VI, bodied by Mulliner Park Ward	1977	PRX4861	Royal court	483, 485, 520, 521, 522, 538, 539, 540, 541
Rolls-Royce Phantom VI, bodied by Mulliner Park Ward	1968	PRX4182	Royal court	541, 542
Rolls-Royce Silver Cloud II Drophead Coupe, bodied by H. J. Mulliner	1960	LSWC418	Shah	315, 325, 326, 404, 522, 523
Rolls-Royce Silver Cloud III, Mulliner Park Ward Drophead Coupe	1965	LCSC83C	Shah, previously BC56LXE	330, 403, 404, 524, 525
Rolls-Royce Silver Ghost	1921	2UE	King Farouk of Egypt	112

MAKE/MODEL	YEAR	CHASSIS/CONSTR.	NOTES	PAGE(S)
Rolls-Royce Silver Ghost Armored	1923	267WO	Iranian Army, renumbered from 7EM	42, 75
Rolls-Royce Silver Ghost Armored	1923	268WO	Iranian Army, renumbered from 76EM	42, 75
Rolls-Royce Silver Ghost Armored	1923	269WO	Iranian Army, renumbered from 77EM	42, 75
Rolls-Royce Silver Ghost Armored	1923	266WO	Iranian Army, renumbered from 8EM	42, 75
Rolls-Royce Silver Ghost by Hooper	1922	38PG	Ahmad Shah Qajar, then Reza Shah	29, 36, 38, 41, 44, 46, 47, 49, 65, 66, 112, 115, 116, 117, 516, 517, 526, 527
Rolls-Royce Silver Ghost Torpedo, bodied by Lachlaverie & Gaches	1914	50AB	Nosrat-ed Dowleh Firouz	47, 49
Rolls-Royce Silver Ghost Touring Phaeton by Hooper	1921	11LG	Vossug ed Dowleh	44
Rolls-Royce Silver Ghost, bodied by Cunard Motor and Carriage Company	1920		J. McMurray	47, 49, 526, 527
Simca Presidence V8			French President	291, 293
Steyr-Puch Haflinger			N/A	379, 380
Straussler truck			Anglo-Iranian Oil Company	31, 33
Stutz Blackhawk	1973	2K57Y3A245367	Shah	542, 543
Talbot-Lago T26 Record Long, bodied by Saoutchik	1951	unknown	King Ibn Saud (King Abdolaziz)	543
Toyopet Crown			Japan visit	241
Vickers Viscount V.816	1961	436	Shah plane	310, 311
TNHP			Tanks, delivered by the Czech Republic	73, 74
Voisin			N/A	102
Volkswagen EMPI Imp	1970		Shah	387, 388, 527
Wegmann & Co. Kassel Royal Carriages	1959	5179	Shah	267, 268, 550
Westinghouse-Marketeer 436			Royal family golf cart	385, 388, 546
Willys-Overland (Jeep) CJ-3A			Iranian Army	156, 158

Bibliography

Books

Asadollah Alam	*The Shah and I*	I.B. Tauris and Co. Ltd.	London/New York	2008
Giovanni Bianchi Anderloni	*Carrozzeria Touring Superleggera*	Fucina S.r.l	Milan	2016
Hooshang Ansari	*Raaz-e-Payandegi*	Pahlavi Political Culture Research and Publishing Center	Tehran	1969
Bahram Ariana	*History of the Iranian Modern Army*	Imperial Army Publication	Tehran	1955
Michael Axworthy	*Iran: Empire of the Mind*	Penguin Press	London	2007
Abbas Gholi Azari	*The Great Reza Shah*	Bank Bazargani	Tehran	1966
Farajollah Bahrami	*The Great Reza Shah, Travel Account of Khuzestan*	Pahlavi Political Culture Research and Publishing Center	Tehran	1976
Martin Bennett	*Rolls-Royce and Bentley: The Crewe Years*	Haynes Publications	Somerset	1995
Carl Benz	*Lebensfahrt eines deutschen Erfinders*	v. Hase & Koehler Verlag	Leipzig	1943
James Buchan	*Days of God*	Simon & Schuster	New York	2012
David Burgess-Wise	*Steam on the Road*	Hamlyn	London	1973
Andrew Scott Cooper	*The Fall of Heaven*	Henry Holt and Company	New York	2016
Lawrence Dalton	*Rolls-Royce – The Classic Elegance*	Dalton Watson Books	Deerfield, IL	1987
Soraya Esfandiary	*Ma Vie*	Pion Publishing	Paris	1963
Ettelaat Newspaper	*The Crown Prince Wedding Memorial*	Ettelaat Newspaper Press	Tehran	1939
Louis F. Fourie	*On A Global mission: The Automobiles of General Motors*	Friesen Press	Altona	2016

Bibliography

Mike Fox and Steve Smith	*Rolls-Royce: The Complete Works*	Faber & Faber	London	1984
Robert Graham	*Iran: The Illusion of Power*	St. Martin's Press	New York	1979
Simon Kidston	*The Lamborghini Miura Book*	Kidston SA	Geneva	2020
Bernard L. King	*Rolls-Royce Camargue: Crewe Saviour*	Complete Classics	Weedon, England	2019
Jacques Lowe, Jay Maisel, Burt Glinn, Gregory Lima	*Celebration at Persepolis*	Creative Communications	Geneva	1985
Jan Melin and Sven Hernström	*Mercedes-Benz, The Supercharged 8 Cylinder Cars of the 1930s, Vol. 2*	Gamla Bilsalongen AB	Sweden	2003
Mohammad Gholi Majd	*August 1941: The Anglo-Russian Occupation of Iran and Change of Shahs*	University Press of America	Lanham, Maryland	2012
Jim Mann	*Beijing Jeep*	Touchstone Books	New York	1989
Abbas Milani	*The Shah*	Palgrave Macmillan	New York	2011
Fakhr ol Molk	*Mozaffar ad-Din Shah Qajar – First and Second European Travel Diaries*	Darbar	Tehran	1902
Farah Pahlavi	*Memorias*	Martinez Roca	Spain	2003
Hossein Manoochehr Parsa	*The Complete Automobile Encyclopedia of Cars in Iran (Third printing)*	Amir Ali Publications	Tehran	2003
Mehdi Parsiaee and Dariush Tahami	*Old Pictures of Tehran, Volume 1*	Bank Ghalam Publications	Tehran	2004
Peter Pugh	*The Magic of a Name: The Rolls-Royce Story, Part 2: The Power Behind the Jets*	Icon Books Ltd	London	2012
Minou Reeves	*Behind the Peacock Throne*	Sidgwick & Jackson	London	1986
Joe Sackey	*The Lamborghini Miura Bible*	Veloce Publishing	Dorchester	2008
Borzou Sepasi	*A Pictorial History of Car Advertisements in Iran*	Ebteda Publications	Tehran	2011
William H. Sullivan	*Mission to Iran*	W.W. Norton & Company	New York	1981
Gail Rose Thompson	*All the Shah's Men*	Outskirts Press	Denver	2016
Gail Rose Thompson	*Iran from Crown to Turbans*	Xlibris Corporation	Indiana	2018
Steven R. Ward	*Immortal: A Military History of Iran and its Armed Forces*	Georgetown University Press	Washington D.C.	2014

Periodicals/Catalogs/Archives/Misc

Source	Title	Details	Date
Aeroplane Monthly	"The Flying Fortress Airliner: The Original Stratofortress?" by Marshall Wainwright	Volume 38, Number 6	June 2010
Amicale Facel Vega archives	Michel Revoy		
Autocar magazine	A Luxury Chrysler ordered by the Shah of Persia		April 1956
Autocar magazine	Advertisement of Maserati Ghibli	API Autoputer	May 1988
Automobiles Classiques magazine	Alain Dollfus	No. 11	Winter 1985
Auto Passion magazine	Maserati 5000GT	L'art d'accommoder de beaux restes	1989
Wolfgang Berger memoirs	Personal Memories of Wolfgang Berger – Former Project Engineer of Porsche	Unpublished Memoirs	
Brooks Europe	Classic Car Auction catalogue	Geneva	March 12, 1997
Bunte Illustrierte	Coronation in Tehran	Burda Druck und Verlag Special Edition	1967
De Auto magazine	Royal Delahaye 135		January 15, 1965
Ettelaat Banovan magazine	The 800,000 Toman Car		
Ettelaat newspaper	Advertisement	The Debut of the Cord 810	1937
Kayhan newspaper	The future Queen of Iran in Paris		November 3, 1959
Kayhan newspaper	Farah drives Mercedes 300SL Roadster		December 1, 1959
Kayhan newspaper	Ferrari 410SA		December 4, 1959
Kayhan newspaper	Report of the royal wedding		December 21, 1959
Khandaniha magazine	The Royal Couple in Rome		1957
Machine magazine	"Tehran International Exhibition" by Arash Behzadi		1993
Magneto magazine	"Maserati 5000GT" by Winston Goodfellow	Issue No. 4	Winter 2019
Magneto magazine	"King Miura" by David Lillywhite	Issue No. 2	Summer 2019
1972 Mercedes-Porsche-VW User Manual			
Motor magazine			September 8, 1948
National Geographic	Iran-Desert Miracle	Page 2	January 1975
New York Times	"The Last of Vienna's Great Carriage Makers" by David A. Andelman		October 29, 1979
Ramp	"If Cars Could Talk" by Simon Kidston	Edition 38	Summer 2017
Road and Track magazine	"1939 Bugatti Type 57C Cabriolet Vanvooren" by Strother MacMinn		October 1986
Road and Track magazine	Plymouth XNR		May 1960
Thoroughbred and Classic Cars magazine	All Four Miuras		July 2000
Sepid-o-Siyah magazine	The Royal Wedding		1951

Web Articles

www.6C2500.org	by Stefano Salvetti	www.maserati-alfieri.co.uk	Maserati 5000GT
www.airport-data.com	The Shah's Jetstar, construction number 5002	www.mashruteh.org	The Shah of Iran Foreign Trips
www.angelfire.com	Coronation	McGrath Maserati Facebook page	Maserati 5000GT
www.aronline.co.uk	The Converters: Panther Lazer	www.mediadaimler.com	Mercedes-Benz G-Class
www.bakhtiarifamily.com	A website dedicated to the Bakhtiary family	www.miuraregister.com	Chassis 4934, December 27, 2011
www.britishpathe.com	The Shah Returns in Triumph, 1953	www.newcaddilacdatabase.org	The Saudi Arabia Royal Cadillac
www.instagram.com/classic_cars_oldpic	The Shah's Lamborghini Miura	www.non14.net	King Ghazi Died in a Car Accident
		www.petromuseum.ir	Oil Industry History in Iran
www.classiccarcatalogue.com	Ferrari 410 Superamerica	www.pieldetoro.net	Pegaso Z-102
www.coachbuild.com	The Customized Chrysler Imperial of Saudi Arabia	www.planespotters.net	The Royal Boeing 707
www.goodingco.com/lot/1957-ferrari-410-superamerica-series-ii-coupe-2	1957 Ferrari 410 Superamerica Series II Coupe	www.prewarcar.com	Comes with an Armed Guard /dick-trenk-shah-iran-rolls-royce-phantom-iv
www.ical.ir	Parliamentary Library of Iran	www.professionalcarsociety.org	
www.influx.co.uk	DeSoto Adventurer II Ghia	www.royalwatcherblog.com	Shah of Iran's Coronation
Iranian Aviation Review e-magazine	"Royal Fleet, the Private Aircraft of the Last Shah of Iran" by Leon Manoucherians	www.truthaboutcars.com	"A Car so Personal Virgil Exner named it after Himself, the Plymouth XNR" by Ronnie Schreiber, December 15, 2014
www.iransupercars.blogspot.com			
www.irishtimes.com	"The Car Connoisseur's Collection of Choice" by Bob Montgomery	www.vickersviscount.net	Vickers Viscount V.816
		www.wikipedia.org	Rolls-Royce Phantom IV
www.JoeSackey.com	Lamborghini Miura SVJ	www.youtube.com	The Royal Wedding
www.Lamborghiniregistry.com	Lamborghini in Iran		
www.madle.org	"The Story of Stutz Rebirth of a Classic Car" by James D. O'Donnell		

Acknowledgments

Mehran Afshar
Alamy Archive
J.N. Alizadeh
Reza Amanatchi
Erfan Arabzadeh
Narodowe Archiwum Cyfrowe, Polish National Archives
Keyvan Banihashemi
Arash Behzadi
Martin Bennett
Ilse Berger
Wolfgang Berger
Brian Bickers
Andreas Birner
André Blaize
Bonhams & Goodman
BP Archive
Jack Braam Ruben, fineautomobiles.nl
Hermann Burst
Kaare Byberg
Jim Cain

Carrozzeria Touring Superleggera Archive
Fabio Collina
Swen Conrad, Yume Vision
Giles Crickmay, Frank Dale & Stepsons, London
Mehrdad Dardashti
Reza Dardashti
Reza Darjini
Oscar Davis Collection
Christian Descombes
Jodi Ellis
Afarin Emami
Ben Erickson
Fathali Esfandiary
Hamed Farrokh Rad
Wolfgang Frei
Getty Images
Ghia Archive
Golestan Palace Archive
Ali Gorji
Tony Haycock, Classic Driver New Zealand

Acknowledgments

The Henry Ford Collection
Alejandro Hernández León
Perry Hoppe, airliners.net
Touraj Hosseini
Johannes Huebner, Automobilclub Von Deutschland e.V
Frank Jung
Hulton Archive
Institute for Iranian Contemporary Historical Studies (www.iichs.ir)
Iran Khodro Archive
Iran National Library
Iran Treasury of National Jewels Archive
Iranian National Royal Jewels, The Naderi Throne, Iran Chamber Society
Islamic Republic of Iran Railways
Islamic Revolution Documents Center (www.irdc.ir)
Ghazal Jami
Rod Jolley
Arthur Jones
Farhad Kashani
Masih Kaviani
Shahab Kazemi
Keystone Archive
Mehdi Khadem Rezaeian
Kasra Kianipour
Simon Kidston
Hamid Kooshanfar
Peter Larsen
Eric Le Moine, Mercedes-Benz 300SL Register
Zarrin Majidi
Makela Auto Tuning
Mehrdad Mani
Skip Marketti, Nethercutt Collection, the Jules Heumann Collection
Alex Marks
Adrian Mashayekhi
Marcel Massini
Nick Mason
Leo McAllam
Ministry of Cultural Heritage Tourism and Handicrafts of the I.R. Iran (MCTH)
Nima Mojtahedzadeh
Ron Monroe
Glyn Morris
Jean Morris
Bonyad Mostazafan Archive
National Automobile Museum of Iran
National Iranian Oil Company Archive
Niavaran Palace Complex
Sam Noroozi

Pierre Novikoff, Artcurial Motorcars, Département Motorcars
Adolfo Orsi
Shahnaz Pakniyat
Hervé Pannier
Hossein Partovi
Petersen Automotive Museum
Pierce-Arrow Museum, Buffalo, New York
Alireza Pourakbari
Edward Quinn
Khashayar Rabbanian
Branko Radovinovic
Michel Revoy, Amicale Facel Vega archives
Mehdi Khadem Rezaian
Teymour Richard
Sonia and Mark Richter, the royal Hispano-Suiza J12 owners
RM Auctions
Rolls-Royce Foundation
Saad Abad Palace Complex
Stefano Salvetti, 6C2500.org
The Samba Collection
Martyn L. Schorr
Mitra Sehhat
Barzin Sepasi
Behrouz Sepasi
Antoin Sevruguin
Hafezeh Shabahati
Parham Shabani
Pedram Shabani
Robert Shaffner (deceased)
Bonyad Shahid Archive
Saeed Shobeiri
Shutterstock Archive
Abbas Soleymani
Lawrence Southward
Rolf Sprenger
Steve Stuckey
Tabatabaie Family Archive
Ladan Tajbakhshian
Tehran Fire Department Archive
Jean-Paul Tissot, President of Club Delahaye France
Top Photo Archive
James Trigwell, Frazer-Nash Archive
TWA Archive
Abd ul-Rahman
Mehrdad Vahid
Shehed Valad Beigi
Dr. V. van der Vinne, vincentvandervinne.nl
Fredi Vollenweider
Kuno Werner
Salman Yarmohammadi

National Automobile Museum of Iran ~ Today

On October 23, 2021, shortly before this book was going to print, the National Automobile Museum of Iran reopened after being closed for renovation since 2016. The National Automobile Museum of Iran was set up in 2003, and since its inception, the author has been involved in identifying, researching and extracting the history of many of the vehicles in the museum, which have been covered in this book.

Many enthusiasts were relieved to see that the connected warehouses have been converted into a new, gleaming structure befitting the status of the cars in this collection. Enthusiasts were further encouraged to note that many of the dust-covered vehicles, which had been sitting in storage for decades, had been refurbished and are now on permanent display.